## The Leading Facts of History Series

# THE

# LEADING FACTS OF AMERICAN HISTORY

BY

### D. H. MONTGOMERY

"America is another word for Opportunity." — EMERSON

## GINN & COMPANY

BOSTON · NEW YORK · CHICAGO · LONDON

# LEADING FACTS
# OF HISTORY SERIES

By D. H. MONTGOMERY

Beginner's American History
(Biographies of Eminent Americans)
List price, 60 cents

An Elementary American History
List price, 75 cents

The Leading Facts of American History
List price, $1.00

The Student's American History (Rev. Ed.)
List price, $1.40

The Leading Facts of English History
List price, $1.12

The Leading Facts of French History
List price, $1.12

D. H. M.

TO

D. A. M. and D. W. M.

# PREFATORY NOTE.

THIS work is based on a careful study of the highest recognized authorities on the subject. Its purpose is to present in a clear, connected, and forcible manner the important events in the history of our country.

The author has had three chief objects in view, — accuracy of statement, simplicity of style, impartiality of treatment.

In the preparation of this work his grateful acknowledgments are due to J. Franklin Jameson, Professor of History in Brown University, for his valuable assistance in the revision of the proof-sheets. The author also desires to express his thanks for the use of books and papers in the Library of Harvard University, the Library of Congress, and the Library of the Massachusetts Historical Society, and he is especially indebted to the Librarian and the attendants of the Boston Athenæum for the aid they have so courteously rendered him.

DAVID H. MONTGOMERY.

☞ *The numbering of the paragraphs or sections in this edition corresponds to the numbering in all earlier editions.*

# CONTENTS.

———◆◇◆———

## LIST OF FULL–PAGE AND OF DOUBLE–PAGE MAPS.

## LIST OF FULL-PAGE ILLUSTRATIONS.

# THE

# LEADING FACTS OF AMERICAN HISTORY.

———∘◦⋅⚬⋅◦∘———

## I.

"He [the Most High] gave to thee [Columbus] the keys of those gates of the Ocean . . . which were fast closed with such mighty chains." — *Dream of Columbus, narrated in his Letter to the King and Queen of Spain,* 1503.

———•◦•———

## THE DISCOVERY AND NAMING OF AMERICA.

### (1492–1521.)

#### COLUMBUS. — CABOT. — AMERIGO VESPUCCI.[1]

**1. Birth of Columbus; Ideas about the Earth; the "Sea of Darkness."** — Christopher Columbus, the discoverer of America, was born in Genoa, Italy, about the year 1436.[2]

At that time the earth was generally supposed to be flat, to be much smaller than it actually is, and to be habitable on its upper side alone.

The only countries laid down on the rude and imperfect maps then in use were the continent of Europe,[3] part of Asia, a narrow strip of Northern and Eastern Africa; and, finally, a few islands, the largest of which were the British Isles and Iceland.

---

[1] Amerigo Vespucci (or Americus Vespucius): Italian pronunciation, Ah-ma ree′go Ves-poot′chee.

[2] The exact year of his birth cannot be determined; several excellent authorities favor 1436.    [3] See Map of the World on page 2.

The Atlantic was popularly called the "Sea of Darkness."
It was believed to be covered with thick black fogs, and to be

guarded by terrible monsters, which alike made it impassable. Long before Columbus was born, storm-driven sailors chanced to discover the Canaries and the Azores. These islands, with Iceland, marked the western limit of voyages. Navigators, even with the help of the mariner's compass, did not dare venture beyond them.

Copy of a map of the world as known in 1436. The faint, dotted outline of the coast of Africa shows the unexplored portion. The monsters represent the terrors of unknown regions.

Europe, at this period, had no true ocean commerce : its trade by sea was confined to the Mediterranean and the Atlantic coast.

2. **The Voyages and Discoveries of the Northmen.** — To these statements one marked exception must be made. The North-men, those daring sailors of Norway and Denmark, from whom our own English-speaking race has largely sprung,[1] braved even the tempests and the terrors of the Atlantic. By acci-dent they made a number of remarkable discoveries several centuries before Columbus. Though they had no compass, — no guide, in fact, but the sun and the stars,[2] — yet they were

[1] The Northmen invaded and permanently settled the northeastern half of Eng-land in the ninth century. In the next century they established themselves in North-western France, which district was called from them Normandy (the country of the Normans, or Northmen). In 1066 the Normans crossed the Channel and conquered England. Hence many English, since the ninth century, and their descendants in America, must have sprung from the Northmen.

[2] Sometimes the Northmen, in their distant expeditions, took ravens with them ; when doubtful which way to steer for land they let the birds loose and followed their flight.

accustomed to make long voyages in rudely built vessels not larger than fishing-smacks.

About the year 850 a famous sea-rover of the Northmen was caught in a violent tempest and driven upon the coast of Iceland. Not long after, an expedition was sent and a settlement made in the new land. In the course of the next hundred years the Northmen pushed their light barks farther and farther west, until at last they reached the bleak shores of Greenland. There, also, they established a colony. But even that distant and dreary outpost was not to be the utmost limit of their wanderings. The coast of North America had already been seen by these adventurous explorers. In the year 1000 Leif, the son of Eric the Red, reached that coast, and was henceforth called "Leif the Lucky."

The place where he and his companions landed, and where they later spent one or more winters, cannot be exactly determined. According to their account they found wild grapes growing in such abundance that they named the region Vinland.[1] This may have been, as many have supposed, a part of Massachusetts or Rhode Island,[2] or it may have been as far north as Labrador. There are no ruins or other remains to mark their temporary settlement on the American coast, although in Greenland the walls of a stone church and of other buildings show where they had a colony.

**3. The Discovery of America by the Northmen had no Practical Result.** — But however interesting it may be to us to know that the Northmen visited our shores as early as the year 1000, still their discovery led to nothing. The reasons are

---

[1] In the account of their return from Vinland to Greenland the records of the Northmen say: "And when spring came they got ready and sailed off ; and Leif gave a name to the land after its sort, and called it Vinland (Vineland). They sailed then . . . until they saw Greenland . . . after that, Leif was called ' Leif the Lucky.' "

[2] It was thought at one time that the ancient round stone tower at Newport, commonly called the "Old Stone Mill," was the work of the Northmen ; but that idea is now pretty generally abandoned, and the old mill is believed to have been built by Governor Benedict Arnold of Rhode Island, in 1676-7.

readily found.    First, they were then only partly civilized, and appear to have made no efforts to establish a permanent settlement here.    Next, their colony in Greenland perished after a while, and a great change for the worse also took place in Iceland.    In the time of Columbus the inhabitants of that island had probably little, if any, communication or trade with any part of the world except Bristol, England.    The energy and enterprise for which these men of the north had once been famous had in great measure died out.    They no longer engaged in daring adventures.

There is a strong probability that Columbus went to Iceland in 1477,[1] but there is little likelihood that he got any information while there of a land farther west.    Had he done so, he certainly would have mentioned the fact when he came to solicit help for his great voyage of discovery a number of years later.    But though he urges every argument in favor of his enterprise, he does not say that the people of Iceland even hinted to him that such a country as Vinland existed.    The truth seems to be that the descendants of "Leif the Lucky" and his brave comrades had lost all remembrance of any traditions or records of that far-off shore where their forefathers declared that they had feasted on American wild grapes.

More than this, we have no evidence that the nations of Europe knew anything of such a country as Leif describes. It is therefore quite safe to say that when Columbus sailed, in 1492, one half the world did not so much as suspect the existence of the other half.

**4.  What Land Columbus wished to reach ; Marco Polo's Travels; First Motive of Columbus.** — What, then, let us ask, first induced Columbus to undertake a voyage that no other man of

---

[1] " In the year 1477, in February, I navigated one hundred leagues beyond Thule [Thule is generally thought to have been Iceland ]. . . .  The English, principally those of Bristol, go with their merchandise to this island, which is as large as England.  When I was there, the sea was not frozen." — *Letter of Columbus.*

that age dared embark upon ? It was not the expectation of finding a new or fourth continent ; for he probably believed as firmly as any one of his day that the three continents of Europe, Asia, and Africa, with some islands, comprised all the land in existence. His object was not to reveal a new world beyond the Atlantic, but simply to reach the Indies by sailing to the westward.

The interest he felt was partly awakened by a noted book, published many years before, and it was partly the result of the condition of the India trade at the time when Columbus matured his enterprise.

Let us see what that book was. In the thirteenth century (1260–1295),[1] Marco Polo, who, like Columbus, was a native of Italy, made an overland journey to Central Asia and the far East. He spent nearly thirty years there, and on his return wrote a volume of travels of great value. In that remarkable work he described India and China, and spoke of the island of Cipango or Japan, whose existence he then first made known to Europe. Polo gave the best account of the countries he visited which had been published since Alexander the Great penetrated India (327 B.C.), and he spoke particularly of the wealth and power of the Great Khan, or Emperor of China, in whose service he had spent upwards of seventeen years.[2]

This book made a deep impression on the mind of Columbus, and later he constructed a map of the world, based in large measure on the geographical discoveries made by Polo. He burned with a desire to visit those marvellous Eastern lands, with which all intercourse, except that of commerce, had long practically ceased. His purpose, as he himself re-

[1] *Dates so enclosed need not be committed to memory*

[2] An eminent authority (M. Walckenaer) says, " When in the long series of ages we search for three men who, by the grandeur and influence of their discoveries, have contributed most to the progress of geography . . . the modest name of the Venetian traveller [Marco Polo] presents itself in the same line with the names of Alexander the Great and Christopher Columbus."

peatedly tells us, was, first of all, that of a missionary,[1] — he hoped to convert the Khan and his people to Christianity. If they rejected the religion he offered them, then, according to the ideas of the time, any Christian king might seize their possessions, and make slaves of them.

Such was one great object with Columbus in going to the Indies, as all Eastern Asia was then called. Throughout his career he never lost sight of this purpose. In fact, he came at length to believe that the Most High had specially chosen him as his instrument to carry the light of faith into the kingdoms of Oriental paganism. That motive, whether wise or not, inspired the great Genoese navigator with a certain enthusiasm and dignity of character which mark his course throughout. His life was not always blameless, — he shared many of the errors of his time, — but it was always noble.

**5. The Second Motive of Columbus; Trade with the Indies.** — But the question naturally arises, if Columbus wished to reach the Indies, why did he not follow in the footsteps of his predecessor Polo, and go overland to that country?

The answer to that inquiry is found in the second motive which actuated him; that was his desire to open up direct commercial intercourse with the East, not by land, but by ocean. Columbus was, as we have seen, a sailor; and for this reason the condition of trade had a great influence on his plans.

Europe had at all times depended on the Indies for much of its supply of silks, cashmeres, and muslins, as well as for dyewoods, perfumes, spices, precious stones, and pearls. How large that trade was in the fifteenth century we cannot say with precision, but it must have been considerable. The control of it was then practically in the hands of the two rival Italian ports of Venice and Genoa. They held such complete possession of this lucrative traffic that it was said

[1] In this respect Columbus may be compared with the celebrated modern missionary and explorer, David Livingstone, who did so much, a number of years since, toward opening up the " Dark Continent " of Africa, not only to religion, but to trade.

THE WORLD AS KNOWN SHORTLY BEFORE AND SHORTLY AFTER THE
SAILING OF COLUMBUS.

Light arrows show voyages made up to 1492; (light track, Da Gama's voyage, 1497).
Dark arrows, voyages of Columbus and Cabot.
White crosses, countries of which something was known before 1492.
White area, including western coast of Africa, the world as known shortly before the sailing of Columbus.

that no one in Western Europe could season a dish of meat or spice a cup of wine, without adding something to the profits of one of those cities.

Each had a route of its own. Genoa took the northern one, and sent her ships by way of Constantinople to the ports of the Black Sea. There they loaded with goods brought either across from the Caspian Sea or up the valley of the Euphrates and the Tigris from the Persian Gulf — part of the way by boats, and part by caravan.

Venice took the southern route, and conducted her traffic by way of Cairo and the Red Sea. This gave her the advantage of a nearly all-water line of communication with the East, though there were points where the navigation was both difficult and dangerous. Trade over these two competing routes had gone on for centuries; but in 1453, when Columbus was a lad of seventeen, a great change suddenly took place.

That year the Turks besieged and took Constantinople, which before that had been a Greek city. When they got possession they refused to allow the Genoese vessels to pass through the straits of the Bosphorus into the Black Sea. This completely broke up the commerce of Genoa with the East, and henceforth Venice had the trade entirely to herself. That result, so disastrous to Genoa, must have made a decided impression on Columbus; for in future he would see no more ships unload their rich cargoes of silks and spices at the wharves of his native city.

6. **Attempt of the Portuguese to reach the Indies by a New Route.** — While these events were happening on the Mediterranean, the king of Portugal, anxious to get the control of the Oriental trade away from Venice, was doing his utmost to find an all-sea route to the treasures of the Indies. His plan was to send out successive expeditions to explore the western coast of Africa, in the hope of finding a way round that continent into the Indian Ocean. But the progress made was very slow. Though they

had already done something, yet it took the cautious mariners of that age more than fifty years to creep down the coast — a distance of over five thousand miles — to the extreme southern point. Finally, in 1487, that feat was accomplished by a Portuguese captain of the name of Diaz.[1] He, however, had such a rough experience that he named the point the Cape of Storms.

It is an interesting and significant fact that Bartholomew Columbus, Christopher's younger brother, accompanied Captain Diaz in that expedition. The elder Columbus must have felt no little interest in the success of the undertaking, since he himself was then maturing a scheme for seeking the Indies in a different direction.

When Diaz returned with the news of what he had achieved, the Portuguese monarch felt sure that he should accomplish his end. To show his confidence in the new route which he foresaw would be opened, he called for Diaz's chart, drew his pen through the name Cape of Storms, and in its place wrote in bold letters that name full of promise, Cape of Good Hope.

7. **Plan of Columbus for reaching the Indies by sailing West.** — But Columbus thought that he could improve on the king of Portugal's project. He felt certain that there was a shorter and better way of reaching the Indies than the track Diaz had marked out. The plan of the Genoese sailor was as daring as it was original. Instead of sailing east, or south and east, he proposed to sail directly west. He had, as he believed, three good and solid reasons for such an undertaking: First, in common with the best geographers of his day, Columbus was convinced that the earth was not flat, as most men supposed, but a globe. Secondly, he supposed this globe to be much smaller than it is, and the greater part to be land instead of water. Thirdly, as he knew nothing, and surmised nothing, of the existence of the continent of America or of the Pacific

[1] Diaz (Dee'az).

Ocean, he imagined that the coast of Asia or the Indies was directly opposite Spain and the western coast of Europe. The entire distance across to Cipango, or Japan, he estimated would probably not exceed about four thousand miles.

His plan was this: he would start from Europe; head his ship westward toward Japan, and follow the curve of the globe until it brought him to what he sought. To his mind it seemed as sure and simple as for a fly to walk round an apple.

If successful in the expedition, he would have this immense advantage: he would enter the Indies directly by the front door, instead of reaching them in a roundabout way, and by a sort of side-entrance as the Portuguese must.

We see that this man who understood practical mathematics, geography, and navigation, as well as any one of his day, was right on the first point, — the shape of the earth, — but utterly wrong on the other two.

Yet, singularly enough, his errors were in one respect a help to him. The mistake that he made in regard to distance was a most fortunate one. Had Columbus correctly reckoned the size of the globe, and the true length of such a voyage, he probably would not have sailed, since he would have seen at once that the proposed Portuguese route was both far shorter and cheaper. Again, could he have imagined or in any way foreseen that the American continent lay right across his path, that in itself might not then have induced him to start on a voyage of discovery, for his object was not to find a new country, but a new way to an old one.

**8. Columbus seeks and obtains the Assistance of Spain.** — This project was not a recent thought of Columbus. He had meditated on it for many years, during which time he sought to get the help first of his native city, then of Portugal, and finally of Spain (1485–1486). He met with nothing but disappointment. He was regarded as a foolish schemer, and the street boys openly mocked him as a lunatic.

At last Columbus, now fast sinking into poverty, received permission from the Spanish rulers to lay his plans before a committee or council. That body listened to his arguments with impatient incredulity. To them such a voyage "appeared as extravagant as it would at the present day to launch a balloon into space in quest of some distant star."

The council ridiculed the idea that the earth is round like a ball. If so, said they, then the rain and snow must fall upward on the under side, — the side opposite where we stand, — and men there must walk with their heads downward : that would be inconvenient, nay more, it would be impossible. Finally, they objected that in case the earth could be proved to be a globe, that very fact would render such a voyage as Columbus proposed a failure. For how, they asked of him, could your ships come back when they had once advanced so far west as to begin to descend the curve of the earth ? Could they turn about and sail up hill to Spain again ? No answer that Columbus could make seemed satisfactory to the council. After much deliberation and vexatious delays they made their report to Ferdinand and Isabella, joint sovereigns of Spain. The report stated that the scheme was "vain and impracticable, and rested on grounds too weak to merit the support of the government."

Sick at heart, Columbus set out to leave the country, when he was recalled. He had a few stanch friends at court who believed, with him, that "wherever ships could sail, man might venture." Through their influence, and especially through the generous encouragement of Queen Isabella, he obtained the assistance he required.[1] Thus, chiefly by a woman's help, the brave sailor got the power to undertake his daring enterprise. It was indeed high time that some one should furnish the means if Columbus was to be the leader; for he

---

[1] The whole amount raised to fit out the expedition was 1,640,000 maravedis, or (according to Harrisse's estimate) about $93,000, of which sum the Queen contributed over two-thirds.

was then a gray-bearded man of fifty-six — an age when not many persons, however fond of adventure, care to embark on new and perilous expeditions.

9. **Columbus sails.** — Columbus had succeeded in getting his own terms, — he had received the rank of admiral, he was to be governor of all lands that he might discover or acquire, and he was to have a tenth of whatever treasure he might find. He now pushed forward his preparations for the voyage as rapidly as possible. When all was ready, he and his men went to church, and implored the blessing of God on their great enterprise. The next day, Friday, August 3, 1492, "half an hour before sunrise," as Columbus himself says, he set sail from Palos, Spain, with three small vessels, and one hundred and twenty men.[1]

Of these vessels, only the largest, the admiral's ship, had an entire deck, and even his was probably of not over one hundred tons' burden, or about the size of an ordinary coasting schooner.

He took his route by way of the Canary Islands, because Cipango, or Japan, the nearest Asiatic land, was supposed to lie in that latitude.[2] At the Canaries he was detained several weeks repairing the rudder of one vessel, and altering the sails of a second.

On September 6th, he hoisted anchor, and resolutely set out to cross that ocean which no civilized man had ever before attempted to pass over. As the last dim outline of the islands

[1] Columbus kept a regular journal of the voyage from the start. In the introduction to that journal he says, respecting one object he had in view: "In consequence of the information which I had given to your Highnesses [the king and queen of Spain] of the lands of India, and of a prince who is called the Grand Khan, which is to say . . . King of Kings . . . therefore your Highnesses . . . determined to send me, Christopher Columbus, to the said parts of India to see the said prince and the people and lands . . . and to discover the means to be taken for the conversion of them to our holy faith; and ordered that I should not go by land to the East, by which it is the custom to go, but by a voyage to the west, by which course, unto the present time, we do not know for certain that any one hath passed."

[2] See chart of Columbus, page 12, and compare also the chart of his course, page 13.

faded from their sight many of the sailors were completely overcome. Some shed tears, as if they "had taken leave of the
world"; others, unable to restrain their grief, broke out into
loud and bitter lamentations.

But Columbus himself had no such fears. He did not feel that
he was making a leap in the dark. He had carefully calculated

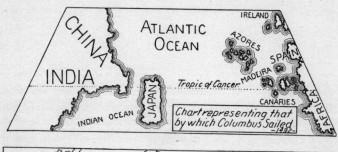

Correct chart of westward route from Europe to Asia, for comparison with the chart
of Columbus given above.

everything and provided for everything. No one understood
navigation better than he. Here was his equipment: First, he
had a chart of the globe, made by himself, and based on the
highest authorities. Next, he had the compass for his guide.
Finally, he carried with him an improved astrolabe, or instrument for determining his position by observation of the sun.

But these were not all. These, in fact, were but the material
and mechanical means of success. He had the conviction that

he was engaged in a Providential work, and that he was certain to accomplish it. There are occasions in life when such a faith is worth everything to its possessor: this was one.

We can judge of the strength of his conviction from the fact that he carried with him, by his own special request, letters of introduction and recommendation from the joint sovereigns of Spain to the Grand Khan of China.

10. **The Voyage; Variation of the Needle; the Crew are greatly Alarmed; the Winged Guides.** — For a time all went well, then a new and strange circumstance was noticed. It was

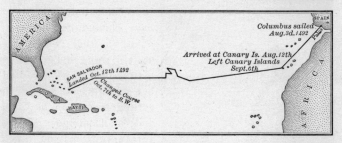

Route of Columbus, 1492.

found that the compass no longer pointed toward the North Star, but that it varied more and more, as they went on, to the west of north.[1]

This astonished Columbus, and greatly alarmed the seamen. They began to think that they had now entered a region where the ordinary laws of nature were suspended, and that to persist in keeping on would be destruction. Columbus pacified their fears as best he could. He however would not hear of turning back then, though he afterward promised to do so if land was not discovered in a few days.

---

[1] Humboldt remarks that it had probably been noticed before this voyage that the magnetic needle varied to the *northeast*. Now it was found that this variation varied; and that from northeast the needle swung round to the northwest. This was the new and startling feature of the situation.

On the 7th of October an event occurred which induced the admiral to change his course.    He was then sailing due west, but that day a flock of land-birds was seen flying to the southwest.    Alonzo Pinzon, captain of one of the vessels, urged Columbus to follow those birds.    He refused ; but at length yielded to entreaty, and reluctantly turned the prow of his ship in the direction of his winged guides.[1]

That seemingly trifling circumstance had important results. Had Columbus kept on in his directly westerly course, he would have struck the mainland of America at the peninsula

Columbus watching for Land.

of Florida.    In that case it is probable that Spain would have planted her first colonies on what is now the eastern shore of the United States, instead of spending her strength, as she did, in getting possession of Cuba and San Domingo.    Such a settlement might have changed — at least, for a long period — the future of this country.    It might have made a second Mexico of the southeast, — planting there a Spanish population, Spanish laws, and the Spanish language.    Had that happened, — and there is no reason to think it would not, — then despotic Spain would have got firm control of a part of the new world that to-day belongs to the American Union, and such a hold, even if but temporary, certainly would not have resulted in our present advantage.

[1] See Paragraph 2, note 2, on the Northmen following ravens.

(By permission of Prang & Co., Art Publishers, Boston.)

COLUMBUS APPROACHING LAND.

**11. Land! San Salvador; the West Indies and the Indians.—** The result of following the birds was that, five days later, Friday, October 12th, at two o'clock in the morning, the cry of "Land! Land!" was heard. It proved to be a small island of the Bahamas, called by the natives Guanahani.[1] It is now thought to be Watling's Island.[2]

When the sun rose, revealing the low sandy shore, — the humble threshold of the new world, — Columbus, clad in complete armor, landed with his men. Kneeling, they kissed the soil, and with tears gave thanks to God for having crowned their voyage with success. Then, with solemn ceremonies, the admiral planted the royal flame-colored banner of Spain, and took possession of the country for Ferdinand and Isabella. To the island he gave the name of San Salvador, or the Holy Redeemer.

Columbus believed this little island to be part of the Indies. Since he had reached it by sailing westward he called the group to which it belongs the West Indies. To the natives he naturally gave the name Indians. However incorrect that designation may seem to us, knowing, as we do, that the Indies are many thousand miles west of the Bahamas, still that name will doubtless cling to that people as long as they continue to exist.

Columbus never found out his mistake in regard to this country. He made three more voyages[3] hither; but he died firmly convinced that America was part of Asia, and that he had discovered a short and direct all-sea westward route from Europe to the Indies.

[1] Guanahani (Gwa'na-ha'nee).

[2] Cat Island, Turk's Island, and Watling's Island, all in the Bahama group, are rivals, each claiming the honor of the first landing of Columbus. The weight of evidence seems now to favor the last.

[3] On his first voyage (1492) Columbus discovered the Bahamas and the West India Islands, including Cuba and San Domingo or Hayti. On his second voyage (autumn of 1493), he discovered the islands of the Caribbean Sea, besides Jamaica and Porto Rico. On his third voyage (spring of 1498), he discovered the Island of Trinidad, off the coast of Venezuela, South America; and on the first of August, the mainland of that continent, at the mouth of the Orinoco River. On his fourth and final voyage (spring of 1502), he explored the coast of Central America and of the Isthmus of Panama. He returned to Spain in 1504, where he died in 1506.

We see an illustration of the strength of that conviction in an incident which happened when he landed at Cuba.[1] He at first thought it must be Japan; but later he came to the conclusion that it was part of the Asiatic mainland, and he compelled his men to swear that they believed that, if they chose, they could go thence, all the way by land, back to Spain.

It should be distinctly understood that Columbus never, in any of his voyages to America, set foot on any part of the mainland of what is now the United States.

**12. Columbus returns to Spain; his Reception; the Pope's Division of the World.** — Having lost his own vessel — the best one in the fleet — by shipwreck on the coast of Hispaniola[2] or Hayti, the admiral built a fort with her timbers on that island.   He left a small colony there, and sailed for Spain, reaching that country in the spring of 1493, after an absence of a little over seven months.

The reception given him by Ferdinand and Isabella was such as the first civilized man who had crossed the Atlantic merited. Those who a year before had laughed at him as crazy, now, cap in hand, bowed low before him.   Yet the only printed account[3] which appeared describing his wonderful voyage was a copy of a letter which he had written to the king and queen.   It was entitled : —

## "A Letter of Christopher Columbus,

(to whom our Age is much indebted)

respecting the

## Islands of India, beyond the Ganges,
lately discovered." [4]

A rhymed version of this letter was sung through the streets of Genoa.   It must have created a stir in that declining city,

---

[1] Cuba was not discovered to be an island until two years after the death of Columbus.

[2] Hispaniola (His-pan-I-o′lah), or Little Spain.

[3] This was in 1493, about forty years after the invention of printing.

[4] This letter may be found complete in Major's "Select Letters of Columbus"

which, forty years before, when Columbus was a boy, had boasted its trade with the East.[1]

One immediate result of this supposed discovery of a western route to the Indies was the division of the world by the Pope. Spain and Portugal were rivals. Both were eager to get the control of Oriental commerce. The Pope had confirmed Portugal in the possession of the islands and countries of Africa she had discovered. Spain now asked him to confirm her claims to countries in the west. The Pope, anxious to keep peace between the two nations, granted the petition. Taking a map of the world (1493), he drew a perpendicular line from the north

Map showing the division of the world made in 1494.

to the south pole, one hundred leagues west of the Azores. Later (1494) the line was fixed at three hundred and seventy leagues west of the Cape Verd Islands.[2] Portugal was to have all lands, not belonging to some Christian prince, found east of this line; Spain all similar lands west of it.

**13. Disappointment of Spain with the newly found " Indies " ; Death of Columbus.** — Meantime Spain was picturing to herself the unbounded wealth she would gain through future voyages of Columbus. But he failed to find any mines of precious metal, and sore was the disappointment. It was said that his men brought back no gold, but only a mockery of it in their yellow, emaciated faces, discolored by disease. The wealth

(Hakluyt Society's Publications, London). Extracts from it are given in Higginson's " American Explorers." In this letter Columbus gives an account of the voyage and describes the West India Islands and their inhabitants.

[1] See Paragraph 5.

[2] The reason for drawing the first line one hundred leagues west of the Azores appears to have been because at that point the compass pointed exactly north. Portugal, however, strenuously objected, and got the line pushed farther west. By the final arrangement Portugal obtained Brazil when it was discovered.

they found consisted of some hundreds of wretched Indians, kidnapped to be sold as slaves in Europe.

Loud was then the outcry against Columbus. The rabble nicknamed him the "Admiral of Mosquito Land." They pointed at him as the man who had promised everything, and ended by discovering nothing but "a wilderness peopled with naked savages."

Broken in health, broken in heart, the great sailor died in Spain, in neglect and poverty.[1] Three years before his death he wrote a touching letter[2] to the king and queen, asking for help, but none was given. Probably, if Queen Isabella had not soon after died, he would have received the assistance he so humbly begged. When she passed away, the admiral lost his best friend. But though his closing days were pitiful, yet none the less the voice that he imagined he once heard in a dream spoke truly.[3] He had not found the Indies; but, as the voice seemed to say, he had unlocked "those gates of the ocean" which until then had been "fast shut with chains,"— the chains of ignorance and fear.

**14. John Cabot discovers the Continent of North America.** — But great as was the merit of Columbus, he was not destined to be the first to look on the mainland of America, nor was he to give it the name it bears. The discovery of the continent

[1] Columbus died at Valladolid, in 1506. He was buried there, but later his body was removed to Seville. In 1536 it was transported to the island of San Domingo. After the cession of that island to France by the Spanish the body of Columbus was exhumed (*as was then supposed*), carried to Havana, Cuba, and there deposited in the cathedral. These reputed remains were sent back to Spain in December, 1898. But there seem to be good reasons for thinking that the true remains of Columbus still rest in San Domingo.

[2] "I was twenty-eight years old [these figures are believed to be a mistake] . . . when I came into your Highnesses' service, and now I have not a hair upon my head that is not gray: my body is infirm, and all that was left to me has been taken away and sold. . . . Hitherto I have wept over others; may Heaven now have mercy upon me, and may the earth weep for me!" — *Letter of Columbus*, 1503.

[3] See quotation from the letter of Columbus at the beginning of this section, page 1. It was while he lay sick and in great trouble, on the Isthmus of Panama, that he fancied he heard the consoling voice.

was reserved for a fellow-countryman, John Cabot,[1] of Venice, then residing in Bristol, England. Influenced by what Columbus had achieved, and encouraged by Henry VII., king of England, Cabot set sail westward in the spring of 1497. His object was to find a northern passage to the Indies and China, in order that he might secure the spice trade to the English sovereign. He failed to discover what he sought; but he did better, for he saw what no civilized man had yet beheld, that was — the continent. The point where he made the discovery was probably in the vicinity of Cape Breton Island, at the entrance to the Gulf of St. Lawrence.[2] On a map drawn by his son Sebastian we read the following inscription:

"*In the year of our Lord 1497, John Cabot, a Venetian, and his son Sebastian discovered that country which no one before his time had ventured to approach, on the 24th of June, about five o'clock in the morning.*"[3]

Cabot planted the English flag on the coast, and took formal possession of the country for the English king.

The next year Sebastian Cabot made a voyage,[4] and explored the coast from Nova Scotia to Cape Hatteras, or perhaps even farther south. He likewise asserted the title of Henry VII. to the land.

That king was notoriously fond of money, and knew how to hold on to it; but in this particular case he tried to be generous. Such services as those of the Cabots could not go wholly unrewarded. He appears to have given the father a small pension. Furthermore, in the royal note-book of that monarch's private

---

[1] Cabot (Cab'ot), and see Note 1, on p. 24.

[2] It is impossible to determine positively where John Cabot first saw land. Different authorities suppose Labrador, Newfoundland, and Cape Breton Island; the last is now strongly supported by special investigators.

[3] Another map, since discovered in Germany, and now preserved in Paris, bears date 1494. Whether this is a mistake for 1497 is matter of discussion. If the date is correct, then Cabot sailed three years earlier than has generally been supposed.

[4] The voyage of Columbus in 1492 "was much talked of," says Cabot, "at the court of Henry VII." He adds, "Then increased in my heart a secret flame of desire to attempt some notable thing."

expenses we find this significant memorandum, which is supposed to refer to the first expedition : —

"*10th August, 1497.  To him that found the new isle, £10.*" [1]

Never, perhaps, in the world's history did any sovereign get so large a territory for so small an outlay ; for on that voyage of Cabot's the English based their claim to this country. Nearly three hundred years later, Edmund Burke, the eminent British statesman, said in Parliament: "We derive our right in America from the discovery of [John] Cabot,[2] who first made[3] the northern continent in 1497."

Thus the continent was found.  Let us see, next, how it was named.

**15.  How the Name America originated.** — Two years after John Cabot's voyage (1499) another Italian, Amerigo Vespucci,[4] a native of Florence, but then engaged in business in Spain, went out in partial command of an expedition of exploration. Following directly in the track of Columbus, and using his charts, he reached the northeastern part of the South American coast, somewhere in what is now Dutch Guiana.  In the course of the next four years he made two more voyages in which he visited Brazil.[5]  On his return to Europe he wrote a pretty full account of what he had seen, which was published soon after (1504).  Though it was nothing but a thin pamphlet, yet, from the fact that it was, so far as we know, the first printed description of the mainland of the Western Hemisphere, it naturally brought the name of the writer into notice.

At this time there was a German professor of geography

---

[1] Ten pounds sterling represented, of course, much more than $50 then.  Perhaps, indeed, it would be safe to call it as much as $700 or $800.  Still, even at that rate, the king got his money's worth.

[2] Burke says Sebastian Cabot by mistake for John Cabot.

[3] "Made," here used in the sense of came in sight of, or reached.

[4] Amerigo Vespucci (Ah-ma-ree'go Ves-poot'chee) : the name also frequently occurs in a Latinized form as Amer'icus Vespu'cius.

[5] Brazil had been discovered by Pinzon, one of the companions of Columbus, in 1499, two years before Vespucci visited that country ; and Columbus had reached the northeastern coast of South America in his third voyage, 1498.

named Waldseemüller,[1] connected with the college of St. Dié,[2] a village now included in Eastern France. He had read Vespucci's

accounts of his voyages and was particularly interested in them.[3]

In the year 1507 he printed a little book in Latin on the college press and entitled it "An Introduction

Map showing the Village of St. Dié, Eastern France.

to Geography." It consisted of only a few pages, and might easily be rolled up and carried in one's pocket. Small as it was, it contained, however, a sentence which was to have a lasting influence on the history of this country. That sentence was this suggestion made by Waldseemüller: *"And the fourth part of the world having been discovered by Amerigo or Americus, we may call it Amerigé, or* **AMERICA**.*"*

Thus one-half the globe received the name it bears. One Italian had found the outposts of the new world, and claimed them for Spain; a second had seen the northern mainland, and taken possession of it for England; finally, a third, coming after both the others, gave to it, perhaps without his own knowledge even, the title it now possesses in every atlas and history.

1 Waldseemüller: German pronunciation nearly Valt'za-miller.

2 St. Dié (San De-ay').

3 Vespucci's voyages: according to what purports to be his own account, Amerigo Vespucci made his first voyage in the spring of 1497, and saw on June 6th of that year "a coast which," he says, "we thought to be that of a continent." If that coast was the continent, he discovered the mainland of America eighteen days before John Cabot did (June 24, 1497); and more than a year before Columbus saw it, on his third voyage (Aug. 1, 1498). In 1499 Vespucci, following in the track of Columbus, visited the northeastern coast of South America, part of which had been seen and described by the great navigator the previous year. Later, Vespucci visited Brazil. Recent authorities on American history generally believe that Vespucci did not make his first voyage until 1499, and that, therefore, John Cabot was the true discoverer of the *continent* of America. (See Winsor ("Narrative and Critical History of America"), Bancroft (revised edition, 1883), and Bryant.)

No man that ever lived before or since has such a monument as Amerigo Vespucci; for a name derived from his is written across the map of two entire continents. If he deserved it, it is right he should have the honor; but most historians think he did not deserve it; that, in fact, he was no true discoverer, but only followed after those who were. In that case he has received by chance fame which he not only did not fairly earn, but which it may be he did not either seek or desire.

16. **How America finally came to be considered a New and Distinct Continent.** — But even after America was named the idea that it was a distinct and separate division of the globe was not gen-

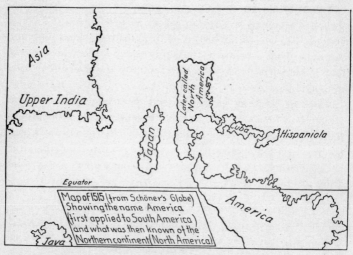

Map of 1515, showing what some geographers then supposed North America to be. This is one of the earliest maps on which the name *America* occurs. It will be noticed that at that time it was confined to South America.

erally accepted. Some, indeed, thought that South America was a great island or southern continent (like Australia); but the majority believed with Columbus that it was simply an immense peninsula projecting from Southeastern Asia. People, indeed, spoke of the "New World," but all that they usually meant by that expression was newly discovered lands.

The real character of America was first found out by Magellan,[1] when, sailing to the southwest (1519–1521), through the straits since known by his name, he passed round South America into that great ocean which he called the Pacific. Coasting up north for some distance, he ended by going across the newly discovered ocean of the west, and one ship of his expedition sailed entirely round the globe.[2] Then men's eyes were opened to the truth. Then they saw that America, instead of being a part of the old world, was in all probability an immense, independent continent, a real NEW WORLD.

Was that discovery hailed with delight? Not at all. Europe was still bent on finding "that hidden secret of nature," a direct passage to Asia, and there stood America barring all progress. It is true that when the Spaniards found gold and silver in Mexico and Peru, they became reconciled in a measure to their disappointment. Still, for more than a hundred years after Columbus, most of the explorers spent their efforts not so much in seeking to find out what was in the new country, as in trying to hit on some passage through it or round it which should be shorter and better than that which Magellan had sailed through.

17. **Summary.** — In 1492 Columbus, while attempting to open up a direct western all-sea route to Asia, accidentally discovered the *West India Islands.* He had no true idea of the magnitude of his discovery; but supposed that land, and all that which he afterward saw, to be part of Asia. His great merit is that he, first of civilized men, dared to cross the unknown sea of the Atlantic. The glory of that bold exploit will always be his.

---

[1] Magellan (Ma-gel'lan).

[2] Magellan himself was killed on an island of the East Indies; but one of his captains succeeded in completing the voyage. Magellan's lieutenant received a coat of arms from the king of Spain, on which a globe was represented with the motto: "*You first sailed round me.*"

John Cabot, a Venetian, discovered the American *continent* in 1497.

The voyages of Amerigo Vespucci, who, like Cabot, was a fellow-countryman of Columbus,[1] suggested the name *America.* Last of all, Magellan's expedition round the world in 1519–1521 proved the earth to be a globe, and showed that America was in all probability a distinct continent, and not a part of Asia.[2]

[1] Columbus, Cabot, and Vespucci were fellow-countrymen in the sense that all of them, though citizens of different Italian republics, were natives of Italy.

[2] **Books for Reference :** The authorities for this and all following sections will be found in the List of Books at the end of this work.

# II.

The discovery of America was "the great event which gave a new world not only to Spain, but to civilized man." — CHARLES SUMNER.

---

## ATTEMPTS AT EXPLORING AND COLONIZING AMERICA.

**THE COUNTRY. — THE NATIVES. — EFFECTS OF THE DISCOVERY OF AMERICA ON EUROPE.** (1509-1600.)

**18. Ponce de Leon's [1] Expedition; Discovery of Florida.** — In 1509 Diego [2] Columbus, son of Christopher Columbus, was appointed governor of San Domingo. Not long afterward he despatched a force to Cuba which conquered that island.

In the spring of 1513 Ponce de Leon, who had been removed by the king of Spain from the governorship of the island of Porto Rico, determined to start on an exploring expedition to the northward. De Leon was getting to be old, but the conquest of Cuba stirred his blood, and he resolved to accomplish something of equal note. He had heard marvellous stories from the Indians of a land not very far distant which was said to possess two things he coveted, — gold, and a fountain which could make the old young again. De Leon readily obtained a royal charter [3] from Spain, which gave him power to go in search of that land of promise, and when found, to hold it as governor for life. The last privilege meant much in the eyes of the

---

[1] Ponce de Leon (Pōn'thā dā Lā-ōn', Spanish pronunciation).

[2] Diego (De-ā'go, Spanish pronunciation).

[3] Charter: a written grant made by the king or head of a government, conferring certain rights and privileges.

veteran adventurer; for if he could once bathe in the waters of the miraculous fountain, and get back his youth, he felt sure of a long term of office. With this tempting prospect of renewed energies and of a governorship lasting for many years, De Leon set sail.

After cruising about among the Bahama Islands for several weeks he struck the mainland of North America. It was Easter Sunday,[1] a day which the Spaniards call Pascua [2] Florida, or Flowery Easter. Shortly after, De Leon landed at a point between where St. Augustine now stands and the St. John's River.[3] There he planted the cross, raised the Spanish flag, and in commemoration of the day when he had first seen the coast, he named the country Florida.[4] Winter is almost unknown in that climate, and the dense foliage and profusion of bright flowers fully justified the name.

De Leon failed to discover gold. Worse still, he found no magical fountain that could make a man approaching threescore a man of twenty. Disappointed in what he most cared for, he set sail for Porto Rico. A number of years later he went back to Florida to colonize the country. He did not succeed; for an arrow shot by an Indian inflicted a wound which ended his days. Thus the old man found death lurking for him in that "Land of Flowers," where he had hoped to get for himself a new lease of life.

19. Balboa discovers a Southern Ocean. — In the autumn of the year when De Leon first saw Florida (1513), Balboa,[5] a fellow-countryman, undertook an exploring expedition on the Isthmus of Panama.[6] His object was to find a great body of water

---

[1] Easter Sunday, and not Palm Sunday, as is sometimes stated.

[2] Pascua (Pas'koo-ah) : meaning Easter.        [3] See Map, page 53.

[4] The name was not restricted to the peninsula now so called, but extended over a vast region beyond.

[5] Vasco Nuñez de Balboa, commonly called Balboa (Bal-bo'ah).

[6] See Map, page 36. Balboa crossed the isthmus (then called the Isthmus of Darien), about 150 miles southeast of Aspinwall, from a point opposite the Bay of San Miguel to that bay (Lat. 8° 50').

which the natives told him could be seen toward the south from the top of the mountains. The way to the mountains was through a country so rough and so covered with dense forest filled with underbrush that the Spaniards did well when they made seven or eight miles a day. At last, after terrible hardships, Balboa reached the summit of the ridge. Looking down, he beheld that magnificent expanse of water which Magellan, seven years later, sailed across on his way round the world.[1] Such a sight was worth all it cost.

A number of days afterwards, Balboa, struggling over rocks, wading streams, and cutting his way through tangled vines, succeeded in getting to the shore.

Drawing his sword with one hand, and bearing a banner in the other, he marched out knee-deep into the smooth sea, and took possession of it and of all lands bordering on it for the sovereigns of Spain. Waving his sword, he said, "I am ready to defend" their claim "as long as the world endures, and until the final day of judgment of all mankind." He named that ocean the South Sea;[2] but Magellan[3] later named it the Pacific.

Six years later the Spanish general, Cortez,[4] landed in Mexico, conquered that country, and thus established the power of Spain on the Pacific slope of the North American continent.

20. **French Explorations ; Montreal.** — Up to this time France had obtained no part of the new world. But the king of that country did not intend to let the other powers of Europe get it all. The Pope had, as we have seen,[5] granted the new lands to rival nations; but that had no effect on Francis I., who then ruled France. "Show me," said he to the sovereigns of those nations, "that clause in the will of 'Father Adam' which divides the earth between the Spanish and the Portuguese, and excludes the French." "Father Adam's" will was not

---

[1] See Paragraph 16.    [2] Because he first saw it to the south of him.
[3] Magellan : see page 23.    [4] Cortez (Cor'tez).    [5] See Paragraph 12.

produced; the consequence was that the king — so the French say — sent out an expedition[1] to obtain his share of America.

But we cannot be sure that France accomplished anything in this way before 1535. That year Cartier,[2] a French navigator, discovered a great river in the northern part of America, to which he gave the name of St. Lawrence. Ascending the stream, he came to an island where there was a little Indian village. Landing, he climbed the lofty hill behind it. He was so delighted with the grand view that he called the height Montreal, or Royal Mountain.

21. **New Attempts of the Spaniards to Conquer Florida; Coronado.** — Meanwhile the Spaniards, under Narvaez,[3] made another attempt (1528) on Florida. The undertaking failed. The disheartened explorers built some boats and crept along the shore of the Gulf of Mexico, toward the west. After cruising in this way for more than five weeks, Cabeza De Vaca,[4] an officer of the expedition, discovered one of the mouths of the Mississippi. Narvaez, the commander of the little fleet, soon after parted company with Cabeza, and was lost. About a week later, Cabeza himself was shipwrecked, probably on the coast of Texas. He was captured by the Indians. After a long captivity, he and three of his companions managed to escape. They plunged into the wilderness, and at length, after nearly two years of wandering, reached a Spanish settlement on the western coast of Mexico.[5]

They were the first white men that had ever crossed so large a portion of the continent. They had only journeyed

[1] This was the expedition said to have been undertaken by Verrazano in 1524. He states that he landed in the vicinity of Cape Fear, North Carolina; then sailed about 150 miles southward along the coast, and then, turning north, sailed to what is now New York Bay, afterward cruising along the coast of New England.

[2] Cartier (Kar-te-ay′, French pronunciation): he made his first expedition in 1534, to Newfoundland and the Gulf of St. Lawrence.

[3] Narvaez (Nar-vah′eth, Spanish pronunciation).

[4] Cabeza De Vaca (Kah-bā′thah Day Vah′kah, Spanish pronunciation).

[5] Compostela, twenty miles from the Pacific. Lat. 21° 10′. From that place they went to the city of Mexico. See Map of America, page 36.

from the Gulf of Mexico to the Pacific, but they probably had a clearer idea of the actual width of that part of the new world than any one else in it; for they literally knew every foot of the way.

De Vaca brought reports of rich cities in the north. Coronado,[1] a Spanish governor in Mexico, set out to find them (1540). He discovered the Great Canyon of the Colorado and the Indian stone[2] cities of New Mexico; he then pushed eastward, and may have reached what is now Kansas. Later the Spaniards made permanent settlements in the southwest.

**22. De Soto's Expedition.** — The next one to undertake the conquest of Florida was Ferdinando de Soto,[3] a Spaniard, as

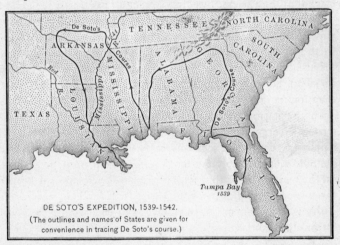

DE SOTO'S EXPEDITION, 1539-1542.
(The outlines and names of States are given for convenience in tracing De Soto's course.)

greedy of gold as he was cruel, and as daring as he was greedy. He sailed from Cuba in the spring of 1539, with a force of about six hundred picked men and over two hundred horses. It was "a roving company of gallant freebooters," in search of fortune. De Soto had provided bloodhounds and chains to hunt and enslave the Indians; finally, he had ordered a drove of hogs

---

[1] Coronado (Ko-ro-nä′do).    [2] And sun-dried brick.    [3] De Soto (Dä Sō′tō).

to be taken along, in order that his men might be sure of an ample supply of fresh meat.

The expedition landed at Tampa Bay,[1] and began its march of exploration, of robbery, and of murder. The soldiers seized the natives, chained them in couples so that they might not escape, and forced them to carry their baggage and pound their corn.[2] The chief of each tribe through whose country they passed was compelled to serve as a guide until they reached the next tribe. If an Indian refused to be a slave or a beast of burden for these insolent Spaniards, his fate was pitiful. They set him up as a target, and riddled his body with bullets; or they chopped off his hands, and then sent him home to exhibit the useless, bleeding stumps to his family.

For two years this march went on. During that time De Soto and his men travelled upwards of fifteen hundred miles through what are now the States of Florida, Georgia, Alabama, and Mississippi. They found no gold worth mentioning; but, in its stead, hunger, suffering, and death. They deserved what they found.

In the spring of 1541 the Spaniards, worn out, sick, disgusted, emerged from the forest on the banks of the Mississippi.[3] Cabeza[4] had seen one of the mouths of the river, but De Soto was probably the first civilized man that ever looked on the main body of that mighty stream which rolls for nearly three thousand miles through the heart of the continent, and, with its tributaries, has a total navigable length of over fifteen thousand miles.[5]

The river at that point is so wide that a person standing on the bank can just see a man standing on the opposite side. Here the Spaniards crossed. They made a long circuit of

[1] See Map, page 29.    [2] Corn: it was pounded in a mortar.

[3] Probably at or near a place now called De Soto Front, De Soto County; in the northwestern corner of the State of Mississippi.

[4] Cabeza De Vaca: see Paragraph 21.

[5] This is the lowest estimate; the highest is from 35,000 to 40,000 miles! See "Encyclopædia Britannica."

many months' march, getting no treasure, but meeting, as they declared, "Indians as fierce as mad dogs." In May, 1542, they came back to the great river at that point in Louisiana where the Red River unites with it.

This was to be the end of De Soto's career. There he died, and was secretly buried at midnight in the muddy waters of the Mississippi. He had made the Indians believe that he was not a human being, but a "child of the sun," and that death could not touch him. When the chief found that he had mysteriously disappeared, he asked where he was. The Spaniards replied that their captain had gone on a journey to heaven; but that he would soon return. What the chief said we are not told; but he doubtless hoped that if De Soto had gone there, that there he would stay.

The survivors at length reached the Spanish settlements in Mexico. Only about half of those that had landed in Florida were alive ; they were a miserable band, half-naked, half-starved, looking worse than the savages they had gone out to subdue.

23. **Attempts of the Huguenots** [1] **to establish Colonies.** — For twenty years after De Soto's death Florida, with the adjacent country, was left to the undisturbed possession of the Indians. Then, in 1562, Jean Ribaut,[2] taking out a small number of Huguenots, attempted to plant a colony at what is now Port Royal, South Carolina.[3] After they had got established Ribaut went back to France.

The settlers numbered less than thirty. That handful of men, shut up in a log fort on the Atlantic coast, represented the first efforts of Admiral Coligny [4] to establish a great Protestant commonwealth in America. But the Huguenots found the wilderness lonesome; at length homesickness made it intolerable.

---

[1] Huguenots (Hū´ge-nots, *g* hard) : a name given to the early French Protestants. For a full account of them, see " The Leading Facts of French History," in this series.

[2] Jean Ribaut (Zhon Re-boh´, French pronunciation).      [3] See Map, page 53.

[4] Coligny (Ko-leen-ye´, French pronunciation) : he **was the champion of the French Protestants.**

They set to work, cut down trees, constructed a rude vessel, took their shirts and bedding to make sails and rigging, and started for France. On the way they were picked up by a passing ship, and taken to England. Without that chance help they would probably have perished.

The next year (1564) a second expedition was sent out under the leadership of Laudonnière.[1] This time the French landed at the St. John's River in Florida, where they built a fort. Later, Jean Ribaut arrived with re-enforcements, determined, it would seem, to hold the peninsula against the Spaniards.

24. Menendez[2] destroys the Huguenot Settlement. — The king of Spain had heard of the new settlement, and resolved to break it up. Pedro Menendez, an officer of the royal navy, was commissioned to drive out the intruders from territory which the Spanish monarch claimed by right, first, of the discovery of America by Columbus,[3] and next, of that of Florida by De Leon.[4]

Menendez started with his fleet in the summer of 1565, and found the French at the mouth of the St. John's River ; but after some manœuvring deferred the attack for that day. He accordingly set sail, and, proceeding southward down the coast about twenty miles, to a point where he had previously landed, there he built a fort at a place which he named St. Augustine.

Meanwhile Jean Ribaut, leaving part of his men in their fort on the St. John's River, set sail with the rest to attack the Spaniards. A tempest came up, and they were wrecked. As soon as Menendez had made his preparations, he advanced to the St. John's, surprised the French garrison, and massacred all but the women and the children.

[1] Laudonnière (Lō-dŏn-yair′, French pronunciation).

[2] Menendez (Mā-nĕn′deth, Spanish pronunciation).

[3] " The nations of Europe adopted the principle that the discovery of any part of America gave title to the government by whose subjects, or by whose authority, it was made, as against all European Governments. This title was to be consummated by possession." — Bouvier's Law Dictionary, " Discovery." It will be seen from this that the Spanish title to Florida was good, but not complete, if by "possession" the actual settlement and holding of the country was meant.

[4] See Paragraph 18.

Shortly after his return, the Indians reported that some of the shipwrecked Frenchmen were on the beach not far off. Menendez soon found them. They were exhausted and practically helpless. They surrendered and were murdered. Next came the news that Jean Ribaut himself, with a large number of men who had been wrecked in like manner, was a few miles away.[1] When Menendez came up to the French, Ribaut with a hundred and fifty of his followers surrendered. The rest, who numbered two hundred, escaped in the night. They were eventually taken, and made slaves for life. Out of those who had surrendered with Ribaut five were for some reason spared. The hands of the others — a hundred and forty-six in all — were tied behind them; then they were marched to St. Augustine, or its vicinity, and deliberately massacred. Thus the foundation of the oldest town in the United States (1565) may be said to have been laid in blood.

**25. Revenge by De Gourgues.**[2] — The king of France treated the affair with indifference; but a French Catholic named De Gourgues vowed vengeance on the murderers of his countrymen. He fitted out an expedition at his own expense and sailed for Florida. Reaching the St. John's River, he surprised and captured the Spanish garrison that Menendez had left there when he took the French fort. Having bound the prisoners, he hanged them. Over their heads he placed a pine board on which these words were burned with a hot iron: "I do this not as to Spaniards; but as to assassins." Then De Gourgues, not having sufficient force to attack the Spaniards at St. Augustine, set sail for France. The French never made a second attempt to colonize Florida, and the Spaniards were left in full possession.

**26. English Exploration : Frobisher : Davis.** — Since the voyages of the Cabots (1497–1498) the English had been occupied with other matters, and hence sent out no more exploring

[1] They appear to have been on Anastasia Island, about five miles from St. Augustine. [2] De Gourgues (Deh Goorg, *g* hard; French pronunciation).

expeditions to the west.[1] But in 1576, nearly eighty years after the English flag had been planted on the North American continent,[2] Sir Martin Frobisher set out to see if he could not discover a northwestern passage to Asia. His object was to reach the Indies, and secure part of the trade for England; for since the Portuguese had opened up a route to that country by way of the Cape of Good Hope,[3] they held the control of that commerce.

Frobisher crossed the Atlantic and cruised about in the seas and straits north of North America, but accomplished nothing. Among the curiosities he carried back was a black stone. When examined in London this was said to have gold in it. The story soon got into circulation that the lucky captain had actually found the spot in those frozen regions of the north where King Solomon dug the gold for his temple in Jerusalem! A stock company was formed, and Frobisher went out and brought back several shiploads of black stones. What became of them does not appear. It was a subject the stockholders preferred not to talk about. That was the last heard of "Solomon's mines"; and a few years later we find Frobisher's wife begging help of the government, and calling herself "the most miserable poor woman in the world." These expeditions were followed by a persistent attempt on the part of Captain John Davis to push his way through the same seas. He, like Frobisher, left his name on the map of that desolate region, but that was all.[4]

27. Sir Humphrey Gilbert's Expedition; Drake's Voyage round the World. — The next two expeditions by the English were of

[1] See "The Leading Facts of English History," in this series.

[2] See Paragraph 14.

[3] Vasco da Gama, a Portuguese navigator (see Map, page 12), succeeded in doubling the Cape of Good Hope in 1497. He reached Calicut on the Malabar coast of India in 1498, and at a later period established a trading post there. The Portuguese thus became "the sole masters and dispensers of the treasure of the East," and held control of India for over a century.

[4] The Map on page 34 is interesting as showing how little was then really known of the North American continent. By examining it, it will be seen that the upper

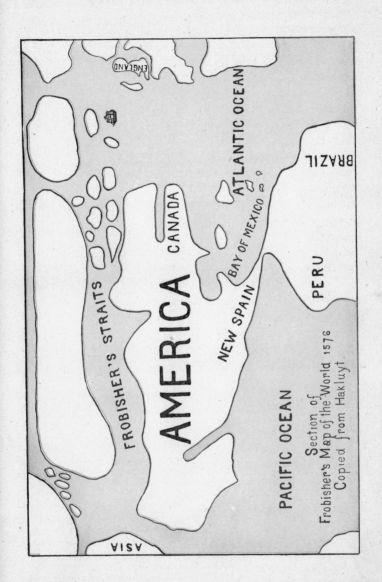

PACIFIC OCEAN

Section of
Frobisher's Map of the World 1576
Copied from Hakluyt.

a different character.  In 1578 Sir Humphrey Gilbert, half-brother to Sir Walter Raleigh, of whom we shall presently speak, obtained a charter from Queen Elizabeth granting him any new lands he might discover in America or the west.  Gilbert started the next year, with his little fleet; but one ship was lost, and he was compelled to turn back.  In 1583 he made a second attempt, and landed on Newfoundland, of which he took possession for the queen.  Not long after, his largest ship was wrecked.  But two vessels of the fleet were now left; and Gilbert started in the smaller of them, a tiny craft of only ten tons, on his homeward voyage.  The weather was tempestuous, and the captain of the larger vessel begged Gilbert to go in the ship with him; but he would not forsake his crew.  "We are as near to heaven by sea as by land," said he.  That was the last heard of him; that night his little vessel was swallowed up by the waves.

Before Gilbert set out on his ill-fated voyage Sir Francis Drake had sailed (1577) on a piratical expedition against the Spaniards and their settlements in South America.  He passed through Magellan's Strait, entered the Pacific, and made havoc as he went along.  He kept on northward until he reached what is now the coast of Oregon.[1]  He hoped, in this part of his voyage, to find a passage opening through to the Atlantic which might be used for trade with the Indies.  He landed at several points, and refitted his ships at a place now called Drake's Bay, about thirty miles north of San Francisco.  The Spaniards, who had been there before him, had named the country California.[2]  Drake took possession of the whole coast, and gave it the name of New Albion.[3]  He then

part was supposed to be very narrow, from north to south, with a broad channel through to the Pacific; for Frobisher Strait and Davis Strait, see Map, page 36.

[1] He reached latitude 43°, in Southern Oregon; or, as some accounts say, 48°.

[2] California : a name probably derived from a Spanish romance of 1510, in which a fabulous island rich in gold and precious stones is so called.

[3] England is called Albion, a name once supposed to mean the Country of the White Cliffs.  Drake saw a part of the shore of the Pacific coast of America, which, perhaps, reminded him of the chalk cliffs of his native land.

crossed the Pacific, and returned to England by way of the Cape of Good Hope,[1] having, as it was said then, "ploughed a furrow round the world." He was the first Englishman who circumnavigated the globe (1577–1580).

**28. Walter Raleigh's Exploring Expedition to Virginia.** — In 1584 Walter Raleigh,[2] a favorite of Queen Elizabeth, received a charter from her granting him the right to explore and settle the eastern coast of America. That charter made Raleigh governor, with full power to enact laws for any colony he might establish; but it expressly said that the settlers were to enjoy all the political and religious rights and privileges which they had in England.

Raleigh was one of the few men of that day who believed that the northern part of the New World was worth settling. Most of the expeditions, as we have seen, had for their object to find a way through or round the continent to Asia; but Raleigh thought that perhaps in the end America might prove to be quite as profitable as the Indies.

He sent out two ships, in the summer of 1584, to explore.[3] The English reached Roanoke Island, off the coast of what is now North Carolina. There they landed, and were hospitably entertained by the Indians. The explorers were delighted with the "native Americans," and spent several weeks, as they said, "eating and drinking very merrily" with the red men. When the explorers returned to England, the queen was so highly pleased with their description of the "Good Land" and the good people in it, that she named it Virginia, in honor of her own maiden life, and knighted the fortunate Raleigh, who now became Sir Walter.

**29. Sir Walter Raleigh's Colony; the New "Root" and the New Weed.** — In the summer of 1585 Raleigh sent out a hundred

---

[1] See Map on page 36, and also Map on page 12.

[2] Raleigh (Raw'le, but usually pronounced Ral'ly in England).

[3] Under the command of Captains Amidas and Barlow.

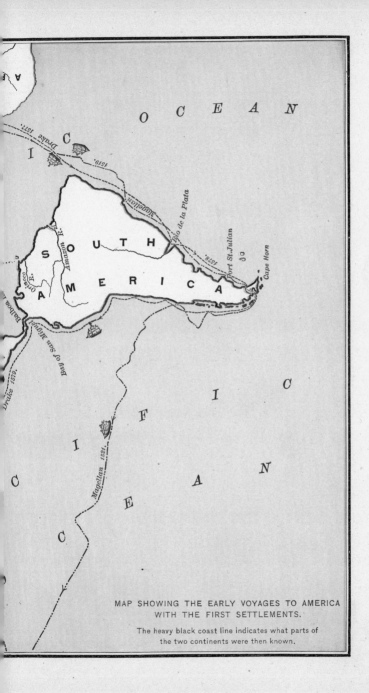

MAP SHOWING THE EARLY VOYAGES TO AMERICA
WITH THE FIRST SETTLEMENTS.

The heavy black coast line indicates what parts of
the two continents were then known.

and eight emigrants under Ralph Lane, who was to act as deputy governor. The new colony established itself on Roanoke Island. It certainly did not lack room; for Virginia, as held by Sir Walter's charter, extended from the southern boundary of what is now North Carolina to beyond Halifax.[1] Westward it reached six hundred miles, or nearly to the Mississippi.

But the colonists had not been well chosen. They would not work. Lane said, "they had little understanding, less discretion, and more tongue than was needful." After less than a year's trial of the country the emigrants returned to England. Still the experiment had not been an utter failure, for they carried back a peculiar kind of "root" — as they called it. When boiled or baked, the English found it excellent. Thus the Potato[2] became an article of food in the British Islands.

But this was not all. The Indians had a weed whose leaves they dried and smoked with great satisfaction. They told the white men of Roanoke that "it would cure being tired." The emigrants tried it, and one of them said that the plant had so many virtues that "it would take an entire volume to describe them all." The courtiers of Queen Elizabeth tested these virtues; and the queen, after smoking a little of it, confessed that it was "a vegetable of singular strength and power." The consequence was that from that time the air of England was never entirely free from tobacco smoke. We shall see later that this plant was destined to have a very important influence on American trade, and also on American history.

**30. Raleigh sends out a Second Colony; Croatoan.[3]** — Raleigh, though disappointed at the return of his first colony, resolved to send out a second (1587). All of the emigrants of 1585 were

[1] That is, from latitude 34° to 45°. The charter gave Raleigh control of the whole territory for six hundred miles in every direction around his settlement.

[2] The potato, by which is meant the common not the sweet potato, was not cultivated by the Indians, and it is supposed that the Spaniards may have brought it to Virginia from some other part of the continent. The potato is an American vegetable; *strictly speaking*, it is not a true root, but an underground stem.

[3] Croatoan (Kro-a-tone′).

men; but many of those who went out in 1587 were men who took with them their wives and families. Sir Walter's hope was that they would make permanent homes in the wilderness, and establish a city named after him. John White, the deputy governor who was to act for Sir Walter, carried a charter, and proceeded to lay the log foundations of the "City of Raleigh."

The governor's daughter, Eleanor Dare, was the wife of one of the settlers. Shortly after her landing, Mrs. Dare gave birth to a daughter. She was the first child born of English parents in America, and was baptized by the name Virginia.

Governor White soon sailed for England to get further help for the colony, leaving his daughter and his granddaughter, little Virginia Dare, to await his return. That was the last he ever saw of them. Circumstances prevented his return for three years. When he did go back Roanoke Island was deserted. The only trace of the missing settlers was the word CROATOAN cut in bold letters on a tree. It had been agreed, before White left, that if the colonists abandoned the settlement, they should carve the name of the place to which they had gone, on a tree or post. If they went away in distress, they were to cut a cross above the name. There was the name, but no cross. Croatoan, as shown on early maps, was an Indian village on an island not far away; but though repeated search was eventually made there and elsewhere, not one of the colonists was ever found. Sir Walter Raleigh was obliged to give up his project; and America was left with not a single English settler, but with many "English graves."

Raleigh had spent over forty thousand pounds on the colony. Such a sum probably represented upwards of a million of dollars now. He could do no more; but he said, "I shall live to see it an English nation." He did live to see a permanent English settlement established in Virginia in 1607. A hundred and eighty-five years after that event (1792) Sir Walter's name was given to the seat of government of North

Carolina, and thus the "City of Raleigh" was enrolled among the capitals of the United States.

Sir Walter's example was not lost; and from his day England kept the colonization of America in mind, until she finally accomplished it. For these reasons Raleigh is rightly regarded as one of the founders of the American nation.

**31. White Settlers in 1600 in what is now the United States.** — As late as the year 1600 there seemed small promise that this country would ever be settled and governed by the English-speaking race. Look at the situation. More than a hundred years had passed since Columbus landed; yet the only white inhabitants of the territory now embraced in the United States were a few hundred Spaniards in St. Augustine, Florida, and perhaps a few hundred more in Santa Fé,[1] New Mexico, the second oldest town. Over the rest of the country, embracing more than three millions of square miles, the Indians ruled supreme. France had tried to get a foothold on the Atlantic coast and had failed; England had tried and failed likewise. Spain alone had succeeded. In 1600 it certainly looked as though her flag was destined to wave over the whole continent from sea to sea.

**32. What America was found to be; its Physical Geography.** — Confining ourselves to the territory now included in the United States, let us see what the explorers of that, and also of a later, age found America to be. In great measure it seemed to them Europe repeated. It had practically the same climate and the same soil. It produced, or was capable of producing, the same trees, the same fruits, the same crops, with the valuable addition of cotton, sugar, and rice. In all ways it was equally favorable to human health and life.

But this was not all. In two important respects America is superior to Europe. That continent commands the Atlantic

[1] Santa Fé (San'tah Fay, Spanish pronunciation) : see Map of United States. St. Augustine, it will be remembered, was settled by the Spaniards in 1565. The date of the settlement of Santa Fé is commonly given as 1582; Winsor gives 1605.

only; this commands two oceans, — the Atlantic and the Pacific. Ships can be sent direct to Europe and Africa from our eastern coast, and direct to Asia and Australia from our western. That is the first advantage. The second is that though America repeats the natural features of Europe in its lakes, mountains, plains, rivers, and forests, yet it repeats them on a far grander scale. Europe has nothing to compare with the Sierras and the Rockies, the Great Lakes, the Mississippi, Niagara, the Canyon[1] of the Colorado, or the Western prairies. "America," says a distinguished English statesman, "has a natural base for the greatest continuous empire ever established by man."[2] As will be seen later, the physical geography of the country was destined to have an important influence on its history. (See Map facing page 50.) Such was the land spread out before the explorers. It seemed to offer to all who were disappointed with the Old World an opportunity to try what they could make of life under new and broader conditions.

**33. The Indians; the Population then and now.** — One strange fact about the country was that east[3] of the Mississippi the whole vast area was well-nigh a solitude. Where to-day fifty millions of white men live, there were then only two or three hundred thousand Indians.[4] In going through the forests, the explorers would sometimes travel for days without meeting a human being. The truth is, that the Indians cannot be said to have occupied the land; they simply possessed it. To them it was mainly a hunting-ground to roam over or a battle-field to fight on.

**34. Personal Appearance of the Indians; the "Scalp-Lock."** — Columbus called the natives Indians;[5] but they called them-

[1] Canyon: the Grand Canyon of the Colorado River in Arizona is a gorge or chasm extending for about three hundred miles. Its rocky walls rise from 3000 to 7000 feet above the river.    [2] Gladstone's "Kin Beyond Sea."

[3] West of the Mississippi the Indian population, in the southwest, was large.

[4] The number of Indians in the United States is estimated at about 250,000.

[5] See Paragraph 11.

selves simply "Men," or "Real Men"; "Real Men" they certainly often proved themselves to be. The most numerous body of Indians in the East was the Algonquins; the ablest and most ferocious was the Iroquois.[1] They were a tall, well-made race, with a color usually resembling that of old copper. Their hair was like a horse's mane, coarse, black, and straight. Their eyes were small, black, and deep-set. They had high cheek-bones and prominent noses.

The women let their hair grow long. The men cut theirs off close to the head, with the exception of a ridge or lock in the middle. That was left as a point of honor. It was called the "scalp-lock." Its object was to give an adversary — if he could get it — a fair grip in fight, and also to enable him to pull his enemy's scalp off as a trophy of the battle. That lock was the Indian's flag of defiance. It waved above his head as the colors do over a fort, as if to say, "Take me if you can!"

**35. How the Indians lived.** — The Indians were savages; but seldom degraded savages.[2] They lived by hunting, fishing, and agriculture. Their farming, however, was of the rudest

---

[1] Iroquois (Ir-o-kwa'). See Map of Indian Tribes facing page 46.

[2] Of the origin of the American Indians, nothing is positively known. They may have come from Asia; or if America is, as some geologists believe, older than the Old World, then the people of Asia may have originated here.

In their structure the different languages of the Indians were apparently unlike that of any other race. Their civilization, customs, and manners varied widely. Those of the northern part of the country were much more barbarous than those of the southwest. The four chief families east of the Mississippi were: I. The Algonquins, extending from that river to the Atlantic. II. The Iroquois, occupying a large part of what is now the State of New York, and surrounded by Algonquins. III. The Mobilians of the southeast. IV. The Natchez of the southwest.

Throughout the Mississippi Valley thousands of remarkable earthworks are found, such as fortifications, burial mounds, enclosures for villages, and ridges of earth shaped like serpents and animals. West of the Mississippi immense buildings are found constructed of stone or sun-dried brick. These *pueblos*, as they are called, are often large enough to accommodate the population of an entire village. They are erected by the Indians of that region. The remains in the Mississippi Valley may have been the work partly of races which preceded the Indians and partly of the Indians themselves. They are of much interest to the antiquarian, but have no known connection with United States history.

kind. For weapons they had bows and arrows, hatchets made of flint, and heavy clubs.

The Indian believed in a strict division of duties. He did the hunting, the fighting, the scalping; his wife did the work. She built the wigwam, or hut of bark.[1] She planted and hoed the corn and tobacco. She made deerskin clothes for the family. When they moved, she carried the furniture on her back. Her housekeeping was simple. She kindled a fire on the

ground by rubbing two dry sticks rapidly together; then she roasted the meat on the coals, or boiled it in an earthen pot. There was always plenty of smoke and dirt; but no one complained. House-cleaning was unknown.

**36. The Moccasin, the Snow-Shoe, the Birch-Bark Canoe.** — The most ingenious work of the Indians was seen in the moccasin, the snow-shoe, and the birch-bark canoe. The moccasin was a shoe made of buckskin, — durable, soft, pliant, noiseless. It was the best covering for a hunter's foot that human skill ever contrived.

---

[1] The wigwams were of various kinds. Some would hold only a single family; others, as among the Iroquois tribe, were long, low tenement-houses, large enough for a dozen or more families. In some parts of the country the wigwams were made of skins stretched on poles; in others, they were built of logs.

The snow-shoe was a light frame of wood, covered with a network of strings of hide, and having such a broad surface that the wearer could walk on top of the snow in pursuit of game. Without it the Indian might have starved in a severe winter, since only by its use could he run down the deer at that season.

The birch-bark canoe [1] was light, strong, and easily propelled. It made the Indian master of every lake, river, and stream. Wherever there were water-ways he could travel quickly, silently, and with little effort. If he liked, he could go in his own private conveyance from the source of the Ohio to the Gulf of Mexico, or from the mouth of the St. Lawrence to the Falls of Niagara.

**37. Indian Government; " Wampum."** — Politically the Indian was free. Each tribe had a chief, but the chief had little real power. All important matters were settled by councils. The records of these councils were kept in a peculiar manner.

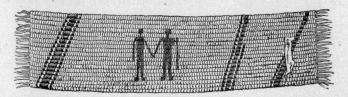

Treaty-Belt made of Wampum.

The Indian could not write, but he could make pictures that would often serve the purpose of writing. The treaty made by the Indians with William Penn was commemorated by a belt made of "wampum," or strings of beads. It represented an Indian and a white man clasping each other by the hand in token of friendship. That was the record of the peace established between them.

But quite independent of any picture, the arrangement of the beads and their colors had a meaning. When a council

---

[1] In some parts of the country canoes were made by hollowing out logs.

was held, a belt was made to show what had been done. Every tribe had its "wampum" interpreters.  By examination of a belt they could tell what action had been taken at any public meeting in the past.

The beads [1] of these "wampum" strings had another use; they served for money, a certain number of them representing

Indian Gravestone showing Totem of the Bear.

a certain fixed value.[2]  But the Indian rarely needed these beads for this purpose.  The forest supplied him and his family with food, clothes, and medicine.  Under such circumstances a pocket full of money would have been as useless to him as to a bear.

**38. Social Conditions of the Indians; "Totems."** — Socially, the Indian had less liberty than the white man.  He was bound by customs handed down from his forefathers.  He could not marry as he pleased.  He could not sit in whatever seat he chose at a council.  He could not even paint his face any color he fancied; for a young man who had won no honors in battle would no more have dared to decorate himself like a veteran warrior than a private soldier in the United States army would venture to appear at parade in the uniform of a major-general.

Each clan [3] had a "totem,"[4] or badge, to designate it.  The "totem" was usually the picture of some animal.  Among the Iroquois the figures of the Bear, Turtle, and Wolf were

[1] Originally all "wampum" was made of white or colored shells strung on strings; after the coming of Europeans glass beads were often used.

[2] For instance, a hundred white beads, or fifty colored ones, would buy a certain quantity of corn.

[3] A clan was made up of kinsmen, — the descendants of a common mother.

[4] To'tem: the animal or other object represented by the "totem" was held in reverence by the tribe.  They believed that they had descended from its spirit, and that it watched over them and protected them.

the coat-of-arms of the "first families" of the Indian aristocracy. The "totem" was also used as a mark on gravestones, and as a seal. Old deeds of land given by Indians often bear these marks, just as a grant of land made now by the United States has the government seal on it.

**39. Indian Religion; Indian Character.** — The Indian usually believed in a Great Spirit — all-powerful, wise, and good;[1] but he also believed in many inferior spirits, some good, and some evil.

Often he worshipped the evil spirits most. He reasoned in this way: The Great Spirit will not hurt me, even if I do not pray to him, for he is good; but if I neglect the evil spirits, they may do me mischief.

Beyond this life the Indian looked for another. There the brave warrior who had taken many scalps would enter the happy hunting-grounds; there demons would flog the coward to never-ending tasks.

It has sometimes been said that "the only good Indian is a dead Indian"; but judged by his own standard of right and wrong, the red man was conscientious. He would not steal from his own tribe, he would not lie to his friends, he did not become a drunkard till the white man taught him.

**40. The Indian's Self-Control; Torturing Captives; Respect for Courage.** — The Indian rarely expressed his feelings in words, but he frequently painted them on his face. You could tell by his color whether he meant peace or war, whether he had heard good news or bad. He sometimes laughed and shouted; he seldom if ever wept. From childhood he was taught to despise pain. A row of little Indian boys would sometimes put live coals under their naked arms, and then press them close to their bodies. The game was, to see which one would first raise his arms, and drop the coal. The one that held

---

[1] Some modern writers question this; but the weight of evidence would seem to show that the Indians worshipped — at least, at times — one omnipotent Power.

out longest became the leader.    If an Indian lad met with an
accident, and was mortally wounded, he scorned to complain ;
he sang his " death-song," and died like a veteran warrior.

The Indians either adopted their captives or tortured them.
They liked to see how much agony a captive could bear without crying out.    The surest way for a prisoner to save his life
was to show that he was not afraid to lose it.    The red man
never failed to respect courage.    An instance is found in the
case of General Stark of New Hampshire.    He was taken
prisoner by the Indians (1752) and condemned to run the
gauntlet.    Two long rows of stalwart young warriors were
formed.    Each man had a club or stick to strike Stark as
he passed.    But Stark was equal to the occasion.    Just as he
started on the terrible race for life he snatched a club out
of the hands of the nearest Indian, and knocking down the
astonished savages right and left, he escaped almost unhurt.
The old men of the tribe, who stood near, roared with laughter
to see the spruce young warriors sprawling in the dust.
Instead of torturing Stark, they treated him as a hero.

**41. The Indian and the White Man ; what the White Man learned
from him.** — The Indian was a treacherous and cruel enemy,
but a steadfast friend.    He thought at first that the white man
was a celestial being who had come from heaven to visit him.
He soon found out his mistake, and acted accordingly.

The Indian could return good for good, but he knew nothing
of returning good for evil; on the contrary, he always paid
bad treatment by bad treatment, and never forgot to add some
interest.    If he made a treaty he kept it sacredly ; it is said
that in no instance can it be proved that he was first to break
such an agreement.    Those of the early white settlers who
made friends with the red man had no cause to regret it.

The Indian's school was the woods.    Whatever the woods
can teach that is useful — and they can teach much — that,
he learned.    He knew the properties of every plant, and the

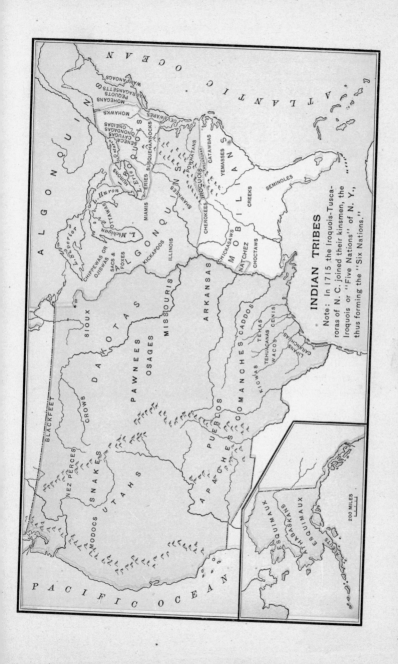

INDIAN TRIBES

Note: In 1715 the Iroquois-Tusca-roras of N. C. joined their kinsmen, the Iroquois or "Five Nations," thus forming the "Six Nations."

200 MILES

habits of every animal. The natives taught the white man many of these things, but the most useful of all the lessons the American barbarians gave the civilized Europeans was how to raise corn in the forest without first clearing the land.

They showed them how to kill the trees by burning or girdling them. Then, when the leaves no longer grew, the sun would shine on the soil, and ripen the corn. There were times in the history of the early settlements of white men when that knowledge saved them from starvation; for often they had neither time nor strength to clear the soil for planting.[1]

**42. Influence of the Indians on the Early History of the Country.** — But the results of contact between the two races did not end here. The alliances formed between the Indians and the English on the one hand, or the Indians and French, who were rivals and enemies of the English, on the other, had important historical results. The hostility of the Iroquois nations of New York to the French in Canada prevented the French from getting possession of the Hudson River, and so separating the English colonies of New England from those of Virginia and Pennsylvania. This was a decided advantage to the English settlers, who thus got a firm foothold on the Atlantic coast.

Finally, the Indian wars prevented the English from scattering over the country. These contests forced them to stand by each other, and thus trained them for union and for independence.

**43. Effects of the Discovery of America on Europe.** — What, now, were the effects of the discovery of the New World on Europe? They may be summed up as follows: —

I. There was a sudden and immense increase of geographical knowledge. That made a new map of the earth necessary, — a

[1] In recent times, the Sibley army tent, which is extensively used at the West by the United States troops, shows that useful lessons may still be learned from the Indians. It is constructed on a plan borrowed from the wigwams of that region.

map representing it not only as a globe, but as a globe enormously larger than had been conceived, for it was found to contain the continents of North and South America and the Pacific Ocean.

II. The New World invited new enterprise: there were vast regions to be explored and conquered. Spain, Portugal, France, and England began to plan western empires beyond the Atlantic. These plans gave rise to a struggle for the mastery, and to important and decisive wars, especially between England and France. Men of every rank turned their attention to America, — some seeking wealth, others political power, others a refuge from religious or political oppression. Here was room and opportunity for all.

III. The discovery of the precious metals in Mexico and South America had far-reaching effects. Before the mines were found there had often been great scarcity of gold and silver in Europe. Kings robbed the Jews, and hired pretended chemists to try to turn lead into gold. Now the treasure obtained from America enabled them to equip armies, build palaces, and make public improvements of all kinds. Thus the riches which poured in from the west gave a new impulse to the life of the Old World.

IV. Intercourse with America had an immense influence on trade and navigation. Before Columbus sailed, the commerce of Europe was confined chiefly to the Mediterranean. Then little vessels crept cautiously along the shore, peddling out their petty cargoes from port to port. Now all was changed. Large and strong ships began to be built, fit to battle with Atlantic storms, and ocean commerce commenced. Trade took its first great step toward encircling the globe.

V. New products were obtained from America. We gave Europe Indian corn,[1] the tomato, the turkey, and the potato, for which tens of thousands of half-fed peasants were grateful.

---

[1] Maize, or Indian corn, if not first introduced to Europe from America, was first practically introduced from here; so, too, was India Rubber.

To these important articles of food should be added such luxuries as cocoa and tobacco, and such drugs, dyestuffs, and valuable woods as Peruvian bark, cochineal, logwood, and mahogany.

VI. Before the discovery of America, sugar, cotton, rice, and coffee, when used at all, were imported by Europe from the Indies.

Only the rich could, as a rule, afford them. Now they were either re-discovered in America, or transplanted here. In time they became cheap and plentiful, and even the poor of the Old World came to regard them as necessaries of life.

VII. The material and scientific results of the discovery and settlement of America were not the only ones. Men's minds grew larger to take in a larger world. The voyage to America was like a journey to another planet. It made Europe acquainted with new races, new animals, new plants, new features of nature, new fields of enterprise. All felt that America meant *opportunity*. That was a great thought — in some respects the greatest that had ever moved the minds and hearts of men. It roused new hope; it stimulated new and independent effort.

**44. Summary.** — The period embraced in this section covers the greater part of a century. In it we have three classes of discoveries and explorations:

1. Those of the Spaniards; these were confined to the south. They comprised Florida, the Pacific, the Mississippi and Mexico.

2. Those of the French; these related to the river St. Lawrence and to expeditions to the eastern coast of Florida and vicinity.

3. Those of the English; these included explorations on the coast at the far north, those of Drake on the Pacific, but, more important than all, those on that part of the Atlantic coast then called Virginia.

We have seen how Ponce de Leon and De Soto attempted to conquer Florida. We have witnessed the struggle between the French and the Spaniards for possession of that country, and have seen it end with the triumph of the Spaniards, and the founding of St. Augustine (1565), the oldest town in the United States.

On the other hand, we have seen that the English expeditions of Frobisher and Gilbert, with Raleigh's project of a Virginia colony, all failed, and that the country was left with no white occupants but the Spaniards.

Finally, we have considered the effects of the contact of the white and the Indian races, and have briefly set forth the important results of the discovery of America on Europe.

# PHYSICAL GEOGRAPHY AND HISTORY.

*(See, in general, Winsor's "America," IV., i.-xxx.; Shaler's "United States," and "Our Continent.")*

The physical geography of the United States has had and must continue to have a powerful influence, not only on the health and industry, but on the character and progress of the American people.

I. The English colonies were planted on rivers or harbors which invited settlement and favored their commercial intercourse with the mother country, with the West Indies, and with each other.

II. The Appalachian range barred the West against the colonists and confined them to a long, narrow strip bordering on the sea. This limitation of soil had important effects on the occupations and the exports of the settlers, while it encouraged the development of union, political strength, and independence.

III. The Canadian French, on the other hand, having control of the St. Lawrence and the Great Lakes, soon got temporary possession of the Mississippi valley. This led to a war which ended by giving the West to the English colonists.

IV. The first English-speaking settlements made west of the Alleghanies were planted on streams flowing into the Mississippi, — a river system 35,000 miles in extent, watering the great central valley of the continent. Later, the steamboat made that vast region accessible in all directions.

V. After the Colonies secured their independence, the boundaries of the American Republic were fixed by successive treaties. These boundaries were determined, to a great extent, by: 1. coast-lines; 2. rivers and lakes; 3. watersheds; 4. mountain ranges. In 1783 our possessions bordered upon the Atlantic only; in 1803 they touched the Gulf of Mexico; in 1846 they reached the Pacific. (See "Table of Boundaries.")

VI. The most pressing question with every rapidly growing people is that of food-supply. Some nations of Europe — notably Great Britain — can only feed themselves by importing provisions. America is so fortunate in soil, climate, and extent of territory, that the people produce not only all the breadstuffs and meats they require, but they have an immense surplus for exportation.

VII. Next in importance to grain and meats are cotton, wool, timber, coal, petroleum, iron, copper, and the precious metals. These products are powerful factors in the development of modern civilization, and it is believed that no continent is richer in them than our own.

VIII. While cotton fastened slavery on the South, the abundant water power of New England gave the first impulse to American cotton manufacturing. On the other hand, the western prairies stimulated agriculture and immigration, and encouraged the building of railroads, which in twenty years did more to open up the country than two centuries had done before. Again, physical geography has influenced legislation respecting labor, the tariff, trade, currency, and the building of roads and canals; furthermore, it determined decisive military movements in the Revolution (see Washington's retreat across the Delaware, § 173) and the Civil War (see §§ 332, 333, 341).

IX. Experience proves that the physical conditions of the United States favor health, vigor, and longevity. Statistics show that in size and weight the American people are fully equal, if not, indeed, superior to Europeans, while their average length of life appears to be somewhat greater. (See Rhodes's "U. S.," III., 73, 74.)

X. The conclusion of eminent scientists is that no part of the globe is better suited to the requirements of one of the master-races of the world than the United States, and such statesmen as Lincoln and Gladstone have declared their belief that this country has a natural base for the greatest continuous empire ever established by man.

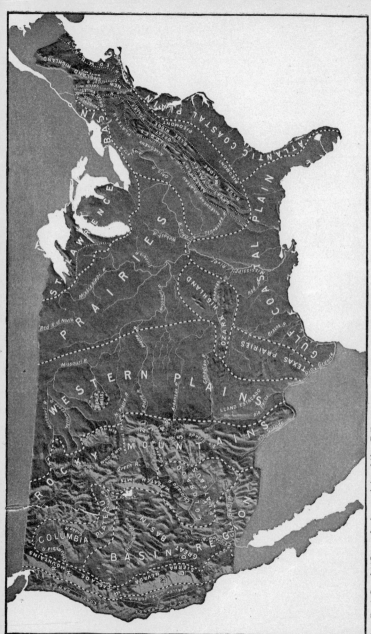

From Frye's Complete Geography, by permission of Alex. E. Frye.

PHYSICAL FEATURES OF THE UNITED STATES.

# III.

"It cannot be denied that with America and in America a new era commences in human affairs." — DANIEL WEBSTER.

---

## PERMANENT ENGLISH AND FRENCH SETTLEMENTS.

THE THIRTEEN COLONIES. — FRENCH EXPLORATION OF THE WEST. — WARS WITH THE INDIANS AND WITH THE FRENCH. — COLONIAL LIFE. — GENERAL VIEW OF THE COLONIES (1607-1763).

**45. Opening of the Seventeenth Century; Gosnold's Expedition.** — The seventeenth century opened with new, and, in the end, successful efforts on the part of both the English and the French to establish colonies on this continent.

In 1602 Gosnold, an English navigator, set sail for Virginia. Instead of taking the usual circuitous route by way of the Canaries and the West Indies, he struck boldly across the Atlantic.[1]

By this course he saved nearly a thousand miles in distance, and at least a week in sailing time. He landed on a cape on the New England coast, which he named Cape Cod, from the abundance of cod-fish found there. Then doubling the cape, and sailing south, he reached Cuttyhunk Island,[2] at the entrance to Buzzard's Bay.

On that island he built the first house erected in Massachusetts, intending to leave a colony there; but when he had got a cargo of sassafras root and cedar logs, the settlers determined

---

[1] Gosnold sailed from Falmouth on the southwest coast of England. Contrary winds drove him to the Azores; thence he sailed a little north of west until he reached the New England coast. See Map of America, page 36.

[2] See Map on page 80.

51

to go back with him. The sassafras root was then in great demand in England as a fashionable medicine and cure-all. Gosnold counted on a handsome profit on it. But Sir Walter Raleigh accused him of trespassing on his land,[1] and seized the cargo, much to the disappointment and disgust of the industrious sassafras-diggers. The expedition, however, had this result: it showed Englishmen a shorter and more direct route to America, and it kept up an interest in the country.

## I. Virginia (1607).

46. **England's Need of America; the King grants a Charter to settle Virginia.** — The population of England was then small, but many were out of employment. There were two reasons for this: first, thousands of disbanded soldiers had returned from the European wars, and could get nothing to do at home; next, many farmers, finding that wool-growing paid better than raising wheat or barley, had converted their farms into sheep-pastures. This threw multitudes of laborers out of work. Everywhere there was distress. So men naturally turned their eyes toward America. Such an opportunity seemed providential. As one preacher declared, Virginia was the door which God had opened to England.

Two companies were organized to send out emigrants. One was called the London, the other, the Plymouth Company. The charter[2] given by King James I. granted to the London Company the exclusive right to settle in Southern Virginia between Cape Fear and the Potomac.[3] To the Plymouth Company he gave the entire control of Northern Virginia between the eastern end of Long Island and the northern limit of the mainland of Nova Scotia.[4] The object of the companies was trade and exploration.

1 It will be remembered that Raleigh's charter gave him control of the American coast from north latitude 34° to 45°. See Paragraph 29.

2 See definition of charter in note on page 25.    3 See map facing page 53.

4 The London Company controlled the territory between the 34th and 38th degrees

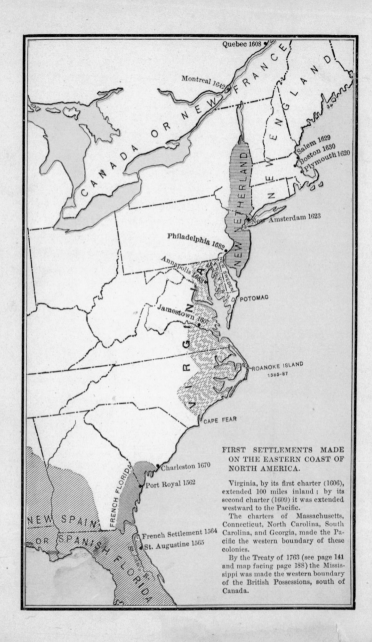

Quebec 1608

CANADA OR NEW FRANCE

Montreal 1642

NEW ENGLAND

Salem 1629
Boston 1630
Plymouth 1620

NEW NETHERLAND

New Amsterdam 1623

Philadelphia 1682

Annapolis 1604

NEW SWEDEN

O POTOMAC

Jamestown 1607

V I R G I N I A

ROANOKE ISLAND
1585-87

CAPE FEAR

Charleston 1670

Port Royal 1562

FRENCH FLORIDA

NEW SPAIN

OR SPANISH FLORIDA

French Settlement 1564

St. Augustine 1565

**FIRST SETTLEMENTS MADE
ON THE EASTERN COAST OF
NORTH AMERICA.**

Virginia, by its first charter (1606),
extended 100 miles inland ; by its
second charter (1609) it was extended
westward to the Pacific.

The charters of Massachusetts,
Connecticut, North Carolina, South
Carolina, and Georgia, made the Pacific the western boundary of these
colonies.

By the Treaty of 1763 (see page **141**
and map facing page **188**) the Mississippi was made the western boundary
of the British Possessions, south of
Canada.

The three most important articles of the charter were these :

I.  The companies were to hold their lands free of any military or other service to the king, but were to give him a fifth part of any precious metals they might find.

II.  Each colony was to be governed by a council appointed by the king, and responsible to him.[1]

III.  The settlers were to enjoy all the rights and privileges ✗ possessed by English citizens in England.

In addition to the charter, the king and the companies gave the emigrants a long list of instructions, and good advice enough for a population sufficient to settle the whole continent.  These instructions ordered —

1.  That the Church of England — that is, the national Episcopal Church — should be established in the colonies.

2.  That for the first five years no land should be given to any one, but that every settler must deposit the products of his labor in the company's warehouse, from which he would receive whatever he needed for his living.

3.  That the colonists should carefully explore all rivers in their vicinity, to see if they could not find "a short and easy way to the South Sea "[2] and the East Indies.

**47.  The London Company's Colony sails, 1607 ; Captain John Smith.** — The first colony[3] was sent out by the London Company on New Year's Day, 1607.  It consisted of 105 persons, all men.  Nearly half of these were classed as "gentlemen ";[4]

of north latitude; the Plymouth, that between the 41st and 45th degrees.  The intervening country (38th to 41st degrees), embracing what is now the coasts of Maryland, Delaware, New Jersey, and New York, was open to settlement by either company ; but neither was to settle within 100 miles of the other.

[1] Each colony was to be under the control of a resident council appointed by the king ; the council chose its own president.  This in turn was to be governed by a general council in London : both were to be subject to the king's will.

[2] The South Sea, that is, the Pacific Ocean.  See Paragraph 19.

[3] The Plymouth Company's colony is mentioned under Paragraph 93, note 1.

[4] In England, a gentleman is usually understood to be a person of good family and of independent income.  One or two of the "gentlemen " who went out to Virginia had property, but most of them were younger sons who had not inherited

that is, persons of good family, not brought up to manual labor. The remainder were mechanics, tradesmen, and laborers. Thus it will be seen that a very large proportion were unfit for such an undertaking — they were going out tenderhanded to struggle with the rough life of the wilderness.

Fortunately there was a young man of decided ability among the colonists. This was Captain John Smith. His energy and courage saved the settlers from starvation.

**48. The Emigrants settle Jamestown, Virginia, 1607 ; Condition of the Colony.** — The expedition went by way of the

West Indies, in order to trade with the natives there, and reached the American coast in the spring. About the middle of May they sailed up a river of Virginia, which they named the James River, in honor of the king; for the same reason they called the settlement which they began on a peninsula on that river, Jamestown.[1]

They found a country abounding in every natural advantage, and well deserving that name of the "Good Land," which the Indians are said to have given it. But they found themselves destitute of those rights and privileges which English citizens enjoyed, and which the charter expressly stated that they should continue to possess. At home many of them had a right to vote, and to take part in making the laws by which they were governed; in the Virginia woods they could do neither, for they were ruled by a council that was in turn ruled by the king.

Next, they owned no land, and the work of their hands did

money. They went hoping to make fortunes in the New World, either in Virginia, or in the Indies, which they supposed could easily be reached from there.

[1] The peninsula is now an island. It is about thirty miles up the river, on the northern bank.

not belong to them. In this last respect they were worse off than the poorest day-laborer they had left behind them. Furthermore, the idle man was certain that he would not suffer, for he could draw provisions out of the common storehouse; the industrious man, on the other hand, knew that by the sweat of his toil he must feed the idle. Considering this discouraging start, the wonder is that the colony not only lived, but lived to lay the foundation of a prosperous, powerful, and independent State.

**49. Sufferings of the Colonists; Search for the Pacific; Pocahontas.** — As the weather was warm, the new settlers built no houses at first, but lived under rude shelters made of branches or of old sails. The provisions they brought with them had partly spoiled, and the river water was unwholesome to drink. Many fell ill with fever. During the hot summer the mortality was terrible. By September, half of the settlers had died. The few who were able to be about had all they could do to tend the sick and dig graves. In the autumn matters somewhat improved; log huts were built, and the settlers were made more comfortable. Later, they urged Smith to lead an exploring expedition to find the South Sea.[1] They set out in high spirits, supposing that, at that point, the country was less than 200 miles across from the Atlantic to the Pacific![2]

In the course of the exploration Smith was captured by the Indians, and taken to their chief, Powhatan.[3] The chief was "a tall, sour-looking old man"; he ordered his warriors to knock Smith's brains out. According to the valiant captain's account, he was saved by Pocahontas,[4] the chief's youthful daughter, who ran up, just as the club was raised, and put her arms round the prisoner's head.[5]

---

[1] See Paragraph 46, No. 3, of the Instructions to the Colonists.
[2] A map of 1651, sold in London at that date, represents Virginia as a narrow strip of land between the two oceans. See a copy of the map in Winsor's "America," Vol. III., page 465. [3] Powhatan (Pow-at-an'). [4] Pocahontas (Pō-ca-hon'tas).
[5] Up to 1866 the truth of the Pocahontas story had never been questioned; but

Some years afterward, John Rolfe, a colonist who had come over to Virginia at a later period, became interested in Pocahontas. He labored for the conversion of the tender-hearted heathen, and labored so effectually that she not only embraced Christianity, but took Rolfe for her husband besides. The marriage was a fortunate one, since it made Powhatan the firm friend of the colony at a time when it needed all the friends it could get. King James, however, shook his head over the matter, and questioned whether Rolfe, being a man without rank, had not committed treason in presuming to marry a native American princess.

**50. Gold! the French settle in Canada, 1608; the Colony's Debt to Smith; the Colonists leave Jamestown.** — Not long after Smith's adventure with the Indians, one of the settlers found a yellowish substance which was said to be gold. In spite of the captain's vigorous protests, the colonists set to work to dig the "gilded dust" and load a vessel with it. When the cargo reached England, it was indeed found to be one sort of gold; that is, it was that worthless kind of glittering iron ore popularly known as "fool's gold."

In the summer of that year (1608) an event occurred destined to have important results. Champlain, a famous French explorer, sailed up the St. Lawrence to Quebec, and there established the first permanent French colony in America. It was the feeble beginning of a rival power which was one day to dispute the right of the English to possess any part of the country.[1]

Shortly after this date Smith was chosen president[2] of the

certain inconsistencies in Smith's account of the affair led the late Mr. Charles Deane in 1866 to deny its authenticity. For a defence of Smith's account, see Professor Arber's edition of Smith's works, and his article in the *Encyclopædia Britannica*, on "John Smith."

[1] De Monts, a friend of Champlain's, attempted to establish a colony in Acadia (Nova Scotia) in 1604, but his enterprise failed. The first permanent settlement in that part of the country was not made until 1610.

[2] See Paragraph 46, Article II., of the Charter, and note 1 on that paragraph.

THE PORTRAICTUER OF CAPTAYNE JOHN SMITH / ADMIRALL OF NEW ENGLAND

CAPTAIN JOHN SMITH.

council, and thus became head of the government at Jamestown.   His rule was an encouragement to the industrious, but
a terror to the lazy.   Those who tried to live without working
soon found that they must also try that harder thing — to live
without eating.   But the captain's term of office was short, for
he met with a fearful accident that made it necessary for him
to return to England.   He never revisited the colony.   After
he had gone, the Indians began depredations.   They had
looked up to Smith as a superior being, and when they
wanted rain used to beg him to pray for it for them.   Now,
they did not hesitate to rob and murder the settlers.   Everything went to rack and ruin.   Sickness and famine set in.   In
six months only sixty persons were left out of five hundred.
A ship came, bringing more colonists and some supplies; but
matters looked so discouraging that it was resolved to abandon the country, and go back to England.   Some of the settlers, when they left, were for setting fire to Jamestown, but
fortunately that was not done.   None shed a tear on going;
for, it was said, "none had enjoyed one happy day" there.

**51.  Lord Delaware; the New Charter; Governor Dale; the Great
Reform.** — The settlers had actually embarked, when they met
Lord Delaware coming up the river with a fleet from England.
Delaware made the settlers turn back.   He came out as governor under a new charter [1] which gave him the entire control
of the colony.   He had the power of ruling by military law,
and could hang a man, without a jury to decide his guilt.

Lord Delaware soon resigned, and was succeeded by Governor Dale.   He was a stern old soldier, determined to preserve order.   If a colonist talked against his regulations, the
governor had a hole bored through his tongue: that kept him

---

[1] This second charter (1609) gave the London Company the entire control of the
colony.   They appointed a governor to act for them.   Virginia was declared by this
charter to extend 200 miles north of Point Comfort, and the same distance south.
"West and northwest" it extended to the Pacific, and included all islands within
100 miles of either coast.

quiet for a while. If a man refused to go to church, he was put on short allowance of victuals, and whipped every day until he repented.

But the new governor was not simply a tyrant. He was a person of excellent judgment, and really sought the welfare of the colony. He practically abolished the old system of living out of the public storehouse.[1] To every settler he gave a small piece of land, and allowed him a certain number of days in the year to work on it for himself.[2] From this time a new spirit animated the community. Up to this year the laborer had been discouraged, for, no matter how hard he toiled, he had nothing he could call his own. Now, owing to the governor's wise provision, every man could look with pride on his little garden, and say, "*This is mine.*" That feeling gave him heart; before, he had worked in silence; now, he whistled while he worked. Before, he had not cared much whether he had the right to vote or not; but now that he was a property-holder, he wanted that right.

52. **What Tobacco did for Virginia.** — In 1612 John Rolfe, the husband of Pocahontas, began the systematic cultivation of tobacco.[3] In the course of a few years it came to be the greatest industry in Virginia.[4] At one time even the streets of Jamestown were planted with it. It took the place of money, and clergymen and public officers received their salaries in it. Before this, America had practically nothing to export. With tobacco, commerce began ; for Europe would buy all the colonists could raise.

[1] See Paragraph 46, No. 2, of the Instructions to the Colonists.

[2] Later, Governor Dale induced the London Company to grant 50 acres to any settler who would clear and settle on them, and pay a trifling rent to the king. For £12. 10s. (or say $300 in modern money), any one could purchase 100 acres where he pleased. Whoever performed a public service to the Company or Colony was to have a grant not exceeding 2000 acres.         [3] See Paragraph 29.

[4] The value of the tobacco crop of the United States is now nearly $57,000,000 annually ; that of cotton, the cultivation of which was begun about the same time, but not then extended, is upwards of $323,000,000. See Abstract of Census of 1900, p. 220.

King James denounced the use of the plant as "loathsome," "hateful," and "dangerous"; but the English people filled their pipes just the same, and smoked calmly on. Then His Majesty had to content himself with laying a heavy tax on tobacco, thus making "the vile weed" help support the throne.

The outlook of the colony now began to change for the better. The cultivation of tobacco had four important effects: 1. It directly encouraged the settlers to clear the land, and undertake working it on a large scale. 2. It established a regular and highly profitable trade with Europe. 3. It induced emigrants who had some money, and also industrious farmers, to come over to Virginia, and engage in the new industry. 4. It introduced the importation of negro slaves, as the cheapest means of carrying on great plantations.

These plantations had a decided influence on the population. They kept it scattered; and as the Virginians did not like to be cooped up in towns, few were built. The tobacco farms were on the banks of the James or other rivers, and vessels could load at them direct for England. Hence there was no need of a port to which to carry the produce. The cultivation of tobacco — especially by unskilled slave labor — exhausted the soil, and so compelled the planters to constantly add new land to their estates, thus pushing the owners farther and farther apart from each other. One result of this separation and of the lack of towns was that neither schools nor printing presses came into existence until very late, and the mass of the people had to get their education from nature, not from books or newspapers. Another result of the want of towns was that men seldom met to discuss public matters.

**53. Virginia becomes practically Self-governing; Importation of Wives.** — The year 1619 was a memorable one in the history of the colony. That year Sir George Yeardley [1] came over from England as governor. Acting under instructions from

---

[1] Yeardley (Yeerd'ly).

the London Company, he summoned a general assembly or legislature, to be elected by all the freemen of Virginia.

The colony now consisted of eleven plantations, or towns,[1] later called boroughs.[2] Each of these boroughs was invited to send two representatives or burgesses.[3] They met in the church at Jamestown, Friday, July 30, 1619.[4] This House of Burgesses, as it was then called, was the first law-making assembly that had ever come together in America. It meant that at last the colonists had practically obtained the right of managing their own affairs. Spain would not grant that power to her colonists in St. Augustine, or elsewhere. France would have refused it to Quebec and to her other settlements. England was then the only country in Europe, except Switzerland, where the people had a share in the government, and England now gave that privilege[5] — the greatest she could give — to her colonists in the New World. Later, the right was restricted, but it was never wholly taken away.

But though the men could now discuss politics and make laws, many of them had no proper homes, for but few unmarried women had emigrated to Virginia. To remedy this serious deficiency, the London Company sent out ninety young women. The cost of the passage for each[6] was fixed at 120 pounds of the best tobacco.

When the long-looked-for ship arrived, the young unmarried

[1] No counties had then been laid out in Virginia. Later, when counties were organized, nearly all the representatives were sent from them. This made the Virginia system of government far less democratic than that of Massachusetts (settled later), for there at first all public affairs were decided by the whole body of voters, and not by a selected number of persons representing them. When the population of Massachusetts became too large for this, the towns, instead of the counties, sent representatives to the legislature.

[2] Borough: an old English name for a town.

[3] Burgess: an inhabitant of a borough or a citizen elected to represent a borough. The House of Burgesses, or the lower house of the Virginia Legislature is now called the House of Delegates.

[4] The date is sometimes, though incorrectly, given as June 30.

[5] Confirmed by a written Constitution sent out by the London Company in 1621.

[6] The best tobacco was then worth about 75 cents a pound in Virginia.

men were waiting at the wharf, and those who had their tobacco ready soon managed to get wives in exchange. The ninety brides liked the country so well that they wrote back to England, and persuaded more maids to come over and take pity on the forlorn bachelors in the American wilderness.

**54. Introduction of Negro Slavery; White "Apprentices."** — In the records of this same remarkable year of 1619 we read these significant words: "About the last of August came in a Dutch man-of-war that sold us 20 Negars." This was the beginning of African slavery in the English colonies of America. At that time every leading nation of Western Europe traded in negroes. No one then condemned the traffic, for no man's conscience was troubled by it, and at a much later period the king of England derived a large income from selling slaves in America. The system gradually spread over the country, and a little more than a hundred and fifty years later (1776) every one of the thirteen American colonies held slaves. There was, however, this marked difference: at the North the negroes were nearly all kept as house-servants, and were not very numerous; but at the South they were employed chiefly as field-hands: so that there the whole system of agriculture depended on them, and many of the wisest and best men did not then see how tobacco and rice could be raised without slave labor.

Still, for a long time the increase of negro slaves in Virginia was very slow, for many white people were sent over from England to be bound out as apprentices [1] to planters for a certain number of years. Part of them were enterprising young men who wanted to get a start in America, but, having no money to pay their passage, bound themselves to work for the London Company, provided they would bring them over. In some cases poor children, picked up in the streets of

[1] They were commonly called "indentured servants" or "indentured apprentices," from the indentures or legal papers which bound them.

London, were sent here to get homes. Others, again, were kidnapped by scoundrels who made it their business to decoy young men, and ship them off as "servants" to America. At a later date, when wars and insurrections broke out in England, many prisoners taken in battle were sent over here, and sold to planters. Finally, in one case at least, King James I. insisted, in spite of the protest of the colonists, on despatching a hundred criminals to this country, thinking, perhaps, and possibly with truth, that ten years' experience here might make honest men of them.

Thus, many elements contributed to build up the new commonwealth. In this respect Virginia resembled the "madeland" of some of our cities. There is good material in it, and there is some not so good; but in time it all helps to make the solid foundation of stately streets and broad avenues.

While the South was thus growing, Dutch and English emigrants had settled at the North. The former established themselves in what is now New York, the latter, a little later, founded Plymouth, Massachusetts.

**55. Virginia becomes a Royal Province; Governor Berkeley; the Puritans and the Cavaliers.** — In 1624 King James took away the Company's charter. In future the colony was to be governed by the king as a royal province; but the assembly was not prohibited, and the people continued to make their own laws to a considerable extent.

The next king, Charles I., sent over Sir William Berkeley as governor. Governor Berkeley was a stanch Royalist. He had small faith in government by the people, in education of the people,[1] or in any religion but that of the Episcopal Church of England.

The majority of the well-to-do colonists and of the rich to-

---

[1] Speaking of the colony in 1671, Governor Berkeley said: "I thank God there are no free schools nor printing, and I hope we shall not have them these hundred years." His reason was that he thought education made the mass of the people discontented and rebellious against authority; but he subscribed toward a college.

bacco planters agreed with the governor. They thought that it was better for a community to confine the privileges of education and of political power to persons of property and standing than it was to give them to everybody who asked for them.

But at that time there was a strong party in England who called themselves Puritans, because they insisted on *purifying*, as they said, the national Church from some of its ceremonies and methods to which they were conscientiously opposed. That party was also opposed to the king, who endeavored in many respects to rule the country contrary to law, and in direct violation of the expressed will of the majority of the people. Many of the Puritans left their native land and sought refuge in New England, where they founded the city of Boston (1630). Next, a body of English Catholics settled Maryland (1634), and the Virginians, who were jealous of the new-comers, made them no little trouble. Later, the English drove the Dutch out of New York and New Jersey, and took possession of the country. But before this last event civil war had broken out in England. On the one side was the king, supported by the Royalists, or Cavaliers; on the other side were the Puritans, many of whom had left the national Church, and, under the name of Separatists or Independents, had set up a form of worship of their own.

The war went against the king. He was taken captive and beheaded. England was then declared a republic under Oliver Cromwell, and Governor Berkeley retired from office. Most of the leading Cavaliers were men of rank, and before the war had been men of property. As they found the new order of things very uncomfortable, hundreds of them emigrated to Virginia, where they knew the Puritans and republicans were few, and the Royalists numerous, rich, and influential.

Some of the most illustrious names in Virginia history are those of Cavalier emigrants. Lee was one, and Washington was probably another.[1]

[1] On the genealogy of the Washington family in England, see W. C. Ford's : *The*

The first was a friend of the late king; and members of the family of the second may have fought for him. The descendants of these men — Richard Henry Lee and George Washington — gave their strength, heart and soul, to the establishment of the United States of America.

**56. Governor Berkeley again in Power; the Navigation Laws; the King gives away Virginia.** — When monarchy was restored in England (1660), Sir William Berkeley put on the governor's silk robe of office again. For sixteen years he, with an Assembly that was in sympathy with him, ruled the colony according to his own imperious will. During that long period no new elections were held, and consequently the mass of the people had no voice in the government.

This grievance was not all. During Cromwell's time certain laws called Navigation Laws [1] had been enacted which forbade the Virginians to send any tobacco out of the country except in English vessels going to England, or to purchase any foreign goods except those brought over in English vessels. The new king, Charles II., now determined to revise and enforce these laws. Governor Berkeley protested, and all the planters with him; but it was useless. The result was that Virginia's chief trade was almost ruined; for the planters had to sell their tobacco for whatever English merchants saw fit to offer them, and then buy their sugar and their cloth at whatever price those merchants pleased to demand.

This was bad enough, but there was worse to come. In 1673 the wasteful and profligate king, with one stroke of his pen, gave away the whole of Virginia — a territory then having a population of 40,000 [2] — for thirty-one years, to the Earl of

*Writings of Washington*, XIV., 319. There is a strong probability that George Washington's ancestors belonged to the Cavalier or Aristocratic party.

[1] The original purpose of the Navigation Laws was not to restrict or injure the foreign trade of the American colonists, but to prevent the Dutch from competing with England in commerce.

[2] The population consisted of 32,000 freemen, 2000 negro slaves, and 6000 " apprentices " or white servants.

Arlington and Lord Culpepper, two of his favorites.  At last the question of ownership was settled in favor of the colonists, but for a long time it caused great anxiety and distress.

Meanwhile, as we have seen, English emigrants, mainly Puritans, had established flourishing colonies in New England; the Dutch had been forced to give up New York, and English Quakers had bought New Jersey.  In the South, English Catholics had settled in Maryland, and colonies of Englishmen had also been founded in the Carolinas.  Thus by 1675 an English-speaking population practically held control of the whole Atlantic coast of America from Maine nearly to the borders of Florida.

**57. Deplorable State of the Colonists ; the Bacon Rebellion.** — The people of Virginia were now in a deplorable state.  They had no homes that they could certainly call their own, they had no Assembly that represented them, the taxes were enormous, and they could get scarcely anything for the tobacco they exported.  Still their lives were safe, and while life was left hope was left.  But in 1676 the Indians suddenly rose, as they had just done in New England, and began massacring the inhabitants.  It was not the first attack, but it was the most terrible.  The people begged Governor Berkeley's help, but he did nothing.  Then a wealthy planter named Nathaniel Bacon raised a force, and took decided action against the Indians.  His influence finally became so great with the colonists that Governor Berkeley was obliged to allow the people to elect a new Assembly.

They did so, chose Bacon for one of their representatives, and enacted a series of reform measures known as the "Bacon Laws."  But as Bacon distrusted the governor, civil war soon broke out, and the "Virginia rebel," as he was called by those in authority, marched on Jamestown.  Seizing a number of the wives of the governor's friends, he placed them in front of his troops.  This "White Apron Brigade" saved him from the fire of the governor's guns. That night Jamestown was abandoned. In the morning Bacon entered it, and applying the torch, burned the place to the ground. It was never rebuilt. As you go up the James River to-day you see the ruined tower of the old brick church standing a melancholy memorial of the first English town settled in America.

Bacon soon after died; but one of his chief supporters,

named Drummond, fell into the governor's hands. "Mr. Drummond," said the governor, "you are very welcome. I am more glad to see you than any man in Virginia. Mr. Drummond, you shall be hanged in half an hour." He was executed forthwith. In all, Governor Berkeley put to death over twenty persons. When Charles II. heard of it, he said, "That old fool has hung more men in that naked country than I did for the murder of my father." [1]

Ruins of Jamestown.

But the colony never wholly forgot the meaning of the Bacon rebellion, and its protest against tyrannical government. The people's Assembly that enacted the "Bacon Laws" met in June, 1676. Just a century later their descendants met at Williamsburg, nearly in sight of the ruins of Jamestown, and there declared themselves independent of Great Britain.

[1] King Charles II. had tried and executed only six out of the fifty-nine judges who had sentenced his father (Charles I.) to death.

**58. Summary.** — Jamestown, the first English town permanently settled in the New World, was founded in 1607. There the first American legislative assembly met in 1619. Negro slaves were introduced the same year. The cultivation of tobacco built up commerce and largely increased the population but did not favor the growth of towns. The colony was strongly Royalist, and received many Cavaliers from England. Later, the Navigation Laws injured its prosperity. There was a period of bad government, and Bacon attempted reform. His undertaking failed. But the people remembered the man and his work, and Virginia, a hundred years later, was the first colony to propose the establishment of American independence.[1]

## II. New Netherland, or New York (1614).

**59. Henry Hudson's Expedition.** — In 1609 Captain Henry Hudson, an Englishman, then in the employ of Holland, crossed the Atlantic in the hope of finding a passage by water through or round America to China and India.

With his Dutch crew he entered what is now New York Bay, and was the first Englishman who sailed up that noble river which to-day bears his name. He reached a point about 150 miles from the mouth of the river, at or near where Albany now stands. It was the month of September, and Hudson had good reason for saying, "It is as beautiful a land as one can tread upon." About a month before, Champlain[2] had come almost as far south as that, on an exploring expedition from Quebec. He gave his own name to the lake, known ever since as Lake Champlain, and claimed the country for France.

**60. The Indians give Hudson a Reception on Manhattan Island; the Strange Drink.** — The Indians thought that the English captain, in his bright red coat trimmed with gold lace, must be the Great Spirit or his direct representative. They gave

[1] See Paragraph 167.      [2] See Paragraph 50.

him a formal reception on Manhattan Island. In the course of the interview Hudson drank the chief's health in a glass of brandy, and then offered him a glass. The chief took it, smelt of it, and passed it to his warriors. Thus it went from hand to hand. At last it came to one more daring than the rest. He thought the Great Spirit would be offended if no one tasted the beverage. Lifting the brandy to his lips, he bade his comrades a solemn farewell, and swallowed it. In a short time he began to stagger, and then fell unconscious to the ground. His friends imagined that he was dead; but before the conference was over the supposed dead man came to life. He declared that it was the "strongest water" he had ever tasted, and that it had made him happier than he had ever been before in his life. Soon, every red man present had tried the new and strange drink. Hudson meant the gift in no unkindly spirit, but to the natives it was simply poison. For them alcohol had a fatal fascination. Since then liquor has probably destroyed more Indians than war and disease combined. The Indians were afraid of the white man's gun; it would have been far better for them if they had been still more afraid of the white man's drink.

**61. The Dutch take Possession of New Netherland; Jealousy of England and France.** — The Dutch, finding from Hudson's report that valuable furs could be bought of the Indians at enormous profit, soon sent over ships, and opened trade with the natives. In 1614 the Republic of the United Netherlands or Holland, took possession of the country on the Hudson River, and gave it the name of New Netherland. That very year Captain John Smith, formerly of Jamestown, Virginia, explored the Atlantic coast east and northeast of the Hudson. He made a map of it, calling the country New England.

Both the English and the French now had good reason for turning jealous eyes on New Netherland, for that province was like a wedge. It separated the colony of Virginia from the

unsettled region of New England, and the point of it at the
north entered that territory which Champlain claimed as part
of New France.　A

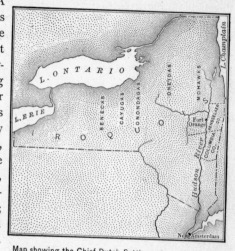

number of years
later (1623) the
Dutch made that
wedge more danger-
ous still by building
a fort on the Upper
Hudson.　This
stronghold they
called Fort Orange,
in honor of the
Prince of Orange,
president of the Re-
public of Holland;
but the Dutch did
better than build a
fort, for they made

Map showing the Chief Dutch Settlements on the Hudson.

a treaty with the Iroquois Indians which was sacredly kept
by those savages.　Many years afterward the English got possession of Fort Orange, and gave it the name of Albany, from
the Duke of York and Albany.

**62. Purchase of Manhattan Island.** — In 1626 the Dutch West
India Company sent out a colony under Governor Peter Minuit.[1]
He landed with his emigrants on the Island of Manhattan,

where a Dutch trading-post already existed.　The governor
bought from the Indians the entire island of 14,000 acres for
twenty-four dollars' worth of scarlet cloth, brass buttons, and
other trinkets, or at the rate of about one-sixth of a cent

[1] Minuit (Min´u-it).

an acre.[1] The city of New York now occupies that land, which is valued and taxed at a good deal more than a thousand millions of dollars.

The new settlement consisted of a fort, a stone warehouse, and a cluster of log huts. Such was the real beginning of the metropolis of America. The Dutch called the place by its Indian name of Manhattan, but later gave it the name of New Amsterdam.

63. The Patroons. — As Holland was anxious to establish a sufficient population in the province to hold it against all intruders, it granted a charter intended to favor emigration. That charter gave to any member of the Dutch West India Company who should take or send out fifty settlers within four years, the right to a large amount of land on any navigable river or bay in New Netherland. Such a proprietor was to receive the honorary title of "Patroon."[2] If he located his estate on one bank only of a river, he was to have sixteen miles of water-front; if on both banks, he was to have eight miles on each. Inland, he might extend his settlement as far as he could occupy the soil to advantage. In all cases he was to purchase the land of the Indians.

The patroon who began a settlement agreed to do three things: 1. To pay the expenses of the emigrant's passage from Holland. 2. To stock a farm for him on his estate with horses, cattle, and all necessary agricultural implements, at a small rent, and free from taxes. 3. To provide a schoolmaster and a minister of the Gospel.

[1]                                        "AMSTERDAM, Nov. 5, 1626.

"HIGH AND MIGHTY LORDS: Yesterday, arrived here the ship 'The Arms of Amsterdam,' which sailed from New Netherland . . . on the 23d of Sept. They report that our people are in good heart and live in peace there. . . . They have purchased the Island of Manhattan from the Indians for the value of 60 guilders [$24.00]. . . .

"Herewith, High and Mighty Lords, be commended to the mercy of the Almighty.
                "Your High Mightinesses' obedient,    "P. SCHAGEN."

[2] Patroon: patron, or protector.

In return, the emigrant bound himself in many ways, of which the three following were the principal ones : He agreed, 1. to cultivate the patroon's land for ten years, and not to leave it without permission. 2. To give the patroon the first opportunity to buy any grain or other produce he might have to sell. 3. To bring all disputes about property and rights to the patroon's court, of which the patroon himself was judge.[1]

A patroon named Van Rensselaer[2] took an estate in the vicinity of Albany, of 700,000 acres. It occupied both banks of the Hudson, extending twenty-four miles along the river, and reaching twice that distance back. Additions were made to the territory, so that eventually it embraced the three present counties of Albany, Rensselaer, and Columbia. The total area of that vast domain was considerably greater than that of the State of Rhode Island. Such a proprietor was richer than many a German prince. He was at once owner, ruler, and judge. He not only had a population of white settlers who were his servants and laborers, but he had moreover the promise from the Dutch West India Company of as many negro slaves as they could "conveniently provide" him. There was no one to contradict the patroon's will. He was clothed with authority which even Governor Minuit might envy ; for he was actually monarch of all he surveyed.

**64. Peter Stuyvesant, the Last Dutch Governor of New Netherland.** — In 1647 Peter Stuyvesant[3] came out to New Amsterdam as fourth and last governor of the province. He was a veteran who had given a leg to the cause of his country, and, having replaced it with a substantial wooden one, bound with

---

[1] In cases involving more than $20.00 value the settler might appeal from the patroon's court to the Company. Other points were these : 1. The settler agreed to bring his grain to the patroon's mill, and pay for the grinding. 2. He could not fish or hunt on the patroon's estate. 3. He was not to weave any cloth, but buy that imported from Holland. 4. If he died without leaving a will, all of his property fell to the patroon.    [3] Stuyvesant (Sti′ve-sant).

[2] Van Rensselaer (Van Ren′sel-ler). Other noted families dating from that period are the Schuylers and Van Cortlandts.

silver, was familiarly known as "Old Silverleg." Governor Stuyvesant was hot-tempered and headstrong; but he was honest, fearless, and determined to have order in the colony at any cost. If turbulent characters came in he disposed of them summarily. In a picture of New Amsterdam at that period two of the most prominent objects are the gallows and the whipping-post — both occupied.

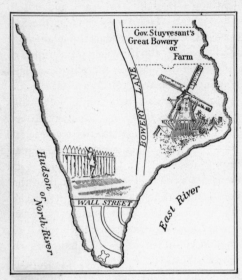

Map of the City of New Amsterdam (New York) in 1660.

The inhabitants complained of taxes, and wished to have a word to say how the money should be raised and spent. The governor resisted such presumption, but finally had to yield, and permit a council of "Nine Men" to be elected to assist him.

Later, when the people asked for still more liberty in this direction, he emphatically refused; for, said he, if citizens elect their own officers, "the thief will vote for a thief, and the smuggler for a smuggler."

Peter Stuyvesant.

In regard to freedom of worship he was equally decided. A minister who ventured to preach doctrines different from those of the Dutch Protestant Church was fined $500, and those who went to hear him had to pay $100 each. This made free thought expensive. Toward a few Quakers, who ventured into the colony, Stuyvesant was horribly cruel. The authorities in Holland rebuked him, and ordered that every man should be permitted to worship God in his own house in his own way; but the governor managed to do as he liked.

Aside from these tyrannical measures, Peter Stuyvesant was a good ruler. He made numerous improvements in the "city" of New Amsterdam — a "city" that in 1656 had a population of only a thousand, many of whom were negro slaves. In order to better defend the place he had a high and strong palisade built on the north of the town. It extended entirely across the island from river to river. Such was the origin of Wall Street, which to-day is the great money-centre of America.

From an early period the population of the town was a mixed one, made up of Dutch, French, and English. The laws had on this account to be published in three languages. Even then New Amsterdam was beginning to represent all nationalities. The Dutch saw that the place had a future, and predicted that the time would come when its "ships would ride on every sea." To-day the miles of wharves on the East and North Rivers, lined with vessels under every flag, and hailing from all the ports of the globe, show how far their judgment was correct. But England, too, understood the value of the Hudson and the harbor. She was determined to get possession of it, first, because of its commercial advantages; next, because, so long as the Dutch held it, Virginia and New England were both in danger.

In fact, Stuyvesant had made attempts to seize the country on the Connecticut River, where English settlers had come in, and he had furthermore succeeded in getting possession of what is now Delaware and New Jersey.

The English king, Charles II., claimed the whole country on the ground that the Cabots had discovered the coast and planted the English flag on it in 1497. For this reason Charles now gave it to his brother James, Duke of York. England and Holland were then at peace; but, suddenly, one day in 1664, a British fleet appeared off New Amsterdam, and demanded its surrender. Governor Stuyvesant was furious. He swore that he would never surrender "as long as he had a leg to stand on or an arm to fight with"; but finding that the citizens positively refused to uphold him he had to submit. The English promised full protection of life and liberty to the inhabitants. Furthermore, they agreed to grant religious liberty, freedom of trade, and a representative government.

The result was that the Dutch flag on the fort was hauled down, the English colors were run up, and thereafter the province of New Netherland became, in honor of James, Duke of York, the British province of New York. In like manner the quiet Dutch "city" of New Amsterdam became "his majesty's town of New York."[1]

Ex-Governor Stuyvesant went back to Holland, but soon returned to spend the rest of his days on his "great bowery," or farm, which was on the east side of the island, just outside the city limits. The street now called the Bowery recalls the "bowery lane" which once led to the stern old soldier's home.

**65. Summary.**— Henry Hudson, in 1609, sailed up the river named for him. The Dutch took possession of the country, and called it New Netherland; on Manhattan Island they founded the city of New Amsterdam. England and France were both jealous of the colony. In 1664 England took possession of the country, and named it **New York,** in honor of James, Duke of York.

---

[1] In 1673 New York was captured by the Dutch during war between Holland and England, but was given up to the English again when peace was made, less than a year later. From that time until the Revolution it remained subject to England.

## III. NEW JERSEY (1617).

**66. The Dutch claim the Country between the Hudson and the Delaware; New Jersey.** — In 1617 the Dutch, crossing over from Manhattan Island,[1] built a small fort at Bergen,[2] on the west bank of the Hudson. Later they built a second fort nearly opposite where Philadelphia now stands. The whole country between these forts they claimed as part of New Netherland,[3] though the English maintained that as the Cabots had discovered the coast, it belonged by right to them.[4]

In 1664, after the English had conquered the Dutch colony of New Netherland, the Duke of York gave the whole territory between the Delaware River and the Hudson to his friends Lord Berkeley[5] and Sir George Carteret. Sir George had

been governor of the island of Jersey in the English Channel. During the Civil War he gallantly defended that island in behalf of Charles I., the Duke of York's father. For this reason the Duke named the country which he granted to him and to Lord Berkeley, New Jersey. An English settlement was made that year at a place which the emigrants called Elizabethtown,[6] in honor of Lady Elizabeth Carteret, wife of Sir George.

Very liberal terms were granted to settlers by the proprietors of this province, and the people had a direct part in the government.

**67. The Friends, or Quakers, buy New Jersey; Treaty with the Indians; Prosperity of the Country; New Jersey becomes a Royal Colony.** — In 1674 some English Friends, or Quakers, bought

[1] See Paragraph 62.  [2] Bergen: pronounced Ber′gen, *g* hard. See Map, p. 112.
[3] See Paragraph 61.  [4] See Paragraph 14.  [6] Now, Elizabeth.
[5] John, Lord Berkeley, and not Governor Berkeley of Virginis.

Lord Berkeley's share, or West Jersey, and later William Penn and other members of the Society of Friends bought the other half, or East Jersey, from the heirs of Sir George Carteret.

The Friends made a treaty with the Indians at Burlington which was so satisfactory to the savages that they declared that if they found an Englishman sleeping in the path, they would not molest him, but would say, "He is an Englishman; he is asleep; let him alone." In the same spirit of good will the Friends granted self-government to the colonists. The people levied their own taxes, made their own laws, and all settlers enjoyed religious liberty. The commerce of the Jerseys increased, and iron manufacture was begun. But eventually trouble arose about titles to land, and the proprietors thought it best (1702) to put the two colonies directly into the hands of the English government. They were united under the jurisdiction of the governor of New York; but in 1738 New Jersey became a separate province. From this time until the Revolution it was ruled by a governor of its own appointed by the king of England. The last of the royal governors was William Franklin, son of Benjamin Franklin.

**68. Summary.** — The Dutch first claimed possession of what is now New Jersey. The English Duke of York seized the country and gave it to two of his friends, naming the province from the British island of Jersey.

A company of English Quakers then bought the land, granting to the settlers most of the privileges of self-government. In 1702, the Quaker proprietors surrendered their rights to the English sovereign, and New Jersey became a royal colony until the Revolution.

### IV. Massachusetts (Plymouth Colony, 1620).

**69. Former Lack of Religious Liberty in England; Catholics; Puritans; Separatists.** — When the English began to settle in America (1607), no country in Europe had that entire freedom of worship which every civilized nation enjoys to-day.  In England the law required every one to attend the Protestant Episcopal Church established by the government.  Furthermore, all persons had to pay taxes for the support of that church.

Three classes of good and loyal citizens objected to that law.  They were, first, the Catholics, who protested against the injustice of being obliged to aid in maintaining a creed they did not accept; secondly, the Puritans,[1] who thoroughly believed in the principle and also in the doctrines of the national Protestant Church, but decidedly objected to some of its ceremonies; lastly, the Separatists, who, like the Puritans, accepted the religious teachings of the Church of England, but, not approving its forms, had separated from it and set up independent congregations of their own.

**70. Emigration of those who sought Religious Liberty; the Separatists go to Holland.** — Not being able to obtain the freedom they desired in England, many emigrants, representing the Catholics, the Puritans, and the Separatists, came to America. Here, they hoped that they might be able to worship God without molestation, according to the dictates of their consciences.

The first who thus emigrated were the Separatists.  In 1607 a congregation of these people held religious services in the little English village of Scrooby.[2]  Finding that they could have no peace, but were, as they said, "hunted," "persecuted," and "clapped up in prison," they fled to Holland, where, they had heard, there "was freedom of religion for all men."

**71. The Separatists, or Pilgrims, resolve to go to America; their Reasons.** — In 1620 a part of the Separatists, or Pilgrims,[3] as

[1] See Paragraph 55.

[2] In the East of England, in the extreme north of Nottinghamshire, at a point where that county joins Lincolnshire and Yorkshire.  See Map, page 78.

[3] "So they left that goodly and pleasant city [Leyden, Holland; see Map, p. 78] which had been their resting-place near twelve years; but they knew they were PILGRIMS [see Hebrews xi. 13] and looked not much on those things; but lifted up their eyes to the heavens, their dearest country, and quieted their spirits." — BRADFORD'S *History of Plymouth*, 1607–1646.  See the MS. in State House, Boston.

they now with good reason called themselves,—for they had no fixed home,—resolved to emigrate to America.

Aside from the prospect of a terrible religious war between Spain and Holland, three chief reasons induced the Pilgrims to leave the country: 1. In Holland, though they were with a friendly people, yet they were among those whose language and customs were not English. 2. As their children grew up, they would naturally marry into the Dutch families, and in a few generations their descendants would become Dutch. 3. Finally, they desired to build up a community on soil belonging to England, where they and those who came after them might enjoy both political and religious liberty, according to the Pilgrim standard of what was just and right.

72. **Where they proposed going; how they got Assistance to go.** — The only English settlement then in America was that at Jamestown, Virginia. The Pilgrims could not go to that part of the country, for no worship but that of the Church of England was permitted there. They eventually determined to establish themselves at some place near the Hudson River.[1] They had first to get the consent of King James of England. He would not openly favor their going, but finally "consented to wink at their departure" for America. As most of the Pilgrims were poor men, they were obliged to get assistance for their passage. A company of English merchants and speculators agreed to help them on these hard conditions: 1. The Pilgrims were to work for seven years without a single day to themselves except Sunday. 2. At the end of that time all that they had accumulated was to be divided equally between them and the company. On these terms a settler would not even own the whole of his house and garden after seven years' incessant toil. But the emigrants could not do better, and the agreement was signed, though it made a number of men

[1] " To find some place about Hudson's river for their habitation."— BRADFORD'S *History of Plymouth*, 1607–1646. The Pilgrims thought at one time of going to New Amsterdam (New York) and settling among the Dutch, but that was given up.

THE HOMES OF THE PI

SCROOBY CHURCH.

NORTH SEA

FOLK
armouth•

FOLK
roton

T

L

AMSTERDAM

• Leyden

Delftshaven

HOLLAND

Meuse R.

BELGIUM

FRANCE

PRUSSIA

NGLAND AND IN HOLLAND.

past the prime of life simply "apprentices and servants" to the company.

**73. The Pilgrims sail; Myles Standish.** — On September 16, 1620, the *Mayflower* sailed from Plymouth, England, carrying the second English colony that was to make a permanent home in the new world.[1]  There were only 102 of the emigrants, all told, and of these, less than ninety could be called Pilgrims.  The others were persons who had joined them, or were servants or sailors hired by them.

Among those who were not members of the Pilgrim congregation, but who chose to cast their lot in with them, was Captain Myles Standish.[2]  He was a man with the heart of a lion in battle, and the hand of a woman for the sick and wounded. Without his counsel and his sword it is doubtful if the colony could have succeeded.

**74. The Pilgrims reach Cape Cod; the Compact.** — On a morning late in November the storm-tossed Pilgrims sighted Cape Cod.  They tried to go south of it, but the weather was against them, and two days later (Nov. 21st) the *Mayflower* finally came to anchor in what is now Provincetown Harbor, at the extreme end of the Cape.

They had no authority to settle in New England, but they decided to do so.  Some of the servants had threatened that if they stopped there, they would be their own masters and obey no one.  To preserve order, the Pilgrims gathered in the cabin of the *Mayflower* and there drew up and signed a com-

[1] The Pilgrims sailed from Delftshaven, the port of Leyden, Holland (see Map, page 78), the last of July, 1620, in the *Speedwell*, for Southampton, England, where the *Mayflower* was waiting.  August 5 both ships sailed for America with about 120 passengers.  Twice the *Speedwell* put back in a leaky condition.  Finally, on September 16 (New Style), the *Mayflower* sailed alone from Plymouth, England, on her ever-memorable voyage to America.

[2] One branch of the Standish family in England has always been Catholic; the other is Protestant.  It is not certainly known to which Myles Standish belonged; but probably to the latter — the family of Duxbury Hall, Lancashire.

pact or agreement. By that agreement they declared themselves "loyal subjects" of the king, and at the same time they

affirmed their purpose of making whatever laws were needful for the "general good of the colony." They elected John Carver for their first governor. Thus the new Commonwealth began: they were but a few score people, but they had the strength that belongs to those who fear God and respect themselves.

**75. They explore the Coast, and land; Plymouth Rock; the First Winter.** — While the *Mayflower* remained at anchor, Captain Standish with a boatload of men went out to explore. On December 21 they reached the harbor which

Plymouth Rock.

Captain John Smith had called Plymouth on the map made by him, in 1614. On the shore of that harbor lies a granite bowlder. It is said to be the only one directly on the water's edge for several miles. According to tradition they landed on that bowlder. It is not a large one, only a few feet square, but it fills a greater place in American history than any other rock on the continent; for Plymouth Rock is the stepping-stone of New England.

A few days later, the *Mayflower* sailed into that harbor, the men all went ashore, and the work of building a log hut for the general use began. Later, another cabin was erected, but it had to be used for a hospital instead of a settler's home.

Such were the hardships of that winter that by spring nearly half of the colony were in their graves. But when the *Mayflower* went back, in April (1621), not one of the Pilgrims returned in her. They had come to stay.

**76. Governor Bradford; Town-Meeting; the Indians.** — Soon after the *Mayflower* sailed Governor Carver died. William Bradford (1621) was chosen to fill his place, and from that time for thirty-six years, until his death in 1657 he was chosen governor every year except five — and those five he begged off. Those thirty years and more of office show what the Pilgrims thought of the man.

All public matters were discussed and decided in town-meeting. There every man met his neighbor on equal terms. There the laws were made. It was pure government by the people — such government as was known nowhere else in either this country or Europe except perhaps in a few districts of Switzerland. The nearest approach to it in America was the

Monument to Captain Myles Standish on " Captain's Hill," Duxbury, Plymouth Bay.

Virginia House of Burgesses, but that was made up of representatives of plantations, — later of counties, — and was not a meeting of the whole people. The laws the Pilgrims made they enforced. The man who resisted was speedily tied neck and heels together on the ground, and left there for a reasonable time to meditate on the error of his ways.

Not long before his death Governor Carver had made a treaty with Massasoit, chief of a neighboring tribe in the southwest. The treaty was faithfully kept — it was not really broken for more than fifty years.  Later, Canonicus, chief of a tribe of hostile Indians, threatened to attack Plymouth.  He sent Governor Bradford a declaration of war in the shape of a bundle of arrows tied round with a rattle-snake-skin.  The governor did not hesitate.  He took the snake-skin, stuffed it full of powder and bullets, and sent it back.  Canonicus, like a prudent savage, decided to let the governor alone.  When trouble with Indians did arise later, Myles Standish soon made them confess that though "he was a little man, he was a great captain."

**77. The Pilgrims buy out the English Company ; what made the Pilgrims Great.** — In 1626 the Pilgrims bought out the English merchants' shares in Plymouth colony.  It cost them a large sum of money, and they had to borrow it in London at from thirty to fifty per cent interest.  But they were determined to be free of the company at any cost.  Henceforth every man had a right to whatever he could gain for himself by fishing, fur-trading, or farming.

The colony increased but slowly.  Even at the end of ten years there were only 300 people in Plymouth.  Massachusetts colony, founded in 1630, overshadowed and finally absorbed it.  It was not what the Pilgrim fathers actually accomplished that made them great ; it was the spirit in which they worked. There is one thing in this world that is better than success — that is to deserve success.  That they had gained ; as their brethren wrote them from England, "Let it not be grievous to you that you have been instrumental to break the ice for others.  *The honor shall be yours to the world's end.*"

IV.  MASSACHUSETTS (MASSACHUSETTS BAY COLONY, 1630).

**78. Settlement of Salem ; Governor Endicott ; Toleration.** — In 1628 John Endicott of Dorchester, England,[1] assisted in

---

[1] Dorchester, in Dorsetshire, in the South of England.

planting a colony on the coast of Massachusetts.[1]  Endicott was a Puritan of the most decided stamp.  He wished to establish a place of refuge in New England for the oppressed people of his own faith, and of his own faith only.

The new settlement received the significant Bible name of Salem, or Peace,[2] because there the Puritans hoped to find rest from persecution.  The year after his arrival Endicott was appointed deputy-governor of the colony by the Massachusetts Bay Company[3] of London which owned the land, the governor-in-chief, Matthew Cradock, remaining in England.  Governor Endicott was conscientious and fearless.  He lived in an age when toleration, or liberty of worship, was not only unknown in England, but when the word itself could not be found in the dictionary.  Had it been there, the governor would probably have cut it out, just as, at Salem, a few years later, he drew his sword and cut the red cross out of the English flag.  That cross represented to his mind the ancient Catholic religion of England; for that reason he would not have it on the royal banner.  The word "toleration" would have seemed to him equally dangerous, and he would have got rid of that in the same way.

Yet Governor Endicott, and those who came with him and after him, sincerely loved their native country and left it with regret.  One of them,[4] as he stood on the deck of the vessel that was bearing him to America, looked back with eyes dim with tears.  "Farewell," said he, "dear England!  Farewell, the Church of God in England, and all Christian friends there."

Yet these were the same men who a little later were so in love with the New World that they wrote back that "a sip of

[1] Massachusetts: an Indian word supposed to mean "the Great Hills."  It was probably given to the Blue Hills of Milton, near Boston.  The English confined the name at first to the vicinity of Boston Harbor.

[2] Salem is about sixteen miles north of Boston.

[3] This company had obtained a grant of land from the Council for New England in London.  The grant was confirmed by royal charter in 1629.

[4] Rev. Francis Higginson of the First Church of Salem, 1629.

New England's air is better than a whole draught of Old England's ale." These were indeed the right sort of emigrants to establish permanent colonies, and to lay the foundations of flourishing states.

**79. Governor Winthrop's Colony ; Settlement of Boston.** — But the great emigration to New England began in 1630. The

Shawmut, or Tri-Mountain, 1630.

Massachusetts Bay Company had determined to transfer their charter* and government from London to Massachusetts. John Winthrop, a wealthy Puritan gentleman of Groton,[1] decided to emigrate, and the Massachusetts Bay Company appointed him to take the place of both Matthew Cradock and Governor Endicott. John Winthrop thus became the first sole and resident governor of Massachusetts.

He came with a fleet of eleven vessels, bringing a colony of over seven hundred persons, with horses, cattle, and all things needed for establishing a thriving settlement. Not finding Salem to his liking, Governor Winthrop and his company went to Charlestown; but at that

Boston To-Day.

place the water was not good, and there was much sickness.

Opposite Charlestown is a peninsula which then had three hills, of which the middle one was divided into three peaks.

[1] Groton, Suffolk County, in the East of England. Governor Winthrop came for the same reason that Endicott did, because the Puritans, as he said, had "no place to fly unto, but the wilderness." He also felt that Great Britain needed an outlet for her unemployed thousands. "This land" [England], said he, "grows weary of her Inhabitants, so as man, who is the most precious of all creatures, is here more vile and base than the earth we tread upon, and of less price among us than a horse or sheep." — WINTHROP's *Life and Letters.*   * See note 3 on page 83.

The Indians called the peninsula Shawmut,[1] but the English named it Tri-mountain.[2]  On that peninsula, where there was an abundance of excellent water, lived William Blackstone,[3] an English hermit.  He was the only white inhabitant of Shawmut.  Blackstone invited Governor Winthrop and his company to move over.  They did so ; and a little later we find the record of an order of the court commanding that Tri-mountain should thereafter be called Boston.[4]  The name was given in affectionate remembrance of the old city of Boston, England,[5] from which place, and its vicinity, many of the colonists had emigrated.

In the course of the next ten years more than 20,000 of Governor Winthrop's countrymen came to New England. Among them were high-born men and women, with graduates of Oxford and Cambridge, besides people of property and influence — "the very flower of the English Puritans."

**80. How Massachusetts was governed; Who could vote; Occupations of the People.** — During the first two years the settlers permitted a governing council [6] to manage all public affairs. Later (1634) the towns sent representatives to the legislature, or General Court, as it was and still is called.  These representatives made the laws.  Not all the inhabitants could vote. We have seen that in Virginia [7] that right was at last restricted to men of property, or "gentlemen " ; in Massachusetts it was confined to church-members.  The object was practically the

---

[1] Shawmut, meaning, it would seem, either a place reached by water, or sweet water.

[2] Tri-mountain, or Tremont: this name is preserved in Tremont Street. It appears to have been given originally to the middle hill — Beacon Hill — because of its three peaks, two of which have since been rounded off.  The other two hills were Fort Hill (since levelled) and Copp's Hill.

[3] Blackstone, or Blaxton: it is supposed that he had been a clergyman of the Church of England.  His house was on the west slope of Beacon Hill, probably not far from the corner of Beacon and Spruce streets.  He moved to the neighborhood of Providence, where he died.

[4] "It is ordered that Trimontaine [Tri-mountain] shall be called Boston."  Sept. 17th, 1630.          [5] Boston, Lincolnshire, on the east coast of England.

[6] "Court of Assistants" : nominally 18 ; really only 12.       [7] See Paragraph 55.

same in both cases; the Virginians wished to keep the government of the colony in the hands of royalist landholders or responsible citizens; the Puritan commonwealth of Massachusetts wished to keep it in the control of Puritans. This corner of the continent, said they, is ours. If others come to it who want a different religion and different kind of government, we give them full liberty — to move on.

Governor Winthrop, like Governor Berkeley of Virginia,[1] did not believe in granting the privilege of voting to all who asked it. He and his friends wanted a state governed not by the majority, but by a select few. "The best part of a com-

munity," said he, "is always the least, and of that part the wiser are still less."

The population of the colony was to a large extent gathered in towns along the coast. Much of the soil was too poor to produce good crops, and there were no great plantations or estates like those of Virginia. But what the colonists could not get from the land, they got either directly or indirectly from the sea. Thousands of men were engaged in the cod fisheries on the banks of Newfoundland, and many were employed in the construction of vessels. Boston, it is said, had then the best shipbuilders in the world. Massachusetts had also a thriving commerce with the West Indies. The colonists sent out cargoes of staves and lumber, and imported quantities of sugar and molasses from which they distilled the famous "New England rum," an article which most people then considered one of the necessaries of life.

**81. Banishment of Roger Williams and Mrs. Hutchinson.** — The fact that the Puritans considered Massachusetts exclusively their own led to the banishment of Roger Williams. He had

[1] See Paragraph 55.

come from England as a minister, and was settled over the church in Salem. He was one of the very few men of that day who thoroughly believed in religious freedom, or, as he called it, "soul liberty." "No one," said he, "should be bound to maintain a worship against his own consent." To say that was to strike directly at the law of Massachusetts, which required every man to attend public worship and to pay for its support. But not only did Roger Williams get into trouble on account of his denial of the right of one man to interfere in any way whatever with the liberty of another's conscience, but he greatly alarmed the Massachusetts authorities by his political utterances. The Company held their territory by a charter given by the king. Mr. Williams denied that the king had any power to give them the land, because it belonged first of all to the Indians. This was a new and startling way of looking at things, and the colonists feared that free utterance of this kind might provoke the English sovereign to take away their charter. Roger Williams was ordered (1635) to leave the colony. Later, an attempt was made to arrest him and send him to England. Williams escaped. It was winter and the weather was bitterly cold. The fugitive took refuge among the Indians, who fed and sheltered him. The next spring he reached Narragansett Bay, and founded what is now the beautiful city of Providence.

Whatever faults the exiled minister may have had, and whatever mistakes of judgment he may have made, we should never forget that he first demanded the right of entire religious liberty for all men.

The same year Mrs. Anne Hutchinson, a woman of remarkable ability and unblemished character, attacked many of the Massachusetts clergy about their religious belief, which seemed to her more a matter of form than of faith. She lectured or preached every week, and her influence was so great that a company of soldiers that had been raised to fight the Indians refused to march because their chaplain did not agree with Mrs. Hutchinson.

The General Court thought it was bad enough to have an Indian war on hand without having also a war of words about creeds. They decided that Mrs. Hutchinson was, as they said, "like Roger Williams, or worse," and compelled her to leave the colony. Later, the Baptists were forbidden to preach in Massachusetts and were punished when they refused to obey the command.

These were harsh measures, but the colonists believed that it was their duty to maintain their Puritan faith at any cost, and they did it.

Roger Williams soon had a chance to show that he could forgive those who had despitefully used him. The Pequots,[1] an Indian tribe of Connecticut, were plotting a massacre of the white settlers of that part of the country, and were trying to stir up the Narragansetts to attack Massachusetts. Williams used his influence with the latter tribe to such good effect that they refused to fight. Thus the exiled minister was probably the means of saving the people of Boston and surrounding towns from the horrors of an Indian war.

**82. Public Schools; Harvard University; Eliot's Work among the Indians.** — In 1635 provision was made for the establishment of a public school in Boston. Twelve years later (1647) a law was enacted practically providing instruction for every white child in Massachusetts. This laid the foundation of the common school system of the United States.[2] Not satisfied with thus doing what no country in Europe had ever done, the General Court voted in 1636 to give four hundred pounds[3] — or what was equal to an entire year's tax of the colony — to found a college at Newtown, afterward called Cambridge.

[1] The Pequots inhabited the valley of the Pequot, or Thames, River, in Eastern Connecticut.

[2] See "The Origin and Growth of Our Public Schools" (D. H. M.), Ginn & Co.

[3] Four hundred pounds: a sum probably equal in cash to $10,000 now; but as the vote was a whole year's tax, it was the same as if the State should give that amount to-day, which would be over five millions!

It is said that "this was the first legislative assembly in which the people, through their representatives, ever gave their own money to found a place of education."

Two years later the Rev. John Harvard of Charlestown left his library of three hundred and twenty volumes, and half of his estate, — or about seven hundred and fifty pounds,[1] — to the college. The General Court out of gratitude ordered the new institution — the first English college in America — to be called by his name: such was the origin of Harvard University.[2]

The interest felt in the college was so great and so universal that at one time (1645) every family throughout New England gave either a peck of corn or twelve pence in money towards its support. The people were poor, but they were determined, as they said, "that learning should not be buried in the graves of their fathers."

Another object of founding the college was to educate and christianize the Indians. Pastor John Robinson, of the Pilgrim church of Leyden, Holland,[3] once wrote of Myles Standish, after that valiant captain had fought a battle with the natives: "O how happy a thing it would have been if you had converted some before you killed any!" The captain never turned missionary, but Rev. John Eliot of Massachusetts resolved that he would convert some.

He labored for many years among the Indians in the vicinity of Boston with great success. After preaching he used to give the men tobacco, and the women apples, to help them digest the sermons, some of which were full three hours long.

Eliot also translated the Scriptures into the Indian language. That Bible is in one respect unlike any other, for it is doubtful whether there is more than a single person now living who can read a chapter of it. When we come to King Philip's War, many years after Eliot began his noble work, we

---

[1] It would represent about $20,000 now.     [3] See Paragraph 71, Note 3.

[2] The next colleges in order of time were William and Mary College, Virginia, 1693, and Yale University, Connecticut, 1701.

shall see how the colonies reaped the fruit of the labors of the
"Apostle to the Indians."

**83. The New England Confederacy.** — In 1643 Massachusetts
Bay united with Plymouth and with the two western colonies
of Connecticut and New Haven in a league for mutual defence.
The league was maintained for over forty years. Rhode Island
and Maine wished to join it, but were refused, because the first
had established freedom of worship, and the second stood by
the king and the Church of England. In that day the Puritans could not conscientiously associate themselves with either.

The object of the confederacy was twofold :[1] First, the colonies sought to protect themselves against hostile Indians and
against the Dutch, who were anxious to get possession of the

territory between
the Hudson and
the Connecticut
Rivers. Secondly,
they wished to
express their sym-
pathy with the
Puritan party in
England, which
was then engaged
in a struggle with the tyrannical king Charles I.,[2] and which
soon after changed England for a time into a republic.

After the confederacy had ceased to exist the remembrance
of it helped the colonists to unite against the French, who
threatened, in 1750, to drive them out of the land. Still later,
when trouble with England came, the fact that there had once
been such an organization as the so-called "United Colonies

---

[1] One object of the confederacy was to secure the return of runaway slaves to
their masters.

[2] The words "you shall bear true faith and allegiance to our sovereign Lord King
Charles" were now dropped from the oath required by Massachusetts of its governors
and chief office-holders.

of New England " prepared the way for that great and permanent confederacy of all the colonies, north and south, known
first as the " United Colonies of America," and finally as the
"United States of America."

**84. The Coming of the Friends, or Quakers.** — In 1656 the citizens of Massachusetts kept a solemn day of fasting and prayer
on account of the news of the doings in England of a strange
people called Quakers. It was said that they were turning the
world upside down with their preaching, and that if they were
not stopped they would destroy all churches and all modes of
government. A fortnight after that fast-day the inhabitants of
Boston heard to their horror that two women, who were Quaker
missionaries, had actually landed in their town. To them it
seemed that the two women had come only to do mischief.

The authorities at once thrust them into jail, boarded up
the window of their cell that they might not speak to any one
outside, and burned the books the women had brought with
them. As soon as possible they put both missionaries on
board ship and sent them to England. But others came, and
all Massachusetts was soon in a fever of excitement.

**85. Why the Coming of the Quakers excited Alarm.** — To-day
there are no quieter, more orderly, or more self-respecting people than the Friends, or Quakers. Boston would welcome a
colony of them now, and feel that the city was the gainer by
their coming. Why did the arrival of a few of them then
excite such alarm? The reason was that the Quakers of that
time stood in decided opposition to the ideas of the great
majority of sober and discreet citizens. When men asked,
"Where shall we find what is right?" the Church of England
answered, "You will find it in the teachings of the Church."
The Puritans replied, "You will find it in the Bible." The
Quakers said, "You will find it in your own heart." To most
persons of that age such an answer seemed like rejecting both
Church and Bible.

But the difficulty did not end there. The Friends, or Quakers, had peculiar ideas about society and government. First, they would not use titles of honor or respect to any one, and they would not take off their hats to a magistrate or a governor — no, not even to the king himself. This appeared to the people then a reckless contempt of authority. Next, the Quakers observed no ceremonies in their worship.

But, acting in accordance with what they believed to be the teachings of the Gospel, they refused to do three things much more important: 1. They would not give testimony under oath in a court of justice, or swear to support the government. 2. They would not pay taxes to support any form of public worship. 3. They would not do military service or bear arms even in self-defence.[1]

**86. Excesses committed by some Quakers.** — These things would certainly have set the Puritans against the Quakers, no matter how conscientious the latter might have been. But there were other reasons why the citizens of Massachusetts regarded them with intense indignation. The persecution the Quakers had suffered appears to have driven some of them half crazy. One of them cried out to the governor that God would smite him. Several others forced their way into Puritan meetings on Sunday and called the ministers hypocrites and deceivers of the people. These things occurred only in Massachusetts. The Quakers in New Jersey and Pennsylvania[2] never interfered with any form of worship, and peace and good order prevailed. In fact, no colony in America prospered more than that founded by the Quaker, William Penn.

**87. The Puritans punish and execute the Quakers; End of the Persecution.** — If such disturbances, as happened in Massachusetts, should occur now, the offenders would be called insane.

1 The religious belief of the Friends, or Quakers, may be summed up as follows: to obey conscience, and, dispensing with forms, to follow literally what they understand to be the commands of Christ.    2 See Paragraphs 67 and 123.

But the Puritans were moved not by compassion, but by anger. They were stern men and they took stern measures. They arrested the Quakers, whipped some of them through the towns, cut off the ears of others, threatened to brand others with red-hot irons, and drove them out into the wilderness.

But the severity was useless; the Quakers felt that they had a mission to the Puritans, and they persisted in returning and preaching it in the loudest manner. They were non-resistants, they would not strike back when persecuted; but they would use their tongues, and their tongues were like two-edged swords. Finally, after repeated warnings, the Massachusetts authorities actually hanged four of these missionaries, one a woman, on Boston Common, and buried their bodies at the foot of the gallows.

The king, however, who was friendly to William Penn, a prominent English Quaker, thought it policy to order that the colony should cease punishing them or other persons on account of their religion, and the excitement gradually died out. From that day to this the Commonwealth of Massachusetts has had no better citizens than the Friends, or Quakers.

**88. King Philip's War.** — In 1675, Philip, son of Massasoit, and chief of the Wampanoags of Rhode Island, began a terrible war against the colonists. While Massasoit lived, the treaty he had made with the English had been faithfully kept; but "King Philip" believed that the great struggle of races was at hand, and that if he and his people did not exterminate the white men, then the white men would certainly exterminate them. Philip succeeded in forming an Indian league, and the savages began a sudden attack on the towns of Southern and Western Massachusetts. At last, after about two years of desperate fighting, in which the loss was very heavy on both sides, and many towns were destroyed, Philip's wife, and his only son, a lad of nine, were both captured. "Now," said the terrible warrior, "my heart breaks. I am ready to die." Shortly after, Philip was killed at his home at Mount Hope, not far from Bristol, Rhode Island. His hands were cut off and carried to Boston, and his head to Plymouth, where it stood exposed on a pole for twenty years. Many of the Indian prisoners were sold as slaves to South America and the West Indies. Among them were King Philip's wife and boy. An aged minister of West Bridgewater remonstrated against this act of cruelty, but without avail. During the war Eliot's "praying Indians," as they were called, remained faithful to the whites, and were the means of saving many lives among the English settlers. With the death of Philip the Indians became discouraged, their power was broken, and Southern New England never again stood in fear of these once powerful tribes.

**89. The Salem Witchcraft.** — In 1692 that extraordinary delusion the Salem witchcraft caused a reign of terror in that town. In Great Britain several thousand unfortunate persons had suffered death for this alleged crime, and the English statute punishing it was not repealed until 1736, or "more than forty years after the excitement in New England had subsided." The whole matter seems to have originated with a few mischief-loving children who accused certain persons of tormenting them. Those so charged were tried for witchcraft, that is, for being in league with evil spirits, and in all nineteen persons were hanged before the terrible error had spent its force. Then the good sense of the Massachusetts people asserted itself; and though in Europe unfortunate old women were still occasionally put to death on charges of witchcraft, no human life was again sacrificed here on such an accusation.

**90. Massachusetts loses her Charter; Governor Andros.** — But before this strange outbreak at Salem occurred, Massachusetts had lost her charter, and was no longer self-governing. For many years the king, Charles II., had watched the Puritan colony with no friendly eye. It was far too independent to suit his arbitrary ideas. The people of Boston were

accused of breaking the Navigation Laws[1] by both importing and exporting goods in other than English ships; they
had also coined money without royal authority, and had
given a warm welcome to two of the judges who had sentenced Charles I.[2] to the scaffold, and then fled to Massachusetts. Furthermore, they were notoriously opposed to the
Church of England, and were believed to be strongly republican in their tendencies.

Charles II. threatened, in view of these facts, to take away
the charter of the colony. The people protested that they
had done nothing but what they had a legal right to do. The
protest had no effect. The charter was withdrawn (1684),
Massachusetts became a royal province, and from that time
until the Revolution it was governed by the king and those
whom the king sent to represent him.[3]

The first royal governor imposed on the colony (1686) was
Sir Edmund Andros,[4] who had been governor of New York.
Three years of his tyranny produced a revolt. The people
took advantage of a revolution in England which forced James
II. to flee the country: they seized Andros and imprisoned
him. They then recovered their former power of managing
their own affairs in their own way, but only for a short time.

In 1692, William III. of England sent over a new charter,
which converted Massachusetts, Plymouth, and Maine into one
province.[5] Henceforth all forms of religion but the Catholic
were permitted, and the right to vote was no longer confined
to church-members. But the people had no power to make
any laws except such as the king approved, and the king
furthermore continued to appoint the governor.

**91. Summary.** — The Separatists, or Pilgrims, settled Plymouth in 1620, and the Puritans settled Boston in 1630. The
object sought by both was freedom of worship for themselves.
To all of their own faith they gave a hearty welcome, but they

---

[1] See Paragraph 56.
[2] See Paragraph 55.
[3] Charles II. died 1685; James II. succeeded him.
[4] Andros (An'drŏs).
[5] With Nova Scotia added.

regarded others as intruders, and the Puritans did not hesitate to drive them out. The colonists of Massachusetts were the first settlers in America who assembled in town-meeting and established government by the people, and public schools for all children. The Pilgrims, for more than half a century, did not restrict the right to take part in the government to church-members,[1] but the Puritans did. The object of both was to build up a strong, free, religious, and intelligent common-wealth; in this they were in great measure successful; but in 1684 they lost the power of making their own laws, and had to accept governors appointed by the king.

## V. NEW HAMPSHIRE (1623).

**92. Grant of Territory to Gorges and Mason; Settlement of Dover and Portsmouth.** — Sir Ferdinando Gorges,[2] a friend of Sir Walter Raleigh's,[3] obtained, with Captain John Mason, a grant[4] of the territory between the Merrimac River and the Kennebec. This region was called Maine, or the Mainland;[5] but later the name Laconia was given to it because it extended back to Lake Champlain and Lake George.[6]

The first settlement, known to be permanent, was made at Dover,[7] on the Piscataqua River, by English colonists, prob-ably about 1627. Four years later (1631) Portsmouth was settled. The chief objects of these colonies were to carry on the fur-trade with the Indians and to establish fisheries. Most

---

[1] Not till 1671, but they excluded Quakers in 1658.

[2] Gorges (Gor'jez).                    [3] See Paragraph 28.

[4] This grant was obtained from the "Council for New England," an English company organized in 1620.

[5] Some have supposed that the name "Maine" was derived from a province of France of that name in which Henrietta Maria, queen of Charles I. of England, held property; but the designation Maine, or Mainland, seems to have been given to the country to distinguish it from the numerous islands along the shore.

[6] Others consider Laconia to refer to the numerous lakes of that territory, or pos-sibly to Lake Ontario, to which some authorities believe the grant originally extended.

[7] A settlement was made at Little Harbor, at the mouth of the Piscataqua, in 1623, but it is not certain that it was permanent.

of the inhabitants of the two settlements belonged, in name at
least, to the Church of England.

**93. Division of the Territory; New Hampshire; Exeter.** — After
a few years the proprietors, Mason and Gorges, decided to
divide the territory.   Gorges took the part east of the Piscataqua — a region now included in the State of Maine;[1] Mason
took that west of the same river.   He gave it the name of New
Hampshire[2] in remembrance of the English county of Hampshire which had once been his home.

In 1638 the Rev. John Wheelwright
was banished from Massachusetts for his
openly expressed sympathy with the religious teachings of Mrs. Anne Hutchinson.[3]   With several of his congregation
who had followed him into exile he settled
the town of Exeter, New Hampshire.

**94. Settlement of Londonderry; Union
with Massachusetts.** — Many years later
(1719) several hundred thrifty Scotch-
Irish[4] emigrants settled Londonderry,
New Hampshire.[5]   They introduced
the manufacture of linen; and soon in every log-cabin the
hum of the housewife's little flax-wheel made cheerful and
profitable music for the family.

---

[1] Maine: under the Plymouth Company (see Paragraph 46) an attempt was
made by Sir George Popham in 1607 to found the colony of Popham at the mouth
of the Kennebec, but the undertaking failed.   The first permanent settlement on
the mainland appears to have been made at Pemaquid Point — about midway between the Kennebec and the Penobscot — in 1625.   Saco and Biddeford were
founded in 1630, and Portland in 1632.   Massachusetts held control of Maine from
1652 to 1820, when it was admitted to the Union as a State.

[2] New Hampshire and New York both claimed the territory of Vermont.   New
York did not give up her claim until after the Revolution.

[3] See Paragraph 81.   [4] Scotch Protestants who had settled in the north of Ireland.

[5] Londonderry: the name was given to the settlement by the Scotch Presbyterian
emigrants who came from Londonderry and vicinity, in the north of Ireland.   A

One of the descendants of an industrious Scotch settler of this class, but who came at an earlier period, was the eminent orator, patriot, and statesman, Daniel Webster.[1]

In 1641 New Hampshire, dreading Indian hostilities, and having but a small and scattered population, petitioned for union with Massachusetts. The petition was granted. Furthermore, the citizens of New Hampshire, in accordance with their request, were permitted to vote and hold office, without first having to prove that they were church-members, as they were obliged to do in Massachusetts.[2]  In 1679 New Hampshire became a royal province,[3] and remained so until the Revolution.

**95. Summary.** — New Hampshire originally formed part of the region called Maine or the Mainland.  English colonists settled Dover and Portsmouth.  Emigrants from Massachusetts, and Scotch-Irish, later founded the towns of Exeter and Londonderry.  The Scotch-Irish set up the manufacture of linen.  Eventually New Hampshire was united with Massachusetts and then became a province of the king.

## VI. CONNECTICUT (1634).

**96. Emigration to the Valley of the Connecticut; Hooker's Colony.** — The rich lands of the beautiful valley of the Connecticut River [4] early attracted the Dutch of New Amsterdam [5] and the settlers of Plymouth.  Both made an attempt to get a foothold on the coveted territory.  But emigration did not

desire to build up an independent community induced the emigrants to come to this country.

1 Mr. Webster was born in 1782, in Salisbury, N. H., about fifty miles northwest of Portsmouth.  He once said, in a public speech: " It did not happen to me to be born in a log-cabin; but my elder brothers and sisters were born in a log-cabin, reared amid the snow-drifts of New Hampshire at a period so early that when the smoke first rose from its rude chimney and curled over the frozen hills, there was no similar evidence of a white man's habitation between it and the settlements on the rivers of Canada."        2 See Paragraph 80.        3 See Paragraph 90.

4 Connecticut, an Indian word, meaning, as is supposed, The Long River.

5 See Paragraph 64.

begin in earnest until 1635. Then a number of settlements were made, which later united under one government. We shall now take up the history of these separate colonies.

1. In 1635 emigrants from the vicinity of Boston founded the towns of Wethersfield and Windsor. 2. In the autumn of that year an English company which held a grant of the territory sent out John Winthrop, son of Governor Winthrop of Boston, with the title of "Governor of the River of Connecticut." He built a fort at Saybrook,[1] at the mouth of the river, and thus effectually shut out the Dutch from that quarter.

3. The next June (1636) the third movement of emigration set in. The Rev. Thomas Hooker of Newtown, now Cambridge, Massachusetts, started with a company of one hundred men, women, and children for what was then called "the West." They travelled on foot, driving a hundred and sixty head of cattle, besides hogs, through the wilderness. There were neither roads nor bridges, and the emigrants had to find their way by the compass, crossing rivers on rafts, sleeping under the stars, and living mainly on the milk of their cows. After a journey of two weeks through a country which express-trains now cross in three hours, they reached Hartford, where a small settlement of English had already been made.

97. The Pequot War. — The next spring (1637) a legislative assembly met at Hartford, and resolved to make war on the Pequot[2] Indians, who threatened to destroy the white settlers. The three towns of Hartford, Wethersfield, and Windsor contributed ninety men led by Captain John Mason. The night before the expedition started was spent in prayer. The Pequots had a fortified village near the present town of Mystic. The little army, accompanied by Indians of tribes hostile to the Pequots, and with some help from Massachusetts, attacked the enemy in their stronghold, and, setting fire to their wigwams,

[1] Saybrook: named in honor of Lords Say and Brook, the two chief proprietors of the company.      [2] See Paragraph 81, page 88.

literally burned them out. The blow was a terrible one to the Pequots. From that time they were hunted down like wild beasts, until in a few months the tribe was practically destroyed.

98. **The Connecticut Constitution.** — In 1639 the inhabitants of the three towns of Hartford, Wethersfield, and Windsor met at Hartford, and drew up the first written American[1] constitution[2] or form of government made "by the people for the people."[3] In the words of that document, its object was "to maintain the peace and union" of the settlers of the colony.

One remarkable fact about that compact is that it made no mention either of the king of England or of the English company which held a royal grant of the Connecticut lands. It was in reality the constitution of a republic; and the men who framed it refused to bow to any authority outside or above themselves, except that of their Maker.

One reason why many of the Connecticut emigrants had left Massachusetts was that they did not believe in the principle of limiting the right of voting to church-members.[4] The Hartford constitution imposed no such restriction, every citizen was politically equal with every other, and there was nothing to hinder his taking part in making the laws. To-day not only the United States but every State in the Union has a written constitution — a safeguard of liberty — similar in that respect to the one drafted at Hartford in 1639. That, then, may be called the parent of all that have followed.

1 See Virginia Constitution of 1621, page 60.

2 Constitution: For the same reason that a game of ball cannot be played successfully without some rules to govern it, so, whenever a number of people join to form a community or a state, they must have some form of agreement or principle of union. Such an agreement is a constitution of government. Its object is to secure individual liberty on the one hand, and order on the other. The advantage of having such an agreement in writing is that it can be readily consulted; and misunderstandings and disputes about its meaning and application are less likely to occur than if it was not so preserved.    4 See Paragraph 80.

3 Bancroft's United States (rev. ed.), I. 270.

**99. The New Haven Colony; Scripture Laws.** — There were now two colonies in the territory: First, that at Saybrook,[1] and next that of the towns settled by the different bands of emigrants who had come into the Connecticut Valley. In 1638 a third colony, that of New Haven, was founded. It

was made up chiefly of people who had arrived at Boston from London the year before. One of its leading men was the Rev. John Davenport, a Puritan minister. The spring after they formed the settlement (1639) all the colonists met in a large barn to listen to a sermon from Mr. Davenport and draw up rules for the government of the new community. What those rules were we can guess from the old verse which tells us how

> " They in Newman's barn laid down
>   Scripture foundations for the town."

Those "Scripture foundations," a few years later, made the severe Jewish laws of the Old Testament[2] those of New Haven. None could vote or hold any public office but members of the church. It was practically the same kind of government as that of Massachusetts.

**100. The Fugitive Regicides; Andros and the Connecticut Charter.** — These stern New Haven colonists believed heartily in jus-

---

[1] Saybrook: this settlement remained an independent colony until 1644, when it was united with the colony of Connecticut.

[2] In 1644 "the judicial laws of God, as they were delivered by Moses," were declared to be binding. Like the laws of Massachusetts, they inflicted the penalty of death for no less than fourteen offences. They were, however, far more merciful than the laws of England, which at a very much later period made upwards of *two hundred* crimes punishable with death — sheep-stealing being one.

tice, and hated royal oppression. In 1661 Whalley and Goffe, two of the judges then known as "regicides," because, during the English Civil War (1649), they had voted to put the tyrannical Charles I. to death, fled to New Haven.

King Charles II. sent orders to arrest them. Davenport concealed the judges, and preached to his congregation from a passage of the Bible[1] containing the words, "Hide the outcasts; betray not him that wandereth."

The sermon had the effect intended, and the disappointed officers went back without capturing the regicides.[2]

Charles II., who was not unfriendly to the colony, had granted to the Connecticut people a charter confirming their right of self-government. By that charter the territory was extended westward to the Pacific, or one-eighth the circumference of the globe, though no one then had any idea of the actual width of the continent. Saybrook had already been united with Connecticut, and New Haven was now joined to it. When James II. came to the throne he determined to take away the charters of Connecticut and Rhode Island, as his brother, Charles II., had done in the case of Massachusetts. His object was to bring them directly under his despotic control. Sir Edmund Andros[3] was made governor of New England, and demanded the surrender of the Connecticut charter. In 1687 he went with a body of troops to Hartford to get it.

The Connecticut people looked upon that document as the title-deed of their liberties, and were resolved never to give it up.

Andros met the legislature, and discussed the matter until evening. At his order, the precious charter was at last brought in, in a box, and placed on the table. Then, according to tradition, the candles were suddenly blown out, and when they

---

[1] Isaiah xvi. 3–4.      [3] See Paragraph 90.

[2] According to tradition, Goffe saved the town of Hadley, Mass. (where he was living concealed in 1675), in an Indian attack during King Philip's War. The savages were on the point of gaining the day, when a venerable man with a long white beard suddenly appeared, rallied the inhabitants, and drove off the assailants. He then disappeared. Some thought they owed their victory to an angel.

were relighted the charter had disappeared. It is said to have been hidden in a hollow oak not far off, which was ever after known as the Charter Oak.[1]

Andros, however, declared that the colony should no longer be governed under the charter, and, to show that the end had come, he ordered the clerk to write "Finis"[2] at the close of the record of the meeting. When the people of Boston[3] compelled Andros to give up the power he had abused, the charter was produced, and Connecticut maintained her government under it not only until the Revolution, but for many years afterward (1818).

**101. Summary.** — Connecticut was settled chiefly by emigrants from Eastern Massachusetts and from England. It was the first colony in America to frame a written constitution of government — one which gave the right of voting to every citizen. The king granted the colony a charter confirming their power of governing themselves. Governor Andros, by the order of James II., tried to get possession of the charter but failed. Except for a very short period, Connecticut practically continued to maintain her own laws.

## VII. Maryland (1634).

**102. The Catholic Pilgrims ; Lord Baltimore ; Maryland.** — We have seen how a band of Protestant Pilgrims[4] settled Plymouth in 1620; fourteen years later (1634) a company of Catholic Pilgrims came to America for a like reason — that they might build up a state where they could worship God without molestation.[5]

---

[1] The famous Charter Oak stood in what is now Charter Oak Place, Hartford. It was blown down in 1856. The spot is marked by a marble tablet.

[2] Finis: a Latin word (the end), formerly put at the end of books.

[3] See Paragraph 90.                    [4] See Paragraph 71.

[5] The English law imposed the ruinous fine of twenty pounds a month — a sum equal to not less than $700 to $800 now — on every Catholic who refused to attend the services of the Church of England. This law was not always strictly enforced, but large sums were frequently extorted by the government from the Catholics by way of compromise.

George Calvert, Lord Baltimore, a Catholic nobleman of excellent ability and high standing, resolved to provide a refuge in the New World for the persecuted people of his faith. From his friend King Charles I. he obtained the promise of a grant of land in Northern Virginia. Lord Baltimore died before the charter was completed, but his son, Cecil Calvert, the second Lord Baltimore, received the grant. It made him practically all but king over a territory north of the Potomac, to which Charles I. gave the name of Maryland, in honor of his queen, who was herself a Catholic.[1]

**103. The Settlement of St. Mary's ; the Wigwam Church.** — In the spring of 1634 a colony of about three hundred persons led by Governor Leonard Calvert, — a younger brother of the second Lord Baltimore, — landed on the northern bank of the

Potomac, near its mouth, and founded the town of St. Mary's.[2] About twenty of the colonists were gentlemen of wealth and standing, — most of them probably Catholics — the rest of the emigrants were laborers, and seem to have been chiefly Protestants. Father White,[3] a priest who accompanied the expedition, had no sooner landed than he got permission from an Indian chief to convert his wigwam into a chapel. This hut was the first English Catholic church in America. Virginia would not have permitted that church to stand; New Eng-

---

[1] Henriette-Marie of France, commonly called Henrietta Maria. The charter gave the territory the Latin name of *Terra Mariæ*, or Mary's Land (Marie, the queen's name meaning the same as Mary in English). Maryland included not only the present State, but also Delaware and part of Pennsylvania and West Virginia.

[2] St. Mary's: this name was probably given because the colonists had celebrated a festival (the Annunciation) of the Virgin Mary two days before.

[3] Father White was the historian of the expedition, and has given us the first account of the settlement.

land would not.   It was only in the wilderness of Maryland, in that mixed population of Catholics and Protestants, that it was safe.

**104. Political and Religious Freedom of the Colony.** — From the beginning all the colonists took part in making the laws by which they were governed, and in a few years Lord Baltimore granted them the power of originating those laws.   In religion absolute freedom of worship was given to all Christians,[1] but to Christians only.   No other colony in this country then enjoyed such liberty, and it was almost unknown in Europe. In 1649 this liberty was confirmed by a Toleration Act.[2]

The result was that Maryland became a refuge not only for the oppressed Catholics of England, but also for many of the oppressed Protestants of the other colonies of America.   Puritans driven out of Virginia, Quakers exiled from Massachusetts, both came to Maryland and found homes there, and in 1649 a Puritan settlement was formed at Providence, since named Annapolis.[3]

**105. The Clayborne and Ingle Rebellion; Lord Baltimore's Government overthrown; Persecution of the Catholics.** — The colony, however, was not to enjoy the peace for which it hoped.   Before Lord Baltimore received his charter, William Clayborne, an influential Virginian, had established a thriving settlement and trading-post[4] on Kent Island in Chesapeake Bay.   He refused to recognize the authority of Governor Calvert and endeavored to hold the island by force, but was driven out.   When the

[1] It is true that Lord Baltimore, holding his charter, as he did, from the Protestant sovereign of a Protestant nation, could not have safely denied liberty of worship to Protestants; but it is also true that he evidently had no desire in his heart to deny such liberty.   The fact that he invited Puritans into the colony and protected them from persecution, shows the man's true spirit.

[2] The Toleration Act of 1649 declared that no person professing belief in Jesus Christ shall be " in any ways troubled, molested, or discountenanced, for or in respect of his or her religion, nor in the free exercise thereof."   This law did not protect those who denied the doctrine of the Trinity.        [3] From Queen Anne of England.

[4] For carrying on the fur trade with the Indians.

Civil War[1] broke out in England, the colonists of Maryland, like the people of Great Britain, took sides for or against the king.

Taking advantage of this division, Clayborne stirred up a rebellion (1645), and kept the whole country in a turmoil for two or three years. Captain Ingle, who asserted that he acted under the authority of the Puritan Parliament of England, but who was practically a pirate, got possession of St. Mary's. He plundered it, and seizing "the venerable Father White," sent him to England in irons on a groundless charge of treason against the Parliament of that country.

But worse was to come. After the king was dethroned and executed, and a republic set up in England, the authorities there sent commissioners to compel the people of Maryland to swear fidelity to the new government. At the same time Lord Baltimore insisted that as Maryland was his property the settlers should swear fidelity to him. The Puritans in the colony objected to taking this last oath, on the ground that Lord Baltimore was a Catholic.

The commissioners went to Maryland, forced the governor[2] to resign, and put one of their own choice in his place. They then caused a General Assembly to be summoned at St. Mary's, but ordered that no Catholic should be elected to it, or should cast a vote for any representative. The new legislature repealed the Toleration Act of 1649, which granted religious freedom to all Christians. In its place they enacted a law prohibiting Catholic worship throughout Maryland.

Furthermore the Assembly declared that Lord Baltimore no longer had any rights whatever in the colony he himself had founded, and to which he had invited many of the very people who now turned against him. Such action must have reminded him of the story of the camel that begged shelter in his master's tent, and, when he had got it, kicked the owner out.

1 See Paragraph 55.

2 Governor Stone, Governor Calvert's successor.

**106. Lord Baltimore restored to his Rights; Loss of the Charter.** — But about four years later (1658), Parliament restored Lord Baltimore to his rights. Freedom of worship was again established and for the next thirty years the colony prospered.

Meanwhile England had again become a monarchy, and in 1689 William and Mary, who were pledged to support the Protestant cause, came to the throne.

In Maryland there was an unavoidable delay on the part of the governor in proclaiming the new sovereigns. The enemies of Lord Baltimore circulated the report that this delay was part of a plot, and that the Catholics of Maryland — who were now not nearly so numerous as the Protestants — had conspired with the Indians to massacre all the people of the colony not of their faith.

The story was wickedly false, but many of the Protestants were so foolish as to believe it. They rose in revolt, and in consequence the new king thought it wise to take the government of the province into his own hands. "The best men and the best Protestants" of the colony stood up for Lord Baltimore, but without avail.

**107. Establishment of the Church of England; Restoration of Maryland to Lord Baltimore; Mason and Dixon's Line.** — The Church of England was now established as the government church in Maryland, and every taxpayer, no matter what his religion, had to pay forty pounds of tobacco yearly towards its support. The Catholic worship was not again allowed to be openly observed until Maryland became independent.

In 1715, on the death of the third Lord Baltimore, his son, who had become a Protestant, was made proprietor and governor of Maryland. He and his descendants held it until the Revolution (1776). Meanwhile (1729), the city of Baltimore was founded, and named in honor of the originator of the colony.

In 1682 William Penn founded the colony of Philadelphia, in Pennsylvania, and from that time for many years there were bitter disputes about the boundary between that Province and Maryland. At length Mason and Dixon, two eminent English surveyors, were employed (1763–1767) to establish a boundary that would be satisfactory to both colonies.

They ran the main border line due west nearly two hundred and fifty miles.[1] When practicable, they set up a stone at every fifth mile, with the coat-of-arms of William Penn cut on the north side, and that of Lord Baltimore on the south. That boundary — the Mason and Dixon's line of history — became famous, for it was looked upon as marking the division between the free and the slave states formed from the original thirteen which entered the Union.

**108. Summary.** — The colony of Maryland was planted by Lord Baltimore, an English Catholic. He, first in America, established freedom of worship for all Christians. The peace of the colony was interrupted by civil war, and enemies of Lord Baltimore, joining with Puritan settlers, who had come in, overthrew the government and forbade the exercise of the Catholic religion. Lord Baltimore succeeded after a time in regaining his power and again granted freedom of worship; but finally the king took possession of the province and compelled the people to maintain the Church of England until the Revolution — though the government of the colony was eventually restored to the Baltimore family, who had become Protestants.

## VIII. RHODE ISLAND (1636).

**109. Roger Williams seeks Refuge among the Indians; settles Providence.** — When in 1636 Roger Williams fled from Massachusetts [2] into the wilderness, his situation was one of extreme peril. It was midwinter and the snow was deep. Williams was in feeble health and a wanderer in a trackless forest. Fortunately he had made the Indians his friends and could

---

[1] The completed line was nearly 280 miles long.    [2] See Paragraph 81.

speak their language. The exile made his way to the hospitable wigwam of the chief Massasoit,[1] at the head of Narragansett Bay. There he found a home till spring.

Then with five friends, who had joined him from Massachusetts, he went to the Seekonk River[2] and built a cabin on its eastern bank. Word was sent to him that the place he had chosen was under the control of Plymouth colony. Such a message meant that he and his companions must move on. Crossing the river a little lower down, in a canoe, they were hailed by some Indians who were standing on a flat ledge of rock on the western bank.[3] "What cheer?"[4] cried the friendly red men to the wanderers.

This welcome from the natives led Williams and his friends to land for a short time. Then, guided perhaps by what the Indians told them, they paddled down the river a little distance, rounded the point, and again landed at the foot of some rising ground, where they found a spring of excellent water. Here (1636) they determined to stay and build homes for themselves. Out of gratitude to "God's merciful Providence to him in his distress" Roger Williams gave to the place the appropriate name of PROVIDENCE. There he, with others, founded (1639) the first Baptist church in America. To-day Provi-

1 See Paragraph 76.

2 Seekonk River: it flows into the Providence River on the east side of the city of Providence.

3 "Slate Rock" or "What Cheer Rock," on the eastern side of the city of Providence, foot of Power Street.

4 "What cheer?": an English salutation the Indians had learned from the whites. It meant How do you do? or, How are you?

dence ranks as the second city of New England in population and wealth. In Roger Williams's case banishment did not mean destruction, but growth and increased influence.

**110. Williams establishes a Colony; Liberty of Conscience; Growth of the Principle.** — Williams had at first no intention of founding an independent colony; his main thought was to build up a mission for the conversion of the Indians. But others came and the town of Providence took firm root. From the beginning entire freedom of conscience was given to every settler. Maryland [1] had granted such liberty to all Christians, but the colony of Providence did not limit it, — not Protestants and Catholics only, but Jews — yes, unbelievers even were protected, and thus men of all religions and of no religion were safe from molestation so long as they behaved themselves.

In all other colonies of America, as in every country of Europe, the government favored some particular worship, and in some degree compelled people to maintain it and conform to it. But here there was nothing of the kind. Roger Williams first laid down and put in actual practice what we may call the American principle — that is, that government has nothing whatever to do with the control of religious belief.

That idea was so new and strange that the other colonies thought it false and dangerous, and predicted that it would soon die out. Instead of that it steadily grew and spread, until in time it became a part of the Constitution of the United States, and there we read this sentence, which Roger Williams himself might have written, " *Congress shall make no law respecting an establishment of religion, or prohibiting the free exercise thereof.*" [2]

**111. Settlement of Rhode Island; the Charter.** — In 1638 William Coddington of Massachusetts, with Mrs. Anne Hutchinson [3]

---

[1] See Paragraph 104.                    [3] See Paragraph 81.

[2] Amendments to the Constitution of the United States, Article I.; compare also Article VI. of the Constitution : "*No religious test shall ever be required as a qualification to any office or public trust under the United States.*"

and a few others, in sympathy with the founder of Providence, bought the island of Rhode Island [1] and there planted the colony of Portsmouth and then that of Newport. A few years after, another colony was planted at Warwick, south of Providence. In 1644 Williams went to England and got a charter which united these colonies into a province and gave them full power to rule themselves by such form of government as they thought best. That charter was confirmed by a second, issued not quite twenty years later, and though Andros,[2] when made governor of New England, tried hard to get possession of it, yet Rhode Island kept it as her form of government until long after the Revolution (1842). Rhode Island always remained true to the principle of "soul liberty," first successfully put in practice by Roger Williams; and though at one time Catholics and Jews were not allowed to vote,[3] yet they had full freedom of worship, and not a single blot of religious persecution rests on the fair pages of the history of the colony.

During the Revolution every male citizen between the ages of sixteen and sixty stood ready to fight for independence.

**112. Summary.** — Roger Williams, an exiled minister from Massachusetts, with others, colonized Rhode Island and first established entire freedom of worship in this country. That principle now forms part of the Constitution of the United States.

## IX. NEW SWEDEN, OR DELAWARE (1638).

**113. The Swedes plant a Colony on the Delaware; it is captured by the Dutch.** — The names of the first European colonies in America were generally expressive of ambition, youth, and hope. The kingdoms of the Old World seemed resolved to establish still grander kingdoms in the New. The Spaniards

---

[1] Rhode Island: a name given to it apparently from its supposed resemblance to the Isle of Rhodes in the Mediterranean, though some accounts state that it was because the Dutch called it Rood or Red Island.

[2] See Paragraph 100.       [3] On this point see Winsor's "America," III, 379, 380.

had founded a New Spain;[1] the French a New France;[2] the Dutch, or Netherlanders, a New Netherland;[3] the English a New England.

In 1638 the Swedes, animated by a like feeling, endeavored to begin here a New Sweden. That year their government sent over a colony of "plain, strong, industrious people," who landed on the western bank of what is now known as the Delaware River.[4]

At a point near where Wilmington now stands the emigrants built a fort which they named Christina in honor of young Queen Christina of Sweden.

But the dream of a New Sweden was not to be realized. The Dutch had attempted to settle Delaware in 1629; they claimed the territory; and in 1654 Governor Stuyvesant[5] came with a fleet from New Amsterdam,[6] captured the country, and sent home those of the colonists who would not swear fidelity to the Dutch government.

**114. The English take the Country; the State of Delaware.** — The Dutch had been in possession of the land a little over ten years when the English Duke of York seized it (1665), as he had already seized that on the Hudson.[7] After holding it for a considerable length of time he sold it (1681) to William Penn. Penn called the country "The Territories," or "The

---

[1] New Spain. This name was given by the Spaniards to Mexico, but Florida was also sometimes called. so.

[2] Canada was also known by the name of New France.

[3] New Netherland (New York). See Paragraph 61.

[4] Henry Hudson called this river the South River, to distinguish it from the North or Hudson River. In 1611 Lord Delaware, then governor of Virginia, was driven, when on shipboard, to take refuge in this river in a violent storm. After his death the English named the river, from him, the Delaware.    [5] See Paragraph 64.

[6] New Amsterdam, or New York City.    [7] See Paragraph 64.

Three Lower Counties on the Delaware." Up to the Revolution it was considered a part of Pennsylvania, and was under the control of the governor of that province, although after a time (1703) the people — among whom were many English Quakers and Welsh — obtained the privilege of having a legislature of their own.

In 1776, when the war against Great Britain broke out, the inhabitants of "The Territories" declared themselves a free and independent state, and took the name of Delaware from the river which forms their northeastern boundary.

Though the smallest of all the states, save Rhode Island, Delaware was foremost in accepting the National Constitution (1787), and was therefore the first to enter the American Union. On that roll of honor her name leads all the rest.

**115. Summary.** — This colony, settled by the Swedes as New Sweden, was taken by the Dutch, and then by the English, who sold it to William Penn. He governed it as part of Pennsylvania. When it became independent it took the name Delaware. After the Revolution it was the first state to adopt the Constitution of the United States.

## X.–XI. NORTH AND SOUTH CAROLINA (1663).

**116. Grant of Carolina; First Settlements.** — In 1663 Charles II. of England granted an immense tract of land south of Virginia to a company composed of Lord Clarendon and seven associates.[1] Out of compliment to the king the territory was called Carolina.[2] On the coast it embraced the entire region

---

[1] The Company consisted of 1. The Earl of Clarendon, Lord High Chancellor of England; 2. General Monk, Duke of Albemarle; 3. Ashley Cooper, Lord Shaftesbury; 4. Lord Craven; 5. Sir John Colleton; 6. Sir George Carteret; 7. Lord Berkeley; 8. Sir William Berkeley, governor of Virginia. Albemarle Sound, North Carolina, and the Ashley and Cooper Rivers in South Carolina, derive their names from those of two of the persons above mentioned.

[2] Carolina: the name was originally given to the country by Charles IX. of France at the time of the attempted French settlements, and was retained out of honor to

now included in the states of North and South Carolina, Georgia, and a part of Florida; westward it extended to the Pacific.[1]

At the time of the making of the grant there were a few planters and farmers in the northern part of Carolina. They had moved in from Virginia, and taken land on the Chowan River and the coast of Albemarle Sound near it. By direction of the Company these settlers were formed into a colony (1663) called Albemarle. Shortly after (1664) a second colony, named Clarendon, in honor of Lord Clarendon, was organized on Cape Fear River, some twenty or thirty miles from its mouth. The colonists were English planters from the West Indies.

117. Settlement of Charleston; the Huguenots. — The first settlement direct from England was made in 1670 when two ship-loads of emigrants sent by the Company landed in the southern part of Carolina, on the western bank of the Ashley River,[2] a short distance from the sea.

Ten years later (1680) the colonists moved across to the

the English king Charles II. The name was derived from *Carolus*, Latin for Charles. It was customary for kings to employ the Latin form for their names.

[1] By his first grant (1663) Charles gave all the territory lying between the St. John's River, Florida, and a point on the coast just south of the present boundary of Virginia. In 1665 the king extended the grant one degree farther south, and half a degree farther north, or from 30° to 36° 30′ north latitude. This would make the original territory of Carolina reach from Virginia almost to St. Augustine, Florida.

[2] Ashley: see note 1 to Paragraph 116.

peninsula between the Ashley and Cooper [1] Rivers, and there laid the foundations of the city of Charleston.[2]

From the outset the Company granted religious liberty to all colonists. One of the results of that wise policy was that many Huguenots [3] or French Protestants fled to Carolina to escape the terrible persecution to which they were subject in their native land.[4] No better class of emigrants could have been desired. They represented not only the best bone and sinew, but the best intellect and conscience of France. They brought with them that power and influence which spring not from rank or money, but from character.

A hundred years later two of the descendants of those South Carolina Huguenots — Henry Laurens, the statesman,[5] and General Marion,[6] the noble Revolutionary leader — won imperishable renown by their services in the cause of American liberty.

**118. The "Grand Model"; Division of the Territory into North and South Carolina.** — Meantime (1670) the eminent English philosopher, John Locke, and Lord Shaftesbury, one of the prominent members of the Company, had drafted a constitution for Carolina. Its authors and their friends believed it to be the most perfect work of the kind ever produced by the human mind. It was called the "Grand Model," and the members of the Company declared when they signed it, that it would remain "the sacred and unalterable form and rule of government forever."

[1] Cooper: see note 1 to Paragraph 116.

[2] The first settlement was called Charles Town, in honor of King Charles II. After the colonists had moved across to the peninsula they still retained the name, but in time it became shortened to Charleston.    [3] Huguenots: see Paragraph 23.

[4] On the persecution of the Huguenots by Louis XIV., see " The Leading Facts of French History," in this series.

[5] Henry Laurens: he was the fourth president of the Continental Congress (1777), and was one of the commissioners sent to Paris to sign the Treaty of Peace with Great Britain at the close of the Revolution.

[6] General Marion: he was one of the heroes of the War of Independence. His epitaph declares with entire truth that he "lived without fear, and died without reproach."

The "Grand Model" established a nobility who practically held all power. It also set up courts of justice intended to regulate everything from the gravest questions of law down to the cut of a man's coat, or the trimming of a woman's bonnet.

But there was one omission in this model constitution: it gave the common people — the very class that had begun to settle Carolina — no rights. They were not permitted to vote; they were not to hold landed property; nay, more, they were not even at liberty to leave the soil they tilled, without permission from the nobleman who owned it. When a wealthy planter bought a tract of land in Carolina it was expected that he would purchase the white settlers on it — they, like the trees and the stones, were considered to be part of the estate.

But the inhabitants of the territory decidedly objected to the "Grand Model." They were resolved to own themselves, to own the labor of their hands, to own all the land they could honestly buy, and lastly, to make their own laws. After twenty years of contest they succeeded; and the boasted constitution, that was to last "forever," was given up: it had never really been in operation at all. In 1712 the province was divided into North and South Carolina,[1] and from that time until the Declaration of Independence (1776) each was subject to a governor appointed by the king.

**119. Growth of the Two Colonies; Introduction of Rice and Indigo Culture; Charleston.** — The growth of North Carolina was very slow. Quite a number of industrious and liberty-loving Scotch, Irish, and Swiss emigrated to the province; but the population was scattered, and the manufacture of pitch, tar, and turpentine, which was the principal occupation, did not tend to build up large towns.

In South Carolina, Charleston made little progress for the first fifteen or twenty years. Up to that time there was no great leading industry, and but little commerce. In 1693 an

---

[1] Some authorities make the date of division 1729.

event occurred which produced a decided change. That year the captain of a vessel from Madagascar gave the governor of the colony a small bag of rice to plant, as an experiment. The grain grew luxuriantly, and the governor distributed the crop among the farmers in the vicinity of Charleston. They began its culture, and soon the few pounds of seed had multiplied to thousands; the thousands gradually increased to millions, and in time South Carolina became, what it still continues to be, the largest rice-producing and rice-exporting state in the Union.

The next great source of wealth was the introduction and cultivation of the indigo plant. About half a century (1741) after the first rice had been sown, the daughter of Governor Lucas[1] planted a little indigo on her father's plantation near Charleston. The frost killed it, so that it never came up. She planted again. The seed came up, but worms destroyed the plants. Not to be discouraged, she tried the experiment a third time, and was successful. To the colonists the news of her crop — small as it was — was like the report of the discovery of a gold mine. Indigo then brought in Europe sometimes a dollar and a half a pound; and shortly before the Revolution Charleston exported over a million pounds in a single year.[2] Later, cotton[3] was found to be more profitable than indigo even, and so the culture of that plant was given up.

The result of this lucrative commerce in rice and indigo was that the city grew rapidly in population and wealth until it became the metropolis of the South. In 1773 Josiah Quincy of Boston visited Charleston, and was so impressed with its general appearance and its commercial activity that he wrote: "In almost everything it far surpasses all I ever saw, or ever expected to see in America."[4]

[1] Governor Lucas: governor in the West Indies; his home was in Carolina.

[2] Indigo is largely used for dyeing cloths blue.

[3] Cotton did not become profitable until Whitney invented the cotton-gin in 1793. Its culture will be considered when that period is reached.

[4] Josiah Quincy Jr.'s Journal, 1773.

**120. Summary.** — Carolina, which was eventually divided into North and South Carolina, was settled by emigrants from Virginia, by English and also by Huguenots or French Protestants. General Marion of the Revolution was a descendant from a Huguenot family. The English Company owning the province undertook to govern it by a constitution called the "Grand Model," but the people refused to accept it and insisted on governing themselves. North Carolina engaged in the manufacture of tar, pitch, and turpentine; South Carolina began the culture of rice and indigo, both of which proved enormously profitable. At the time of the Revolution Charleston was one of the chief cities of America.

## XII. Pennsylvania (1681).

**121. Grant of Pennsylvania to William Penn; the "Holy Experiment."** — Charles II. owed William Penn, the most influential of the English Friends, or Quakers,[1] a large sum of money. As that good-natured but extravagant monarch always contracted as many debts as possible and paid as few, Penn suggested to his majesty that he might easily settle his claim by granting him a tract of land in America. The proposition pleased the king, and he gave Penn a territory of forty-eight thousand square miles fronting on the Delaware River. Charles named this vast region, which was nearly as large as the whole of England,[2] Pennsylvania,[3] or Penn's Woods.

In those woods the proprietor resolved to begin what he called his "Holy Experiment." That experiment consisted in establishing a "free colony," or Christian community, on the basis of that Golden Rule which commands us to do unto others as we wish them to do unto us. The Quaker founder thought that even the North American savages could understand that principle, and would let the people who practised it

[1] Friends, or Quakers: see Paragraph 85.
[2] The area of England, not including Wales, is about 50,000 square miles.
[3] Pennsylvania: from Penn and the Latin word *sylva*, a wood.

grow up in peace. The king suggested that the savages would be more likely to respect a well-armed regiment of soldiers; but Penn had no faith in the virtues of gunpowder, and would not send so much as a single musket to protect his colony.

122. **Emigration to Pennsylvania; Philadelphia; Landing at New-castle.** — The first emigrants were sent out under the charge of Penn's commissioners in 1681. They appear to have spent the winter on the western bank of the Delaware at a Swedish settlement which was subsequently named Chester. The following year (1682) Penn himself sailed with a company of a hundred English Quakers, to found the city of Philadelphia,[1] or Brotherly Love. The location had already been selected by Penn's commissioners, in accordance with instructions which he had given them. The city

was planned by its founder before he left England. It is said that not even a thousand dollars have since had to be spent in straightening or widening streets, — that work having been done once for all in Penn's orderly brain before the first house was built in 1683.

Penn landed at Newcastle, in what is now Delaware. That territory he had purchased of the Duke of York,[2] so that it then formed part of Pennsylvania. The whole population of the region gathered to welcome him and to witness the interesting ceremony of his taking possession of his vast estate. First, a piece of turf was handed to Penn — that meant that he owned the land and all that grew on it; next, a dish filled from the Delaware River was given to him — that signified that he owned the water; finally, the key of the fort was solemnly presented to him — that act completed the transfer, for it

[1] A Bible name: see Rev. iii. 7–8.     [2] See Paragraph 114.

acknowledged his right to hold both land and water by military force.

**123. The "Great Law."** — Less than two months after that, Penn called an assembly at Chester, and he with the people enacted the "Great Law."

That constitution had a twofold foundation — liberty of the people to make their own laws, and obedience to the laws they had made; for, said Penn, "Liberty without obedience is confusion, and obedience without liberty is slavery."

By the "Great Law" it was provided: 1. That all colonists should be protected in their worship of God, but that no one should be compelled to support or attend any form of worship against his will.[1]   2. That all resident tax-payers should have the right to vote, and that every member of any Christian church might hold office and become a member of the legislative assembly.[2]   3. That every child, after reaching the age of twelve, should be brought up to some trade or useful occupation.   4. That the death penalty should be inflicted for two crimes[3] only, — murder and treason,[4] — and, for the first time in the history of the world, it was further ordered that every prison should be made a workshop and a place of reformation.[5]

**124. The Great Treaty; Growth and Importance of Philadelphia.** — Penn's next act (1682)[6] was a treaty with the Indians.

---

[1] No person believing in God and living peaceably and justly "shall in any wise be molested." *The Great Law*, Section 1, Hazard's "Annals of Pennsylvania."

[2] This is according to Section 65 of *The Great Law;* but Section 2 of the same would appear to limit the right to elect members to the assembly to "such as profess and declare they believe in Jesus Christ."

[3] On the number of crimes then punishable with death in England, see note 2 on page 101.

[4] Treason: that is, an open and deliberate attempt to overturn the government by force of arms.

[5] The prisons of Europe at that time were dens of idleness and disorder. Instead of reforming the criminal they often taught him new crimes, so that he usually came out of his place of confinement actually worse than he entered it.

[6] See Hazard's Pennsylvania, p. 635; but some authorities fix the date at 1683, and consider the treaty to have covered the purchase of lands.

According to tradition he met the Red Men under the branches of a wide-spreading elm in what was then the vicinity of Philadelphia.[1]  There solemn promises of mutual friendship were made.  In accordance, however, with the principles of the Quaker faith, no oaths were taken. Each trusted to the other's simple word.  That treaty was "never broken,"[2] and for sixty years, or as long as the Quakers held control, the people of Pennsylvania lived at peace with the natives.  The tree under which that memorable transaction took place no

TREATY GROUND
OF
WILLIAM PENN
AND THE
INDIAN NATION
1682
UNBROKEN FAITH

Treaty Monument.

longer stands, but its site is marked by a monument.  The Indian record of the treaty — a belt of wampum representing Penn[3] and the chief clasping hands — is still preserved.[4]

---

[1] The treaty was made at Kensington, in the northeastern part of the city.  The Treaty Elm was blown down in 1810.  So great was the regard for the old tree that during the Revolution, when the British forces occupied Philadelphia, General Simcoe, their commander, stationed a sentinel under it to prevent his soldiers from cutting it down for firewood.  The monument marking the spot where it stood is on the west side of Beach Street, north of Columbia Street, Kensington.

[2] Voltaire, the French historian, said that it was "the only treaty which was never sworn to, and never broken"; if he had heard of Carver's treaty (see page 81), he would have mentioned that too.

[3] William Penn set sail for England, Aug. 12, 1684, having spent not quite two years in Pennsylvania.  He visited the colony again in 1699, and returned to England in 1701, where he spent the remaining seventeen years of his life.  His outlay in Pennsylvania had involved him heavily in debt, and in 1709 he was obliged to mortgage his province for £6600.  Other misfortunes fell upon him, and at one time he was a prisoner for debt in London.  He was negotiating a sale of his right in Pennsylvania to the English government at the time of his death.  His successors were unlike him, and their greedy and unjust policy created constant irritation.  In 1779 the state of Pennsylvania purchased their rights for $650,000.

[4] See Paragraph 37, and picture of the belt.  Penn is the right-hand figure.  The

Philadelphia grew rapidly, and at the beginning of the Revolution it was the largest and in every respect the most important city in the American colonies. Its history is closely connected with many decisive events in the early history of the country.

There the first Continental Congress met (1774), there independence was declared (1776), there too the present Constitution of the United States was framed (1787), and there the seat of government remained (1790–1800)[1] until it was removed to Washington, then "a backwoods settlement in the wilderness."

**125. Summary.**—William Penn founded the colony of Pennsylvania, which was named from him. He gave the people the right to take part in making the laws, and all persons believing in God were protected in their religion. He made a treaty of peace with the Indians which was sacredly kept. At the opening of the Revolution Philadelphia was the chief city of the country, and long the seat of government.

## XIII. Georgia (1733).

**126. Oglethorpe's Project for the Settlement of Georgia; his Two Motives.** — In 1732 General James Oglethorpe, a member of the English Parliament, obtained a charter for settling a tract of country in America between the Savannah and Altamaha rivers.

Oglethorpe was a man of high character and of distinguished ability. His objects in establishing a new colony were both patriotic and benevolent. South Carolina was exposed to attacks from the Spaniards in Florida, and it was desirable

belt is in the possession of the Pennsylvania Historical Society, Philadelphia. See their Memoirs, Vol. VI.

[1] Philadelphia was virtually the capital of the country after independence was declared, although Congress did not always meet there. Pennsylvania attracted a large emigration; and in 1776 about half the population were English, one-third Germans, and the rest Irish and Swedes.

to have a body of men so placed that they might repel such attacks. The proposed colony would serve therefore as a barrier against the enemies of Charleston on the south. That was the first object. The second was one of pure benevolence. Thousands of poor debtors were then confined in the prisons of England. Many of them were honest, hard-working men, who through sickness or misfortune had contracted some trifling debt, — it might be no more than a single shilling even, — and not being able to pay had been cast into prison. There their condition was most pitiful. They could earn nothing, and unless their friends supported them they were actually in danger of starvation, some of them having to subsist by begging in an iron cage from the passers-by. The jailors often treated these poor creatures with revolting cruelty, and never failed to extort fees and fines from them on every possible occasion. Cases occurred in which men were kept in confinement for years after their creditors had withdrawn all claims against them, simply because they could not raise money to pay the jail fees, which sometimes amounted to much more than the original debt.

Oglethorpe had spent a good deal of time in visiting and investigating these prisons in London; his heart was touched by the misery he saw, — the misery of those who had committed no crime, — and he resolved to help them. His scheme was to select the most deserving of the prisoners, to discharge their debts, to furnish them transportation, with their wives and families, to America, and thus give them, what England could not — a chance to begin life anew.

Such a charity was as honorable as it promised to be useful. The English government subscribed a large sum toward it, so too did the Bank of England, and private individuals increased the fund until it reached what would be equal to half a million of dollars to-day.[1]

[1] The House of Commons gave £10,000, and private subscription £26,000; or in all £36,000, equal, probably, to not less than $500,000 now.

**127.   The Settlement at Savannah ; Silk Culture.** — An association of twenty-two persons was formed with Oglethorpe as leader.   Out of compliment to King George II., who favored the undertaking, the new colony was called Georgia.   The first emigrants sent out settled under Oglethorpe on the Savannah River, from which they named the town Savannah (1733).

Later, German Protestants [1] who were persecuted in their own country on account of their religion, and sturdy Scottish peasants from the Highlands,[2] made settlements in Georgia.

It was hoped that wine could be produced on a great scale, so as to rival Madeira itself.   Mulberry-trees grew wild in the

territory, and it was expected that silk could be raised in large quantities. The first seal of the colony represented the silkworms at their work, with the words, "Not for themselves, but for others."[3] Such a seal not only expressed the industry of the inhabitants, but its motto told the story of the unselfish purposes of the founders.   The silk culture, however, never went very far, cotton being found in the end far more profitable.

**128.   Restrictions on the Colony.** — From the outset, however, the enterprise was hampered by certain regulations that caused

---

[1] Moravians and Lutherans:  The Moravians were from Austria ; in several respects they resembled the Quakers.        [2] They settled at Darien, on the coast.

[3] The motto was in Latin, — "*Non sibi sed aliis.*"

discontent and tended to prevent the rapid growth of the province.   The first of these was the provision that for twenty-one
years all laws should be made by the Association.   This kept
the people like children, and made that best of all educations
— the education of self-government — impossible.   The next
forbade that land should descend to women — the object being
to keep it in the hands of those who could do military service.
The third regulation prohibited the importation of rum or
spirituous liquors, thus cutting off the Georgians from commerce with the West Indies, which was the most lucrative
trade they could then hope to obtain.   Fourthly, the importation of slaves was denied to the settlers, and they therefore
could not compete agriculturally with the other colonies, all
of which had them.   Lastly, entire religious liberty was not
allowed, no Roman Catholic being permitted to settle or hold
land in the colony.

129.  The Wesleys; Whitefield; the Restrictions removed; the
Spaniards; Resources of Georgia. — John and Charles Wesley,
the two distinguished brothers who founded Methodism, were
both interested in Oglethorpe's project, and went out with him
on his second voyage,[1] the first for the purpose of doing
missionary work among the Indians.   Later, another noted
preacher of that denomination, the Rev. George Whitefield,[2]
established an orphan asylum near Savannah.   In strong con-
trast to John Wesley, he conscientiously believed in slave-
labor, and partly supported his asylum from the produce of
his plantation in the adjoining colony of South Carolina.
Through his persistent efforts, joined to those of others, the
purchase of negroes was at last (1750) allowed; the prohibition on the importation of rum from the West Indies was also
removed, the land laws changed for the better, and Georgia
soon had a flourishing commerce, and could hold her own with
the Carolinas.

[1] Oglethorpe went back to England in 1743.  He was a member of Parliament
for many years, and died in 1785.          [2] Whitefield (Whit'field).

With respect to checking the attacks of the Spaniards the colony was highly successful. Oglethorpe defeated an expedition sent to conquer and drive out the settlers, and did the work so thoroughly that the enemy had no desire to make his further acquaintance.[1]

In 1752 Georgia became a royal province, and was governed by the crown until the Revolution. No colony planted by the English possesses greater natural resources or natural wealth — in cotton, coal, and iron — than the territory that was first settled by that philanthropist who sought the prosperity of all. If he could see what Georgia has become, and better still, see its probable future, he would feel that he could not have chosen more wisely.

130. Summary.—Georgia, the last of the thirteen colonies, and one of the richest in its natural advantages, was settled by English emigrants brought over by General Oglethorpe, as a work of charity. One chief object of the colony was the raising of silk. That, however, was unsuccessful. In the outset the settlers had no power of self-government, and the land laws caused much discontent. Slavery and the importation of spirituous liquors were forbidden, but later, both were allowed, the people got the management of the colony, in considerable measure, and Georgia opened a large trade with the West Indies.

THE FRENCH EXPLORATION OF THE WEST.

131. French Exploration of the Great Lakes and the Mississippi Valley ; the Jesuit Missionaries. — But while the English colonists had been getting firm possession of the coast from Maine to Georgia, the French in Canada [2] had not been sitting still. In fact, it was they, and not the English, who were the ex-

[1] The defeat of the Spaniards had the effect of extending the southern boundary of Georgia to the St. John's River, Florida. In 1763 it was fixed at the present line.
[2] See Paragraph 50.

plorers of the West.    Among the first Europeans who dared to push their way into the wilderness were Jesuit missionaries,[1] who had come here to convert the Indians.    In their zeal for this work they braved all dangers — enduring hunger, cold, and torture without a murmur.    Long before William Penn's emigrants had felled the first tree for the first log cabin in Philadelphia, the Jesuits had reached the western shore of Lake Michigan (1669),[2] and had planted missions among the Indians at Mackinaw, Sault Ste. Marie, and Green Bay.[3]

132.  **Joliet and Marquette on the Mississippi.** — A few years later (1673) Joliet,[4] a famous French explorer and fur-trader, and Father Marquette, a Jesuit priest, set out from Mackinaw to find a great river which the Indians told them lay west of Lake Michigan.   Making their way in birch-bark canoes[5] to the head of Green Bay, they paddled up the Fox River to a place which they called Portage,[6] — now Portage City, — then carrying their canoes across, a distance of less than two miles, they embarked on the Wisconsin River.   Borne by the current, they dropped down the Wisconsin until, on a beautiful day

[1] Jesuit missionaries: missionaries belonging to the Roman Catholic order of the Jesuits, or "Company of Jesus."   The order was founded in 1540, for the double purpose of checking the spread of Protestantism, and of carrying the Catholic faith to the heathen.   The French Jesuits accomplished a great work among the Indians of Canada and the West, but made but little impression on the ferocious Iroquois, who captured several of the missionaries and put them to death with horrible tortures.   Before the Jesuits came, a Catholic friar had founded a mission on Lake Huron in 1615.

[2] *Dates so enclosed need not be committed to memory.*

[3] Mackinaw, Michigan, at the northwestern extremity of Lake Huron.   Here is Fort Mackinaw.   Sault Ste. Marie (usually pronounced Soo Sent Mā'ry), on the river of that name, about fourteen miles from the outlet of Lake Superior.   Green Bay, Wisconsin, on western shore of Lake Michigan.   See Map, page 128.

[4] Joliet (pronounced in the United States, Jo'le-et): Marquette (Mar-ket'): both names frequently occur in the West, especially in Michigan, Wisconsin, and Illinois, where counties, cities, and towns have been named for the French explorers.

[5] See Paragraph 36.

[6] Portage: a French word, meaning a carrying-place, because at such points canoes or goods were carried across from one stream to another.   See Map, page 128.

in June, they floated out on the broad, shining bosom of the upper Mississippi. The sight of it was enough : they knew that they had found that mighty stream which the Indians called the "Father of Waters" — at the point where the voyagers reached it, it is full two miles from bank to bank. Turning their canoes southward, they let the river bear them where it would. Day after day they kept on their silent journey; now gliding by castle-shaped cliffs, now coming into the sunlight of open prairies, now entering the long shadow cast by miles of unbroken forest. Thus they drifted on, past the muddy torrent of the Missouri, past the mouth of the beautiful Ohio. In about three weeks the explorers came to the spot where De Soto [1] had crossed the river more than a hundred years before; then pushing on, they reached the mouth of the Arkansas. There the Frenchmen stopped and feasted with friendly Indians. The Indians warned them not to go further south, telling them that the tribes below were hostile to strangers. Joliet and Marquette took their advice, and after resting for some time with the hospitable red men, they got into their canoes and patiently paddled their way back.[2] It was a tremendous piece of up-hill work, that battling for hundreds of miles against the powerful current, but they felt fully repaid for the labor. They had not followed the Mississippi to the Gulf, as they intended ; but who will say that they had not made a good beginning?

133. **La Salle reaches the Mouth of the Mississippi.** — Six years later (1679) La Salle,[3] the greatest of the French explorers, a man of active brain and iron will, set out from Canada to complete the work of Joliet and Marquette. He had already explored a good part of the Ohio, and he now started with high hopes on this still more important expedition. On the Niagara River, not far above the falls, he built the first sailing-vessel

---

[1] See Paragraph 22, page 30.

[2] They worked their way up the river to the Illinois, then up that river and across to Lake Michigan.          [3] La Salle (Lah Sal').

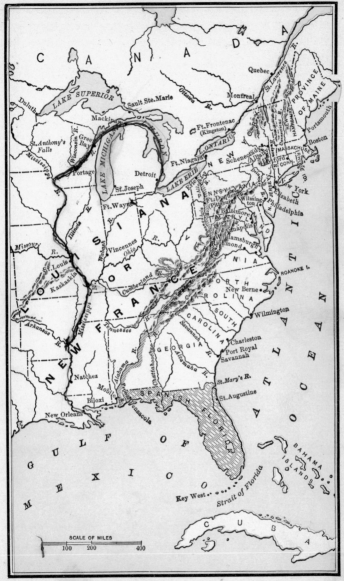

MAP SHOWING THE THIRTEEN ENGLISH COLONIES AND THE FRENCH
EXPLORATIONS AND SETTLEMENTS IN THE WEST.

ever launched on the upper Great Lakes.   In her he sailed to
Green Bay, then, sending the vessel back for supplies, La Salle
and his companions went in canoes to the St. Joseph River,[1]
near the southeastern corner of Lake Michigan.   There they
built a fort; then, crossing over to the head waters of the
Kankakee, a tributary of the Illinois, they descended that
river to the point where Peoria now stands.   There they built

a second fort.[2]  Leaving a small
garrison to hold this position, La
Salle, near the end of winter, went
back on foot to Canada[3] — a journey of a thousand miles — to get
the supplies which had failed to
reach him, and which he needed
for the exploration of the Mississippi.   While he was gone, Father
Hennepin, a Catholic missionary
in La Salle's expedition, set out
from the fort to explore the country.   After many startling adventures, he finally reached a cataract
on the upper Mississippi, which he
named the Falls of St. Anthony.

La Salle at the Mouth of the Mississippi.

The next year (1681) La Salle returned to Illinois, only to
find his fort deserted and in ruins.   But the brave Frenchman
knew no such word as fail.   In the autumn he set out on his
great expedition for the third time.   Landing at the head of
Lake Michigan, where Chicago[4] now stands, he crossed over
to the Illinois and, going down that river, entered the Missis-

---

[1] La Salle paddled from Green Bay, along the shore, round to the St. Joseph
River, Michigan.

[2] La Salle called the second fort Crèvecœur, the Broken Heart, a name generally
supposed to refer to his misfortunes there.

[3] He went back to Fort Frontenac (now Kingston), on the Canada shore of Lake
Ontario.

[4] Chicago: here the French built a fort, or fortified trading-post, a few years later.

sippi in February (1682).  The weather was "bitter cold,"
and the river full of floating ice; La Salle did not hesitate,
but started with his company on his perilous voyage.  Nine
weeks later — having stopped on his way to build a fort — he
reached the sunny waters of the Gulf of Mexico.  There he set
up a rude wooden cross on which he fastened a metal plate
bearing the arms of France.[1]  Then with volleys of musketry
and loud shouts of "God save the King!" La Salle took possession of the entire vast territory watered by the Mississippi
and its tributaries.  To that region of unknown extent — twice
as large as France, Spain, and Germany united — he gave the
name of Louisiana, in honor of Louis XIV., then the reigning
sovereign of France.

**134. The Founding of Mobile and New Orleans.** — Many years
later John Law, an enterprising Scotchman, got permission
from France to establish a colony in Louisiana.  The country
was believed to possess mines of precious metals rich as those
of Mexico or Peru.  Law promised to open these mines,[2] and
every needy and greedy Frenchman who could muster a few
dollars bought the right to take part in the speculation.  It
failed, and made thousands beggars.  Still the undertaking
had some permanent results for good.  A Frenchman named
Iberville[3] had established a colony at Mobile,[4] on the Gulf of
Mexico (1701).  His brother, Bienville,[5] was appointed governor of Louisiana.  It was hoped that he would send ship-
loads of gold to France.  He sent nothing of the sort, but did
far better; for he founded the city of New Orleans (1718).[6]

[1] Arms of France: a shield decorated with representations of the heads of lilies,
(here resembling small crosses).   The latest French life of La Salle says he fastened
the arms of France to a post, and erected a cross beside it.

[2] On John Law and the Mississippi Company, see " The Leading Facts of French
History," in this series.          [3] Iberville (E-ber-veel').

[4] Mobile: the name is Indian.          [5] Bienville (Be-an-veel').

[6] New Orleans: Bienville named the city from the Duke of Orléans, who was
then, during the minority of Louis XV., at the head of the government of France.
The word New seems to have been given to distinguish Orleans in America from
Orléans in France.

The settlement was merely a cluster of huts round a fort; but in time it was destined to become the commercial metropolis of the richest agricultural valley in the world, — a valley capable of producing food enough to feed all the civilized races of the globe.

Meanwhile what had the English colonists in the East done toward exploring and occupying the country? Practically nothing. They simply continued to hold their first settlement on the Atlantic coast: in other words, the mere rim or edge of what is now the United States. The long range of the Alleghany Mountains, rising like an immense wall, had prevented their spreading further. France, on the other hand, had, as we have seen, got possession of the interior; by her claim to the Mississippi and its tributaries she held the great West, extending from the Alleghanies to the Rocky Mountains. What France held she intended to keep; that was what the forts meant that La Salle had built at so many points of his explorations from the Lakes to the Gulf.

## The French and Indian Wars.

**135. War with the French; Attacks on Schenectady, Haverhill, and Deerfield; the French lose Acadia.** — In Europe, the French and the English had long been enemies. The desire of each to get possession of America did not make them any better friends. In 1689 war broke out between the rival colonists. With intervals of peace that contest[1] extended over seventy years (1689–1763). In Europe the same war was fought between England and France, and it lasted even longer. The struggle in this country is usually represented as four distinct wars, but in reality it was but one; though, here, the combatants made one long stop of thirty years to get breath.

[1] This war and those that follow were simply the *American* side of a hundred years' struggle waged in Europe and Asia, between the English and the French for the possession of India and of the continent of America. See Seeley's "Expansion of England," Lecture II.

In the first war [1] which lasted eight years (1689–1697), Frontenac, the French governor of Canada, sent an expedition of French and Indians to attack the colonies on and near the Hudson. They secretly marched from Montreal in mid-winter, and falling on the little village of Schenectady, New York,[2] at midnight, they burned it and massacred most of the inhabitants. In a similar attack on Haverhill,[3] Massachusetts, the savages met their match. A small party of Indians carried off Mrs. Hannah Dustin captive. She got possession of some tomahawks, and with the help of another woman and a boy, also prisoners, she split the heads of the sleeping Indians, and carried home their scalps, ten in all, in triumph. A regiment of such women would have soon made both French and Indians beg for peace. During this war, an expedition from Boston, led by Sir William Phips of Maine, captured the French fort at Port Royal, Acadia,[4] but it was returned to the French the next year (1691).

In the second war,[5] which lasted eleven years (1702–1713), a party of French and Indians attacked Deerfield, Massachusetts,[6] and reduced the place to ashes. On the other hand, the New England colonists recaptured Port Royal, which they named Annapolis, in honor of Queen Anne, then reigning in England. They also undertook an expedition against Quebec, which ended in shipwreck and terrible loss of life. When peace was made (1713), Great Britain not only kept Annapolis, but got possession of Acadia, which the English now named Nova Scotia.

**136. The Third War; Taking of Louisburg.** — There was a long interval of peace, and then the third war [7] broke out. It lasted

1 "King William's War," so called because King William reigned in England.

2 Schenectady (Ske-nek'ta-dy): 17 miles west of Albany. See Map, page 172.

3 Haverhill: 33 miles north of Boston. Both Schenectady and Haverhill were then, in a sense, frontier towns. See Map, page 157.

4 Acadia : now Nova Scotia. See Map, page 133.

5 Known as "Queen Anne's War," from Queen Anne of England.

6 Deerfield: in Northwestern Massachusetts, near the Connecticut River.

7 Called "King George's War," from George II., then on the throne of England.

four years (1744–1748).　During this contest, the New England colonists gained a remarkable victory.　France had spent millions in fortifying Louisburg, on Cape Breton Island, — a position of great importance to the French, because it stood guard at the entrance to the Gulf and the River St. Lawrence.[1] The fort was of immense extent, and had walls of solid masonry thirty feet high.　The French believed this stronghold could not be taken; but Colonel Pepperrell[2] of Maine, with a force of a few thousand Yankee farmers and fishermen, set out to capture it.　The expedition seemed so foolhardy that even Benjamin Franklin[3] ridiculed it.　Though himself a native of New England, and full of faith in New England grit, he wrote to his brother that Louisburg was far too hard a nut for their teeth to crack.　But, with the help of a British fleet, Pepperrell and his men, after six weeks' fighting, did crack it (1745), and Boston fairly went wild over the great news.[4]

[1] France needed the fortified harbor of Louisburg as a shelter for her vessels, as a protection to her commerce and fisheries, and for maintaining free communication with Canada.　　　　[2] Usually, but incorrectly, spelled Pepperell.

[3] Benjamin Franklin: born in Boston, 1706; died in Philadelphia, full of years and honors, in 1790.　He was the son of a soap-boiler and candle-maker.　He learned the printer's trade and went to Philadelphia, where, in 1729, he became editor and proprietor of the *Pennsylvania Gazette*.　Later he entered public life, went abroad as agent of the colonies, and rendered the whole country his debtor by his eminent services in the cause of American independence.　The succeeding pages of this history will show that his name deservedly ranks with that of Washington as one of the founders of the United States.　For a full account of his life, see Ginn & Co.'s "Benjamin Franklin."

[4] Notwithstanding the bravery of Pepperrell and his gallant little force, it is not likely that they, even with the help of the British fleet, could have taken Louisburg

The victory had two important results: 1. It broke up the nest of French pirates at Louisburg, and so put an end to their capturing and plundering Massachusetts fishing-vessels. 2. It inspired the New England people with the faith that they could not only beat the French, but beat them when entrenched behind granite walls. At the end of the war England gave Louisburg back; but one thing Great Britain could not do,— she could not give back the confidence the French once had in the famous fortress. The "Yankees" had taken it; and what men have done, they can do again.

137. **The Fourth, or French and Indian, War; the Great Line of French Forts.** —In 1754–1763 came the fourth and final struggle, known as the "French and Indian War." It was to decide a greater question than any that had yet been fought for; that was, whether the French or the English should control the continent of America. The English outnumbered the French fifteen to one; but the French had got possession of the two chief rivers of the country, — the St. Lawrence and the Mississippi. To clinch their hold they built fort after fort, until by this date they had a line extending from Quebec to the Great Lakes, and thence down the Wabash, the Illinois and the Mississippi to the Gulf.[1] Where many of those and succeeding forts stood, flourishing cities have since risen which still keep the old French or Indian names of Detroit, Chicago, St. Louis,[2] Natchez, New Orleans. That shows the forethought of the French explorers. When they selected a spot to fortify, they seem to have thought not only of its military strength,

had that fort possessed an efficient garrison and a competent commander. It had neither, and hence it fell. England was astonished, and the king was so delighted that he made the American commander a baronet, — Sir William Pepperrell. He was the first native of New England who received that honor; though William Phips (see p. 132) had been *knighted* more than fifty years before.

[1] See Map, page 128.

[2] There were two forts named St. Louis; that marking the site of the modern city of St. Louis was built by French emigrants after the war (1764), on territory then belonging to Spain.

but also of the possibilities of its growth as a centre of business and commerce.

**138. The Ohio Company; Governor Dinwiddie's Messenger.** — But at last, after all the important points had passed into the hands of the French, the English began to open their eyes to the danger which threatened them. They saw that unless they bestirred themselves, and moved into the rich territory west of the Alleghanies, they would lose the heart of the continent. To prevent such a disaster a wealthy London merchant, with certain influential Virginians, organized the Ohio Company (1748) for planting a colony of emigrants on the east bank of the upper Ohio.[1] The French at once resolved to stop the movement, and began a new line of forts, extending southward from Erie on Lake Erie to the point where the Alleghany and the Monongahela rivers unite to form the Ohio. That point at the head of inland navigation was with good reason called the "Gateway of the West." Both parties knew its importance; both meant to seize and fortify it.

Governor Dinwiddie of Virginia determined (1753) to send a messenger to Venango, — one of the new line of French forts, — and warn off those whom he considered intruders.[2] Whoever undertook such a journey must travel at least three hundred miles on foot, climb a succession of mountain ranges, cross rivers, as best he could, and risk his life among hostile Indians.

The governor, after due deliberation, finally decided to entrust this difficult and dangerous work to the brother of the late chief manager of the Ohio Company, a young man of twenty-one, who was a skilful surveyor, knew all about life in

[1] The first Ohio Company (formed in 1748), whose chief manager, Lawrence Washington, died in the summer of 1752, received a grant of 500,000 acres on the east bank of the Ohio, between the Great Kanawha and the Monongahela rivers. The region is now embraced by West Virginia and Southwest Pennsylvania.

[2] The English maintained that they had purchased the Ohio Valley region of the Iroquois Indians, who declared that they had conquered it many years before. There is no evidence that the Iroquois had any right to sell the land.

the wilderness, and did not know what fear meant.    The name of that young man may still be read on a lofty limestone cliff in Virginia,[1] where, when a lad, he climbed up higher than any of his companions dared to go, and cut it with his hunting-knife, — GEORGE WASHINGTON.[2]

**139. Results of Washington's Journey.** — Washington performed the journey (1753), but the French commander sent back an unsatisfactory reply to the governor.    The expedition had, however, two important results.    In the first place, it may be said to have made Washington "a Western man," for the journey seems to have impressed him with the immense value and future growth of that region.    In time he came to hold more lands there than any one else in the country; and throughout his life he used his influence in every way to build roads and canals to open up and settle the West, or what was then known by that name.    In the second place, the answer which Washington brought made it evident that if the Ohio Company was to hold its own, it must do so by force.    The

[1] At Natural Bridge, in the mountains of Western Virginia.   The walls rise over two hundred feet, and it is exceedingly difficult and dangerous to climb them.

[2] George Washington was born at Bridges Creek, Virginia, on the Potomac, about fifty miles south of where Washington now stands.   His father, soon after the birth of George, removed to an estate on the Rappahannock opposite Fredericksburg.   Nothing remains of the old homestead at Bridges Creek; but a stone slab marks the site of the house, and bears this inscription: "Here, the 11th of February, 1732, George Washington was born."   Difference of reckoning now makes the 11th the 22d.   Washington's great-grandfather, John Washington, emigrated from England to Virginia about 1657.   It is generally thought that he belonged to one of the old Cavalier families that fought in behalf of Charles I. during the English Civil War.   George Washington received a fair English education, but nothing more.   He excelled in athletic sports and horsemanship, and was fond of life in the woods.   He became a skilful surveyor, and found the work highly profitable.   By the death of Lawrence Washington, an elder brother, George came eventually into possession of the estate at Mount Vernon, on the Potomac, a short distance below the present city of Washington.   Washington's mission to the French commander at Venango first brought him into public notice.   In 1759 he married Mrs. Martha Custis, a wealthy widow.   From this time until his death, in 1799, he will stand prominent in this history.   For a full account of Washington, see "Washington and His Country," Ginn & Co.

WASHINGTON BEFORE THE REVOLUTION.

Company accordingly began a fort at the "Gateway of the West"; but before they could complete it, the French drove them out, finished building it, and named it Fort Duquesne[1] in honor of the French governor of Canada. Washington then began a small fort, which he called Fort Necessity, about forty miles south of Fort Duquesne; but the French came in overwhelming force, and compelled him to surrender it.

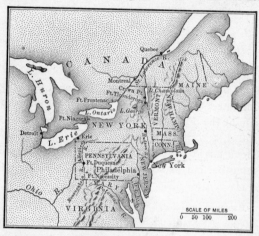

**140. The Albany Convention; Benjamin Franklin's Snake; General Braddock.** — Matters now looked so serious that a convention of the Northern colonies met at Albany (1754) to consider what should be done. The Iroquois Indians, who were stanch friends of the English, sent some of their people to the convention, and warned the colonists that if they did not take up arms, the French would drive every Englishman out of the country. Benjamin Franklin, delegate[2] from Pennsylvania, headed an appeal in his paper, the *Pennsylvania Gazette*, with a rude woodcut, which told its own story. It represented the colonies in the form of a snake cut in pieces,

---

[1] Duquesne (Du-kane´).

[2] Delegate: a representative, a person sent to act for others.

with the motto, "Unite or die." Franklin furthermore proposed an excellent plan for banding the colonies together for self-protection, but it was not adopted. The English government rejected it as too democratic, though the colonists thought it not democratic enough. Even then, the authorities in England "dreaded American union as the key-stone of independence." [1]

. The next year (1755) England sent over General Braddock with a body of troops to drive the French out of the Ohio Valley. He was a good soldier, but did everything by rule. He and his men could fight any enemy that would meet them openly face to face; but he did not know how to fight the French and Indians, whose plan was to hide in the forest, and fire from behind trees.

Braddock might have got useful hints from either Franklin or Washington, but he scorned consulting men who had never been regularly trained in the European arts of war.

**141. Braddock's Defeat; Washington.** — Braddock advanced (1755) from Alexandria, Virginia, across the mountains to attack Fort Duquesne. Washington accompanied him. All went well until the British army had nearly reached the fort. Suddenly a savage yell rose from the woods through which the men were marching, followed by a murderous volley of musket-shots which killed many. The English general did everything a brave man could to repel the attack, but it was useless. Both he and his army were simply "a living target to an unseen foe." A panic set in; the men ran like sheep, and were shot down as they ran. Finally Braddock, who was himself mortally wounded, had to order a retreat. A few days later he died, and was secretly buried at night. Colonel Washington read the funeral service over his grave by torchlight.

---

[1] Part of Franklin's plan was that the colonies should have a president appointed by the crown, and a council chosen by the people.

It was said in Virginia that Braddock lost the victory, but that Washington's coolness and courage saved the army. It was true; for without Washington's aid the defeat would have become a massacre. An eminent Virginia clergyman, who preached on the disaster shortly afterward, said of Washington, that he believed that "Providence had saved him for some important service to his country."

142. The Acadians; Pitt and Victory; Fort Duquesne; the French driven to Canada. — In the course of the next two years the English took the French province of New Brunswick, and drove many thousands of Acadians, or French inhabitants of Nova Scotia, into exile.[1] But up to 1758 the war languished. Then a great change took place. William Pitt, later known as Lord Chatham, had now become the chief councillor in the English government. He was a man of immense energy, of spotless integrity, and one of the truest friends that America ever had. He sent fresh troops to fight for the colonists; and, what was better, he seemed to inspire them with his own spirit. Louisburg was now retaken, never to be given back. Then a second expedition was sent against Fort Duquesne. Colonel Washington took part in it as before. The fort was captured, and named Fort Pitt in honor of the distinguished statesman who had made the victory possible. To-day we know the place as Pittsburg, the centre of the most extensive iron works in the United States.

This victory gave the English the control of the Ohio country. Then, by the help of his Iroquois "braves," Sir William Johnson of Johnson Hall, New York,[2] took Fort Niagara.

---

[1] Longfellow has made this exile of the 7,000 Acadians the subject of his poem of "Evangeline." Burke called the expulsion "an inhuman act," but recent investigation seems to show that the English were justified in driving out the French, since they positively refused to take the oath of allegiance to England, and their sons were secretly fighting against her. (See Parkman's "Montcalm and Wolfe," I. 234–284.)

[2] Johnson Hall, near Schenectady. Sir William and his son had unbounded influence over the Iroquois tribes, and at this period they used that influence for the advantage of the colonies.

Next, the French were compelled to give up Fort Ticonderoga and Crown Point on Lake Champlain, and were driven back to Canada.

**143. Fall of Quebec; Pontiac's Conspiracy.** — The French had lost Fort Frontenac (Kingston), but they still held Quebec; and so long as they had possession of that formidable stronghold, they could continue to threaten the American colonies. The fortress was built on a lofty rock, overlooking the St. Lawrence. It was rightly believed to be one of the strongest

in the world; in fact, the "Gibraltar of America." Montcalm, one of the ablest and noblest generals of France, held the fortress. General Wolfe, an English soldier of equal character and courage, undertook to wrest it from him. The death struggle came in the autumn of 1759, when Wolfe, with his troops, climbed the Heights of Abraham. In the terrible battle both commanders found the truth of the words, "The paths of glory lead but to the grave,"[1] which Wolfe quoted to his brother officers on the eve of the contest; for both were killed. They met death as only heroes can.

The Heights of Abraham.

The English general exclaimed when he heard that his men had gained the hard-fought field, "Now, God be praised, I die in peace." The French leader, when told that he must soon breathe his last, said, "So much the better; I shall not live to see the surrender of Quebec."

The fall of Quebec practically ended the war; but four years later, Pontiac, chief of a Michigan tribe and friendly to the French, rose in revolt. He formed a secret league with other

[1] Gray's "Elegy written in a Country Churchyard," 1749. "Gentlemen," said Wolfe to his officers, "I would rather have written those lines than take Quebec."

tribes, — the Iroquois refusing to join, — to drive the English from the whole Western country. A young Indian girl betrayed the plot to the commander of the fort at Detroit. Pontiac's attack failed, though many frontier settlers were massacred, and he himself was forced to beg for peace. It was the last general attempt on the part of the Indians to reconquer the land that the white man had taken from them.

144. **What the French and Indian War settled.** — The fall of Quebec was a turning-point in American history. When Wolfe with his brave men climbed the rocky heights back of that great fortress on a starlight autumn night of 1759, the whole West, from Quebec to the Mississippi and New Orleans, belonged to France.

When the sun went down the following day, France had lost her hold on America forever. By the treaty of peace of 1763 the French king gave up the whole of his possessions in this country to England. Of all the magnificent territory that he had held on this continent, nothing was left that he could call his own but two little barren islands off the coast of Southern Newfoundland [1] which the English permitted him to keep, to dry fish on.

The war settled the fact that America was not to be an appendage of France, but was to become the home of the chief part of the English-speaking race. Spain had owned Florida since its discovery by Ponce de Leon [2] — more than two centuries and a half. She had fought on the side of France against England : now that France was defeated Spain was forced to give up Florida to Great Britain; so that by the end of 1763 the flag of England and of the English colonies floated over the whole eastern section of this continent, from the Atlantic to the great river of the West, with the single exception of New Orleans, which, with the Louisiana territory west of the Mississippi, France had secretly transferred to Spain.

[1] Miquelon and St. Pierre.        [2] See Paragraph 18.

**145. Results of the Wars.** — The long series of wars between the English and the French in this country accomplished four great results: 1. They united the inhabitants of the colonies — especially of those north of the Carolinas — and inspired them with new strength. 2. They trained thousands of resolute men in the use of arms, taught them to face an enemy, and thus, in a measure, prepared them for the war of Independence not many years distant. 3. By removing all danger of attack by the French they made the colonists feel less need of British protection. 4. They cleared the ground east of the Mississippi of rival and hostile forces, and so left it open for our ancestors to lay — when the right time should come — the corner-stone of the United States.

### GENERAL STATE OF THE COUNTRY IN 1763.

**146. The Thirteen Colonies in 1763; Growth of the Country; Number and Character of the Population.** — The growth of the colonies from the first settlements in 1607[1] and 1620[2] to the end of the French and Indian War had been slow but steady. When a gardener finds that a healthy young plant shows but little progress, he is not discouraged. He says cheerfully, "It is all right; it is making roots, and will last the longer." For a century and a half the colonies had been "making roots," — getting that firm hold so necessary for the future growth of a free and powerful nation.

In 1763[3] the entire population probably did not greatly exceed half that of New York City now.[4] Of this about one-sixth were negro slaves; every colony had some, but by far the larger part were owned south of the Potomac. This population was nearly all east of the Alleghanies. West of those mountains the country was really a howling wilderness. The

---

[1] See Paragraph 47.                    [2] See Paragraph 73.

[3] The date of England's treaty of peace with France.

[4] No exact estimate of the population can be given, as the first census was not taken until 1790. It was probably about 1,800,000.

majority of the colonists — especially in Virginia and New England — were English or of English descent. Next in number came the Germans in Pennsylvania,[1] the Dutch in New York,[2] the Irish and Scotch-Irish[3] who had settled to some extent in all of the colonies, and finally, the descendants of the Huguenots, or French Protestants, most numerous in South Carolina.[4]

147. **Language; Religion; Social Rank; Cities; Trade.** — Nearly all of the colonists spoke English, and nearly all were Protestants.[5] Most of them had sprung from the same social class in the mother-country. A witty Frenchman of that day said that the people of England reminded him of a barrel of their own beer — froth on the top, dregs at the bottom, but clear and sound in the middle. It was from that energetic, industrious, self-respecting middle class that the greater part of the emigrants to this country came. In none of the colonies was there a titled aristocracy holding land, and established by law as in Europe. In Virginia, however, the great plantations were usually handed down to the eldest son after the English fashion. America had men of intelligence and wealth, but no lords; she had learned and influential clergymen, but no bishops.

Philadelphia, New York, Boston, and Charleston were the chief cities, yet even Philadelphia, then the largest, had only about twenty thousand inhabitants, and not one of these cities published a daily paper and did not until more than twenty years later.[6]

The foreign trade of the country was prosperous. The South exported tobacco, rice, indigo, tar, and turpentine; the North, fish, lumber, furs, and iron. New England built and

---

[1] See Note 1, page 122.                [2] See Paragraph 61.

[3] See Paragraph 94.                      [4] See Paragraph 117.

[5] The greatest number of Catholics were in Maryland; there they may have constituted a fifteenth of the population.

[6] The *Boston News Letter*, 1704 (weekly), was the first regular newspaper published in America. The *American Daily Advertiser*, Philadelphia, 1784, is said to have been the first daily.

sold so many sailing-vessels that the ship-carpenters of Great Britain complained that the Americans were ruining their business. Manufactories were comparatively few. England treated her colonies in a broader and more generous spirit than any other nation in Europe, but she wished, so far as practicable, to compel the Americans to buy all their goods from her. On this account she refused to let them make so much as a yard of fine woollen cloth, an iron pot, or print a New Testament. The people of this country did not openly dispute this right, or supposed right, of the mother-country to restrict their trade; but they smuggled goods, especially tea and other luxuries, from Europe; and the British custom-house officers pretty generally winked at the landing of such articles.

**148. Government of the Colonies; Law; Unity of the People.** — The colonies did not all have the same form of government. Connecticut and Rhode Island held charters,[1] by which they practically managed their own affairs in their own way without interference of any sort. Eight of the remaining colonies[2] were under a governor appointed by the king; the three others, Pennsylvania with Delaware,[3] and Maryland were governed by their proprietors,[4] the descendants of William Penn and of Lord Baltimore.

All the colonies had legislative assemblies elected by the people; by means of these assemblies they levied their own taxes and had the chief voice in making their own laws.[5] In New England all matters of public interest were openly and fearlessly discussed in town-meeting; in Virginia, county meetings were held occasionally for the same purpose. Every

---

[1] See Note 3, page 25.

[2] Massachusetts had a charter, but could make only such laws as her governor, appointed by the king, saw fit to approve.          [3] See Paragraph 122.

[4] Proprietors: those to whom the land was originally granted.

[5] The laws enacted by the colonial assemblies required the governor's approval, except in Rhode Island and Connecticut, where the people elected the governor and could legislate, if they chose, without his consent.

white man had the right to trial by jury and to the protection given by the common law of England.

The colonists, though loyal to the king, were full of sturdy independence of character. In 1775 some of them adopted a flag on which was a rattlesnake coiled ready to strike, and the words, "DON'T TREAD ON ME"; but they might have hoisted such colors just as well a dozen years before, for that flag expressed what their real spirit had always been. Though there was but little communication between the colonies, yet they were essentially one people, — they spoke the same language, they appealed for justice to the same general law, they held, with some few exceptions, the same religion.

**149. Life among the Farmers.**—Few of the colonists were very rich; fewer still were miserably poor. The mass of the people lived simply but comfortably. The farm-houses were generally built of huge timbers covered with rough, unpainted clapboards, often with the upper story projecting so that in case of an attack by Indians, the owner could fire down on the savages and give them a reception they would remember. Usually the centre of such houses was taken up by an immense

By the Fireside.

open fireplace, so big that it was a fair question whether the chimney was built for the house or the house for the chimney. On a snapping cold night there was no more cheerful sight than such a fireplace piled up with blazing logs, round which our forefathers and their sturdy families sat contentedly, watching the flames as they leaped up the chimney. But these roaring fires meant work. During the day the wood-chopper seemed to hear them forever crying "more, more," and if by ill-chance they went out at night, there were no matches to rekindle them. That had to be done by striking a spark with flint and steel, catching it on a bit of old half-burnt rag, and then blowing that spark to a flame. If we are tempted to envy our ancestors their cosy winter evenings, probably few envy them their winter mornings in case the fire failed to keep over.

The cooking was done either over or before these open fires, or in huge brick ovens. The food was very simple, — often nothing more than mush and molasses for breakfast, — but there was plenty of it, and no lack of healthy appetite.

The farmer bought little at the store. He raised his own food; his sheep furnished wool, and his wife and daughters

spun and wove it into stout "homespun" cloth. In such households there were few idle days, but many happy ones; and for recreation the young people had sleighing parties, husking-bees,[1] general-trainings,[2] and other merry-makings.

150. **Life in the Cities, and on the Great Virginia Plantations.** — In the cities and large towns, and on the great planta-tions at the South, there was a good deal of luxury. The rich lived in stately man-sions, furnished with solid oak and ma-hogany imported from England. Their

Life at the South.

tables shone with silver plate, and sparkled with costly wines. They owned their servants instead of hiring them. Gentlemen,

---

[1] Husking-bees: at these gatherings the young people met to husk corn; there was usually quite as much fun as work on such occasions.

[2] General-trainings: meetings for military drill. They occurred once or twice a year, and were regarded as holidays.

when in full-dress, wore three-cornered cocked hats, long velvet coats, lace ruffles at their wrists, knee breeches,[1] white silk stockings, and shoes with silver buckles. They kept their hair long, powdered it white, and tied it back in a twist or queue with a black silk ribbon. Ladies wore gowns of brocade[2] and rich silk almost stiff enough to stand alone. They also powdered their hair, so that all people of fashion, whether young or old, looked stately and venerable. In general, life moved in somewhat the same stately way : there was no hurrying to catch trains, no flashing of telegrams from one end of the country to the other, no newsboys shouting daily papers, no instantaneous photographs, no pushing and hustling in overcrowded streets. On Sunday every one, or practically every one, went to church ; and, in New England, if a man was absent more than once without some very good reason, he was in great danger of making the acquaintance of the whipping-post.

**151. Travel; Letters; Hospitality; Severe Laws.**—People seldom travelled. When they did, they generally preferred going by water if possible, in order to avoid the bad roads. But as such travelling was wholly in sailing-vessels, the time when a man reached his destination depended altogether on the wind, and the wind made no promises. Knowing this fact, some chose to go by land. To accommodate these venturesome people a lumbering covered-wagon ran once a week between New York and Philadelphia, travelling at the rate of about three miles an hour.

The " Flying Machine."

Later (1766), an enterprising individual put on a wagon which actually made the trip of ninety miles in two days.

---

[1] Knee breeches: breeches coming down to the knees; before the introduction of trousers they were worn by men of all classes.

[2] Brocade: cloth or stuff richly embroidered with raised flowers or other figures in silk or gold and silver thread.

On account of its speed it was advertised as the "Flying Machine"; the cheaper conveyances, which did not "fly," took a day longer to make the journey. In the wet season of the year the passengers often worked their passage as well as paid for it, for they were frequently called on to get out and pry the wagon out of the mud with fence-rails.

The expense of carrying the mails made postage so high that but few letters were written. These were rarely prepaid; and as a charge of twenty-five cents on a single letter was not very uncommon, most persons preferred that their friends should think of them often but write to them seldom.

Yet if people rarely wrote to each other and travelled but little, they were quite sure of being hospitably entertained

Pillory and Stocks.

along the way when they did venture from home. This was especially the case in Virginia. The rich planters in that section considered a guest a prize. He brought the latest news and the newest gossip. It was no strange thing for a planter to send out one of his negroes to station himself by the roadside to watch for the coming of some respectable looking stranger on horseback. Then the servant, smiling and bowing, begged him to turn aside and stop over night at his master's mansion. There he was sure to be treated to the best there was in the house; and as no temperance society had then come into existence, the best, both North and South, always meant plenty to drink as well as plenty to eat, followed perhaps by a fox-hunt, or some other sport, the next day.

But if the times were hospitable, they were also somewhat

rough and even brutal. A trifling offence would often send a man to the stocks for meditation, and something more serious to the pillory, where the passer-by might stop to pelt him with a handful of mud, a rotten apple, or something worse. Imprisonment for debt was an every-day occurrence, and criminals who committed highway robbery or murder were first paraded through the principal streets and then hanged in public.

**152. Education; Books; Jonathan Edwards and Benjamin Franklin.** — Most of the colonists, especially in New England, where free schools had long been established by law, could read and write fairly well; and a small number, particularly clergymen, were highly educated. Very few books were published, but the rich imported a stock of the best English authors, and, what is more, they read them. The two ablest American writers of that day were the Rev. Jonathan Edwards of Massachusetts [1] and Benjamin Franklin of Philadelphia. Edwards wrote his great work "On the Freedom of the Will" for that small number of readers who like a book that forces them to think as well as read. Not many can grasp Edwards' thought about the "Will," but we can all understand how nobly he used his own will when he made these two resolutions: 1. "*To do whatever I think to be my duty.*" 2. "*To live with all my might while I do live.*"

Franklin's best-known work was his Almanac, commonly called "Poor Richard's Almanac," [2] which he published for many years. It was full of shrewd, practical wit and wisdom, and it suited a hard-working people. Men who had begun life with no help but such as they got from their own hands and their own brains liked to read such sayings as these: "*Diligence is the mother of good luck.*" "*He that can have*

[1] Edwards was born in Connecticut, but spent most of his life in Massachusetts.

[2] Because Franklin represents a curious old fellow, whom he calls "Poor Richard," as uttering the sayings which made the almanac famous. Franklin wrote his famous "Autobiography" many years later (1790).

*patience can have what he will."* *"Heaven helps those who help themselves."* Thousands of young men learned these maxims by heart, put them in practice, and found their reward in the prosperity and independence to which they led.

But Franklin did not confine himself to writing; he was also greatly interested in scientific experiments. Everybody has noticed that the fur of a cat's back, when stroked vigorously the wrong way on a winter's night, will send out a multitude of electric sparks. Franklin asked himself, Are these sparks the same as the flashes of lightning seen in a thunder-shower? He resolved to find out. To do this he sent up a kite during a shower, and fastened a door-key near the end of the string. Touching his knuckle to the key he got an electric spark from it. This, and other experiments, convinced him that his conjecture was right; electricity and lightning, said he, are one and the same thing. That discovery, simple as it now seems, made Franklin famous. When he went to England on business for the colonies he needed no introduction, — everybody had heard of the American who had found the key to the clouds and to electrical science as well. Even George III., though he heartily hated Franklin for his independent spirit, actually put up a bungling kind of Franklin lightning-rod — one with a ball instead of a point — on his palace in London.

To-day we light our cities, propel our street-cars, ring our fire-alarms, and send our messages across continents and under oceans by this mysterious power. We owe the practical beginning of much of this to Franklin. He said, "There are no bounds . . . to the force man may raise and use in the electrical way." In view of what is now being done in this "electrical way," the words of the Philadelphia printer, philosopher, and statesman — written more than a hundred years ago — read like a prophecy.

**153. General Summary.** — The thirteen colonies were settled, mainly by the English, between 1607 and 1733, — Virginia was

BENJAMIN FRANKLIN.

the first colony founded (1607), Massachusetts the second (1620), Georgia (1733) the last.   During the closing seventy years of this period (1689–1763) the colonists were engaged nearly half of the time in a series of wars with the French settlers in Canada, who had explored the West and claimed it for themselves.   In these wars many Indian tribes (but not the Iroquois [1]) fought on the side of the French.   The colonists, with the aid of England, gained the victory, and thus obtained possession of the country from the Atlantic to the Mississippi.   Up to that time (1763) the people had been growing in prosperity, in intelligence, and in the determination to maintain all those rights to which as English colonists they were justly entitled.

[1] Iroquois: the Indians of New York.   See Paragraph 42.

# IV.

"Resolved, That these United Colonies are, and of right ought to be, FREE AND INDEPENDENT STATES." — *Motion made in the Continental Congress at Philadelphia, June 7, 1776, by Richard Henry Lee of Virginia, seconded by John Adams of Massachusetts.*

————◆————

## THE REVOLUTION; THE CONSTITUTION.

### (1763–1789.)

1. THE COLONISTS RESIST TAXATION WITHOUT REPRESENTATION, 1764–1775.
2. THE COLONISTS MAKE WAR AGAINST ENGLAND IN DEFENCE OF THEIR RIGHTS AS ENGLISH SUBJECTS, 1775–JULY 4, 1776.
3. THE WAR OF INDEPENDENCE, JULY 4, 1776–1783.
4. THE FORMATION AND ADOPTION OF THE CONSTITUTION, 1787–1788.

154. **American Commerce ; the New King ; George III. ; how he interfered with Trade.** — Up to the close of the war by which England had compelled the French to give up their hold on America the people of this country had prospered. During the war, and for a long time before it, the laws which forbade the colonists to trade with any country except Great Britain had not been enforced. The result was that the New Englanders had made a great deal of money by trading with the French and the Spanish West Indies — sending them lumber and fish, and bringing back molasses and sugar from the French islanders, and bags of silver dollars from the Spaniards.

Now, all this profitable commerce was to stop. A new king — George III. — had come to the throne in England (1760). He was conscientious but narrow-minded, obstinate, and at times crazy.[1] The new government was determined that the old laws should be carried out. Ships of war were stationed along the American coast to stop free trade with the French and the Spaniards. In Boston and other large towns the king's officers, armed with warrants called "Writs of Assistance," began to break into men's houses and shops and search them for smuggled goods.[2] They did not ask for proof of guilt; they entered and searched when and where they pleased. New England saw her trade broken up. It began to look as though the king and his "friends"[3] meant to ruin every merchant and ship-builder in the country. James Otis and other leading citizens of Boston protested, but it was useless.

155. **The King proposes to tax the Colonies; Object of the Tax; Protest of the Americans.** — This, however, was only the beginning of evil. The cost of the late war had been enormous and English tax-payers groaned at the thought of paying out any more money. But the king was determined to send at least ten thousand troops to America, to protect, as he said, the colonies against the Indians and the French. In order to raise money to pay these soldiers — whom the Americans did not want — George III. and his "friends" proposed an entirely new measure — that was to tax the people of this country. But the colonists believed that according to the principles of English law the king had no just power to demand his people's money except by consent of the men whom they should

---

[1] The king had his first attack of insanity — a mild one — in 1765, while the Stamp Act was under discussion. In 1788 he felt that his mind was seriously affected; bursting into tears, he exclaimed that "He wished to God he might die, for he was going mad." He soon became so.

[2] These "Writs of Assistance" were general search-warrants in blank. In an ordinary search-warrant the person applying to the magistrate for it must swear that he has good reason for suspecting the person he accuses, and must have his name, and no other, inserted by the magistrate in the warrant. In the case of the "Writs of Assistance" it was entirely different. The officers wrote any name they pleased in the warrants, and then entered and rummaged the man's house from attic to cellar. Sometimes this was done purely out of spite.

[3] Those who supported the king in England were called the "King's Friends."

elect to represent them in Parliament.[1]  The Americans had
no such representatives, and, what is more, they were not permitted to send any.  For this reason they protested against
the tax as a direct and open violation of their rights.  The
best men in Parliament — such men as William Pitt[2] and
Edmund Burke — took the side of the colonists.[3]  Burke said
that if the king undertook to tax the Americans against their
will he would find it as hard a job as the farmer did who tried
to shear a wolf instead of a sheep.

156.  **The Stamp Act.** — But the king and his "friends,"
with many others, thought that the Americans were like

British Stamp.

lambs and that they would stand any
amount of shearing without once showing their teeth.  Accordingly, Parliament
passed the Stamp Act in 1765.  That
act required that the colonists should
use stamps — resembling our postage-
stamps — on all important law and business papers, and also on pamphlets and
newspapers.  The stamps cost all the
way from a half penny (one cent) up to
ten pounds (fifty dollars).  Such a law,
if enforced, would tax everybody in spite of himself; for every
one would have to pay that tax when he bought a newspaper
or an almanac, took out a policy of insurance on his house,
or made his will.

157.  **Resistance of the Colonists.** — Benjamin Franklin,[4] who
was in London as agent for the colonies when the law was
proposed, fought against it with all his might, but, as he said,

---

[1] The British Parliament, which sits in London, is to England what Congress is
to the United States.  It is a law that no tax shall be levied on the British people
except by members of Parliament elected by the people as their representatives.

[2] See Paragraph 142.

[3] Pitt thought it was not right to tax America; Burke thought it was not wise to
do so.                                    [4] See page 133, note 3.

he might as well have tried to stop the sun from setting. In Boston, Samuel Adams, the "Father of the Revolution," denounced the act at a town-meeting held in Faneuil[1] Hall — the "Cradle of Liberty," as it was called. But the law passed, and the colonists got the news in the spring of 1765.

Then the indignation of the people blazed out in an unmistakable manner. In Virginia, Patrick Henry, in a speech — now familiar to every school-boy — fired all hearts by his eloquence. James Otis[2] had already declared that "Taxation without representation[3] is tyranny." Delegates from nine of the colonies met in New York to protest against the Stamp Act. When the hated stamps came the people destroyed them, and even the boys shouted, "Liberty, property, and no stamps!"

Faneuil Hall, the "Cradle of Liberty," as it appeared in 1765.

**158. Repeal of the Stamp Act; the Declaratory Act; the "Boston Massacre"; Destruction of the *Gaspee*.** — When news of these vigorous proceedings reached London, William Pitt[4] said in Parliament, "In my opinion, this kingdom has no right to lay a tax on the colonies. . . . I rejoice that America has resisted." The Stamp Act was speedily repealed (1766),[5] much to the delight of many people in

---

[1] Faneuil: commonly pronounced Fan'il.    [2] See Paragraph 154.
[3] See Paragraph 155.    [4] See note 3, page 154.
[5] *All dates in parentheses [as in this case (1766)] are given simply to enable the pupil to follow the order of time readily; dates not so enclosed — for instance, 1765, on this page — should, as a rule, be committed to memory.*

England as well as of the colonists.    Parliament, however, put a sting in its repeal, for it passed a Declaratory Act, maintaining that the British government had the right to bind the colonies " in all cases whatsoever."    At the time, the Americans did not see the full force of that declaration.

But they saw it when the king sent troops to be quartered here at the expense of the people.    New York promptly refused to pay the bill.    Later, General Gage, the British commander at New York, was sent with two regiments to Boston (1768). These troops were quartered in the very centre of the town, and they had frequent quarrels with the citizens.    Finally (1770) a fight occurred in which the soldiers fired, in self-defence, and killed several of the people.    This was called the " Boston Massacre "; the citizens never forgot or forgave the blood stains then made on the snow of King Street.[1] Later, that feeling showed itself in the destruction by the Rhode Islanders of the *Gaspee*, an armed British vessel stationed off the coast to prevent smuggling.

**159.  The New Taxes; the " Boston Tea Party."** — Meanwhile (1767) the king and his party tried a new scheme of taxation.    They imposed a duty on glass, paper, paints, and tea.    The object of the Stamp Act had been to raise money to pay the king's soldiers in this country.    This new tax had not one object, but three: 1. To pay the soldiers sent here to do the king's will.    2. To pay the governors, judges, and other officers of the crown in the colonies.    This would make them wholly dependent on the king, and they would no longer feel that they were responsible to the people or must do their best to serve them.    3. To give large sums of money to leading citizens and thus hire them to use their influence for the king.

---

[1] King Street, now State Street.    The soldiers were tried for murder; John Adams and Josiah Quincy, Jr., of Boston, defended them.    All but two were acquitted.    They were convicted of manslaughter, and branded in the hand in open court.

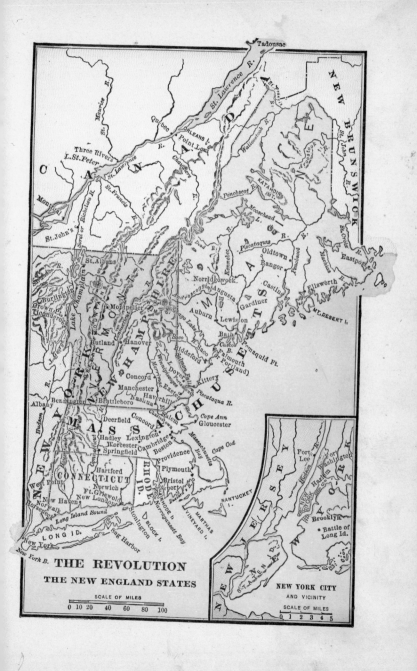

# THE REVOLUTION
## THE NEW ENGLAND STATES

SCALE OF MILES

0  10  20    40    60    80    100

NEW YORK CITY
AND VICINITY

SCALE OF MILES

0  1  2  3  4  5

But the Americans were not to be caught in this trap. They saw that George III. was endeavoring to exalt his own power and deprive them of theirs, and that the tax was for that purpose.

The great body of merchants throughout the colonies now agreed not to import the taxed articles. Others, like Samuel Adams, bound themselves "to eat nothing, drink nothing, wear nothing" imported from England until all the duties on goods should be taken off.

Parliament then decided to take off all taxes on these goods except one of a few cents a pound on tea. This duty was retained, not for the money it would yield, but to maintain the right of the British government to tax the colonies. The price of the tea was purposely put so low

Samuel Adams, the "Father of the Revolution."
(From Miss Whitney's Statue of Adams, in Adams Square, Boston.)

that the Americans could actually buy it, tax and all, cheaper than they could smuggle it from Holland.[1]

But though the colonists wanted the tea, they declared that they would not take it, even as a gift, if any tax, even the smallest, was demanded. Parliament again made the mistake of supposing that our forefathers did not mean what they said. Three tea-ships were accordingly sent to Boston, and cargoes

[1] Up to this time the colonists smuggled most of their tea from Holland; only about one pound in ten came from England.

were likewise despatched to New York, Philadelphia, Charleston and Annapolis;[1] but they were sent back or destroyed. In Boston (1773) the citizens refused to permit the tea to be landed. But if the ships were not unloaded within twenty days the custom-house officers had the right to unload them. The nineteenth day came, and unless something decisive should be done the tea would be brought ashore at sunrise the next morning. An immense meeting was held in the Old South Meeting-House. After discussing the matter all day, until evening set in, it was found impossible to get the vessels sent back to England. Samuel Adams then rose and said, "This meeting can do no more to save the country." These words were the signal for action. Suddenly a company of citizens disguised as Indians appeared at the church door and gave a war-whoop. Then they rushed down to the wharf, and, going on board the vessels, emptied every chest of tea — about $100,000 worth — into the harbor. A Bostonian had jokingly asked, "Will tea mix with salt water?" The patriots settled that question and the tax at the same time.

160. **Parliament closes the Port of Boston and places a Military Governor over the People; the First Continental Congress; Action of Massachusetts; the "Minute Men."**— When Parliament heard of the destruction of the tea the wrath of the king's party rose to white heat. They passed a law (1774) which closed the port of Boston to all trade until the people should pay for the tea, and make humble submission to the king. A second law took the government entirely out of the hands of the people, and put the colony under the rule of General Gage,[2] who was sent from England to Boston with several regiments of soldiers. Two other arbitrary measures enacted by Parliament completed the "Intolerable Acts," as the Americans called them.[3]

---

1 In 1774 the patriots of Annapolis burned the brig *Peggy Stewart* bringing tea.

2 General Gage (see page 156) was one of those who took part in Braddock's disastrous expedition. (See Paragraph 141.) He was in England in 1773.

3 These were the Transportation and the Quebec Acts. The first gave British

Patrick Henry of Virginia was so indignant at this treatment of Massachusetts that he said in the Virginia Convention, "There is no longer any room for hope.  We must fight.
I repeat it, sir; we
must fight."  "Com-
mittees of Corre-
spondence" had
prepared the colonies
for united action, and
in 1774 a Continental
or General Congress
— the first ever held
in America — met in
Carpenters' Hall,
Philadelphia, to con-
sider what course
the colonies should
take.

A "Minute Man."

The spirit of that
Congress was unmis-
takable.  It was per-
fectly calm, perfectly respectful, but perfectly determined.  The
delegates who met there, of whom George Washington was
one, did not demand representation in Parliament — they had
got beyond that — they demanded the right to levy all taxes,
and make all laws (except those respecting foreign commerce
and the like), in their own colonial assemblies.[1]

officers who were accused of committing murder — as in the case of the "Boston
Massacre" — the right of trial in England, where, of course, everything would be in
their favor.  (By a law of a different date, Americans who committed murder, in
resisting oppression, might be sent to England for trial, where, of course, everything
would be against them.)   The Quebec Act united the territory north of the Ohio and
east of the Mississippi — which the colonists considered theirs — with Canada.   The
object was to conciliate the French Canadians, and, if need be, to get their help in
punishing the colonists.

[1] They declared (Declaration of Rights, October 14, 1774) that since they "cannot
be properly represented in the British Parliament, they are entitled to a free and

Not long after this, Massachusetts set up a government quite independent of the military rule of General Gage, and made John Hancock, a wealthy and influential merchant of Boston, head of it. The colony[1] next raised twelve thousand volunteers, of whom one-third were "Minute Men"; that is, men ready to march or fight at a minute's notice. The spirit of liberty was universal—as a South Carolina paper said, "One soul animates 3,000,000 of brave Americans, though extended over a long tract of 3000 miles."

1. From the Beginning of the War in 1775 by the Colonists in Defence of their Rights as English Subjects, to the Declaration of Independence, July 4, 1776.

**161. The British Expedition to Lexington and Concord; Paul Revere; the Battle; the Retreat.**—General Gage having learned that the colonists had stored a quantity of powder and provisions for the use of their militia, at Concord, about twenty miles from Boston, sent a secret expedition to destroy both. The soldiers were instructed to go by way of Lexington, and there arrest Samuel Adams and John Hancock, who were known to be stopping with a friend in that village. The London papers

exclusive power of legislation in their several Provincial Legislatures." Yet this same Congress (October 26, 1774) sent a petition to the king, imploring him, "as the loving Father of your whole People," to redress their wrongs. They might as well have petitioned the "Great Stone Face" in the White Mountains of New Hampshire.

[1] Practically Massachusetts had possessed an independent government ever since Governor Hutchinson, in 1772, refused to convene a legislature to settle the question of how the judges' salaries should be paid. Samuel Adams then organized "Committees of Correspondence" by means of which the towns could consult on all public matters by letter. This method was extended by Virginia (1773) to other colonies, and thus prepared the way for calling a Continental Congress.

boasted that the heads of these two prominent "rebels" would soon be on exhibition in that city; but, as Gage found out, Adams and Hancock were not the kind of men to lose their heads so easily.

The British troops left Boston just before midnight of April 18, 1775. Paul Revere, a noted Boston patriot, was on the watch; at his request two signal lanterns flashed the news abroad from the steeple of the Old North Church, — a church still standing, — and he galloped through the country giving the alarm. When he reached the house in Lexington where Hancock and Adams were asleep, a man on guard cried out to him, "Don't make so much noise." "Noise," shouted Revere,[1] "you'll have noise enough before long; the 'regulars'[2] are coming."

Just before daybreak of April 19 the "regulars" marched on to the village green of Lexington where a number of "minute men" had collected. "Disperse, ye rebels!" shouted Pitcairn, the British commander. No one moved; then Pitcairn cried, "Fire!" A volley blazed out, and seven Americans fell dead. Some scattering shots were fired in return. Advancing to Concord, the soldiers destroyed such military stores as they could find; at Concord Bridge they were met by the patriots. It was the opening battle of the Revolution, — several men fell on each side. There the first British were killed, there the first British graves were dug. The "regulars" then drew back, leaving the Americans in possession of the bridge, and began their march toward Boston.[3]

But the whole country was now aroused. The enraged farmers fired at the British from behind every wall, bush, and tree. The march became a retreat, the retreat something like

[1] Longfellow's "Paul Revere's Ride" is not strictly historical.
[2] The soldiers of the regular British army.
[3] When the news of the attack on Lexington and Concord reached England, a number of friends of the Americans and their cause made up a purse of $500 which they sent to Benjamin Franklin to distribute among the wounded patriots, and the wives and mothers of those who were killed by the British.

a run. When the "regulars" got back to Lexington, where Lord Percy met them with reinforcements, they dropped panting on the ground, "their tongues hanging out" like those of tired dogs.[1] From Lexington the "minute men" chased the British all the way to Charlestown. Nearly three hundred of the "red-coats," as the Americans nicknamed the English soldiers, lay dead or dying on the road.

Percy had marched gaily out of Boston to the tune of "Yankee Doodle," played in ridicule of the Americans, but it was noticed that his band did not play it on re-entering the town — they had had quite enough of all that was "Yankee" for that day.

The next morning the British army found themselves shut up in Boston. The Americans had surrounded it on the land side; they dared the British to come out and fight — the siege of Boston had begun.[2]

**162. Meeting of the Second Continental Congress; Ethan Allen's Victories.** — The Second Continental Congress met at Philadelphia on May 10, 1775. It recognized George III. as the "rightful sovereign" of the American colonies, but it voted to raise 15,000 men to defend the liberties of the country. On the very day that Congress met, Ethan Allen, a "Green Mountain Boy,"[3] surprised the sentinel on duty and got entrance with his men to Fort Ticonderoga on Lake Champlain. It was early in the morning and the garrison was asleep. Allen burst into the commandant's room and demanded the immediate and unconditional surrender of the fort. "By what authority?" asked the astonished officer. "In the name of the great Jehovah and the Continental Congress," thundered Allen.[4] The commandant surrendered; the Americans got

---

[1] So says an English officer, see Stedman's "American War," I. 118.

[2] See Map, page 163.    [3] Allen was born in Litchfield, Connecticut (1737), but early removed to Bennington, Vermont, the "Green Mountain State."

[4] It is now denied that Allen used these words, but it is admitted that he used some that were even more emphatic. One thing is certain: the British commander understood him, and gave up the fort.

possession of cannon, arms, and military stores which they sorely needed. Crown Point, a little fortress on the lake, north of Ticonderoga, was taken the next day.

**163. Washington appointed Commander-in-chief of the Continental Army; Battle of Bunker Hill.** — Not long after this exploit, Congress appointed Washington commander-in-chief of the army around Boston. General Gage had received reinforcements from England under the command of Generals Howe, Clinton, and Burgoyne. He now had a force of about eight thousand men. Near the middle of June (1775), he planned an expedition to seize Bunker Hill.[1] This hill is in Charlestown, and overlooks part of Boston. Gage was afraid that the Americans might get possession of it; if so, they could fire into his camp and make him very uncomfortable.

What then was his surprise when he found on the morning of the 17th of June that the "rebels" had got the start of him and had actually seized and fortified the hill. During the night, while the British commander was peacefully sleeping, Colonel Prescott, aided later by General Putnam of Connecticut and General Warren of Boston, had entrenched himself there with about fifteen hundred men. General Gage saw that he must drive the Americans from Bunker Hill or they would drive him out of Boston. He sent Howe to make the attack with three thousand British "regulars." The American officers ordered their men to wait — they had but little powder and that little was very precious. The word was: "Don't fire till you see

[1] The name Breed's Hill did not then exist. See Frothingham's "Joseph Warren," 507; and Winsor's "America," VI, 135.

the white of their eyes." They obeyed; when they did fire the destruction of life was terrible. The smoke lifted and there lay "The 'red-coats' stretched in windrows as a mower rakes his hay."[1]

The British fell back; rallied, made a second attack and again fell back. A third time Howe led his men up the hill. This time he was successful. The Americans had fired their last round of ammunition, and fighting desperately with the butt ends of their muskets — they had no bayonets — and even with clubs and stones, they slowly retreated — driven back not because they had been defeated, but because they no longer had the means to continue the battle.

In an hour and a half the British lost over a thousand men, out of three thousand. The American loss was also very heavy;[2] among those who fell was the distinguished patriot, General Warren. During the engagement Howe ordered Charlestown to be fired, and by night the greater part of the town was in ashes.

This act roused Benjamin Franklin's indignation and he wrote a letter to his former friend Strahan, a member of the English Parliament, which showed that though he was a man of peace yet he knew when to be angry.[3] When General Washington heard how the Americans had fought at Bunker Hill he exclaimed, "The liberties of the country are safe!"

164. Washington takes Command of the Army; Expedition against Quebec. — Washington reached Cambridge and took command of the army — a force of about fifteen thousand poorly armed and untrained men — early in July (1775). Nothing was done that summer. But meanwhile Congress had learned that the British in Canada were intending to march down and attack

---

1 See O. W. Holmes's fine poem, "Grandmother's Story of Bunker Hill."

2 Our loss was 449, that of the British, 1054. When the English government got the news of the battle, Gage was ordered to return to England, and the command of all the British forces in the colonies was given to General Howe.

3 See copy of this letter in Franklin's handwriting on page 165.

Philad.ᵃ July 5. 1775

Mr Strahan,

You are a Member of Parliament, and one of that Majority which has doomed my Country to Destruction.— —You have begun to burn our Towns, and murder our People.— Look upon your Hands! — They are stained with the Blood of your Relations! — You and I were long Friends: —You are now my Enemy, —and

I am,

Yours,

B Franklin

FRANKLIN'S LETTER TO STRAHAN.

points in Northern New York.   To give them something else
to think of nearer home, General Montgomery of New York
set out to take Quebec.   He descended Lake Champlain and
captured Montreal.   Benedict Arnold of Connecticut, one of
the bravest soldiers of the Revolution,
started with a force of over a thousand
men to join in the attack.   Setting out
from Newburyport, Massachusetts, Arnold
undertook to make his way from the mouth
of the Kennebec through the forests of
Maine.   He was six weeks getting across
the wilderness.   The suffering was so terrible that many men deserted, and the rest,
after having been compelled to eat their
moccasins, nearly perished.   At last Arnold
reached Quebec with his ragged, barefooted,
half-starved, and sadly diminished little
army.   Montgomery joined him with a few
hundred men, and with this small force they
attempted, on the last day of the year

Map showing Arnold's
Route to Quebec.

(1775), to storm "the strongest fortified city of America."
Montgomery was killed at the head of his troops, and Arnold
badly wounded — it would have been a happy thing for the
latter if he, too, had fallen dead on the field.   A few months
later the Americans were driven out of Canada.

**165. Washington enters Boston; the British repulsed at Fort
Moultrie.** — Throughout the winter of 1775–76 want of artillery and powder prevented Washington from doing anything
more than simply keeping up the siege of Boston.   At length.
General Knox succeeded in dragging fifty cannon on ox-sleds
all the way from Ticonderoga [1] to Cambridge.   Early in March
(1776) Washington seized Dorchester Heights (South Boston)

---

[1] See Paragraph 162.   A distance of about 200 miles, most of the way through a
country that was practically a wilderness.

overlooking Boston on the south.   He got his cannon into position and then gave General Howe — who had succeeded Gage in command — his choice of withdrawing his forces from the town or having it battered to pieces about his ears.   Howe took a good look, through his spy-glass, at the American guns on the Heights, and then gave the order to his men to embark

Reduced Copy of the Gold Medal presented to Washington by Congress.

(March 17 — St. Patrick's Day — 1776) for Halifax.

The following day Washington entered Boston in triumph.   The British had left it never to return. With them went about a thousand Tories, as those Americans were called who opposed the war and wished to submit to the king.   The Whigs, or patriots, now held a day of rejoicing, and Congress voted Washington a gold medal to commemorate his bloodless victory.

About midsummer (June 28, 1776) a British fleet[1] attacked Fort Sullivan, on Sullivan's Island, in the harbor of Charleston, South Carolina. Their hope was to get possession of the city; but Colonel Moultrie, aided by such heroes as Sergeant Jasper,

defended their log fort with such energy that the enemy were not sorry to withdraw.   Thereafter it was called Fort Moultrie in honor of its brave commander.

**166.  "Common Sense"; the Americans decide to separate from Great Britain.** — Up to 1776 the Americans had been fighting

1 General Clinton left Boston in the winter of 1776 and sailed to attack the Carolinas.   He was joined there by a fleet from England under Sir Peter Parker and Lord Cornwallis.   After their defeat at Fort Sullivan, Cornwallis and Clinton, with their men, went to New York.

in defence of their rights as British subjects. Washington said: "When I first took command of the Continental army I abhorred the idea of independence." But in January, 1776, the king's proclamation reached Congress. In it he called for troops to put down "the rebellion" in America. That was the only answer he gave to their humble petition [1] for justice. Congress now saw that there was no hope of reconciliation. The very day that proclamation came, a remarkable pamphlet was published in Philadelphia. It was entitled "Common Sense." The writer withheld his name,[2] but he boldly said that the time had come for a "final separation" from England, and that "arms must decide the contest." The pamphlet sold by tens of thousands, because it gave voice to what tens of thousands were thinking. The English people would not volunteer to fight the Americans, and the king had to hire, in all, nearly thirty thousand Hessians [3] for the work.

"Independence Hall," Philadelphia, as it appeared in 1776.

The knowledge of that fact cut the last thread that held us bound to the mother-country. The Americans had not sought separation; the king — not the English people — had forced it on them. There was no choice left.

167. **The Declaration of Independence.** — In June, 1776, Richard Henry Lee of Virginia offered this resolution in Congress: "Resolved: that these United Colonies are, and of right ought to be, FREE AND INDEPENDENT STATES." John

---

[1] See note 1 on page 159.    [2] The writer was Thomas Paine, an Englishman who had come to this country and espoused the cause of American liberty.

[3] Hessians: Germans from the province of Hesse and vicinity. The Prince of Hesse sold their services to the English king. The Germans had no voice in the matter, and had to go and fight where they were sent. Eighteen thousand were sent over the first year and eleven thousand afterward.

Adams of Massachusetts seconded the resolution. A committee of five — Thomas Jefferson of Virginia, John Adams of Massachusetts, Benjamin Franklin of Pennsylvania, Roger Sherman of Connecticut, and Robert R. Livingston of New York — was chosen to draw up a declaration embodying that resolution. Thomas Jefferson did the work. On the Fourth of July, 1776, John Hancock, President of Congress, signed the Declaration of American Independence in that bold,

And for the support of this declaration] we mutually pledge to each other our lives our fortunes, & our sacred honour.

*John Hancock*

*Sam'l Adams   Phil. Livingston*

Reduced copy of the last line of the Declaration of Independence (in Jefferson's handwriting) with the first three signatures.

decided hand which "the king of England could read without spectacles." Then the patriots of Philadelphia rang the "Liberty Bell" in the Old State House till it nearly cracked with the joyous peal. In New York City the people pulled down a gilded lead statue of the king and melted it up into bullets.

Later, the representatives of the colonies added their names to the Declaration. That completed the work; the thirteen British colonies had ceased to exist; in their place stood a new nation — the UNITED STATES OF AMERICA, — your country and mine.

**168. Summary.** — George III. endeavored to tax the colonists against their will, and in violation of their rights as

THOMAS JEFFERSON.

English subjects. They resisted, and finally took up arms in their defence. The king refused to listen to the demands of the Americans, hired a foreign army to subdue the people, and so drove them, at last, to separate from Great Britain and to declare themselves independent.

Liberty Bell, Independence Hall, Philadelphia.
(It was cracked in 1835, while tolling for the death of Chief Justice Marshall.)

2. THE WAR OF INDEPEND-
ENCE, FROM JULY 4, 1776,
TO THE VICTORY OF SARA-
TOGA, 1777.

**169. What the British hoped to do in New York.** — Driven out of Boston and defeated at Fort Moultrie the British determined to strike their next blow at New York. Their plan was to get pos-session of the city and of the Hudson River. They could then prevent the New England colonists and those south of New York from giving each other any help; for our force on land was small, and we had no vessels of war to attack the enemy by sea.

If the British were successful in thus cutting the colonies in two, they could then send a large force against Boston or Phila-delphia, whichever they thought best, and feel sure that the people of the two sections could not unite to defend either.

**170. Washington's Preparations to receive the British; Fort Washington and Fort Lee.** — Washington foresaw this design of the enemy and prepared for it. When General Howe, with his brother, Lord Howe, commander of the English fleet, reached New York in the summer (1776) they found Washington in possession of the city. Furthermore, they found, to their disappointment, that they could not send their ships up the Hudson so easily as they had hoped, for the Americans had built two forts expressly to prevent it. One of these was Fort Washington, on the upper part of Manhattan Island, on the bank of the Hudson ; the other was Fort Lee, nearly opposite, on the Jersey shore.[1] Between these two forts vessels had been sunk, so that if any of the enemy's ships tried to go up the river they would first be checked by the sunken vessels, and next, they would be exposed to the cross fire from the cannon of both forts.

**171. The Two Armies; the Battle of Long Island.** — But the British were confident that they could win the day. Howe and his brother were experienced military commanders. They had the aid of Clinton and Cornwallis,[2] both of whom were good generals, and over thirty thousand well-armed soldiers — men who fought for a living — while Washington had less than eighteen thousand, most of whom knew nothing of war, while many had no muskets fit to fight with. On the other hand, Washington had the advantage of position. He not only held

the city and the forts on the Hudson, but he had possession of Brooklyn Heights on Long Island directly opposite the city on the south. General Howe, with his army, was on Staten Island. He saw that if he could take Brooklyn Heights, and plant his cannon there, he could drive Washington out of New York, just as Washington, by seizing Dorchester Heights, had driven him out of Boston.[3]

General Putnam was in command of the Heights with a

---

[1] See map of New York City and vicinity, page 156.

[2] See note 1, page 166. Cornwallis, though he fought against us, was strongly opposed to the war, and believed that the Americans were right in protesting against taxation so long as they were denied representation.

[3] See Paragraph 165.

force of nine thousand men. Believing that the British meant to attack him, he sent about half his force to meet the enemy. The British, twenty thousand strong, or nearly five to one of the Americans, came across from Staten Island to the south-western shore of Long Island and marched toward the Heights. They defeated [1] the gallant little American army, although the Maryland and Delaware men made a desperate fight to win the battle of Long Island (August 27, 1776). The British then got ready to besiege Putnam.

Putnam with his whole army would certainly have been captured if it had not been for Washington's energy and skill. During the night a dense fog came up. Washington took advantage of it and succeeded in getting all the men across the river in boats to New York. In the morning, when the British commander stretched out his hand to take the "nest of rebels," as he called it, he got the nest indeed, but it was empty — the birds had flown.

**172. Washington retreats Northward; Fort Washington taken; Lee's Disobedience.** — Washington was now forced to abandon New York and retreat up the east side of the river. Captain Nathan Hale of Connecticut, who volunteered to discover the English plans, was arrested and hanged as a spy. On the gallows he said: "I only regret that I have but one life to lose for my country." Washington ordered West Point,[2] the strongest place on the Hudson, to be fortified, so as to prevent the enemy from going up to Albany. Meanwhile a deserter had carried plans of Fort Washington to the British commander. He now knew just where to strike, and took the fort with three thousand prisoners. It was a terrible blow. Washington had crossed to the west bank of the river, but could not hold his ground against Lord Cornwallis, for he had left quite a large force of his best soldiers on the east side of the Hudson under command of General Charles

---

[1] Each side lost about 400 in killed and wounded; but over 1000 Americans were taken prisoners. Many of these prisoners died in the British prison pens.

[2] West Point, 45 miles above New York. See Map, page 172.

Lee,[1] and when Washington ordered him to come over and join him, Lee wilfully disobeyed.

**173. Fort Lee taken; Washington retreats across the Delaware; General Lee captured.** — It was of no use for the Americans to try to hold Fort Lee now that the fort opposite was taken. Cornwallis threatened to attack it and it was abandoned. Washington with his small force now began to retreat across

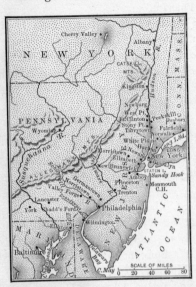

New Jersey. He broke down bridges after he had crossed them; destroyed the provisions Cornwallis hoped to get for his army, and so delayed the enemy that it took them nearly three weeks (November 19 to December 8) to march less than seventy miles across a level country. Washington hoped to save Philadelphia from falling into the hands of the British. If he could not, and everything went against him, he intended to escape with his little army to the mountains of Western Virginia, which he knew perfectly. There he could fight for years in the cause of liberty. Cornwallis and his "redcoats" followed the retreating Americans sometimes at a distance, then again close on their heels. There

[1] General Charles Lee was born in England. He had been an officer in the British army, but had left that service, come to this country, and had obtained the rank of major-general in the American army. He was in no way connected with the Lees of Virginia. While he was in command on the Hudson he was trying to prejudice Congress against Washington, in hope of getting his place. Later he showed himself to be utterly unprincipled and treacherous.

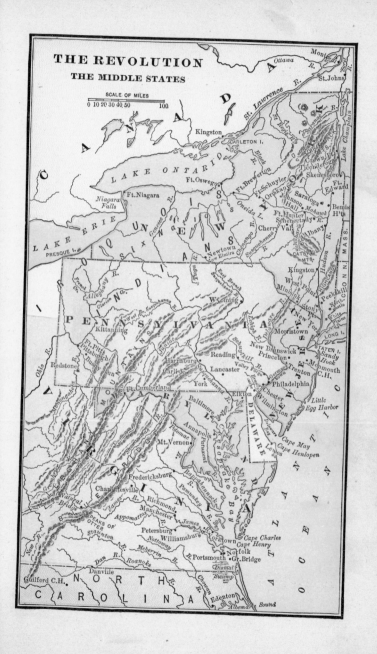

THE REVOLUTION
THE MIDDLE STATES

SCALE OF MILES
0 10 20 30 40 50    100

were times when the British would be entering a town just as our men were hurrying out of it. Many patriots began to despair of success. What, they asked, can we hope from a fugitive army of three thousand men, miserably armed, scantily clothed, half-fed, not paid? How can they escape their pursuers? Under any other general they could not have escaped; but they had Washington for their leader; and he was the heart, strength, and soul of the Revolution. Finding that he could not hold New Jersey, he was forced at last (December 8, 1776) to cross the Delaware at Trenton. The British would have pushed on after him; but the American general had thought of that, and had seized every boat for nearly a hundred miles up and down the river. All the British could do was to sit down on the bank and wait for the stream to freeze over.

Not long after Washington had reached Pennsylvania in safety the false-hearted Lee crossed the Hudson and marched with four thousand men toward Morristown, New Jersey. While he was asleep in a tavern, several miles from his men, a squad of British soldiers surprised and captured him. His army thus fortunately rid of him, advanced and found an opportunity to join Washington.

**174. The Victory of Trenton.** — On Christmas night (1776) Washington, with a force of less than twenty-five hundred men, re-crossed the Delaware — then full of floating ice — and marched on Trenton in a furious snow-storm. There he surprised a body of Hessian [1] soldiers, and took a thousand prisoners and a large quantity of arms and ammunition.

All this he did with scarce the loss of a man. It was not only a bold stroke, but a great victory, because it had great results. Thousands of patriots had begun to despair; now their hearts leaped with joy. It was a Christmas long to be remembered.

**175. What Robert Morris did for Washington.** — But it was near the end of the year; the time for which many of Washington's

[1] See note 3, page 167.

men had enlisted would be out in a few days, and he needed money to get them to re-enlist. Congress had indeed tried hard to manufacture money. It had printed bills[1] by the wagon-load. But the poor soldiers, barefooted, half-starved,

Robert Morris collecting Money

ragged and miserable, did not want what Congress offered them. They had left wives and children at home who were crying for bread, and the men wanted to send them something that would buy it. They knew by sad experience that a dollar bill issued by a government that had no silver or gold to make it good was worth just as much as any other dingy scrap of paper of the same size — and worth no more.

Washington sympathized with the men. He felt that on this occasion he must have money that had the genuine *ring* in it. He wrote to his friend Robert Morris, merchant and banker, of Philadelphia, imploring him to send him $50,000 in hard cash. Morris set out on New Year's morning (1777) before it was light, went from house to house, roused his friends from their beds, and at last got the money. He sent it forthwith to Washington. It was as good as another victory. It saved the army.

**176. Cornwallis outwitted; Victory of Princeton; Winter Quarters at Morristown; coming of Lafayette, De Kalb, and Steuben.** — Cornwallis, leaving part of his force at Princeton, New Jersey, hurried south to catch Washington. He found him between Trenton and a bend of the Delaware. That night the British general went to sleep, certain that Washington could not get away. For how could he hope to escape, with the British army in front and the broad, deep Delaware River full of

[1] These bills were called "Continental Currency"; they finally became utterly worthless, so that it was said of anything absolutely good for nothing that it was "not worth a Continental."

floating ice behind him? Cornwallis told his brother officers that they would "bag the old fox" in the morning. While the English general lay dreaming, Washington like an "old fox" crept stealthily round him, and got to Princeton. In the battle there (January 3, 1777), the American advance force was driven back. Just then Washington came up. He saw that if beaten our army would be lost. Calling on his troops to follow him, he rode to within thirty yards of the British force, and stood facing the foe, exposed to the fire of both sides. For some moments he was completely hidden from sight by the smoke of the battle. When it lifted, both sides expected to find that he had fallen; but he was unhurt — not a bullet had touched him. Our men, inspired by the bravery of their commander, defeated the enemy with heavy loss to the British; and soon after, the American general with his little army made themselves snug and safe in the hills about Morristown, in northern New Jersey.

Cornwallis knew that he could not drive Washington out of his strong position without a desperate battle, so he hurried back to New Brunswick, New Jersey, for fear that the Americans would cut him off from his supplies at New York City.

Washington spent the rest of the winter of 1777 at Morristown, raising new troops and getting his army into good fighting condition. The next summer the Marquis de Lafayette, a French nobleman of nineteen, came from Paris to offer his services to the cause of American liberty. He became one of Washington's generals, and not only gave his services to the country, but equipped many of the men under his command with arms and clothing furnished at his own expense. Lafayette brought with him Baron de Kalb, a German military veteran, who also became a general in the United States army. Later, Baron Steuben, a Prussian military engineer, joined the Americans and made himself of the greatest use in drilling and disciplining our troops.[1]

---

[1] Kosciusko and Pulaski, two eminent Polish patriots, joined our army in 1777.

**177. Burgoyne's Expedition ; Battle of Bennington.** — Meanwhile the British made a new move.  General Burgoyne[1] marched down from Canada (1777) with eight thousand men by way of Lake Champlain, and took Fort Ticonderoga.  He then pushed

SCALE OF MILES
0    25    50    100

forward toward the Hudson, expecting to join a part of Howe's army there.  Another British expedition started from Oswego with a force of Iroquois Indians and Tories to unite with Burgoyne. The three English armies expected to get control of the state of New York and the Hudson River, and so cut off New England — "the head of the rebellion" — from the other colonies.

The enemy coming from Oswego might have taken Fort Stanwix,[2] had not General Herkimer met them at Oriskany. In the battle he received his death wound ; but the brave old man propped himself against a tree and kept up the fight until British, Indians, and Tories fled from the field.

All went well with Burgoyne until he struck into the wilderness south of Lake Champlain.  There General Schuyler[3] broke down all the bridges, felled trees across the only road there was through the woods, and made Burgoyne's life miserable.  To add to his misfortunes, the British general's horses and provisions gave out.  He sent an expedition with a thousand men to Bennington, Vermont, to get more.  Colonel John Stark,[4] one of the heroes of Bunker Hill, started with a small force to meet the enemy.

[1] See Paragraph 163.  Burgoyne returned to England from Boston in the autumn of 1775.  In June, 1776, he came over to America to serve under Sir Guy Carleton, the British commander of Canada.        [2] Later, Fort Schuyler.

[3] General Philip Schuyler of Albany, New York.        [4] See Paragraph 40.

Pointing to the "red-coats," he said, "There they are, boys; we beat them to-day or Mollie Stark's [1] a widow." Mrs. Stark had no occasion to put on mourning; for her husband, with his men, whipped the British (August 16, 1777) so badly that less than a hundred out of the thousand ever got back to Burgoyne. Washington called the victory a "great stroke." It was, indeed; for by weakening Burgoyne's force, and preventing his getting provisions, it prepared the way for his final downfall.

**178. Howe's Expedition to Pennsylvania; Battle of Brandy-wine; Philadelphia taken; Battle of Germantown.** — While these events were happening Howe started to march to Philadelphia. Washington had not men enough to meet him in open fight, but he so worried him, and wasted his time, that the British general finally went back with his army to New York in disgust. He then started by sea. Finding that he could not go up the Delaware, which was fortified against him, he sailed south, entered Chesapeake Bay, and landing at the head of it, marched against Philadelphia. Washington met him at Brandywine Creek, and tried to check his advance; but Howe had a much stronger force, and the bat-

tle (September 11, 1777) delayed but did not stop the British. Two weeks later the enemy entered the city which was then the

---

[1] As Mrs. Stark's name was Elizabeth, this story has been called in question; but the fact remains that Stark thrashed the enemy.

capital of the United States.   Leaving a small force at Germantown, now a part of Philadelphia, Howe went down the Delaware to capture the forts and get possession of that river. While he was gone Washington attacked the British at Germantown, but was repulsed.   He then fell back to the hills on the Schuylkill at Valley Forge, about twenty miles northwest of Philadelphia.

**179. Saratoga ; the " Stars and Stripes " ; Help from France.** — Meanwhile, great events had happened in the North.   Burgoyne had fought two battles in the neighborhood of Saratoga (1777),[1] had been utterly defeated, and his entire army, numbering about six thousand men, captured.   If to this number we add that of the prisoners taken by us before the surrender, and the loss of the enemy at Bennington,[2] it will give a total of nearly 10,000 — or about one-third the entire British force then in America.[3]   The captured army was marched off by the American officers triumphantly bearing the " stars and stripes,"[4] which had just been adopted as our national flag. General Gates[5] got the credit of the victory; but Benedict Arnold, and Daniel Morgan,[6] with his sharpshooters, were the

1 The first battle was at Bemis Heights, between Saratoga Lake and the Hudson, September 19; the second, at Stillwater, south of the Heights, October 7.   Burgoyne surrendered at Saratoga, October 17 (1777).   See Map on page 176.

2 See Paragraph 177.

3 The estimates of Burgoyne's loss vary from about 6,000 at Saratoga to a total (for his entire campaign in New York) of 14,000.

4 The first United States flag (adopted by Congress, June 14, 1777) having the stars and stripes, was made, it is said, out of a soldier's white shirt, an old blue army overcoat, and a red flannel petticoat.   It was hoisted by our army at Fort Stanwix (near Rome), New York, during Burgoyne's campaign in 1777.   Paul Jones appears to have first raised this flag at sea.   The flag raised by Washington at Cambridge when he took command of the army was the English flag with thirteen red and white stripes added.   In the flag adopted by Congress the stars represent all the states; the stripes, the first thirteen states.

5 General Gates, like General Charles Lee (see Paragraph 172), was born in Great Britain, and had served in the English army.   He appears to have taken no direct part in these battles ; in fact, he was not actually on the field in either.

6 Daniel Morgan of Virginia.   He commanded a force of five hundred picked riflemen — " sharpshooters " — with aim so accurate that it was humorously said

men who really won it, partly by gallant fighting, and partly by cutting off all supplies from the enemy, and at last literally starving them into a surrender.

In the wars of over twenty centuries an eminent English writer finds only fifteen battles that have had a lasting influence on the world's history. The American victory at Saratoga, he says, was one of them.[1] It had indeed these two immense results: 1. It completely broke up the English plans for the war. 2. It secured for us the aid of England's old and powerful enemy, France.

Some time after the victory, Lafayette received letters from Paris. When he had read them he ran to Washington, and embracing him with tears of joy, cried out, "The King, my master, has acknowledged the independence of America, and will sign a treaty to help you establish it." It was true. Men are usually willing to help those who show that they are able to help themselves. We had shown it, and now France held out her hand to us. The next year (February 6, 1778) Benjamin Franklin, our minister[2] at Paris, obtained the treaty or agreement by which the French king pledged himself to send us men, ships, and money to complete the war. Franklin and Washington were, in fact, the two great men who carried the war through to final success: Washington by destroying enemies, Franklin by gaining friends; Washington by the sword, Franklin, like Morris, with the purse.[3]

**180. Summary.** — The war of Independence began with the Declaration of Independence, July 4, 1776. In the first battle,

that any one of them could toss up an apple and shoot all the seeds out of it as it fell. The enemy who had to face these riflemen never disputed the story.

[1] "The Fifteen Decisive Battles of the World," by Sir Edward S. Creasy.

[2] Minister: see note 1, page 188.

[3] Franklin lent all his ready money — about fifteen thousand dollars — to the country, to fight the battles of the Revolution, and lent it when everything looked against us. His influence got us a gift from France — nearly two million dollars — and a loan of over three million dollars more. Thus he used his own purse and the purse of the French king to help us.

that of Long Island, the Americans were defeated. Washington retreated across the Delaware, but returned and gained the brilliant victory of Trenton. Howe took Philadelphia; but shortly after, the Americans captured Burgoyne and his whole army at Saratoga; in consequence of that success France recognized the independence of America, and pledged herself to help us fight our battles by land and sea.

## 3. THE WAR OF INDEPENDENCE: FROM THE TREATY WITH FRANCE TO THE END OF THE WAR, 1778–1783.

**181. Washington at Valley Forge, Winter of 1777–1778; Peace offered; Howe leaves Philadelphia.** — But though the great victory of Saratoga filled the land with joy, yet the winter which followed was a terrible one. While Howe and his officers were living luxuriously in Philadelphia, Washington's men, "naked and starving," were dying of putrid fever on the frozen hillsides of Valley Forge. They were dying, too, before the good news could reach them — for news from Europe travelled very slowly in those days — that the French king would certainly aid America.

But the next spring (1778) England, alarmed at the action of France in taking our part, offered us peace, representation in Parliament — anything, everything in fact, but independence. But it was independence that we were fighting for, and the offer was rejected. Fear of the approaching French fleet now compelled the British[1] to abandon Philadelphia and start for New York.

**182. Battle of Monmouth; Lee's Disgrace; Indian Massacres; Clark's Victories in the West.** — Fifteen thousand of the English forces were to go by land across New Jersey. Now was

[1] General Howe resigned in the winter of 1777–78. His brother, Lord Howe, resigned the next summer (1778). Sir Henry Clinton succeeded General Howe in command of the army (May, 1779), and Admiral Byron succeeded Lord Howe in command of the British fleet.

Washington's opportunity.   With about the same number he followed them up sharply.   A battle was fought at Monmouth (June 28, 1778).   It would have ended in a brilliant victory for our side, if General Charles Lee,[1] who unfortunately had come back to us,[2] had done his duty.   He acted like a lunatic or a traitor.   Washington sternly rebuked him, and shortly after ordered him to withdraw from the battle and go to the rear.   Later, Lee was tried by court-martial[3] for disobedience and misbehavior, and suspended from the army; eventually Congress dismissed him in disgrace, and in disgrace he died.

Washington won the fight at Monmouth.[4]   It was the last battle of note fought on northern soil.   The British forces had now returned to New York and vicinity.   Washington, with his army stretched out from Morristown, New Jersey, to West Point on the Hudson, watched them day and night.

In the summer and autumn horrible Indian massacres were committed by bands of ferocious Iroquois led by Tory[5] captains at Wyoming, Pennsylvania, and Cherry Valley, New York; there were also towns attacked and burned to ashes along the coast ; but no great battle was fought.   In the West, Captain George Rogers Clark of Virginia by his resolute bravery drove the British out of Illinois and later from Indiana, thus securing that immense region to the United States.   It began to look as though the British were losing their grip on America.

183.  The British attack the South ; Savannah taken ; Wayne's Victory ; Paul Jones. — The enemy now transferred the war to the South.   Their plan was to begin at Georgia, and conquer northward.   Then, in case the English government was forced to make peace, they hoped to be able to keep the southern territory — King George was prudent : " Half a loaf," said

---

[1] See Paragraph 173.

[2] While Lee was a prisoner, the English government thought of hanging him as a deserter from their army.   Washington saved him from the gallows — it was one of the few mistakes that great man ever made.   [4] Monmouth : see Map, page 177.

[3] A court composed of military officers.   [5] See Paragraph 165.

he to himself, "is better than none." The last of the year
(December 29, 1778) an expedition attacked Savannah. The
British had three men to our one; they took the city.[1] The
next year (1779) there was a lull. The British had got possession of the fort at Stony Point,[2] in the Highlands of the Hudson.
So long as they held it, our men could not cross the river at
King's Ferry — then the principal crossing-place between New
England and the southern states. "Mad Anthony Wayne,"[3]
under Washington's direction, stormed and took the fort (July,
15, 1779), at midnight, at the point of the bayonet — never
firing a shot during the battle. The capture of the fort stopped
the British plans for ravaging Connecticut. They found that
they must use all their forces to hold the Hudson.

The next autumn brought glorious news. Captain Paul
Jones,[4] the first man to hoist an American flag over an Ameri-

can warship, had, with the help of
Benjamin Franklin, fitted out three
or four vessels in our defence. With
three, one of them a half-rotten old
hulk, he boldly attacked and captured
two British men-of-war. The fight
took place on the North Sea, off
Flamborough Head on the English
coast. After that most humiliating
defeat England still boasted that she
was "mistress of the seas"; but the
boast was in a lower tone: if Paul Jones had only had a few
more ships, he would have made the tone a whisper.

### 184. The British take Charleston; Marion and Sumter's Mode of Fighting. — In the spring (1780) the war in the South was

---

[1] Here later (1779) Count Pulaski (note, page 175) fell fighting for American liberty.
[2] Stony Point: see Map, page 177. [3] General Anthony Wayne of Pennsylvania. He
was called "Mad Anthony Wayne" on account of his daring. The British thought
that the Americans could not use the bayonet; Wayne showed them their mistake.
[4] Paul Jones was by birth a Scotchman. He entered the American service in 1775.
His name was originally John Paul.

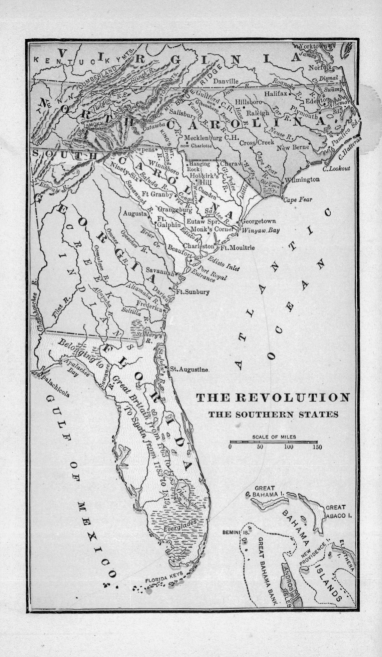

THE REVOLUTION

THE SOUTHERN STATES

SCALE OF MILES
0    50    100    150

renewed with vigor.   The British took Charleston (May 12, 1780), and Lord Cornwallis held the city.   But Marion [1] and Sumter, with their bands of resolute men armed with a few guns, and weapons made of old scythes and saw-blades, did good service in the American cause.   When the British forces went out to conquer the country, the Carolina patriots attacked them as the mosquitoes of Alaska attack a bear.   They buzz, sting, retreat; advance, buzz, sting; till at last the unwieldy brute, with eyes swollen so that he can no longer see, wanders around helpless, and dies of starvation.

### 185. Loss of Camden; Brilliant Victory at King's Mountain. —

The British had a small force at Camden,[2] South Carolina — a great centre for roads, and hence of much importance from a military point of view.  General Gates with General De Kalb resolved to attempt the capture of the place before Cornwallis could arrive there, but Cornwallis reached Camden first.   A battle was fought (August 16, 1780) in which Gates was compelled to retreat, losing artillery and baggage, and narrowly escaping capture himself.

But while Cornwallis was chuckling over his victory, the backwoodsmen of this part of the country, sharpshooters, every man, attacked a British force at King's Mountain (October 7, 1780), on the borders of North and South Carolina, and in a terrible battle completely defeated the enemy.

### 186. Arnold's Treason; the Terrible Winter at Morristown. —

Meanwhile (September 22, 1780), the most startling and the saddest event of the Revolution occurred.   Benedict Arnold, Washington's trusted friend, commander at West Point, had turned traitor.   The discovery was made through the arrest of André,[3] a British spy by whom Arnold attempted to send a plan of the fort to the British commander at New York.   André was tried and hanged, but Arnold escaped to the British army.

[1] See Paragraph 117.     [2] Camden: see Map, page 185.     [3] André (An'dray).

Later, the traitor led an attack on Richmond, Virginia, and burnt it, and, last of all, one on New London in his native state of Connecticut.

Arnold died in London twenty years later. It is said that the last request he made was that the epaulettes and sword-knot which Washington had given him might be brought. "Let. me die," said he, "in my old American uniform, in which I fought my battles. God forgive me for ever having put on any other!"

The gloom of Arnold's awful act of treason seemed to be reflected in the American camp at Morristown in the terrible winter (1780–1781) which followed. In some respects it was worse even than that at Valley Forge; and the men, unpaid, half-fed, freezing, were driven to desperation and partial revolt.

**187. Greene's Campaign in the South ; Cornwallis leaves the Carolinas.** — But it was the gloom that precedes the dawn. General Nathanael Greene of Rhode Island had been placed in command at the South. Next to Washington he was by far the ablest soldier in the Revolution. With a little force that seemed, as he said, but "the shadow of an army," he accomplished wonders.

Early in the year (January 17, 1781) a part of Greene's men, led by Morgan,[1] gained the battle of Cowpens, South Carolina. Then Greene, who was master of the game he was now playing, retreated toward Virginia, thus drawing Cornwallis, who followed him, further and further away from his supplies at Charleston. But the American general had many anxious days during this retreat, and often the chances of success seemed wholly against him.

On one such occasion he reached Steele's tavern at Salisbury after midnight and wet to the skin with the heavy rain that had fallen all day. Steele looked at him in astonishment and asked if he was alone.

[1] See Paragraph 179.

"Yes," answered the general, "tired, hungry, alone, and penniless." Mrs. Steele heard his reply; she made haste and set a smoking hot breakfast before the weary, despondent soldier. Then she carefully shut the door, and drawing two bags of silver from under her apron she held them out to her guest.

"Take these," said she, "you need them and I can do without them."

It was such noble-hearted women as Mrs. Elizabeth Steele who helped our men to keep up heart to the end. The honor shall be theirs so long as history lasts.

At Guilford Court House (now Greensborough), North Carolina, Cornwallis defeated the Americans (March 15, 1781), but he himself lost so heavily that he could not hold his ground, and had to retreat to Wilmington, North Carolina. He arrived there (April 7, 1781) in miserable plight, having lost about half of his small army by battle, sickness, or desertion. At Wilmington Cornwallis found, as he expected, some provisions and military supplies which a British expedition from Charleston had landed there; but he also found what he did not expect, that was, news that Greene had suddenly gone back to attack the English force under Lord Rawdon left at Camden, South Carolina. Cornwallis was in no condition to wheel about and follow Greene. What, then, should he do? He turned that question over and over in his mind; finally he decided that his best plan was to march northward to Petersburg, Virginia. There he hoped to unite with a British force sent from New York; then, having conquered Virginia, he would go back and reconquer the Carolinas.

**188. Greene's Campaign in South Carolina.** — Cornwallis started on his long march of 200 miles. Meanwhile Greene, aided by Marion, Sumter, and Pickens, had driven the British from Camden (May 10, 1781). Through the summer he struck the enemy blow after blow, and ended with a battle, which was practically a victory, at Eutaw Springs, South Carolina (September 8, 1781). After that the British — what there was left of them — fled to Charleston, shut themselves up there, and did not venture out. Greene had in fact won back the Carolinas; and he had won them, thanks to the help given by Marion, Sumter, and Pickens, with an army which did not number more than about two thousand men. To accomplish much with small means is a sure sign of greatness. Greene had done this, and Washington was the man who taught him.

**189. The Crowning Victory of the War.** — Cornwallis reached Virginia, and after vainly pursuing Lafayette and destroying millions of dollars' worth of property he entered Yorktown, on a narrow peninsula at the mouth of the York River. He went there not because he wanted to, but because he must. Cornwallis had been chasing Lafayette; he boastingly said, "The boy cannot escape me." But "the boy," Lafayette, with a larger army had turned round and begun chasing him. Cornwallis moved to Yorktown (July 30, 1781) to get help by sea from New York. There the British general fortified himself. He did not know it, but he was building his own prison — one that he would never get out of except by surrender. While he was waiting for soldiers to arrive from New York a French fleet of war-ships under Count de Grasse [1] was coming to block him in. Now was Washington's chance to strike a tremendous blow. His plan was to march rapidly south from the Hudson to Yorktown, and with the help of the French fleet and French troops and of Lafayette and his army to capture Cornwallis with his whole force. Such a move required a large amount of money for provisions, pay, and powder. Robert Morris [2] came to the rescue and is said to have furnished

nearly a million and a half of dollars for the good work.

Clinton, at the head of the British force in New York, thought Washington was getting ready to attack him. Washington encouraged him to think so. He went on making every possible preparation for moving against New York. Even Washington's own army supposed that was his intention. When at length everything was ready Washington suddenly broke camp and marched his entire force with all possible speed across the country to the head of Chesapeake Bay and thence by vessels to Yorktown.

Cornwallis looked over the walls of his fortified town. He saw the French fleet on one side, and the American and the French army, 16,000 strong,[3] on the other. He held out man-

---

[1] De Grasse (Deh Grahss).    [2] See Paragraph 175.  Professor Sumner **thinks** that Morris furnished means of transportation and subsistence but not **money**.

[3] The allied army comprised 9000 Americans and 7000 French.

fully for more than a week against solid shot, shell, red-hot balls. Then seeing that it was useless to struggle against fate he surrendered. His army marched out October 19, 1781, to the tune of "The World's Upside Down" — it was true; the British world in America was "upside down," and the fall of Yorktown practically ended the war of the Revolution. Washington had conquered. It was "the victory of a great and good man in a great and good cause."

When the news reached London and was announced to Lord North, then the prime minister [1] of the British government, he threw up his arms as though a cannon-ball had struck him, cried out wildly, "It is all over!" and then resigned his office.

**190. Summary of the Revolution.** — The king of England insisted on taxing the American colonies without their consent. The Americans refused to pay, and took up arms in defence of their rights as loyal English subjects. The king and his party endeavored to put down the rebellion; and on July 4, 1776, the colonists declared themselves independent of Great Britain.

The war for independence then began. At Saratoga, in 1777, the Americans gained a great victory over Burgoyne. In consequence of that victory the king of France acknowledged the independence of the United States, and sent money, ships, and men to fight in our behalf.

In 1781, Washington, with the help of the French ships of war, defeated Cornwallis at Yorktown, and took him prisoner with all his army. That decisive victory practically ended the Revolution, and not long after, the British gave up the contest.

**191. George III.'s Speech on the United States; England makes a Treaty of Peace with us; the King's Meeting with John Adams.** — At the opening of Parliament [2] (1782), the king, in a voice choked with emotion, announced that he was ready to acknowledge the independence of the United States. He closed his

---

[1] Prime minister: the king's chief adviser.    [2] See note 1, page 154.

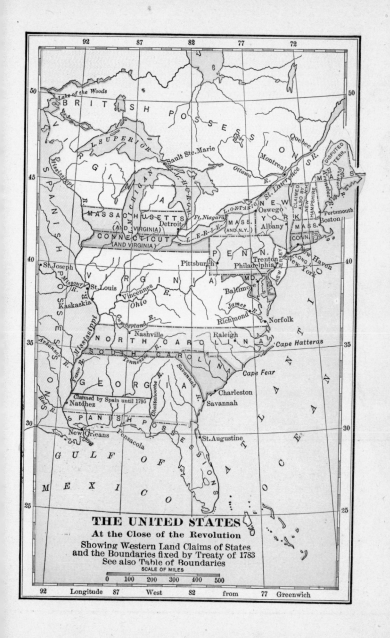

# THE UNITED STATES

### At the Close of the Revolution

Showing Western Land Claims of States
and the Boundaries fixed by Treaty of 1783
See also Table of Boundaries

SCALE OF MILES

0    100    200    300    400    500

speech by saying that it was his earnest prayer that 'religion, language, interest, and affection might prove a bond of permanent union between the two countries.'

A final treaty of peace between Great Britain and this country was signed at Paris in 1783.[1]  It secured to us the thirteen states, with Maine, and the territory west of them to the Mississippi.[2]  Our first minister[3] to England was John Adams of Massachusetts.  The king said to him, "Sir, I will be very free with you.  I was the last to consent to the separation, but the separation having been made ... I have always said, as I say now, that I would be the first to meet the friendship[4] of the United States as an independent power."[5]

## 192. The American States Independent but not really United; Congress destitute of Power. — But though America had won her independence, she had not secured harmony and union.  While the war lasted the states fought like brothers, side by side; now that the danger was over, they threatened to fall apart. We were like a barrel made of thirteen stout staves, but yet without a single hoop to hold us together.  Under the Articles of Confederation or Constitution adopted in 1781, the nation had no President — no head.  It had only a Congress, and that Congress was destitute of power.  It might pass good and useful laws, but it could not compel the people to obey them. It might beg the people to give money, but it could not make them furnish it.  It might ask for soldiers to defend the country, but it could not draft[6] them.

## 193. Distressed Condition of the Country; Jealousy of the States; Lack of Freedom of Trade. — The truth is, that the people had

[1] The Revolution, from its first outbreak at Lexington (April 19, 1775) to the virtual disbanding of the army (April 19, 1783), lasted just eight years to a day.

[2] In all, the treaty secured to us something over 800,000 square miles of territory.

[3] Minister: here the word means a person sent on public business by one government to another.     [4] Later, however, the king treated Mr. Adams very coldly.

[5] "Power" is here used for nation or people.

[6] Draft: to compel men, chosen by lot, to do military service.

come out of the war in a distressed condition. They were
heavily in debt. Business was at a standstill. Gold and silver
coin was scarce. The states had an abundance of paper stuff
which pretended to be money, but nobody knew what it was
worth, and what passed for a dollar in one state might not
pass at all in another. Distress and discontent grew worse
and worse. The states quarrelled with each other about
boundary lines, about commerce, about trade. Instead of
being a united and friendly people, they were fast getting to
be thirteen hostile nations ready to draw the sword against
each other.

This feeling was shown in the fact that a man could not buy
and sell freely outside of his own state. If, for instance, a
farmer in New Jersey took a load of potatoes to New York, he
might have to pay a tax of five or ten cents a bushel to that
state before he could offer them for sale. On the other hand,
if a New York merchant sent a case of boots to New Jersey to
sell to the farmers, that state might, if it chose, tax him ten cents
a pair before he could get a permit to dispose of his goods.

194. "Shays' Rebellion." — The people of Massachusetts
were perhaps more heavily loaded with debt than those of
any other state. It is said that the heads of families owed
on the average two hundred dollars apiece. They were willing to pay, but could get nothing to pay with. When great
numbers of poor people were sued and thrown into prison,
multitudes became desperate. In the western part of the
state Daniel Shays raised an army of nearly two thousand
excited farmers. (1786.) They surrounded the court-houses
at Worcester and Springfield, and put a stop to all lawsuits
for debt. It was not until a strong military force was sent
out against them that the "rebellion" was finally quelled,
and Shays compelled to fly to New Hampshire.

195. The Northwest Territory. — The most powerful influence which kept the nation from dropping to pieces was the

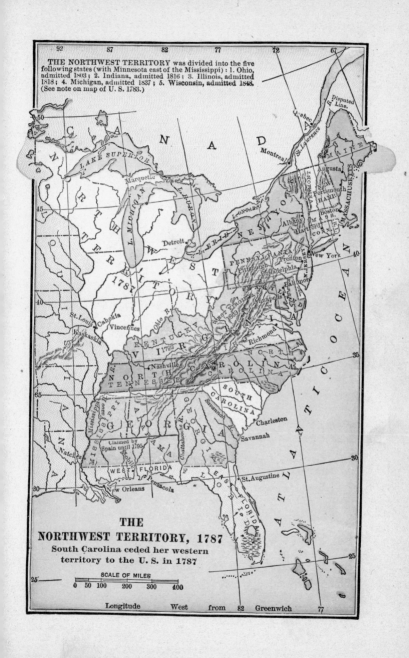

THE NORTHWEST TERRITORY was divided into the five following states (with Minnesota east of the Mississippi) : 1. Ohio, admitted 1803 ; 2. Indiana, admitted 1816 ; 3. Illinois, admitted 1818 ; 4. Michigan, admitted 1837 ; 5. Wisconsin, admitted 1848. (See note on map of U. S. 1783.)

THE
NORTHWEST TERRITORY, 1787
South Carolina ceded her western
territory to the U. S. in 1787

SCALE OF MILES
0  50 100    200    300    400

Longitude    West    from    82    Greenwich

fact that the states had an interest in the Northwest Territory. Up to the middle of the Revolution, seven of the thirteen states claimed the country west of them as far as the Mississippi River.[1]

Four of these states, — New York, Virginia,[2] Massachusetts, and Connecticut, — claiming land northwest of the Ohio River to the Mississippi, agreed (1781–1786) to give it to the United States to be disposed of for the common good. In 1787 Congress made an ordinance or body of laws for the government of this Northwest Territory. That ordinance (1) forbade the holding of slaves in the territory (though it made provision for returning fugitive slaves who should escape to that region) ; (2) it granted entire religious freedom to every settler ; (3) it encouraged " schools and the means of education." The states believed that Congress could sell lands in that vast region, — now forming the great and prosperous states of Ohio, Indiana, Illinois, Michigan, Wisconsin, and Eastern Minnesota, — and thus get money to pay off the war debt of the Revolution.[3] That belief helped to hold the country together.

**196. The New Constitution.** — Still, even with this hope to brighten the sky, the outlook was dark enough. Washington, Franklin, Madison, Hamilton — in a word, the ablest men of that day — thought the prospect anything but encouraging. It seemed to them that unless something was done promptly the new-born republic was likely to die in its cradle.

[1] The seven states were Massachusetts, Connecticut, New York, Virginia, North Carolina, South Carolina, and Georgia (the claim of New York rested on treaties with the Iroquois Indians). South Carolina, North Carolina, and Georgia ceded their western lands (1787–1802) to the United States. The last two mentioned states stipulated that the territory they gave should be kept open to slavery. The remaining six states, of the thirteen, had fixed western boundaries, so they could not claim any part of the territory, but they would have an interest in the land sales — if the nation held together as one whole. See Map, page 188.

[2] Virginia giving by far the greatest part.

[3] It was provided that new states, of equal standing with the original thirteen, should be formed in this northwestern territory as soon as there was sufficient population in that region.

At last (1787) a convention of fifty-five members was held in Philadelphia to make a new Constitution [1] — one that should "form a *more perfect* union." [2]  Washington presided at this convention, and a majority of the state legislatures sent their chief men to take part in it.  The convention held a secret session of nearly four months, and had many stormy debates before the articles of the new Constitution could be agreed upon.  At one time Franklin and other eminent men nearly despaired of any successful result.  But by judicious compromises [3] the great work was finally completed, and the Consti-

[1] That is, a new set of laws for the government of the whole nation adopted in place of the Articles of Confederation.  See p. 189, and Appendix, p. vi ; and see p. 100.

[2] See the opening words of the Constitution, page vi (following this history).

[3] The first important question of debate was between the delegates from the small states and those from the large ones in regard to representation in Congress. If the representation rested wholly on population then the large states would, of course, have entire control.

By a compromise or mutual concession it was finally agreed that Congress should consist of two houses : 1. The House of Representatives chosen by the people of the different states and representing them. 2. The Senate, or Upper House, consisting of two members from each state. (See the Constitution, page vii, Section 3, Paragraph 1.)  In the Senate, therefore, the small states stand equal to the large ones. This arrangement satisfied all.

The second great question was whether slaves should be counted in reckoning the number of the population with reference to representation in Congress.  The North insisted that they should not ; the South (where slaves were very numerous) that they should.  The contest on this point was long and bitter.  Finally it was agreed that three-fifths of the slaves should be counted with reference to both representation and taxation (though the slaves themselves were of course neither represented nor taxed). (See the Constitution, page vii, Section 2, Paragraph 3.)  " *Three-fifths of all other persons.*"  These " other persons " were slaves.

The last question was in regard to commerce and to protection of slaveholders. It was agreed that Congress should have the entire control of commerce (the states had had it before).  (See the Constitution, page ix, Section 8, Paragraph 3.)  It was agreed that the importation of slaves might be prohibited after 1808.  (See the Constitution, page x, Section 9, Paragraph 1 ; these slaves are called " such persons." The word slave does not occur in the Constitution.)  It was also agreed that runaway slaves should be returned to their owners.  (See the Constitution, page xiv, Article IV., Section 2, Paragraph 3, " No person [*i.e. slave*] held to service," etc.)

If the compromise between the small states and the large, and the North and South, had not been made, the Constitution would have been rejected, and we should in all probability have split up into two or three hostile republics.

tution was adopted.    After the convention had accepted the
new Constitution, it was sent to the different states to be
voted upon by the people.[1]   Many of the people were strongly
opposed to it.    They thought it gave the national government too much power.    But in time all of the states decided
to adopt it.    The man who did the most to convince them of
the wisdom of such a course was Alexander Hamilton of New
York.   When the city of New York celebrated the adoption of
the Constitution (1788) a ship on wheels representing the

The "Ship of State."

"Ship of State," or the Union,[2] was drawn through the streets
by ten milk-white horses.    Hamilton's name was painted in
large letters on the platform upholding the vessel.

**197. What the Constitution did for the Country.** — The Constitution went into effect in 1789.    It accomplished these four
chief objects: 1. It gave the nation a head — the President
of the United States — whose duty it is to see that the laws

---

[1] Delegates voted in state conventions called by the legislatures.

[2] See Longfellow's "Building of the Ship," last part, lines beginning —

> "Thou, too, sail on, O Ship of State !
> Sail on, O Union, strong and great !"

are executed.[1]  2. It gave Congress power to raise money by taxation to carry on and defend the government.[2]  3. It gave every citizen of the United States equal rights in all the states, with liberty to buy and sell in all parts of the country.   Thus entire freedom of trade was secured throughout the Union.[3]  4. It established the Supreme Court of the United States, to decide all questions and disputes about the powers of the national government.[4]

A few years later ten very important amendments were added to the Constitution.[5]   They were called a "Bill of Rights." They secured still further protection to the rights and liberties of the people.   For this reason many who had strongly opposed the original Constitution now gave it their hearty support.

**198.  Summary.**— The Revolution made us an independent people; the Constitution completed the work by making us a united people — a true American nation.   Now, to use the words of John Adams, 'the thirteen clocks all struck together.'

[1] Constitution, p. xi (II., 1).          [2] Constitution, p. ix (8, Pars. 1, 12).
[3] Constitution, p. x (9, Pars. 5, 6).    [4] Constitution, p. xiii (III., 1, 2).
[5] Amendments to the Constitution, p. xvi ; two more amendments were adopted between 1798 and 1804.

Map showing the Westward Movement of Population in the United States from 1790 to 1890, inclusive.   (See Note 2 on page 198.)

The census of 1900 showed that the centre of population had moved about fourteen miles westward, nearly in a straight line, to a point about six miles southeast of Columbus, Indiana. The total movement (1790-1900) has been five hundred and nineteen miles.   Through this entire distance the centre of population has kept close to the 39th parallel of latitude.

# V.

"This government, the offspring of your own choice, . . . adopted upon full investigation and mature deliberation, completely free in its principles, . . . and containing, within itself, a provision for its own amendment, has a just claim to your confidence and respect." — PRESIDENT WASHINGTON'S *Farewell Address to the People of the United States, September 17, 1796.*

---

## THE UNION. — NATIONAL DEVELOPMENT.

### (1789–1861.)

### GEORGE WASHINGTON.

**199. Political Parties; Washington elected President (Two Terms, 1789–1797); his Inauguration; and Administration.**[1] — There were now two political parties in the United States: the Federalists[2] who had voted for the adoption of the Constitution; and the Anti-Federalists[3] who had voted against it. The first party believed that the country needed a strong government, — one able to make its power respected both at home and abroad; the second party thought such a strong government dangerous to the liberties of the people, and wished the chief power to be exercised by the different states. In the course of time this last class came to be known as the Democratic party;[4] while the Federalists

---

[1] Administration : presidency.

[2] Federalists (from *fœdus*, a Latin word, meaning a league or union), those who supported the union of states formed by the Constitution.

[3] Anti-Federalists (from the Latin words *anti*, against, and *fœdus*, league or union), those opposed to the Constitution until it was amended; see page 194.

[4] The Democratic party was at first called Republican, or Democratic-Republican. Eventually the name got shortened to its present form. Care should be taken not to confound the early Republican (or Democratic) party with the modern Republican party which did not come into existence until 1856.

were succeeded by the Whigs,[1] and later by the Republicans. Both parties united in electing Washington to be the first President of the United States (1789–1793) ; and when, at the end of four years, his time of office expired, they again united to re-elect him (1793–1797). In both cases John Adams was chosen Vice-President. New York City was then the capital of the country,[2] and Washington was to be inaugurated [3] there on March 4 (1789), the day the new Constitution went into operation ; but the ceremony was delayed until April 30. The President took the oath of office,[4] standing on the balcony of a building in front of Federal Hall,[5] the hall where Congress met, in the presence of an immense multitude. There, amidst ringing of bells and firing of cannon, a great shout went up: " Long live George Washington, President of the United States ! "

**200. Washington's Cabinet; how the Government raised Money.** — Washington chose four eminent men, as members of his Cabinet or private Council, to aid him in the discharge of his presidential duties. They were Thomas Jefferson, the author of the Declaration of Independence ;[6] Alexander

1 After the Federal party expired (between 1815 and 1825), it was succeeded by one called the National Republican; this was followed in 1835 by the Whig party, and this in 1856 by the present Republican party.

2 By Act of Congress the national capital was established at Philadelphia from 1790 to 1800. In 1800 it was permanently located at the city of Washington, on land given for that purpose by the states of Virginia and Maryland.

3 Inaugurated : introduced into office (made President) with solemn and appropriate ceremonies.

4 The following is the oath taken by the President : " *I do solemnly swear (or affirm) that I will faithfully execute the office of President of the United States; and to the best of my ability, preserve, protect, and defend the Constitution of the United States.*"

5 Federal Hall (the old City Hall) : it stood on the northeast corner of Wall and Nassau streets, on ground now occupied by the United States Sub-Treasury Building.

6 Thomas Jefferson was appointed Secretary of State; his duties were to attend to the foreign business and relations of the government.

Hamilton;[1] General Henry Knox;[2] Edmund Randolph.[3] To John Jay[4] he gave the very important office of Chief Justice of the Supreme Court of the United States. These men did not all agree with Washington in political matters; but they all reverenced him, and they were ready, like him, to do their utmost to promote the welfare and prosperity of the country.

The new government had no money; but a government can no more hope to live and pay its bills without money than you or I can. In order to obtain funds, Congress (1789) imposed a duty or tax on all foreign ships and on many foreign goods entering our ports. Thus, if a French vessel of six hundred tons loaded with wine came into New York, the owners would have to pay a duty of fifty cents a ton — or three hundred dollars on the vessel, and eighteen cents a gallon on the wine. Other articles, such as tea, silk, and sugar, were charged different rates.

201. **Paying our Just Debts.** — By this duty, or revenue-tariff, as it was called, a very large amount of money was obtained. Hamilton, who was Secretary of the Treasury, got permission from Congress (1790) to use all of this money, not needed for the expenses of the government, to do three things : 1. To pay back to France and to other countries what we had borrowed of them during the Revolution. 2. To pay the debts we owed at home to our soldiers, and to those who had lent money to the government during the war. 3. To pay the debts which the different states were owing to their own citizens.[5] Hamil-

[1] Alexander Hamilton of New York (see Paragraph 196) was appointed Secretary of the Treasury.

[2] General Knox of Massachusetts, one of the leaders in the Revolution (see Paragraph 165), was appointed Secretary of War.

[3] Edmund Randolph of Virginia was appointed Attorney-General; his duty was to give the government advice in law matters.

[4] John Jay of New York, one of the commissioners who, with Franklin, had secured and signed the treaty of peace with Great Britain (1783). He was Secretary of Foreign Affairs (or Secretary of State) from 1784 until 1790, when Jefferson took his place. He then became Chief Justice of the Supreme Court of the United States.

[5] That is, debts incurred in carrying on the war.

ton's wise and honest dealing put the credit of the United States on a sure foundation; it enabled us to pay debts amounting to nearly six millions of dollars, and to provide for the payment of many millions more. From that day to this, we have always been able to borrow all the money we wanted.

**202. The First Census; Establishment of a United States Bank and a Mint.** — Meanwhile (1790), the first census was taken. It showed that we had a population of nearly four millions.[1] It also showed that nearly the whole body of people lived along the Atlantic sea-coast, on a strip of country about two hundred and fifty miles wide. Since then the population has doubled, on the average, every twenty-five years, and has moved steadily westward.[2]

Within two years after taking the census Congress established a United States bank (1791) and a mint at Philadelphia (1792). Both supplied the country with a kind of money, which, unlike that in circulation before, could be used throughout the states. This was an immense help to all business men.

With the opening of the mint we began our decimal system of coinage, — ten cents make a dime, ten dimes a dollar, — a system so clear, simple, and convenient, that the time is probably not very far distant when England, and every leading country of Europe which has not already adopted it, will do so.

**203. Arrival of "Citizen" Genêt; Washington's Proclamation of Neutrality.** — During Washington's second presidency France was engaged in a terrible revolution. The people had declared themselves a republic, and beheaded their king. This led to a war between France and England. The French sent a

---

[1] In 1776 we had, it was supposed, about 2,750,000.

[2] In 1790 the centre of population (that is, the geographical point where the population is equal in number in all directions) was about twenty-five miles east of Baltimore. It has since moved westward, on nearly the same parallel, at the rate of about fifty miles every ten years. See Map, page 194.

minister[1] to this country (1793) to get help toward fighting the English.   He was styled " Citizen " Genêt,[2] — for, having abolished all titles of honor and respect, the French could not endure even so simple a title as Mr.   He came here expecting to obtain ships, money, and aid from the government. Thousands of our people welcomed him with wild enthusiasm. Washington, however, knew that if " Citizen " Genêt was allowed to have his way, we should soon be dragged into a war with England, at a time when such a war would have been terribly disastrous to us.   The President therefore issued a proclamation of neutrality, stating that we should take no part in European quarrels.   This proclamation so maddened the excitable Genêt that he endeavored to stir up a mob in Philadelphia, to pull Washington from his seat of office, overturn the government of the United States, and set up one more in accordance with his French tastes.   The result was that, at Washington's protest, France recalled her minister, and nothing more was heard of him.

204. **Emigration to the West; Cincinnati.** — Meanwhile, a great movement of population had begun toward the country west of the Alleghanies — that section in which Washington had so deep an interest.[3]   Sevier, Robertson, and other pioneers had built cabins in the Tennessee country ; and Daniel Boone, the famous hunter of North Carolina, with his bold companions, had chopped a narrow path across the wilderness to Kentucky; and by the beginning of the Revolution the Americans had got a firm foothold in that fertile region.   Emigrants crossed the mountains, and formed settlements on the rich lands of the Ohio valley.   Marietta, on that river, was already established (1788).   A cluster of log huts, which had been built further down the river in the same year, now (1790) received the name of Cincinnati.[4]   There, not long after (1793), the first

---

[1] Minister: see note 3, on page 189.   [2] Genêt (Zhen-ay').   [3] See Paragraph 139.
[4] Cincinnati: named in honor of the Society of the Cincinnati, organized by the officers of the Revolutionary army headed by Washington.

Western newspaper was published,[1] and the corner-stone laid of the state of Ohio, the first of all that magnificent group of states formed from the Northwest Territory[2] which were one by one (1803–1848) to knock at the doors of Congress and gain admission to the Union.

But these settlements were made at heavy cost of life. The Indians rose, resolved to kill or drive out the invaders. After four years of fighting the savages were defeated in a final battle. General Wayne[3] — "the chief that never slept" — forced them to sign a treaty of peace (1794) by which they gave up the greater part of the Ohio country to the whites.

205. **Whitney invents the Cotton-Gin ; Results.** — The year (1793) that the printing-press in that enterprising log city of the West began sending out its weekly budget of news, a great

event occurred at the South. Eli Whitney, of Massachusetts, but then living in Georgia, invented the cotton-gin.[4] Whitney's invention has had more influence on the industry, wealth, and political history of this country than any other labor-saving machine ever constructed in America. Up to that time, small quantities of cotton had been raised at

The Cotton-Gin.

the South ; but it was of little use, for no practical method had then been contrived of freeing the cotton fibre, or wool, from the multitude of seeds it contains. By working a whole day, a negro could clean only about a pound. This made cot-

---

[1] *The Centinel of the Northwest* — Cincinnati, 1793.
[2] See Paragraph 195.     [3] See Paragraph 183.
[4] Gin : a contraction of the word engine, meaning a machine.

ton so expensive that none but the rich could buy it. Now, everything was changed. By the use of Whitney's machine one man could clean a thousand pounds in a single day.

The result was soon seen. In 1784 we had exported eight bags, or about three thousand pounds, of cotton to Liverpool. The cotton was seized by the English custom-house officers, on the ground that the United States could not have produced such a "prodigious quantity," and that the captain of the vessel must have smuggled it from some other country. Ten years after Whitney had put his machine into operation (1803) we were exporting over one hundred thousand bags of cotton, or more than forty millions of pounds, and every year saw an enormous increase. The effect at home was equally marked. A great number of mills for the manufacture of cotton cloth were built in New England. At the South the raising of cotton became immensely profitable, and planters gave more and more land to it.

Up to this period, many men in both sections of the country had deplored the holding of slaves. They had earnestly discussed how to rid the country of what was felt to be both an evil in itself and a danger to the nation. The invention of the cotton-gin put a stop to this discussion in great measure; for now the Southern planters and the Northern manufacturers of cotton both found it for their interest to keep the negro in bondage, since by his labor they were rapidly growing rich. Few, even of the ablest minds of that time, realized what we all see to-day: that in the end free labor is cheaper, safer, and better than any other.[1]  To sum up: Whitney's great

[1] Whitney received fifty thousand dollars for his invention from South Carolina, besides something from several other Southern States. Other notable American inventors of this period were: 1. Oliver Evans of Newport, Delaware, who, about 1780, invented the grain-elevator, and made such improvements in milling that he "effected a revolution in the manufacture of flour." In 1803 he constructed the first steam dredge for deepening the channels of rivers. 2. Jacob Perkins of Newburyport, Massachusetts, invented (1790) the first practical nail-machine — it was capable of cutting out two hundred thousand nails a day. Formerly all nails were made by hand. Later, he invented a greatly improved machine for calico-printing. 3. Asa

invention of 1793 did four things: 1. It stimulated the production of cotton and made it one of the leading industries of the country.  2. It increased our exports enormously.  3. It caused the building of great numbers of cotton-mills at the North.  4. It made a large class, both North and South, interested in maintaining slave-labor.

**206. The Whiskey Rebellion.** — During Washington's second term of office, the government, finding that it needed more money, imposed (1794) a heavy duty or tax on the manufacture of whiskey.  The rough Pennsylvania backwoodsmen were in the habit of distilling large quantities of that liquor, which was then freely used by all classes and conditions of men. The whiskey producers refused to pay the duty, tarred and feathered one officer sent to collect it, and gave a second a tremendous flogging with beech rods.  Then they proceeded to arm themselves in order to resist the law.  Washington sent an army of fifteen thousand men, mostly Pennsylvanians, to teach them how to behave.  When the whiskey distillers and their friends caught sight of the muskets, they prudently dispersed.  They saw that if any shooting was to be done the President could do a good deal more than they could.  There was no more trouble.

**207. Jay's Treaty with England.** — The treaty of peace with Great Britain, made in 1783, had not been satisfactorily carried out by either party.  We had promised to pay certain debts due to British subjects, and they complained that we did not keep our word.  On the other hand, England persisted in holding forts at Detroit and elsewhere along our northern frontier, though she had agreed to give them up to us.  The English also interfered with our trade with France.[1]  Chief-

Whittemore of Cambridge, Massachusetts, invented (1797) a machine for making wire cards for carding wool, 'which operated, and still continues to operate, as if it had a soul.'  On later American inventions see notes on pages 262, 351, 375.

[1] This was while France and England were at war.  The English seized American vessels loaded with grain for French ports and took them into English ports.

Justice Jay[1] went to England and obtained a new treaty (1795). It did not satisfy the people, who thought that the English were getting the best of the bargain; but the forts were given up to us. Washington signed the treaty for the reason that he, like Jay, considered that we were not then able to demand anything better. Certain newspapers attacked him and Jay in the most violent manner, and Washington, worn out with their abuse, declared that "he would rather be in his grave than in the presidency." But the majority of the people stood firmly by the man who had brought them through so many dangers, and the treaty[2] was duly confirmed by Congress. When Washington retired from office — refusing to be a candidate for a third term — he left the nation in every way stronger and more prosperous than he had found it; and with the three new states of Vermont, Kentucky, and Tennessee (1791–1796) added to the Union.

208. **Summary.** — Washington, the first President of the United States, held office for two terms (1789–1797). During that time he, with his Cabinet,[3] got the new government into practical operation, and through the wise counsel of Hamilton, our national credit was solidly established. Washington's efforts prevented the nation from getting entangled in European wars at a time when our greatest need was peace. Three new states had been added; Marietta and Cincinnati had taken firm root, and the vigorous life of the West had begun. Whitney's invention of the cotton-gin had an immense effect on manufacturing and commerce, greatly increasing the wealth of both North and South, but unfortunately it also fastened slave labor on the country.

They paid for the cargo, or else permitted the Americans to sell them to countries at peace with Great Britain. Our complaint was that England had no right to interfere in any way with our commerce.

[1] See Paragraph 200.

[2] See Fisher Ames's speech in favor of the Jay or "British" Treaty.

[3] Cabinet: see Paragraph 200.

## JOHN ADAMS.

209. Adams's Administration[1] (Second President, One Term, 1797–1801); the "X. Y. Z. Papers." — Mr. Adams's[2] presidency began with strong prospects of war with France. The French were enraged because we did not take sides with them in their contest with Great Britain.[3] They captured our merchant vessels, sold them openly in French ports, and insulted the statesman sent by us to France to represent the United States. Finally, certain private agents of the French authorities made demands threatening war unless we bribed them with money — "much money" — to keep peace. Pinckney, one of our representatives in France, indignant at such treatment, replied, "Millions for defence; not one cent for tribute."[4] President Adams, substituting the letters X. Y. Z. for the names of the French agents, sent a full report of the demands to Congress. The X. Y. Z. papers roused the whole country, and Pinckney's defiant words were echoed throughout America — for sooner than spend a single copper in buying peace we were ready to fight at any cost. War soon broke out, and our sailors, with shouts of "Hail Columbia," — the new song which every American was then singing, — fought and captured several French vessels. When Napoleon Bonaparte came into power in France (1799), he speedily made peace.

[1] Administration : presidency.

[2] John Adams was born in Braintree, near Boston, in 1735; died 1826. Thomas Jefferson said of him that "he was the ablest advocate and champion of independence" in the Congress of 1776. He was one of the commissioners who negotiated the treaty of peace with Great Britain at the close of the Revolution; and he was shortly after sent as minister from the United States to England. He was elected by the Federalists (see Paragraph 199) by only three electoral votes over Thomas Jefferson, the Republican (or Democratic) candidate (Adams had 71 votes, Jefferson 68). Mr. Adams used to call himself "the President of three votes." According to the law (since changed), the candidate for President getting the largest vote next to the one elected was made Vice-President. This law gave that office to Jefferson.                     [3] See Paragraph 203.

[4] Tribute : money paid by one nation to another as a token of submission, or for the purpose of procuring protection or favor.

**210. The Alien and the Sedition Laws ; Death of Washington.** — Several of the American newspapers were edited by foreigners, or by men who sympathized with France and were anxious to force us into a war with England. To put a stop to their constant abuse of the government, Congress, with the approval of Mr. Adams, passed (1798) the Alien and the Sedition Laws. The Alien Law gave the President the power to banish any alien or foreigner from the country whose influence he thought dangerous to our welfare. The President never enforced the law. The Sedition Law undertook to punish persons who should speak, write, or publish anything false or malicious against the President or the government of the United States. Under this last-named law several persons were heavily fined, and at least one was imprisoned.

The legislatures of Kentucky and Virginia denounced both the Alien and Sedition Laws as dangerous, and contrary to the Constitution. They furthermore declared that should the President persist in enforcing them, the states would have the right to refuse to obey his commands. Both laws soon passed out of existence ; but the idea that states might resist the national government, if they saw fit, was destined to make trouble many years later, and in the end was to result in civil war.

During the excitement caused by these unpopular laws, Washington died at his home at Mt. Vernon (1799). The whole country united to do honor to the memory of him who was "first in war, first in peace, and first in the hearts of his fellow-citizens " ; Bonaparte ordered public mourning for him in France, and Lord Bridport, commander of a British fleet of nearly sixty men-of-war, lying off the coast of England, testified his respect by ordering his flags to be lowered to half-mast.

**211. Summary.** — The four chief events of Adams's presidency were the excitement caused by the " X. Y. Z." papers, followed by war on the sea with France; the passage of the Alien and the Sedition Laws denounced by Kentucky and Virginia, and the death of Washington.

## THOMAS JEFFERSON.

**212. Jefferson's Administration** [1] **(Third President, Two Terms, 1801-1809); " Republican Simplicity " ; the New National Capital.** — The new President was a Democrat [2] — a man who took his stand with the people. In dress, [3] manners, and ideas he was quite different from the Federalist Presidents, Washington and Adams. They both thought it proper for the head of the nation to stand a little apart from the people; and though both were opposed to monarchy, yet they kept up something of the dignity and ceremony of a king. Jefferson preferred, on the contrary, "republican simplicity " in all

---

[1] Administration : see note 1, page 195.

[2] Thomas Jefferson was born 1743, at Shadwell, Virginia; died 1826. He was a member of the Continental Congress and drafted the Declaration of Independence, and drew up the Act of Religious Freedom adopted by Virginia through Madison's influence (see page 215, note 1) in 1785. He proposed our present decimal system of coinage and secured its acceptance. In 1785 he was sent to France to succeed Franklin as minister of the United States. On his tombstone is the following epitaph written by himself : " Here was buried Thomas Jefferson, author of the Declaration of Independence, of the Statute of Virginia for Religious Freedom, and the Father of the University of Virginia." The presidential election of November, 1800, was a time of great excitement, and of bitter strife between the Federalists and the Republicans (or Democrats. See Paragraph 199). Thomas Jefferson of Virginia and Aaron Burr of New Jersey were the Republican candidates. Each received 73 electoral votes; while John Adams, the Federalist candidate, got but 65. In such a case the House of Representatives — a majority of whom were Federalists — had to decide the election ; they finally voted in favor of Jefferson ; and he was declared President, with Burr for Vice-President (for according to the law then the candidate for President who received the greatest number of votes next to those of the successful candidate, became Vice-President). This period marks the downfall of the Federalists; for the next forty years the Democrats held control.

[3] It was about this time that a marked change took place in men's dress, and breeches and long stockings began to give way to trousers — a product of the French Revolution. The British minister, Mr. Merry, says Jefferson wore " pantaloons and slippers " when he received him.

things, and was ready to receive and shake hands with any one and every one that wanted to shake hands with him.

Jefferson took the oath of office [1] in the new capitol, which was ridiculed as a "palace in the woods." It stood on a hill in the " **city** of Washington," then nothing but a straggling village of a few hundred inhabitants. Washington, for whom it was named, had himself chosen the ground for the city ten years before. Many people preferred Philadelphia, thinking that the new national capital was too far west.

**213. What was thought of the Probable Extent of the Republic.** — Eminent men of that day thought it very doubtful whether the American republic could extend into the wilderness beyond the Alleghany Mountains. Many agreed with them, and believed that in time the country would be divided into several nations — for it seemed impossible to them that a territory reaching from the Atlantic to the Mississippi could be efficiently and safely governed by a single President. When we consider that there were then no steamboats, canals, or railroads, to bind the states together, and in fact very few good ordinary roads, it does not seem so strange that men of sound judgment should have thought so.

**214. The Pirates of Tripoli ; they declare War against the United States ; the Result.** — For many years Tripoli and other towns on the north coast of Africa had been nests of pirates. The people were Mohammedans, and they were in the habit of sending out fast-sailing armed vessels to capture the ships of Christians coming to the Mediterranean to trade.

European nations had made repeated efforts to break up this system of robbery, but had not succeeded. Even Great Britain was obliged to pay the governors of Algiers and Tripoli large sums of money every year in order to protect her commerce in that quarter of the globe. During Washington's and

[1] See page 196, note 4.

Adams's presidencies the United States, having no ships of war worth mentioning, had to buy the good will of these pirates.  At one time we paid the ruler of Tripoli twenty thousand dollars a year to let our merchant vessels sail the Mediterranean in peace.  But even this did not satisfy him, and we had to give him costly presents, and purchase the liberation of many of our sailors whom the people of Tripoli had seized, held as slaves, and worked like beasts of burden under the lash.  We had spent a million to rescue these unfortunate men.  Part of the money was given by the government and part of it was collected in the churches on Sunday.

The governor of Tripoli, disappointed because we did not yield to his demands and give him a still larger tribute, declared war (1801) against the United States.  Jefferson was a man of peace, but he believed with Benjamin Franklin that, "if you make yourself a sheep, the wolves will eat you."  He thought we had been sheep long enough.  We now had a small fleet of war-ships commanded by such men as Bainbridge, Decatur, and Preble.  The President sent them out to Tripoli, and they soon made the ruler of that place confess his sins and beg for mercy.

The Pope declared that the Americans had done more toward punishing the insolent power of the Mohammedan pirates than all the nations of Europe put together.  The result of the war was that the people of Tripoli were glad to make a new treaty (1805) with the United States.  By it they agreed to let our merchant ships and sailors alone in future, without asking pay for their good behavior to us.

215. **Purchase of the Territory of Louisiana.** — While this war with Tripoli was going on, the greatest event of Jefferson's presidency occurred.  France owned the province of Louisiana,[1] including New Orleans.  Napoleon Bonaparte, who was

---

[1] Just before the close of the great war between England and France in 1763, France ceded Louisiana with New Orleans to her ally, Spain.  In 1800 Napoleon Bonaparte induced or forced Spain to cede them back to France.

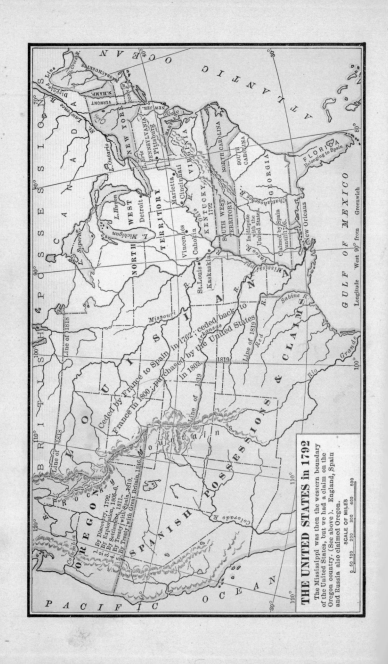

THE UNITED STATES in 1792

The Mississippi was then the western boundary of the United States, but we had a claim on the Oregon country. (See above). England, Spain and Russia also claimed Oregon.

SCALE OF MILES

0 50 100    200    300    400    500

OREGON

1. By Discovery, 1792.
2. By Exploration, 1805-6.
3. By Settlement, 1811.
4. By Treaty with Spain, 1819.
5. By Treaty with Great Britain, 1846.

Ceded by France to Spain in 1792; ceded back to France in 1800; purchased by the United States in 1803.

then about to engage in a tremendous contest with England, was afraid that when war broke out the English would send over a fleet and take Louisiana out of his hands. For that reason he was willing to sell it to the United States — especially as the money would help him to fit out his armies against Great Britain. In 1803, the year that Ohio entered the Union, President Jefferson bought the whole territory of Louisiana for fifteen millions of dollars. By so doing he got the very heart of the American continent, reaching from the Mississippi back to the Rocky Mountains. He thus, at one stroke, more than doubled the area of the United States, getting nearly nine hundred thousand square miles, or over five hundred and sixty millions of acres, for less than three cents an acre.

There were people who grumbled at the purchase, — some denying that he had the right to make it, — but the majority heartily supported the President. He himself confessed that he had stretched his power "till it cracked," in order to complete the bargain. In reality Jefferson showed his statesmanship in the act. The possession of Louisiana secured to us four most important points: 1. It prevented any disputes with France about the territory. 2. It prevented England from getting control of it. 3. It gave us the Great West — that is, the West beyond the Mississippi to the Rocky Mountains. 4. It made us masters of the entire Mississippi River, with the city of New Orleans to boot.

**216. Lewis and Clark's Exploration of the Far West.** — The next year (1804) the President sent out an expedition under Lewis and Clark[1] to explore the new territory. They started from St. Louis (May 14, 1804), then nothing but a little village of log-cabins, and worked their way up the Missouri in boats, until they reached (July 19, 1805) what they called the

---

[1] Lieutenant William Clark, brother of the brave soldier (see Paragraph 182) who conquered the Illinois and Indiana territory for the United States during the Revolution.

"Gates of the Rocky Mountains,"[1] a long, deep, narrow gorge, through which the river forces its way. This point is over twenty-six hundred miles from St. Louis, and it had taken the explorers more than a year to get to it. With an Indian girl for their guide, they made their way across the mountains to the head waters of a stream flowing westward. Launching their canoes (October 7, 1805) on its swift current they floated down till they entered a far larger river. Down this they drifted, sometimes through perilous rapids, until they came at last (November 7, 1805) to its mouth. A dense fog hid everything. When it lifted, they found themselves within sight of the Pacific Ocean. The river they had descended was that which Captain Robert Gray of Boston[2] had entered from the Pacific in 1792, and had named the Columbia; he thus gave us our first claim to Oregon.

The explorers returned the next year (September 23, 1806) to St. Louis. They had been absent nearly two years and a half. They had travelled, in all, over eight thousand miles, in boats, on horseback, and on foot, through a wilderness peopled only by savages. Lewis and Clark's remarkable expedition gave the people of this country their first idea of the immense extent, unlimited natural wealth, and almost fabulous wonders of the Far West. But the most important result of the expedition was that it enabled the United States to claim the Oregon territory, which Captain Gray had entered, but which Lewis and Clark first actually crossed. Five years later (1811) John Jacob Astor[3] of New York established a fur-trading post called Astoria, at the mouth of the Columbia River.

[1] The "Gates of the Rocky Mountains" are near the point where Helena, the capital of Montana, is now situated. A short distance above, the Jefferson, Gallatin, and Madison rivers unite to form the Missouri. Lewis and Clark ascended the Jefferson to its source, crossed the Rocky Mountains and embarked on a branch of the Snake or Lewis River, which flows into the Columbia.

[2] Captain Robert Gray, born in Tiverton, Rhode Island. He named the river from his vessel, the *Columbia*. Captain Gray was the first man to carry the American flag around the globe.

[3] Astor planned the extension of a line of trading-posts.

**217. Effect of the French and English War on the United States; The *Leopard* and the *Chesapeake*.** — During all this time France and England continued at war. Each of these nations forbade the United States to trade with the other. This in itself was disastrous to our commerce; but, as if this was not enough, England insisted on stopping our vessels on the ocean and searching them for British sailors. Unless a man could prove that he was an American by birth, the English seized him — especially if he was an able-bodied seaman — and compelled him to enter their service. In this way they had helped themselves, in spite of our protests, to several thousand men, whom they forced to fight for them on board their ships of war. Finally (1807), the British man-of-war *Leopard* stopped the *Chesapeake*, one of our war-vessels, at a time when the latter could make no effectual resistance, and seized four of her men, one of whom they hanged as a deserter.

**218. The Embargo and the Non-Intercourse Acts.** — Congress passed the Embargo [1] Act (1807) to put an end to these outrages. The Embargo forbade any American vessel's sailing from one of our ports — even a fishing-smack found it difficult to leave Boston to get mackerel. [2] Congress hoped that by stopping all trade with Europe we should starve France and England into treating us with respect.

But we did not starve them; our exports fell off forty millions of dollars in a single year, and the loss of trade caused great distress and discontent.

At last New England grew desperate; there seemed danger of rebellion, possibly of disunion, if the Embargo Act was not repealed. Congress did repeal it; and (1809) passed an act

---

of different kinds west from the Great Lakes to the Pacific, and thence to the Sandwich Islands and China. The war of 1812 put a stop to this immense undertaking. He died in 1848, leaving a property of twenty million dollars, which has since increased enormously.

[1] Embargo: an order by the government forbidding ships to leave port.

[2] Coasting and fishing vessels might sail by special permission.

called the Non-Intercourse Act,[1] which forbade the people to
trade with Great Britain and France, but gave them liberty to
trade with other foreign countries.    But though our exports
rose, yet many men who had been engaged in commerce
turned their attention now to manufacturing.    This was one
of the important results of the Non-Intercourse Act, since
many of the manufactories of the country had their beginning
at that time.[2]

219. **Burr tried for Treason.** — Meanwhile (1807), Aaron
Burr, the former Vice-President of the United States,[3] was
tried for treason.[4]    Burr had shot Hamilton,[5] his political
opponent, in a duel.    That act, hardly different from down-
right murder, brought him into disgrace.    Later, Burr planned
an enterprise for conquering Texas, which was then part of
Mexico, and belonged to Spain.    He hoped to draw some of
the Western states to join him, and so to set up an independent nation in the Southwest, with New Orleans for its capital,
he, of course, to be its chief ruler.    Burr's guilt could not be
proved, and he was permitted to go free.    He lived to be a
very old man, and died at last in obscurity and poverty in
New York.

220. **"Fulton's Folly."** — In the summer of the same year,
1807, Robert Fulton[6] launched his newly invented steamboat

[1] Non-Intercourse: from *Non*, a Latin word meaning not; and Intercourse
(here, meaning commerce or trade), hence a law forbidding trade.

[2] Later, Congress imposed new and heavier duties on many foreign goods, in
order to enable the American makers to manufacture similar goods in this country,
which it was thought they could not do at a profit if the foreign goods came in free.

[3] See page 206, note 2.

[4] Treason: an attempt to overthrow the government or break up the Union by
force of arms.    Burr was indicted for treason on the ground that he or his party
intended to seize New Orleans by force of arms.    This charge of treason was set
aside by the court for the reason that the Constitution did not uphold it.    (See the
Constitution, page xiii, Section 3.)          [5] See page 197.

[6] Robert Fulton, born in Fulton, Lancaster County, Pennsylvania, 1765.    He
was of Irish descent.    John Fitch of Windsor, Connecticut, had invented a steamboat many years before, and tried in vain to get Benjamin Franklin to help him

on the Hudson.   He gave notice that he should start from
New York City for Albany.   Up to that date, all the trade
and travel on the river had been either by sailing-vessels
or row-boats.   Men called the steamboat "Fulton's Folly."
Thousands gathered at the wharf (August 11, 1807), to laugh
and jeer at the expected failure of the invention.

The steamboat — the *Clermont* — was a rude affair, with
uncovered paddle-wheels and clumsy machinery.   Men said
that she was as "helpless as a log."
Presently the paddles began to re-
volve.   Then the "log" was no
longer helpless.   "She moves!"
"She moves!" shouted the astonished crowd.   Sure enough, she did
move ; and she kept on moving
against both wind and current,
going steadily up stream, until, in
thirty-two hours, she reached Albany.   Sailors on the Hudson, seeing this puffing monster coming up
the river after dark, sending out a
shower of sparks from her smoke-
pipe, were frightened almost out of

The "Clermont."

their senses.   Many who had never prayed before, ran below,
and begged, on their knees, to be saved from the Evil One.

In a few years, Fulton's great invention made a complete
change in modes of travel.   Steamboats were put on the
Ohio, the Mississippi, and the Great Lakes, and had a most
important influence in helping to open up and to settle the
western part of the United States.   A number of years later
(1819), the *Savannah* — the first ocean steamship — started
from Savannah, Georgia, and crossed the Atlantic.   Thus the

make it a success.   In 1798 he became discouraged, and committed suicide.   In
his journal he left these words : "The day will come when *some more powerful
man* will get fame and riches from *my* invention."

honor of accomplishing that great feat belongs to a Southern state.   She set the example which Great Britain was to follow twenty years later.

**221. The Importation of Slaves forbidden.** — The year of Fulton's triumph (1807), Congress put a stop to the importation of slaves into the United States.[1]   The law had the hearty support of the President.   He, like Washington and most leading men of that day of the South, was a slaveholder.   But, like Washington and hundreds of other influential Southerners, he hoped that the country would find some peaceful means of freeing the negroes.[2]   Jefferson, in particular, was beloved by his slaves, and would gladly have given them their liberty, if he could have clearly seen how to do it.   He continued to hold them, as many other good men did, but he said, "I tremble for my country, when I reflect that God is just."

**222. Summary.** — Jefferson was the first Democratic President.   He purchased the territory of Louisiana, thereby more than doubling the area of the United States, and sent Lewis and Clark to explore the country to the Pacific.   During Jefferson's administration,[3] Fulton invented the first practicable steamboat, and established steam navigation on the Hudson; the pirates of Tripoli and Algiers were conquered; the importation of slaves was stopped; and on account of trouble with Great Britain and France, Congress passed the Embargo and the Non-Intercourse Acts restraining our foreign trade.

### JAMES MADISON.

**223. Madison's Administration (Fourth President, Two Terms, 1809–1817); Re-opening of the Trade with Great Britain.** — When

---

[1] After January 1, 1808.   See note 3, page 192.

[2] When slavery was prohibited in the Northwest Territory, in 1787 (see Paragraph 195), every Southern member of Congress voted in favor of the prohibition.

[3] See note 1, page 195.

Madison [1] became President, Great Britain and France were actively at war, and our ships were still forbidden by Act of Congress [2] to trade with either country. The President was anxious to re-open commerce with one or both. The British minister [3] at Washington gave Madison to understand that England would let our vessels sail the seas unmolested, if we would promise to send our wheat, rice, cotton, fish, and other exports to her and her friends, but refuse them to her enemy, France. The agreement was made. More than a thousand of our vessels, loaded with grain and other American products, were waiting impatiently for the President to grant them liberty to sail for Great Britain. He spoke the word, and they 'spread their white wings like a flock of long-imprisoned birds, and flew out to sea.' A great shout of joy went up from the people; farmers, merchants, shipowners, — all believed that the fleet of vessels that had gone forth would return to fill thousands of empty pockets with welcome dollars. But England refused to carry out the agreement, — said it was all a mistake, as in truth it was,[4] and so, to the disappointment and anger of multitudes, especially in New England, trade stopped as suddenly as it began.

**224. How Napoleon deceived us.** — Next, Napoleon, Emperor of the French, had a word of promise for us. He had seized

[1] James Madison of Virginia and Alexander Hamilton of New York were the foremost of the distinguished statesmen who framed the Constitution and aided Washington in organizing the government. Madison not only drafted the main features of the Constitution, but offered the first ten amendments, adopted 1791.

Madison furthermore obtained the passage of the Religious Freedom Act of Virginia (originally drawn by Jefferson in 1778), 1785, by which entire religious liberty was granted, and all taxes for the support of public worship, and all religious tests for holding office in that state were forbidden. In this great reform, Virginia led every state, not excepting Rhode Island, in some respects, and set an example followed in the Constitution of the United States (see Constitution, page xv, Paragraph 2). Madison was born in King George County, Va., in 1751; died 1836.

Madison (with George Clinton of New York, Vice-President) was elected President by the Republican, or Democratic, party (see Paragraph 199, and note 4).

[2] See Non-Intercourse Act, Paragraph 218.     [3] Minister: see page 189, note 3.
[4] It was the mistake of Mr. Erskine, the British minister.

and sold hundreds of our ships, because we would not aid him in his war against England. He now agreed to let our commerce alone, provided we would bind ourselves not to send any of our produce to Great Britain, but would let him and his friends have what they wanted to buy. Napoleon's offer was a trick to deceive us, and to get us into trouble with England. We agreed to his terms; he did not keep his word, and the ill-feeling between England and America was made more bitter than ever.

**225. Tecumseh's Conspiracy; Battle of Tippecanoe.** — Meanwhile, it was discovered that Tecumseh, a famous Indian chief, of Ohio, had succeeded in uniting the savage tribes of

the West in a plot to drive out the white settlers. General Harrison, who became President thirty years later (1841), met the Indians at Tippecanoe, in the territory of Indiana, and defeated them in a great battle (1811). Tecumseh himself, however, was not in that battle; but he took a leading part in later ones, led by the English. Many Americans believed that England had secretly encouraged Tecumseh's plot. This belief helped to increase the desire of the majority for war with Great Britain.

**226. The War of 1812; the Henry Letters; the Real Cause of the War; its Declaration.** — It was still further increased by a man named Henry. He declared that the English government in Canada had employed him to endeavor to persuade the New England states to withdraw from the Union and join themselves to Canada. In proof of what he alleged, he produced a package of letters, which he stated contained positive evidence of what he said. Madison paid Henry fifty thousand dollars for the letters. They were a fraud, and Henry was a villain; but for a time both the President and

Congress were completely deceived by this artful swindler, and his letters made our hatred of Great Britain burn hotter than ever.

The real, final cause of the war, however, lay in the fact that England persisted in stopping our ships, taking American seamen out of them, and forcing them, under the sting of the lash, to enter her service and fight her battles.[1] Her excuse was that she seized men who were British subjects and who had deserted and entered our service. This was true in some cases, but England made no discrimination, but took any able-bodied sailor she fancied. This was an outrage that we could no longer bear — thousands of our citizens had been kidnapped, but England refused to stop these acts of violence. For this reason Congress declared war, in the summer of 1812. New England, knowing that such a war would ruin what commerce she had, was opposed to fighting; but the rest of the country thought differently, and, with a hurrah for "Free Trade and Sailors' Rights,"[2] the war began.

**227. Hull's March to Detroit; his Surrender.** — Our plan was to attack Canada, and, if all went well, to annex it. In expectation of the war, General William Hull had been ordered to march from Urbana, Ohio, to Detroit. Hull had served in the Revolution, and Washington had spoken of him as "an officer of great merit." In order to reach Detroit he had to build two hundred miles of road through forests and swamps. It was a tremendous piece of work. Hull did it, and reached Detroit. He did not get the news that we had declared war, until after the Canadians had got it, and had

[1] England denied that a British subject could become an American citizen. This was at a time when she could not get her own people to enter her navy, and used to send gangs of sailors ashore in England at night, with hand-cuffs and gags, to seize men and drag them off to fight against France.

[2] By "Free Trade," we meant freedom to send our merchant ships to what ports we pleased; by "Sailors' Rights," we meant the protection of American seamen against seizure by the British.

cut off most of the supplies of provisions and powder that he was expecting to receive. The forests back of Detroit were full of hostile savages; in front was the English general, Brock, with a force of Canadians and Indians. Brock sum-

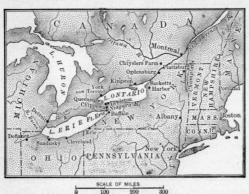

moned Hull to surrender. Without waiting to be attacked, without firing a single gun at the enemy, he hoisted a white tablecloth as a signal to Brock, gave up the fort, and with it Detroit and Michigan. For this act Hull was tried by a court of American army officers, convicted of cowardice, and sentenced to be shot; but President Madison pardoned him on account of his services during the Revolution.[1]

**228. The *Constitution* and the *Guerrière*.[2]** — But though we were beaten on land, we were wonderfully victorious at sea. England had been in the habit of treating America as though she owned the ocean from shore to shore. She had a magnificent navy of a thousand war-ships. We had twelve! One of our twelve was the *Constitution*, Captain Isaac Hull[3] — and certainly a braver officer never trod a ship's deck. While cruising off the coast of Nova Scotia, Captain Hull fell in with the

[1] General Hull's defence was that he surrendered in order to save the women and children of Detroit from the scalping-knives of the Indians who formed part of Brock's force. James Freeman Clarke says, "Public opinion has long since revised this sentence [against Hull], and the best historians disapprove it."

[2] Guerrière (Ghĕ-rē-air'). The British had captured this vessel from the French; hence her French name, meaning the *Warrior*.

[3] He was nephew of General Hull.

British man-of-war *Guerrière*. The fight began (August 19, 1812) without delay, and in twenty minutes the *Guerrière* surrendered, a shattered, helpless, sinking wreck.[1] The *London Times* said, 'Never before in the history of the world did an English frigate haul down her colors to an American';[2] but before the war was over, England had prac- tised hauling down her flag to Americans so much that it had ceased to excite surprise. Out of fifteen such battles, we won twelve. Captain Hull brought his prisoners to Boston. The *Constitu- tion*, almost unhurt, and henceforth known as *Old Ironsides*,[3] was hailed with ringing cheers. Hull and his brave officers were feasted in Faneuil Hall; Congress voted him a gold medal for the victory, and gave his men fifty thousand dollars in prize money.

Battle of the "Constitution" and the "Guerrière."

229. **Progress of the War; Perry's Victory.** — Later that year (1812), the Americans attacked Queenstown, Canada, and General Harrison, commander of the army of the West, tried to drive the British out of Detroit, but accomplished nothing of note.

But in the autumn (September 10, 1813), Commodore Perry gained a grand victory on Lake Erie. Perry had gone to the shore of the lake, and, with the help of a gang of ship-carpen- ters, had built five vessels from green timber cut in the wilder-

[1] The *Constitution* carried heavier guns and more men than the *Guerrière*.

[2] The *Times* had forgotten Paul Jones (see page 182).

[3] See Holmes's poem on "Old Ironsides," written when it was proposed to break the old ship up.

ness back of them.    He added four more vessels, and with that
little fleet captured the British fleet carrying more guns and

more men.    Before the fight began,
he hoisted a flag over his vessel —
the *Lawrence* — bearing the words,
"Don't give up the ship." [1]    During
the battle, the *Lawrence* was literally
cut to pieces, and her decks covered
with dead and dying men.    Perry
saw that if he persisted in staying
where he was, he must be defeated.
Taking his little brother — a boy of twelve — with him, he
jumped into a boat, and ordered the crew to pull for the
*Niagara*.    It was a peril-
ous undertaking.    The
British shot broke the
oars to pieces, and young
Perry's cap was torn with
bullets; but the boat
reached the *Niagara*, and
Perry gained the battle.    Then — on the back of an old letter
— he wrote this despatch to
General Harrison, —

> "*We have met the enemy, and
> they are ours.*"

That victory gave us con-
trol of Lake Erie, and the
British abandoned Detroit.

### 230. Jackson's Victory at Tohopeka. — The next year (1814) General Andrew Jack-son — destined to be Presi-

---

[1] These were the last words of Captain James Lawrence (June 1, 1813), when he
fell mortally wounded in a battle between his ship, the *Chesapeake*, and the English
ship-of-war *Shannon*.    Perry had given Lawrence's name to his ship.

dent of the United States — marched against the Creeks, a strong Indian tribe in the southwest territory, now forming the states of Alabama and Mis-

sissippi. The Creeks had fought against us from the beginning of the war; and the summer before Jackson set out to attack them they had massacred five hundred men, women, and children at Fort Mimms, near Mobile. Jackson was a man who never did things by halves. He drove the Indians before him, but at last they turned and met him (March 27, 1814) in battle at Tohopeka, or Horseshoe Bend, on a branch of the Alabama River. Here Jackson killed so many that he completely destroyed their power, and the result was that the Indians surrendered the greater part of their territory to the United States.

**231. Battles of Chippewa and Lundy's Lane; Burning of Washington.** — In the summer of the same year (1814) General Brown, with General Winfield Scott and General Ripley, gained the battle of Chippewa, in Canada (July 5, 1814). Later, they drove the British from a hard-fought field at Lundy's Lane (July 25, 1814), near Niagara Falls.

Meanwhile, the British had blockaded all our ports along the Atlantic coast, and had plundered and burned a number of towns. Later in the summer (August 24, 1814) they entered

Washington. The sudden appearance of the enemy created a panic. President Madison fled in one direction; Mrs. Madison, filling her work-bag with silver spoons, snatched from the table, fled in another. The President's dinner, which had just been served, was captured and eaten by the enemy. After

dinner, Admiral Cockburn, the English commander, and his officers, paid a visit to the House of Representatives. Springing into the Speaker's chair, he cried out, "Shall this harbor of Yankee Democracy be burned? All for it will say 'Aye!'" A general shout of "Aye!" "Aye!" settled the question. The torch was applied, and soon the evening sky was red with the glare of the flames, which consumed the Capitol, the President's House, and other public buildings. A recent English historian [1] says of that deed, "Few more shameful acts are recorded in our history; and it was the more shameful in that it was done under strict orders from the government at home." [2]

**232. Macdonough's Victory on Lake Champlain; British Attack on Fort McHenry.** — A few weeks after the burning of Washington, a British expedition fourteen thousand strong moved down from Canada by way of Lake Champlain to attack Northern New York. Commodore Macdonough had command of a small American fleet on the lake. A British fleet — carrying more guns and more men — attacked him (September 11, 1814)

[1] Green's "History of the English People."

[2] The English justified the burning of Washington on the ground that we had burned (May 1, 1813) the Canadian government buildings at York (now Toronto), then the capital of Canada. The truth is, that both sides perpetrated many acts which time should make both forgive and forget.

in Plattsburg Bay.[1]    At the first broadside fired by the enemy, a young game-cock kept as a pet on board Macdonough's ship, the *Saratoga,* flew up upon a gun ; flapping his wings, he gave a crow of defiance that rang like the blast of a trumpet.  Swinging their hats, Macdonough's men cheered the plucky bird again and again.  He had foretold victory.  That was enough.  They went into the fight with such ardor, and managed their vessels with such skill, that in less than three hours all of the British ships that had not hauled down their flags were scudding to a place of safety as rapidly as possible.  That ended the invasion from Canada.

The next British attack was on Baltimore, by the same force and fleet that had taken Washington.  That city was guarded by Fort McHenry.  All day and all the following night (September 13, 1814) the enemy's ships hammered away with shot and shell at the fort.  Would it, could it, hold out ? was the anxious question of the people of Baltimore.  When the sun rose the next morning, the question was answered — "our flag was still there," the British had given up the attack, and were sailing down Chesapeake Bay.  Baltimore was safe.[2]

**233.  Jackson's Victory at New Orleans ; the Hartford Convention ; End of the War.** — Early the next year came the final battle of the war.  The contest had now lasted over two years.  The British determined to strike a tremendous blow at New Orleans.  If successful, it might give them a foothold on the Mississippi River.  Ten thousand picked men under Sir Edward Pakenham made the attack (January 8, 1815).  General Andrew Jackson defended the approach to the city with for-

[1] See Map, page 218.

[2] It was on this occasion that Francis S. Key, of Baltimore, wrote " The Star-Spangled Banner."  Key was a prisoner at the time on board of one of the British men-of-war.  All night long he watched the bombardment of the fort.  By the flash of the guns he could see our flag waving over it.  In the morning, when the mist cleared away, he found it was " still there."  His feelings of delight found expression in the song, which he hastily wrote in pencil on the back of an old letter.  In a few weeks the people were singing it from one end of the country to the other.

tifications made of banks of earth and logs.   He had just half as many men as the British commander, and they were men, too, who knew practically nothing of war.

In less than half an hour after the fight began, Pakenham was killed, and the enemy had lost so heavily[1] that they gave up the battle.   It was the end of the war.   Great Britain had already made peace with our commissioners at Ghent, in Belgium (December 24, 1814); but as it often took even fast sailing-vessels a month or six weeks to cross the Atlantic, the news did not reach us until several weeks after Jackson's victory.   The treaty said nothing about the British claim of the right to search American vessels; but there was hardly need to mention it, for our ships were no longer molested.

While the news of the treaty of peace was on its way, delegates from most of the New England states met in Hartford, in secret session.   The enemies of New England said that the Convention wished to dissolve the Union.   The delegates declared that they met to secure defence for the New England states, and to propose certain amendments to the Constitution.

234. **Results of the War.** — The war, sometimes called "the second war for independence," had three chief results: 1. Though our military operations had generally been far from successful on land, yet we convinced Great Britain that we were able and determined to make our rights on the ocean respected.   2. The war showed foreign nations that any attempt to establish themselves on the territory of the United States was likely to end in disastrous failure.   3. By cutting off our foreign commerce for a number of years, the war caused us to build many cotton and woollen mills, thus making us to a much greater degree than before a manufacturing people — able to clothe ourselves, instead of having to depend on the looms of Great Britain for our calico and our broadcloth.

[1] Only 8 Americans were killed; 2600 British were killed and wounded.

**235. Summary.**— Madison's administration was mainly taken up with the second war with Great Britain, begun in 1812 and ended early in 1815. The cause of the war was the refusal of England to stop seizing our sailors on board our ships and forcing them into her service. The war had the good effect of putting an end to this practice. That was over eighty years ago. Since then England and America have been at peace with each other. May that peace never again be broken!

### JAMES MONROE.

**236. Monroe's Administration (Fifth President; Two Terms, 1817–1825); Monroe a Soldier of the Revolution; his Inauguration.**— Monroe,[1] like Washington, got the best part of his education on the battle-field. When the Revolution broke out he was a student in the College of William and Mary,[2] Virginia. Knowing that the country needed her young men to fight for her, he laid down his books and went to do his part in the cause of liberty; among the gallant officers who helped to gain the victory of Trenton[3] James Monroe, then only eighteen, was one.

Mr. Monroe stood near the ruins of the Capitol at Washington when he took the oath of office,[4] and delivered his inaugural address. The British had burned,[5] but had not wholly destroyed that edifice, and the foundations remained unharmed. Workmen were then busily engaged in rebuilding it.[6] The President's address to the people was full of encouragement. It seemed to him that the solid foundations of the

[1] James Monroe of Westmoreland County, Virginia (born 1758; died 1831), was elected President by the Republican or Democratic party (see page 195, note 4) by a very large majority over the Federalist candidate. Daniel D. Tompkins of New York was chosen Vice-President. On Monroe's second election, see page 226.

[2] The College of William and Mary, near Williamsburg, Virginia, is the oldest college, except Harvard, in the United States, and at the outbreak of the Revolution it was the wealthiest.

[3] See Paragraph 174.   [4] See note 4, page 196.   [5] See Paragraph 231.

[6] The Capitol has since been greatly enlarged, and a new dome erected.

Capitol stood an image of the nation, and that, like them, the government was sure to continue to exist.

**237. The President's Journey through the North; the "Era of Good Feeling."** — Mr. Monroe spent the summer (1817) in travelling through New England and the Northern states. New England had been bitterly opposed to the war of 1812, because the stoppage of commerce had ruined many of her merchants and ship-builders. The President's journey in this part of the country did great good. He went as a peacemaker. All knew that he had fought under Washington; all respected the man's unblemished character and honest purpose. When the New England people saw him dressed in the military costume of the Revolution, the sight brought back the old days that had 'tried men's souls.'[1] In Boston and other cities the citizens brought out the shot-torn and smoke-stained battle-flags of '76[2] to decorate the streets. Gray-haired men, scarred with wounds received at Bunker Hill, at Trenton, at Saratoga, gathered to welcome the new President. When he spoke, it was of the inestimable worth of the Union, of the need that the North and the South had, and always must have, for each other. Men listened, and forgot their political differences and hatreds; party lines seemed to fade away. Every one declared that the "Era of Good Feeling" had begun. When Mr. Monroe was chosen President for the second time (1821) the people showed their respect for him and their confidence in him by their electoral vote, which lacked but a single one of being unanimous.[3]

[1] No country ever made more generous provision for its old soldiers than the United States did (in Monroe's administration) for those who had fought in the Revolution. The government pensioned the veterans of the war, and their widows, spending in all about $65,000,000 in that noble work.    [2] 1776.

[3] Out of 232 electoral votes cast by the twenty-four states then constituting the Union, Monroe received 231. The elector who cast the remaining vote (for John Quincy Adams) did it simply because he had vowed "that no later mortal should stand in Washington's shoes" — that is, receive, like Washington, every vote for the presidency.

**238. The First Seminole War; the Purchase of Florida.** ―
Florida, which belonged to Spain,[1] was a constant source of
trouble to the people of the South.   Pirates, robbers, desperadoes of all kinds, had got complete control of that territory.
Many Seminoles, or wandering Indians,[2] had gone there from
the country west of Georgia, and, uniting with runaway negroes
from the South, they sallied out and attacked the Georgia
planters, burning houses, murdering families, and carrying off
property.   Several attempts had been made (1817) to put a
stop to these outrages ; but, as it was no easy matter to fight
the Indians and negroes in the swamps and thickets of Florida,
nothing satisfactory had been accomplished.   Finally, General
Jackson[3] was sent (1818) to see what he could do.   His measures were sharp and energetic ; in three months he had conquered the country, though it still continued to belong to
Spain.

The Spanish government found that these troubles were
likely to break out again, and that the people of Georgia would
never rest until they got possession of Florida ; Spain therefore wisely decided to sell it to us.   We obtained the entire
territory, about sixty thousand square miles (1819), for five
million dollars, thus adding another large area[4] to the United
States.[5]   At the same time Spain gave up all claim to the
Oregon country, and so strengthened our title to it.

**239. The Question of the Western Extension of Slavery.** ―
The year in which we purchased Florida the question came
up, whether slavery should be permitted to establish itself
beyond the Mississippi, in the northern part of the territory

---

[1] See Paragraph 144.   Great Britain ceded Florida back to Spain in 1783.

[2] Seminoles (wanderers).   The name was given to the Indians of Florida by the
Indians of Georgia and the Southwest.   The second Seminole War began in 1835.

[3] See Paragraph 230.            [4] See Map, page 183.

[5] When the United States made the treaty with Spain for the purchase of Florida
(1819) we gave up to Spain all claim to the country west of the Sabine River (later
known as Texas) ; and on the other hand, Spain agreed to make over to the United
States all her title and claims to Oregon.   (See " Table of Boundaries.")

of Louisiana,[1] then called Missouri.  Congress had shut out slavery (1787) from the Northwest Territory;[2] now the discussion began whether it should in like manner shut it out from that part of the country beyond the Mississippi, north of a line drawn west from near the point where the Ohio joins that river.

Jefferson was afraid that this discussion would lead to trouble between the states.  He said that the suddenness with which it arose terrified him "like a fire-bell in the night."

**240. Change of Feeling in Regard to Slavery ; Condition of Things at the North and at the South.** — The reason for this fear was that a great change had come over the country.  Before, and even during, the Revolution, every colony held negroes in bondage. But in the North the slaves were chiefly house-servants, and their number was never very large.  In the South, however, the planters raised all their crops by slave labor, and the number of negroes was constantly increasing.  At first, few persons considered slavery an evil; but after a time many able men in both sections of the country came to believe it a bad thing for both the whites and the blacks.

In the North, this feeling gradually led to the passing of laws which gave the slaves their freedom.  This was not the case at the South, because there the planters did not see how they could free their negroes without ruining themselves.

Later, as has been shown,[3] the invention of the cotton-gin made slave labor immensely profitable.  The natural result was that the planters wished to keep the system up.  At the same time, a good many Northern men who made money by manufacturing and dealing in cotton cloth became interested in maintaining slavery.

---

1 See Paragraph 215, and compare Map, page 209.  Slaves were held in the southern part of that territory (in New Orleans and vicinity) when we purchased the territory from France ; hence the *State* of Louisiana came in with slavery, in 1812.

2 That is, the territory north of the Ohio and east of the Mississippi, forming now the five states of Ohio, Indiana, Illinois, Michigan, and Wisconsin, with Eastern Minnesota. See Paragraph 195.        3 See Paragraph 205.

**241. How Slavery divided the Country in Regard to Trade with Europe.** — On the whole, the effect of the slave system was now to divide the nation, instead of uniting it. The people of the two sections not only thought differently about the right and the wrong of holding the negro in bondage, but their business interests had come to be different. The South devoted all its strength to raising cotton, rice, and tobacco. Whatever manufactured goods — such as cloth, shoes, hats — it needed, it had to buy ; and as Europe could make such goods much cheaper then than we possibly could, the South naturally wished for free trade, in order that it might import its supplies from the other side of the Atlantic.

The North, however, had gradually come to devote much of its labor and its money to making cloth and other goods ; for this reason it was opposed to free trade in these articles. It wished to tax the importation of whatever it could manufacture to advantage, and so keep foreign goods high, and induce people to buy our own instead. Hence, while the South wanted liberty to send abroad for goods, the North believed that the country would thrive better if manufacturers were protected by government in making them here.

**242. Why the North opposed the Extension of Slavery West of the Mississippi ; why the South demanded it.** — The great majority of the Northern people, believing slavery to be an evil, had therefore two chief reasons for opposing its establishment in the new territory west of the Mississippi : 1. They thought it would be a serious injury to that part of the country, and as great a mistake as for a farmer to take the thistles and weeds which grew on his old land and deliberately plant them on a field of freshly cleared soil. 2. They objected to it because, if the new territory should be admitted as slave states, the South would thereby gain such a great number of representatives in Congress that it would have a large majority. That section could then, by its votes, strengthen and extend slavery, and at the same time secure the passage of laws which would permit the free importation of all kinds of manufactured goods.

The South, on the other hand, was firmly convinced that its prosperity depended on the extension of slave labor, and on free trade with Europe. The people there saw that the North was rapidly outstripping them in growth of population. If, then, the new territory should come in as free soil, the result would be that the North would soon get control of Congress, and so control of trade.

Both sides were the more eager because since 1812 five states — Louisiana, Indiana, Mississippi, Illinois, and Alabama — had entered the Union. This made the number of free and of slave states (1819) equal, each section having eleven. The next state admitted would throw the power on the side of either freedom or slavery.

243. The Missouri Compromise. — When, therefore, Missouri took steps to gain admission as a slave state, the South urged the measure with all its might, and the North fought against it with equal determination. After nearly two years of angry debate, Henry Clay[1] of Kentucky succeeded in persuading Congress to make a compromise.[2] It was this: Missouri was to be allowed to enter the Union as a slave state, but on the express condition that in all future cases the states formed out

[1] Henry Clay was born in Virginia in 1777; died at Washington, 1852. He studied law, and in 1797 removed to Lexington, Kentucky. In 1799, when the people of Kentucky were about adopting a state constitution, Clay urged them (but without success) to abolish slavery. He entered Congress in 1806, and continued in public life from that time until his death. He was a man of remarkable personal influence, a "peacemaker" by temperament, and the greatest orator the Southwest ever possessed. Although ardently attached to his adopted state of Kentucky, yet he declared in 1850 that he owed his first allegiance to the Union, and a subordinate allegiance to his state. See Carl Schurz's admirable "Life of Henry Clay" in the "American Statesmen Series."

[2] It was called a compromise because, as will be seen, each side promised to give up something to the other for the sake of making a peaceful settlement of the dispute.

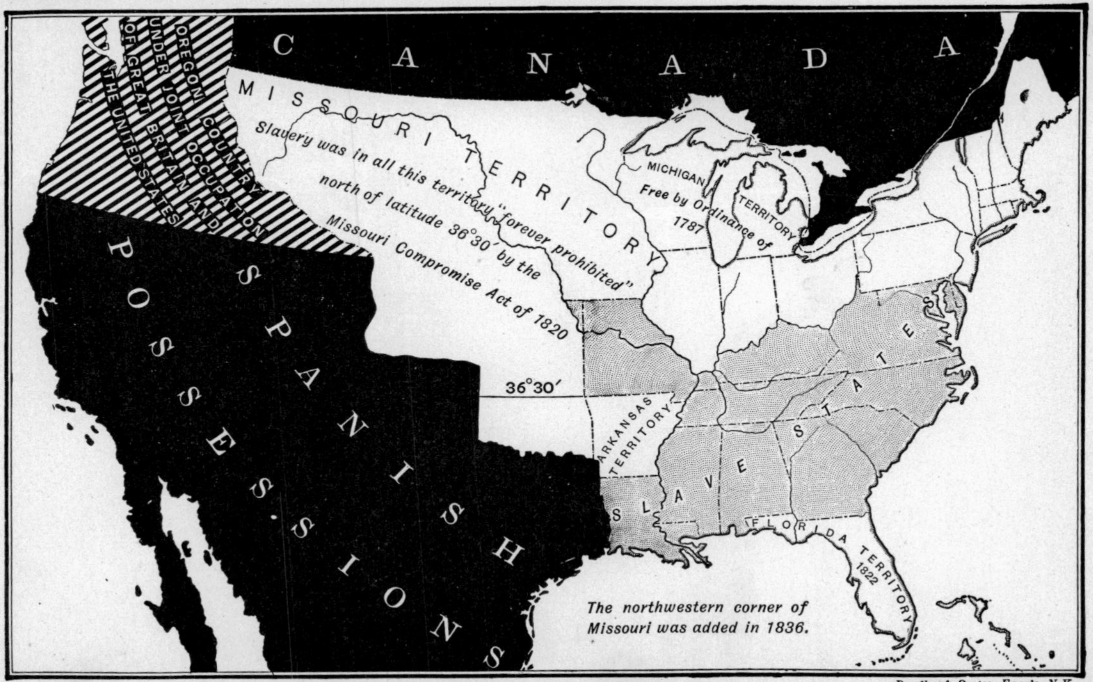
CANADA
OREGON COUNTRY UNDER JOINT OCCUPATION OF GREAT BRITAIN AND THE UNITED STATES
MISSOURI TERRITORY
Slavery was in all this territory "forever prohibited" north of latitude 36°30′ by the Missouri Compromise Act of 1820
MICHIGAN TERRITORY
Free by Ordinance of 1787
36°30′
ARKANSAS TERRITORY
SLAVE STATES
FLORIDA TERRITORY 1822
SPANISH POSSESSIONS
The northwestern corner of Missouri was added in 1836.
Bradley & Poates, Engr's, N.Y.

THE MISSOURI COMPROMISE ACT.

of the territory west and northwest of Missouri — that is, north of the parallel of 36 degrees and 30 minutes on the map — should come in free.[1]   Congress passed this law in 1820, under the name of the Missouri Compromise.[2]   Meantime, Maine had been admitted (1820) ; so that, when Missouri entered the Union (1821), the balance between the free and the slave states was still kept, — each section had just twelve.

Many people now believed that the debate about the extension of slavery was settled "forever."   But facts proved that in this case "forever" meant something less than twenty-five years ;[3] then, as we shall see, the question was to come up again, and in a more dangerous form than before.

244.  Desire to reach the West ; the " National Road." — Next to the extension of slavery, one of the greatest questions of this period was how to reach the West.   To-day, we find it difficult to understand this.   To get West, we simply step into an express train, and steam whirls us to our destination at the rate of forty miles an hour.   If mountains block the way, the train either climbs over them or goes through them.   In President Monroe's time the railroad did not exist, and, although the steamboat did, that could only go where some navigable river or lake opened the way.   Look on the map of the United States, and you will see that the Alleghany Mountains shut out the East from the West.   As the steamboat could not find a passage leading through those rough walls of rock, Congress resolved to build a road over them.   Such a national road had already been begun on the banks of the Potomac, at Cumberland, Maryland.   It was now (1825) gradually extended across the forest-covered mountains to Wheel-

[1] See Map facing page 230.

[2] John Randolph of Virginia called the Northern men who voted for the Compromise " Doughfaces," because he thought they had no more character than a piece of dough.

[3] That is, until the question of the Wilmot Proviso came up in 1846, followed by that of the Compromise of 1850 and that of the admission of Kansas in 1854.

ing, on the Ohio River, where it would connect with steamboats running to Cincinnati, or even to New Orleans.

But that was not enough. There were millions of acres of fertile lands in Ohio and the country beyond it, that emigrants wished to reach more directly than the steamboat would help them to do. For this reason it was proposed to extend the National Road from Wheeling through to the Mississippi. President Monroe earnestly favored this and similar enterprises, but did not think that he had lawful power under the Constitution to spend the people's money for such purposes. Indirectly, however, he used every effort to help it forward. The road was gradually built farther and farther west. It was the first great work of the kind undertaken by the United States, costing, in the end, over six million dollars. It stretched across the country for hundreds of miles, — broad, solid, smooth, — a true national highway.[1]

245. Traffic on the National Road; Emigrant Wagons. — The traffic over it was immense. Gayly painted stage-coaches ran through the more thickly settled parts. Beyond, toward the west, there was a constant stream of huge canvas-covered emigrant wagons, often so close together that the leaders of the teams could touch the wagon ahead of them with their noses. To see that procession of emigrant families going forward day after day gave one an idea of how fast the people were settling that wild western country, which is now covered with cultivated farms and thriving towns.

It was the beginning of that great march toward the setting sun which was to keep steadily advancing until the Pacific said "Halt!"— that is, until we had taken possession of the whole breadth of the continent.

246. The "Monroe Doctrine"; "America for Americans." — While the National Road was being pushed westward, Mexico and several South American countries had declared themselves

[1] The Road was carried nearly to the Mississippi by the State governments.

# THE MONROE DOCTRINE.

From President Monroe's Message to Congress, December 2, 1823.

*Fellow-Citizens of the Senate and House of Representatives :*

(I.) "At the proposal of the Russian imperial government . . . a full power and instructions have been transmitted to the minister of the United States at St. Petersburg, to arrange, by amicable negotiation, the respective rights and interests of the two nations on the northwest coast of this continent." [Russia at that time, not satisfied with owning Alaska, claimed the greater part of the Oregon country, and was attempting to plant colonies on the coast of the Mexican State of California.] . . . "The occasion has been judged proper for asserting, as a principle in which the rights and interests of the United States are involved, *that the American continents, by the free and independent condition which they have assumed and maintain, are henceforth not to be considered as subjects for future colonization by any European powers.*"

(II.) "In the wars of the European powers, in matters relating to themselves, we have never taken any part, nor does it comport with our policy so to do. It is only when our rights are invaded, or seriously menaced, that we resent injuries or make preparations for our defence. With the movements in this hemisphere we are, of necessity, more immediately connected and by causes which must be obvious to all enlightened and impartial observers. The political system of the Allied Powers is essentially different in this respect from that of America. . . . We owe it, therefore, to candor and to the amicable relations existing between the United States and those Powers to declare *that we should consider any attempt on their part to extend their system to any portion of this hemisphere as dangerous to our peace and safety.* With the existing colonies or dependencies of any European power we have not interfered and shall not interfere. But with the governments who have declared their independence " [i.e. the Spanish South American Republics, and the Republic of Mexico] "and maintained it, and whose independence we have, on great consideration and on just principles, acknowledged, we could not view any interposition for the purpose of oppressing them, or controlling in any other manner their destiny, by any European power, in any other light than as *the manifestation of an unfriendly disposition toward the United States.''*

**Note on the Monroe Doctrine.** — The essential part of what is popularly known as the Monroe Doctrine will be found in the passages printed in italics in the above message.

Shortly after the defeat of Napoleon at the battle of Waterloo (1815) the sovereigns of Austria, Prussia, and Russia, who had been leagued against the great French commander, formed a " Holy Alliance." The object of this treaty or compact was to suppress any attempts to establish liberal and popular governments on the continent of Europe.

In 1823 the report reached the United States that the Holy Alliance was preparing to help Spain conquer Mexico and the Republics in South America which had declared themselves independent of the Spanish monarch.

About the same time Russia undertook to extend her possessions on the northwest coast of America so as to endanger our hold on Oregon. (See Paragraphs 216, 286.)

John Quincy Adams, who was then Secretary of State, told the Russian minister that "we should contest the right of Russia to any territorial establishment on this continent, and that we should assume distinctly the principle that the American continents are no longer subjects for any new European colonial establishments." Mr. Adams believed that the whole of North America belonged to the United States by what he called a "law of nature."

Later in the same year (1823) Mr. Canning, who was a member of the English cabinet, proposed to Mr. Rush, the American minister in London, that the United States should coöperate with England in preventing the Holy Alliance from interfering with the Spanish American Republics.

President Monroe consulted Jefferson on this point and Jefferson replied : "Our first and fundamental maxim should be, **never to entangle ourselves in the broils of Europe. Our second, never to suffer Europe to intermeddle with cis-Atlantic affairs.**"

In these utterances of John Quincy Adams and Ex-President Jefferson we have the idea which President Monroe formulated in his Message. The late Dr. Justin Winsor says (Winsor's "America," vii. 524) that " Popular estimation has given a more defiant meaning to Monroe's language than was intended." But it is noteworthy that the Holy Alliance abandoned the project of interfering with the Spanish American Republics, and that Russia, by treaty of 1824, gave up all claims to territory south of 54° 40′, or the southern boundary of Alaska. See Gilman's " James Monroe"; Morse's "John Quincy Adams" ; and Prof. Woolsey on the " Monroe Doctrine" in Johnson's " Universal Cyclopædia " (new edition).

republics, independent of Spain. The Czar of Russia and the European kings looked with a jealous eye on republics. We suspected that these rulers had promised to help the king of Spain to force the new American nations to bow their heads again under the old despotic yoke from which they had just freed themselves. President Monroe cried, Hands off! In his message to Congress (1823) he declared that, while the United States was resolved not to meddle with the affairs of the nations of the Old World, we were equally determined that they should not meddle with the affairs of the New. That declaration is called the " Monroe Doctrine." [1]  It means that we consider that " America is for Americans." We stand by the right of the different nations on both the American continents, North and South, to manage their own affairs in their own way, without interference from Europe.

247. **Visit of Lafayette.** — Near the close of Monroe's administration, Congress requested the President to invite Lafayette, then a venerable man verging on seventy, to revisit the United States after forty years' absence. He came (1824), and spent more than a year travelling through the country as the guest of the nation. He visited every one of the twenty-four states, and all of the principal cities and towns. He had spent much of his fortune in our cause. Congress gratefully voted him two hundred thousand dollars, and made him a grant of twenty-four thousand acres of land.[2] He was everywhere received with enthusiasm and affection. Some of the old soldiers of the Revolution, who had fought under him, were completely overcome by their feelings on seeing their former commander, and fainted when they grasped the hand that had so generously helped them

---

[1] President Monroe, in his message of December 2, 1823, says, speaking of the proposed interference of European governments in America, " We should consider any attempt on their part to extend their system to any portion of this hemisphere *as dangerous to our peace and safety*." And again, in the same message, the President says that we should consider such interference " *as the manifestation of an unfriendly disposition toward the United States*." These two passages contain what is to-day regarded as the " Monroe Doctrine."     [2] The land was in Florida.

in the dark days of the war.   Lafayette took part in laying the corner-stone of Bunker Hill Monument (June 17, 1825), just fifty years after the battle.[1]   When he returned to France that autumn he was followed by the grateful prayers of the powerful nation he had done so much to establish.

248. Summary. — Three chief events marked the period of the presidency of James Monroe.   They were: 1. The debate on the extension of slavery west of the Mississippi River, ending in the Missouri Compromise.   2. The pushing forward of the National Road into Ohio, which opened up a large section of the West to emigrants from the Atlantic states.   3. Just before Lafayette's visit we declared by the Monroe Doctrine that Europe must keep her hands off both American continents.

## John Quincy Adams.

249. John Quincy Adams's Administration (Sixth President, One Term, 1825–1829);[2] Governor Clinton and the Erie Canal. —

[1] See Webster's address at the laying of the corner-stone of the Bunker Hill Monument, June 17, 1825.

[2] John Quincy Adams, son of President John Adams, was born in Braintree (now Quincy), Massachusetts, in 1767; died, 1848.   He was independent in politics, though his sympathies were with the National Republican or early Whig party.   This party, the successor of the Federalists (see Paragraph 199), desired, like them, to give a broad interpretation to the Constitution.   They favored a protective tariff (that is, a heavy tax imposed on imported goods for the purpose of "protecting" our manufacturers against foreign competition — a revenue tariff is a lighter tax imposed merely to obtain money or revenue for the government).   They also favored public improvements — such as the building of roads, canals, and the like — at the expense of the nation, in opposition to the Democratic party, which insisted on a strict interpretation of the Constitution, favored free trade, or a simple revenue tariff, and believed that each state should make its own improvements at its own expense.

John Quincy Adams and Andrew Jackson were the two leading candidates for the presidency in 1824; the latter represented the Republican, or Democratic party, though party lines at that time were not very clearly defined.   Neither candidate got a majority of the electoral votes; and the House of Representatives finally chose Mr. Adams President (John C. Calhoun of South Carolina Vice-President).   Mr. Adams had refused to make any exertion to secure his own election; and when asked by his friend Edward Everett if he did not intend to do something to obtain it, he replied, "I shall do absolutely nothing."   It was one of those rare cases in which the office sought the man, and not the man the office.

HENRY CLAY.

The year that Mr. Adams became President (1825) the Erie Canal was completed by the state of New York. It was the most important public improvement yet made in the United States. It connected the Hudson River at Troy and Albany with Lake Erie, at the point where the city of Buffalo now stands.

Governor De Witt Clinton of New York carried the great work through. When he proposed it, many denounced and ridiculed the undertaking as a sheer waste of the people's hard-earned money. They nicknamed it "Clinton's Big Ditch." They said that it never would be completed, that it would swallow up millions in taxes, and in the end yield nothing but mud.

250. **How the Canal was built; its Opening.** — Governor Clinton had indeed put his hand to a stupendous task. Lake Erie is three hundred and sixty-three miles west of the Hudson, and it is nearly six hundred feet above the level of that river. The country between the Hudson and the lake is in some places rough and broken. There were people in New York who knew these difficulties, and who asked the governor whether he could make water run up hill. He replied that he could do better: he could build locks which would make the water lift the canal-boats over the hills.

Locks at Lockport, on the Erie Canal.

When all was ready, he set his army of laborers at work. They toiled eight years in the wilderness, cutting down forests, excavating the earth, blasting their way through ridges of rock, building aqueduct-bridges to carry the canal across rivers, constructing locks of solid masonry to carry it up the hillsides.

In the autumn of 1825 the great undertaking was finished, and, when the water was let in, a row of cannon about five miles apart, extending from Buffalo to New York, flashed the news the whole length of the state. Governor Clinton travelled from Buffalo to Albany by the canal, and thence by the Hudson to New York City. He brought with him a keg of water from Lake Erie. When he reached the city, he solemnly poured the water into the harbor, to commemorate, as he said, "the navigable communication opened between our Mediterranean seas [1] and the Atlantic Ocean."

**251. What the Canal has done for New York and for the Country.** — The Canal has since done far more than Governor Clinton expected. The expense of building it was easily paid by means of a small tax levied by the state on boats and freight.[2] Before the canal was built, the charge for hauling a barrel of flour from Albany to Buffalo was ten dollars, and it took three weeks' hauling to get it there. After the canal was opened, a barrel of flour could be sent through in a week, at a cost of thirty cents! Since its completion to the present time, over six thousand million dollars' worth of freight has been carried on its waters.

The canal originally ran through a country in great part unsettled. It was the means of bringing in great numbers of emigrants from the East. On its banks now, there are scores of flourishing towns and rapidly growing cities. New York City gained immensely by the trade with the West which began to spring up as soon as this water-way was opened. To-day the canal is free; a constant procession of boats laden with grain is seen going eastward day and night; a similar procession, laden with merchandise, is seen going westward. This movement is a means of growth and a source

---

[1] He gave this appropriate name to the Great Lakes.

[2] Before the completion of the New York Central Railroad, the canal carried thousands of passengers and emigrants; it now carries freight only.

of wealth to both sections of the country. On the one hand it makes food cheaper all through the East, on the other it makes imported goods cheaper throughout the West.

252. **Experiments with " Steam-Wagons."** — A few years later a work was begun in Maryland which was destined to have greater results even than the Erie Canal. Fulton had shown the world that the steam-engine could be successfully used to propel boats; the next question was, why could not the steam-engine be put on wheels, and made to propel itself on land? After many experiments and many failures, George Stephenson [1] invented a "steam-wagon," or locomotive, in England, which would draw a train of cars on a track, at the rate of ten or fifteen miles an hour. Meanwhile, Oliver Evans and other ingenious American mechanics had been experimenting with "steam-wagons" in this country.

253. **Breaking Ground for the First Passenger Railroad in America.** — In 1828, the venerable Charles Carroll of Carrollton, Maryland, performed the ceremony of breaking ground for the construction of a railroad from Baltimore westward. The road now forms part of the Baltimore and Ohio railway system. Mr. Carroll, then over ninety years of age, was the only person living who had signed the Declaration of American Independence (1776). As he struck the spade into the ground with a firm hand, he said, "I consider this among the most important acts of my life, second only to that of signing the Declaration of Independence, if second even to that."

254. **The First American Locomotive; the Road opened; the Race.** — The first locomotive which ran over the road (1830) was built at Baltimore by Peter Cooper, since widely known for his noble gift of the Cooper Institute to New York City. His engine had little resemblance to our modern ones; but it drew a rudely constructed open wagon filled with passengers,

[1] See the " Leading Facts of English History," in this series.

and that in itself was no small triumph. The road at first extended only to Ellicott's Mills, about thirteen miles from Baltimore. The trip was made in somewhat less than an hour. On the return, the train had a race with a spirited gray horse belonging to one of the Baltimore stage-coach lines. The gray did his best; the puffing, wheezing little locomotive did its best likewise. Finally, steam conquered; and a great shout of victory went up from the dozen passengers in the open wagon. That shout meant that the days of stage-coaches were numbered.

**255. Growth of Railroads in the United States; Results.** — The same year (1830) six miles of the Charleston and Augusta Railroad were opened; a year later (1831) the Mohawk and Hudson Railroad began to carry passengers

First Steam Train (1831) on the Mohawk and Hudson Railroad, New York.

in New York. In ten years the thirteen miles of track in Maryland had multiplied to nearly three thousand miles in different states. These have since increased to over two hundred thousand miles — or nearly seventy-fold — binding the nation together in all directions with bands of steel, and making every part of it quickly, cheaply, and easily accessible to every other part. The men of Jefferson's time who lived to see what the railroad accomplished no longer doubted whether the United States could reach beyond the Alleghanies. Steam convinced them that the republic was destined to get possession of the West as well as of the East.

**256. The Temperance Cause; Drinking Habits in Early Days.** — Side by side with this wonderful material advance, the country was now beginning to make progress in moral reforms, especially with respect to temperance. One of the great evils of the times was drunkenness. In the early days of our history the use of liquor was almost universal. People quite usually began the day by taking a glass of whiskey or rum; they had another glass in the middle of the forenoon; another at dinner; perhaps another, to help them through the afternoon, especially if it was a long afternoon; and, in order to make sure of getting enough, they seldom, if ever, missed taking a last glass before going to bed, that they might, as they said, make certain of pleasant dreams. No well-to-do farmer thought he could get in his hay without a good-sized jug of whiskey to refresh himself and his men; no house or church was built without plenty of spirits to help get the timbers into place; no bargain was clinched without their aid; and no gentleman called on another without being asked to take a social glass.

**257. The First Successful Temperance Society; what has been done.** — In 1826, the "American Society for the Promotion of Temperance" was formed in Boston; and a number of years later (1840), six men, who knew the evils of the vice of intemperance from their own sad personal experience, met in Baltimore, signed a total-abstinence pledge, and founded the "Washingtonian Temperance Society."[1] That movement did immense good, and restored, it is said, a hundred and fifty thousand drunkards to the manhood they had lost through

[1] The first temperance societies did not insist on total abstinence from all alcoholic drinks, but only from the use of distilled spirits such as whiskey, brandy, and the like. Later, they required — like the Washingtonians — a pledge of "*total* abstinence from all that can intoxicate"; but they still retained the name of temperance societies, though strictly speaking, they had now become total abstinence societies. In 1851 the state of Maine enacted a prohibitory law forbidding the manufacture or sale of intoxicating liquors as beverages. Since then, a number of other states have passed similar laws.

drink. Since then a great change for the better has come over society. "Strong drink" still slays its thousands in the United States as elsewhere; but the young man beginning life now has this in his favor: all the best influences are opposed to intemperance — seventy years ago a majority of influences seemed to encourage it.

**258. Summary.** — The presidency of John Quincy Adams was marked by three important events: 1. The completion of the Erie Canal. 2. The building of the first passenger railroad in the United States. 3. The first successful attempt at temperance reform.

## ANDREW JACKSON.

**259. Jackson's Administration (Seventh President, Two Terms, 1829–1837); Character of the New President.** — Up to this date all the Presidents had been chosen from Virginia or from Massachusetts, and all were known to the country as statesmen of a high order. General Jackson[1] came from Tennessee. He was

[1] Andrew Jackson was of Scotch-Irish descent (see note 4, page 97). He was born in 1767, in the Waxhaw Settlement, Mecklenburg County, North Carolina, close to the South Carolina boundary line. In his will and elsewhere he speaks of himself as a native of the latter state. He died in 1845. He got his early education rather from the hard, rough, dangerous life of the backwoods than from books and schools. No one could excel him in handling a rifle, or in breaking and riding a wild or vicious horse.

During the Revolution, Jackson, then a lad of fourteen, was taken prisoner by the British, and was nearly starved to death by them. Once the commanding officer ordered him to clean his boots. Young Jackson refused, saying that he was a prisoner of war, and therefore not obliged to perform such acts of drudgery for his captors. The officer, in a rage, struck him with his sword, cutting a gash on the boy's head and another on his hand. Jackson carried the scars of this brutal treatment to his grave.

In 1784 he began the study of law in Salisbury, North Carolina. Four years later he emigrated to Nashville, Tennessee, where he opened a law-office. In 1797 he was elected United States Senator, but soon resigned the office, "partly," says Parton, "because he felt himself out of place in so slow and dignified a body, but chiefly for pecuniary reasons." He was again elected in 1823.

During the War of 1812 Jackson was appointed a general in the regular army, and served the country with distinguished ability. When he fought the British,

considered a western man, and a man of the people. His military services, and especially his victory over the British at New Orleans,[1] had made him famous throughout the United States.

Andrew Jackson.

In character, Jackson was headstrong, absolutely honest, and utterly fearless. When he was roused, there was a flash in his gray eyes that startled one like the gleam of a suddenly drawn sword. His blunt speech and decided action made many bitter enemies, but he had also many devoted friends. They knew him to be a warm-hearted, true-hearted, high-minded man.

**260. President Jackson's " Political Revolution."** — The new President began his administration with what his Secretary of the Treasury called "a great political revolution." The President's friends demanded government offices. In a short time he turned out about two thousand men from their positions, and gave their places and salaries to those who had voted for him. Jackson believed the change would be an advantage to the country; but such removals by wholesale had never been made before. During the forty years which had passed since the adoption of the Constitution, the six Presidents who had governed the country had dismissed only seventy-four[2] persons holding office, and of this small number five were removed because they had stolen public money.

they found, to their cost, that he had not forgotten how they used him in the Revolution. He also gained great popularity with his men in his battles with the Indians, and his wonderful endurance of hardships got for him the affectionate nickname of " Old Hickory."

In 1828 General Jackson (with John C. Calhoun, of South Carolina, for Vice-President) was elected President of the United States by the Democratic party, by a large majority over John Quincy Adams, the National Republican or Whig candidate. In 1832 he was again elected (Martin Van Buren of New York, Vice-President), over Henry Clay, the Whig candidate.     [1] See Paragraph 233.

[2] Some recent authorities believe that about one hundred and forty persons were removed in all, and that Jefferson turned out nearly one hundred of that number.

**261. Jefferson's Removal of Government Officers ; the " Spoils System."** — Jefferson had removed more persons than any previous President. His object was to give each political party an equal share of offices. When he had made that division he said that he should ask only three questions respecting an applicant : "Is he honest ? Is he capable ? Is he faithful to the Constitution ? " If the answer was " Yes," that was enough.

When Jackson became President he began, as we have seen, by making sweeping dismissals of the men who did not agree with him in politics. He filled their places with those — and those only — who voted as he thought right. In doing this he intended, as he said, to effect a great "reform " ; but his action established the "spoils system,"[1] which Webster, Clay, Calhoun, Benton, and other eminent statesmen denounced.

In fact, such a system seems to contradict sound business principles. If a bank should adopt it, and turn out the majority of its faithful officers and experienced clerks every few years only to put new and untried men in their places, we should say that it must fail — yes, we should go farther ; we should say it ought to fail. Many prominent men of all political parties think that the "spoils system " is just as great a mistake. They have labored in the past to free the Government from its influence, and they are determined to continue the good work.

**262. William Lloyd Garrison ; Dr. Channing ; the Anti-Slavery Movement.** — On New Year's Day, 1831, William Lloyd Garrison, then a "poor, unlearned young man," [2] published in Boston the first number of a paper called the *Liberator*. Mr. Garrison

---

[1] Because, in 1832, Senator Marcy of New York declared that "to the victors belong the spoils"; or, in other words, that the successful political party in an election have the right to make all they can out of it in the way of offices and salaries.

[2] See James Russell Lowell's poem " To W. L. Garrison," beginning, —

> " In a small chamber, friendless and unseen,
> Toiled o'er his types one poor, unlearned young man."

was its editor, owner, publisher, printer, and carrier. The *Liberator* demanded the " immediate and unconditional emancipation of every slave held in the United States."

Mr. Garrison was resolved to free the negro, even if he had to destroy the Union to do it.[1]

The Southern planters believed the editor of the new paper had lost his reason; most people at the North agreed with them.[2] Even many warm friends of the negro thought Mr. Garrison was wholly wrong in his methods. They felt as Dr. Channing did. That eminent man wrote to Daniel Webster, declaring that what we should say to the South was this : "We consider slavery as your calamity, not your crime ; and we will share with you the burden of putting an end to it."[3]

**263. Insurrection of Slaves in Virginia ; Mr. Garrison mobbed in Boston.** — It so happened that in the summer following the publication of the *Liberator*, a terrible negro insurrection broke out in Virginia. The slaves engaged in it massacred over sixty white men, women, and children. Many Southern people believed that Mr. Garrison's object was to stir up the negroes

---

[1] After laboring many years in the cause of emancipation, Mr. Garrison finally came to the conclusion that the Constitution of the United States upheld slavery, and that the dissolution of the Union, by depriving the South of the support of the North, would hasten the liberation of the slaves. In consequence of this conviction, he violently denounced the Constitution (in words taken from Isaiah xxviii. 15) as "a covenant with death and an agreement with hell." These words were then regularly printed at the top of the *Liberator* until the outbreak of the Civil War, when they were dropped.

[2] Mr. Garrison said that he found the prejudice and contempt of Northern men harder to deal with than that of the slaveholders. In an address to the public in the first number of the *Liberator* he used these words: "I am in earnest — I will not equivocate — I will not excuse — I will not retreat a single inch — and *I will be heard.*" See Life of W. L. Garrison, by his Children.

[3] See Dr. W. E. Channing's letter to Daniel Webster (Webster's Works), May 14, 1828. Dr. Channing proposed that the United States should appropriate the money from the sale of the public land, buy the slaves from their owners, and set them free. Could that have been done, it would have saved us from four years of civil war. England bought her West India slaves, and freed them, in 1833, at a cost of one hundred million dollars.

to rise and murder their masters.  There was not a grain of truth in the belief, but it spread at the South and powerfully increased the excitement.

In the North, Mr. Garrison's appeals in behalf of the freedom of the blacks roused almost equal excitement.  Gangs of "roughs" broke up meetings held to discuss emancipation, and on one occasion a howling mob dragged the editor of the *Liberator* through the streets of Boston with a rope round his body.  It was with great difficulty that the police saved his life.

These violent outbreaks were not made out of hatred to the negro, but out of fear that Mr. Garrison was putting the country in peril.  Many thoughtful men who were opposed to slavery believed that, on the whole, it was better to save the Union with slavery than to deliberately destroy it for the sake of liberating the negro.  Daniel Webster held that idea, and so, as we shall see later, did Abraham Lincoln.

**264.  Formation of Abolition Societies; Petition to Congress for Emancipation; what John Quincy Adams did.** — Mr. Garrison believed that he was right, and persisted in demanding the emancipation of the slaves, Union or no Union.  His influence spread.  In a few years nearly two thousand societies had been formed in the North for the abolition of slavery.

Then a flood of petitions began to pour into Congress, praying that the slaves held in the District of Columbia might be set free, and that the trade in slaves between the different Southern states might be stopped.

Congress finally passed resolutions refusing to receive such petitions.  John Quincy Adams, then a member of the House of Representatives, denounced these resolutions as "gag-rules," which forbade debate and were contrary to the Constitution.[1]

[1] On the right of the people to petition the government, see Amendment to the Constitution, No. I., page xvi; but compare the right of Congress to make rules for its proceedings, — Constitution, page viii, Section 5.

He insisted on presenting every petition that was sent to him, and sometimes offered two hundred or more in a single day, amid cries of "Treason!" and yells of "Put him out!" From this period the discussion of slavery never ceased until the North and the South took up arms to settle it on the battle-field.

265. The President puts an End to the United States Bank. — While the great question of emancipation was being hotly debated, the President was attacking the United States Bank.[1] He believed, as did Senator Benton of Missouri,[2] that it was badly managed and unsafe. For these reasons he refused to sign a bill[3] (1832) to renew the right of the bank to continue business. This refusal put an end to its existence in a short time. The year following this action the President removed nearly ten million dollars of the public money which the government had kept in the bank. This amount, with about thirty million dollars more, was deposited later (1836) in a number of small banks in the different states. Speculators borrowed large sums of this government money and used it to buy land; their course excited others, and soon people all over the country were crazy with wild schemes for getting suddenly rich.

266. South Carolina resists the Duty or Tax on Imported Goods. — The South was at this time strongly opposed to having heavy duties or taxes imposed on goods brought into the

[1] See Paragraph 202. The United States Bank obtained a new charter (or right to do business) in 1816, good for twenty years. Jackson refused to sign a bill granting it a charter to go on after 1836.

[2] Colonel Thomas H. Benton was one of the most decided opponents of the bank. He thought paper money was unsafe, and urged Congress to adopt gold and silver currency instead of bank bills. His able speeches on this subject of "hard money" got for him the nickname of "Old Bullion."

[3] Bill: a law proposed by Congress; except in certain cases, it requires the President's signature to make it complete. When he returns a bill unsigned he is said to *veto* it. See the Constitution, page ix, Section 7.

United States. The reason for this opposition was that the people of the South had never established manufactories in any number, and therefore had to buy their woollen and cotton cloth either from the Northern states, where large quantities were made, or from Europe. As labor was cheaper in Europe than in this country, the wealthy mill-owners in England could afford to make cloth, send it to the United States, and sell it at a much lower price than it could be made here. In order to prevent this, the manufacturers in the Northern states had obtained the passage of a law establishing a protective tariff ; that is, a heavy duty or tax levied on imported goods to protect the American manufacturer, and enable him to sell the same articles cheaper than a merchant bringing in foreign goods could afford to sell them after paying the duty.[1]

[1] From the outset a division of opinion existed in regard to the power of the government to levy duties. One party contended that, strictly interpreted, the Constitution did not give Congress authority to impose duties beyond what would be sufficient to defray the expenses of the government and furnish money for the payment of the national debt. This party demanded simply a Revenue Tariff. The opposite party held that the Constitution gave Congress the right to levy duties not only for revenue, but also to encourage the production of goods at home, as opposed to their purchase from foreign producers. This party advocated a Protective Tariff.

The first tariff had its origin as follows: When, after the adoption of the Constitution, the new government went into operation, Congress found the national treasury empty. The great question was how to obtain a revenue. Finally, after prolonged discussion, an act was passed (1789) which imposed a moderate duty on certain imported articles. The object of this tariff, as stated by the act, was "for the support of the government, for the discharge of the debts of the United States, and the encouragement and protection of manufacturers." Later, after we had begun to manufacture goods quite largely, many people came to believe that we ought to impose a protective tariff which would levy a heavy tax on foreign goods, similar to those we were making, and thus encourage buyers to purchase those made here rather than pay a much higher price for the imported articles. Such a protective tariff was imposed in 1816, and again in 1824, 1828, 1832, and 1842.

In 1846 England began to let in our products free, or nearly so. From that date until the Civil War, in 1861, we took off our protective duties, and levied only a small tax for revenue. During the war we again put on a very heavy tax, in order to raise all the money we could to carry on the war. Since peace was declared, efforts have been made (1865–1899) to reduce the tariff to a lower rate, by those who believe that free trade between nations is, in the end, for the advantage of all.

JOHN C. CALHOUN.

267. **John C. Calhoun ; Nullification ;** [1] **Preparations for War.** —
John C. Calhoun [2] of South Carolina, who was then Vice-
President, protested against this "Tariff of Abominations,"
as he called it.  He asserted that it compelled the South to
pay such a price for cloth and other goods that the people
were constantly growing poorer, while the Northern manufacturers, on the other hand, were getting rich at their expense.
He therefore demanded free trade.  To this the North answered that free trade would ruin the factory-owners and
compel them to close their factories.  Congress refused to
abolish the protective tariff.  Then the feeling of opposition
grew so hot in South Carolina that the people declared through
a state convention that, after February 1, 1833, they would not
pay duties on goods imported into Charleston from Europe.
They considered that every state had the right to refuse to
obey a law which it believed to be contrary to the Constitution.[3]  This refusal was called *nullification*.  In Charleston
preparations were made to resist the collection of the duty.
Governor Hayne, of South Carolina, threatened that if the
government used force, his state would secede or withdraw
from the Union and declare itself independent.

268. **Webster's Reply to Hayne and Calhoun ; what we owe to
Webster.** — When, in the Senate of the United States, Governor Hayne (1830) boldly upheld the right of nullification,

1 Nullification : the refusal of a state to obey a law enacted by Congress, on the
ground that the law objected to is a violation of the Constitution.

2 John C. Calhoun, born in Abbeville district, South Carolina, 1782 ; died 1850.
Like Jackson, he was of Scotch-Irish descent.  He entered Congress in 1810.  He was
elected Vice-President in 1824 and in 1828.  In 1832 he resigned his office, and was
chosen U. S. Senator.  He was at first a supporter of a protective tariff, but later became
a strong advocate of free trade.  He was one of the few leading men who taught that
slavery is "a positive good," an advantage alike to the negro and to his owner.  His
nature was "as great as it was pure."  Webster, his chief political opponent, said of
him that nothing "low or meanly selfish came near the head or the heart of Mr.
Calhoun."

3 This was the doctrine of "State-Rights" (see Paragraph 210) ; but the Constitution expressly established the Supreme Court to settle all such disputes.

Daniel Webster [1] replied to him, closing with the well-known words : "Liberty and Union, now and forever, one and inseparable." Later, when Calhoun in the United States Senate defended the right of secession, Webster made a powerful speech, in which he declared that "there can be no secession without revolution." He saw that if a state is resolved to leave the Union, the national government, sword in hand, must insist that it shall remain in its place and obey the laws.

We owe an immense debt to Webster's commanding eloquence on this subject. In the remarkable series of speeches which he delivered at this period (1830–1833), he made Americans realize the inestimable value and sacredness of the Union as they had never felt it before. When, thirty years later, the Civil War threatened to destroy the nation, the reverence for the Constitution and the Union with which that great statesman had inspired so many hearts, made thousands willing to die to save it. The North and the South are now one. All discord has passed away, and as brothers we can join in honoring the memory of Daniel Webster for his services to our common country.

**269. Jackson's Fidelity to the Union ; his Orders to General Scott ; Henry Clay obtains a New Tariff.** — President Jackson had the same feeling that Webster had of the necessity of preserving the Union. He did not like the tariff, but he was resolved to enforce it so long as it remained law. He saw that what was called the doctrine of "State-Rights," that is, the

---

[1] Daniel Webster, born at Salisbury, New Hampshire, 1782 (see note 1, page 98) ; died at his residence at Marshfield, near Boston, 1852. He graduated at Dartmouth College, and began the practice of law in 1805. In 1812 he was elected to Congress, and again in 1822. From this time forward he was constantly in public life, as representative, senator, or in the Cabinet. He was unquestionably the greatest orator this country has produced, and as a statesman he stood second to none. His defence of the Union in his second reply to Hayne, January 26–27, 1830, has been called "the most remarkable speech ever made in the American Congress." Webster's "Reply to Calhoun" was delivered February 16, 1833.

DANIEL WEBSTER.

so-called right of a state to decide for itself when it would obey Congress and when it would not, was destructive of all government.

The Union, said he, is at present like a bag of meal with both ends open. Whichever way you try to handle it, you will spill the meal. " I must tie the bag and save the country."

So saying, the President ordered General Scott (1832) to go forthwith to Charleston and enforce the law. It was done, and the duties on imported goods in that city were collected as usual.

A few months later (1833) Henry Clay, the "great peace-maker," succeeded in getting Congress to adopt a new tariff more acceptable to the South. The country could well afford to reduce its taxes on foreign goods, for we did not owe one dollar of public debt. Every claim against the government had been paid.

**270. Growth of the Country; Extension of Railroads and Canals; Use of Coal; the Express System.** — With the exception of a very destructive fire in New York City (1835), Jackson's presidency was a period of great prosperity, and of rapid growth for the entire country, but especially for the West. Canals had been opened, steamboats were running on the Great Lakes and the Western rivers, and the whistle of the locomotive was beginning to be heard beyond the Alleghanies. Arkansas and the rapidly growing territory of Michigan were admitted to the Union (1836–1837), making twenty-six states in all.

Both hard and soft coal[1] had been found in immense quantities in Pennsylvania, and they were now coming into use for manufacturing as well as for other purposes.

The increased activity of the country, in connection with steamboats and railroads, gave rise to a new enterprise. A

[1] Hard or anthracite coal was not discovered until 1790. The first load taken to Philadelphia, in 1803, was used as stone to mend roads with. This bed of Pennsylvania hard coal has been worth more to the country than all the gold mines of California.

young man named Harnden[1] conceived the plan of making a business of carrying parcels between Boston and New York, and shortly after (1839) began it.   At first a small hand-bag

Chicago in 1833.

was sufficient to hold all the articles sent.   In that humble way he laid the foundation of the American express system, which now extends to every town of the United States, and employs millions of money and an army of men to do its work.

**271.  Indian Wars ; Growth of the West ; Chicago.** — The increased growth of the country alarmed Black Hawk, a famous Indian chief at the West, and he (1832), at the head of a large body of Indians, attempted to prevent emigrants from taking possession of public lands in the state of Illinois and the territories of Iowa and Wisconsin.   He was defeated and driven beyond the Mississippi. The removal of the Indians beyond that river greatly encouraged emigration to the Western states and territories.

Chicago To-Day.

Shortly after this a second Seminole[2] war began (1835) in Florida.  The Indians were led by Osceola, a celebrated chief, who had been badly treated by the whites.   The war lasted

---

[1] William Frederick Harnden was born in Reading, Massachusetts, in 1813; died 1845.  On his monument, erected at Mount Auburn cemetery, near Boston, by the " Express Companies of the United States," he is called the " Founder of the Express Business in America."

[2] On the Seminoles see Paragraph 238.

nearly seven years. The Indians were defeated by Colonel Zachary Taylor, and were finally conquered, and, all but a few, sent west of the Mississippi by General Worth. The war cost nearly $40,000,000.

On the southwestern shore of Lake Michigan stood Fort Dearborn. It was garrisoned by a small number of soldiers, and around the fort a dozen white settlers, with their families, had built as many rude wooden houses. Two years later (1833), the little settlement took the name of Chicago.[1] It had then grown to be a town of between five and six hundred inhabitants, and some of its people were bold enough to think that it might grow to be still larger. To-day the city has more than a million of inhabitants, and stands the great metropolis of the Northwest.

272. **American Art, Books, and Newspapers.** — America had already produced five eminent painters — West, Copley, Stuart,[2] Trumbull,[3] and Allston.[4] We also had three noted writers. They were Cooper, the novelist, who wrote exciting tales of life on the sea and in the wilderness; Bryant, our first great poet; and Washington Irving, the author of "Rip Van Winkle" and of scores more of delightful stories.

But when Jackson was first elected, a book had just been published (1828) in this country which was in one respect more remarkable than any that had yet appeared, for it contained the whole English language.[5] This was Webster's Dic-

[1] Chicago: an Indian name originally given to the Chicago River. It is supposed to be the name of the god of thunder; but on this point authorities differ.

[2] See Stuart's portrait of Washington (frontispiece).

[3] Thomas Cole was another noted artist of a somewhat later period, but he was not an American by birth.

[4] Born in South Carolina, 1779, died in Cambridge, Massachusetts, 1843.

[5] The best English dictionary before Webster's was Johnson's, first published in London in 1755. It had not really been revised for seventy years, and was very unsatisfactory to Americans, since it did not contain many familiar American words, such as "congress" (in the sense of a national legislature), "savings-bank," "prairie," and hundreds of others. Webster thought that America had as good a right to coin new words as England had. He accordingly included these words in his dictionary; in his definitions he was generally far superior to Johnson.

tionary, by Noah Webster of Connecticut. It had cost the author and compiler nearly twenty years of almost continuous labor, and it was destined to make his name and work known in every schoolhouse of the United States.

Following Webster came the poets Whittier, Longfellow, Holmes, Lowell, and Poe; Emerson, with his wonderful essays on nature; Hawthorne, with his stories of New England; Audubon, with his magnificent work on the "Birds of America";[1] Bancroft, with his history of the United States, followed by the historians Prescott, Motley, and Parkman. It was the beginning of American literature.[2]

About the same time (1833) the first cheap newspaper ever published, which sold for one cent,[3] appeared in New York. From that time forward the poorest man could afford to carry home in his pocket at night a daily history of the world's doings.

**273. Summary.** — Six important events marked the administration of Andrew Jackson. They were: 1. The beginning of the system of removals from government offices for political reasons; 2. The commencement of the anti-slavery movement by William Lloyd Garrison; 3. The overthrow of the United States Bank; 4. The "nullification" of acts of Congress by South Carolina; 5. Indian wars in the West and South; 6. The rise of American literature and of cheap newspapers.

### MARTIN VAN BUREN.[4]

**274. Van Buren's Administration (Eighth President, One Term, 1837–1841); Business Failures; Financial Panic.** — In his fare-

---

[1] Audubon (Aw′du-bon), born in Louisiana, 1780.

[2] For interesting examples of poems connected with American history, see Whittier's "Laus Deo" and "Our State," Longfellow's "Paul Revere's Ride," Holmes's "Grandmother's Story of Bunker Hill," Lowell's "Present Crisis," Emerson's "Concord Hymn," and Bryant's "Song of Marion's Men."

[3] The *New York Daily Sun*, 1833.

[4] Martin Van Buren was born in New York in 1782; died in 1862. He was United States Senator from 1821–1828; governor of New York later, and Secretary of State

well address, President Jackson had said, "I leave this great
people prosperous and happy." But Mr. Van Buren had
scarcely entered upon the duties of his office, in 1837, when
a large business house in New Orleans failed. It was the
beginning of a panic [1] in trade and money matters which swept
over the country like the waters of a destroying flood.

In ten days, one hundred merchants in New York City had
lost everything; and within two months, the total business
failures in that city reached the enormous sum of one hundred millions of dollars. Next, the banks began to fail; and
the difficulty of getting gold or silver became so great that
even the United States government had to pay the army and
navy in paper money, which, if it chanced to be good to-day,
might be worthless to-morrow. John Quincy Adams declared
that, "without a dollar of national debt, we are in the midst
of national bankruptcy."

**275. Stoppage of Trade; Distress among Workmen; Failures of
States; Causes of the Panic.** — Soon factories and mills stopped
running, and nearly all trade came to a standstill. Thousands
of workmen were suddenly thrown out of employment, and
saw no way of earning bread for themselves and their families.

Many states had borrowed large sums of money in Europe
for the purpose of building roads, canals, and railways. In
1830, the total debt of this kind was only thirteen millions;
in seven years it had risen to nearly two hundred millions.
It was exceedingly difficult, if not impossible for a number

under Jackson, 1829–1831. In 1836 he was elected President (R. M. Johnson of Kentucky, Vice-President) by the Democratic party, over General W. H. Harrison, the
Whig candidate.

[1] Panic: sudden fright or alarm — particularly alarm without any real cause.
Such periods occur in business from time to time, especially after several years of
great activity and speculation ending in reckless investments and loss. The chief
cause of a panic appears to be want of confidence. When men cease to put trust in
each other, then the trouble begins. There may be as much money in the country as
before; but it has shifted into the hands of a few, and they are afraid to use it
themselves, or to let others use it. The consequence is that prices fall, business stops
in great measure, and much distress is produced.

of these states[1] to raise money to meet the interest; and one positively refused to pay anything whatever, whether interest or principal.

There were three chief causes for this desperate state of things. 1. After the United States Bank[2] had ceased to exist, a great number of worthless banks sprang into existence; 2. the ease with which people could borrow money led to wide speculation in land; men eagerly bought town lots at enormous prices, in the backwoods of Maine; and speculated in property in so-called Western "cities" that had no existence except on paper, or that were six feet under water; 3. the government suddenly called in the gold and silver which it had deposited in certain state banks, — nicknamed "pet banks," — and at the same time it refused to sell any more public land except for hard cash. This suddenly checked the fever of speculation, and made every one anxious to get coin at a time when coin was not to be had. The result was, property of all kinds fell in price, men could neither collect debts nor pay them, the banks could not redeem[3] their bills, and the crash came.[4]  After a time confidence began to be restored, business sprang up, and a new period of prosperity commenced.

**276. The Government establishes an Independent Treasury.** — This panic in business had at least one good result. Up to this time, the national government had never taken entire

---

[1] Seven states — Arkansas, Illinois, Indiana, Louisiana, Maryland, Michigan, Pennsylvania, and Florida, then a territory, — suspended payment of interest. Mississippi repudiated her entire debt on the ground that it had been incurred in violation of the state constitution.  Sydney Smith's "Letters on American Debts," Dickens's "American Notes" and "Martin Chuzzlewit" show how sore the English creditors felt about these failures.          [2] See Paragraph 265.

[3] A bank is said to redeem its bills when, on demand, it pays gold or silver for them.  If it cannot do this, its bills are worthless.

[4] During this period a rebellion broke out in Canada, and many Americans living on the border were eager to take part in it, with the hope of annexing Canada to the United States.  The President's proclamation of neutrality compelled them to keep quiet.

charge of its own money, but had let one or more banks have the care of it. The disastrous failure of these "pet banks" taught Congress a lesson; and the United States now established (1840) an independent treasury [1] at Washington, with branches, known as sub-treasuries,[2] in the chief cities. In this way the government was protected against loss. We owe this excellent system mainly to President Van Buren.

**277. Rise of the Mormons; Nauvoo.** — Toward the close of Van Buren's presidency, a new religious community, called Mormons, settled in Illinois. Its founder was Joseph Smith, a native of Vermont.[3] While living in New York he declared that an angel from heaven gave him a number of golden plates — like sheets of tin — on which a new scripture was written called the "Book of Mormon."[4]

Smith went to Ohio, to Missouri, and, finally, to Illinois, where he and his followers — the "Latter Day Saints" or Mormons — built the "Holy City" of Nauvoo [5] on the banks of the Mississippi. There he stated that he received a revela-

---

[1] The independent treasury system was, however, not fully and finally established until 1846. During the Civil War (1863) a great many new banks were created. These give security (by the deposit of government bonds at Washington) to the United States for the bills they issue; for this reason they are called National Banks. The government has the right to deposit public money (except that received for duties) in these banks, as well as in the treasury.

[2] Sub-treasuries: from the Latin word *sub*, meaning under; hence, subordinate, or smaller treasuries. The chief treasury is in the Treasury Building at Washington; the sub-treasuries are in (1) New York, (2) Philadelphia, (3) Chicago, (4) Boston, (5) St. Louis, (6) Cincinnati, (7) San Francisco, (8) New Orleans, (9) Baltimore.

[3] Joseph Smith was born in 1805 in Sharon, Vt., and was murdered at Carthage, Ill., in 1844. While living near Manchester, N. Y., in 1827, he states that the angel gave him the golden plates of the Book of Mormon. The plates, he says, were written in an unknown tongue, but he alleges that the angel provided him with a peculiar kind of glasses by which to read and translate them. The Mormons declare, "We believe the Bible to be the Word of God, so far as it is translated correctly; we also believe the Book of Mormon to be the Word of God."

[4] Mormon: a name derived from that of the alleged writer of the Book of Mormon, a Jew, who, as the Mormons believe, lived in this country about a thousand years before Columbus discovered it.

[5] Nauvoo: meaning the Beautiful City; it had, it is said, no idlers and no drunkards.

tion from God declaring that every true Mormon marriage would last forever, and sanctioning the marriage of more than one wife by those deemed worthy. Those, said he,[1] who keep this law will, in the next world, "pass by the angels" in glory.[2]

Shortly after this, several persons who had belonged to the Mormons began publishing a paper in Nauvoo, in which they accused Smith of leading an evil life. Smith broke up the paper. For this he was arrested, and while in jail at Carthage (1844) was shot by a mob who had no faith in him or his religion.

**278. Emigration of the Mormons to Utah; what they have accomplished there.** — Brigham Young of Vermont — a man as keen-sighted in the things of this world as it was said Smith had been in those of the other — now became leader of the Mormons; but the people round Nauvoo forced the "Saints" to leave, and they crossed the Mississippi. In 1847 Young started for the far west, and, with about a hundred and fifty followers, reached Salt Lake, in what is now Utah. Later, he led a much larger number of Mormon emigrants to the same place. It was a journey of fifteen hundred miles through the wilderness. The country bordering on the lake was a desert. The hunters of that desolate region predicted that the Mormons would starve. But Young saw what could be done to prevent that. He set his company to work digging ditches to bring water from the mountains; every street in the village had two of these ditches running through the length of it, one on each side. The abundant supply of water soon made the dead, dry soil green with waving crops of wheat and corn. Industry transformed the desert into a garden.

---

[1] But a very small number of Mormons have ever married more than one wife.

[2] This doctrine (see the Mormon "Book of Covenants and Doctrine") was not fully published to the world until 1852. One branch of the Mormons — the "Josephites" — deny that Smith ever taught the doctrine, but say it was invented by Brigham Young and others.

Since then the Mormons have prospered and grown strong. Many non-Mormons, also, attracted by climate and resources, have taken residence there.   The village has become a city and the territory a state with a population of about 250,000.[1]

**279. Emigration to the United States ; Ocean Steamships ; Growth of the West.** — While the Mormons were getting a foothold in the far West, an immense emigration from Europe to the United States had begun.   A regular line of steamships was established between Liverpool and Boston in 1840,[2] and, soon after, similar communication was established with New York.   By means of these steamers, and of lines of passenger vessels, emigrants now began to pour in at the rate of over three thousand a week; and in the course of the next ten years (1840–1850) nearly two millions had come to settle here — or almost twice as many as had landed in this country during the preceding forty years.   Since then the stream of emigrants has never ceased, and the whole number who have thus become American citizens is estimated at nearly twenty millions.[3]

A very large part of these emigrants went West, where the rich prairie lands could be converted into farms with but little labor.   Then again that comparatively level and treeless region stimulated the rapid building of railroads, which did a great work in helping to fill the country with settlers.

[1] In 1887 the Edmunds-Tucker law was passed, declaring the property of the Mormon church forfeited to the United States for violation of the laws of Congress against polygamy.   The Supreme Court in 1890 sustained the law of 1887; the church then declared that it would obey the United States law in relation to plural marriages.   Utah adopted a constitution prohibiting polygamy and entered the Union in 1896.

[2] The first English steamships which came here were the *Sirius* and the *Great Western ;* they arrived at New York in 1838.   Sir Samuel Cunard, son of Abraham Cunard, a Philadelphia merchant, established the first regular line (between Liverpool and Boston) in 1840.

[3] The Irish famine in 1845–6 was one cause of this unusual increase of emigration.   Ireland, Germany, and England sent the greatest number of emigrants.

**280. Summary.** — This period began with a disastrous panic in trade by which great numbers were ruined ; it was followed by the establishment by the government of the independent treasury system; then came the movement of the Mormons to Utah, and vastly increased emigration from Europe to the United States.

### WILLIAM HENRY HARRISON AND JOHN TYLER.

**281. Harrison and Tyler's Administrations (Ninth and Tenth Presidents, One Term, 1841–1845); how Harrison was elected ; his Death.** — General Harrison,[1] "the hero of Tippecanoe," was elected President amidst the wildest excitement. The Democrats had carried the day for forty years ;[2] now their opponents, the Whigs,[3] were to be victors. Harrison was then living on his farm, in a clearing on the banks of the Ohio. He was popularly known as "the Log-Cabin candidate." The farmers of the West gathered to his support with a will. They had monster out-door meetings, and processions miles long,[4] in which a log-cabin on wheels was always a conspicuous object, with its live coon fastened on the roof, and its barrel of

---

[1] William Henry Harrison was born in Virginia in 1773. His father, Benjamin Harrison, was one of the signers of the Declaration of Independence. From 1801 to 1813 Harrison was governor of what was then the territory of Indiana. In 1811 he defeated the Indians in a great battle at Tippecanoe, Indiana (see Paragraph 225). During the war of 1812 he was appointed a major-general in the regular army. Later, he returned to his farm at North Bend, on the Ohio, near Cincinnati. In 1840 he was elected President (John Tyler of Virginia, Vice-President) by the Whig party, by an immense majority over Van Buren, the Democratic candidate.

[2] Since the election of Jefferson in 1800.

[3] The Whigs wished (1) to have the government carry on the building of canals, roads, and other internal improvements; (2) to protect manufactures by a high tariff; (3) to re-establish the United States Bank, and part of the Whigs wished to restrict the extension of slavery. The Democrats held that each state should make its own improvements; that free trade was better than protection; that an independent treasury was better than a United States bank; and that the slavery question should be left to the people of the different states.

[4] This was the beginning of our modern presidential "campaigns," with their bands of music and torchlight processions.

hard cider standing handy by the open door.   The enthusiasm increased more and more as election day drew near ; the rousing song of " Tippecanoe and Tyler too " stirred the blood of every true Whig ; and, with shouts of exultation, the Whigs triumphed, and the occupant of the Ohio log-cabin entered the White House at Washington.

. A month later, President Harrison died, and the joy of his friends was suddenly changed into mourning.   Vice-President Tyler, who was practically a Democrat,[1] now became President ;[2] and he and the Whig Congress were soon quarrelling over political questions about which there was no chance of their coming to any agreement.

282. The Dorr Rebellion ; the Webster-Ashburton Treaty ; the Anti-Renters. — In Rhode Island, the right to vote was confined to persons holding real estate, and to their eldest sons. Newport, where there were many land-holders, had six representatives in the state legislature, while Providence, with a population nearly three times as great, had only four.   The party in favor of reform finally framed a new constitution, and elected (1842) Thomas W. Dorr for governor.   The opposite, or state government party, headed by Governor King, denied Dorr's right to hold office.   Both sides took up arms, but no blood was spilt, and nobody was even hurt.   Dorr was arrested and thrown into prison, but was released a few years later, and lived to see his party successful in the reform they had attempted.

In the summer of 1842, Daniel Webster, representing the United States, and Lord Ashburton, representing Great Britain, settled the question of the boundary between Maine and Canada, by an agreement known as the Webster-Ashburton

---

[1] Tyler was in most respects a Democrat, though he had acted, to some extent, with the Whigs.  The Whigs nominated him to the Vice-Presidency in order to secure Southern votes, and thus make sure of electing Harrison.

[2] In case of the death of the President, the Constitution provides that the Vice-President shall succeed him.  See the Constitution, page xii ; see, too, page 369.

Treaty.[1] The dispute in regard to the true line between the two countries had been very bitter, and threatened to bring on war; for this reason the friendly settlement of the controversy was of the greatest advantage to both England and America.[2]

In New York, the tenants of the Van Rensselaer family, on the Hudson,[3] refused to pay rent for their farms, on the ground that the Revolution had swept away the old Dutch methods of letting land. It became necessary to call out a military force to protect the sheriff in his attempts to collect the rents; finally, a political party was formed (1843), favoring the anti-renters,[4] and a change was made (1846) in the state constitution for their benefit.

### 283. The Electric Telegraph; Dr. Morton's Discovery. — In the spring of 1844, travellers from Baltimore to Washington saw a force of men engaged in putting up several lines of copper wire on a row of lofty poles extending between the two cities. It was the first telegraph line erected in the United States, or in the world. After four years of weary waiting, Professor Morse[5] had at length got a grant of thirty thousand dollars from Congress, for the purpose of proving that a message could be sent by electricity a distance of forty miles!

On the morning of May 24, 1844, Professor Morse took his

[1] During the progress of the negotiation of the treaty, Mr. Webster practically settled another question of equal importance, by his formal declaration to Lord Ashburton, that in future the United States would insist that our flag should protect our vessels against the so-called " right of search," on the part of Great Britain; and that any attempt to make such search would be considered by us a reason for war. See further on this treaty, page 265, note 1.

[2] See " Table of Boundaries."          [3] See Paragraph 63.

[4] Anti-renters: from the Latin word *anti*, against; hence, those opposed to paying the rent demanded by the proprietors of the land.

[5] Samuel F. B. Morse was born in Charlestown, Mass., 1791; died in New York, 1872. He became an artist, and, in 1830, Professor of the Literature of the Arts of Design in the University of the City of New York. He conceived the idea of the electric telegraph in 1832. Later, his associate, Mr. Alfred Vail of N. J., rendered very important services in perfecting the work. See *Century Mag.*, April, 1888.

seat at the telegraphic instrument placed in the Supreme Court Room in the Capitol.   Many of the chief officers of the government were present.   The professor pressed the key of the instrument with his finger.   In an instant, the waiting operator at Baltimore received the message, and it was sent back to the Capitol.   Here it is:

In a minute of time these words had traversed a circuit of eighty miles.   When they were read in the Court Room a thrill of awe ran through those who reverently listened ; it seemed as though the finger of God, not man, had written the message.[2]

In 1871, at a celebration held in New York in honor of Professor Morse, the original instrument invented by him was exhibited, connected, at that moment, by wire, with every one of the ten thousand instruments then in use in this country. At a signal, a message from the inventor was sent vibrating throughout the United States, and was simultaneously read in every city and in most towns of the republic, from New York to New Orleans, from New Orleans to San Francisco.

Thought had conquered space ; it was to make its next conquest in a wholly different direction.   While Professor Morse was building the first telegraph line, Dr. W. T. G. Morton of Boston, acting on the suggestion of Dr. Charles T. Jackson, was endeavoring to produce artificial sleep by the breathing of the vapor of ether.   He believed that, if successful, all suffering under the surgeon's knife would be at an end.   He did suc-

[1] The characters over the printed letters represent the letters of the telegraphic alphabet.   The words are quoted from the Bible; Numbers xxiii. 23.

[2] Before the completion of the first line of telegraph, Professor Morse wrote to a friend (1843) : " Telegraphic communication may with certainty be established across the Atlantic Ocean.   Startling as this may now seem, I am confident the time will come when this project will be realized."   He lived to see it accomplished in 1858, and permanently in 1866.

ceed; and shortly after (1846), the great fact was made known to the world by tests made at the Massachusetts Hospital in Boston.   As the inscription on Dr. Morton's monument truthfully declares: "Before that discovery, surgery was agony; since, science has controlled pain."[1]

**284. Annexation of Texas.** — The great political question of the times was the admission of Texas.   Many years before this period, Stephen F. Austin, General Sam Houston, with other Americans, had settled in that country, — then a part of Mexico, — and had finally, by force of arms, made it an independent republic.   That republic now asked to be annexed to the United States.   A powerful party at the South was anxious to obtain it for the purpose of making a number of new slave states, and thus maintaining their influence in Congress.[2]   The Anti-Slavery party at the North strongly opposed the annexation;[3] but Congress, after much debate, decided to make it. Thus, in the spring of 1845, we obtained a territory so vast that, as Daniel Webster said, a bird could not fly over it in a week—a territory large enough to make nearly five countries the size of England, or more than that number of states, each larger than New York.

[1] Dr. Horace Wells, of Hartford, began to make use (1844) of nitrous oxide gas as an anæsthetic in the extraction of teeth.   Between 1820 and 1846 there were invented in this country: 1. Blanchard's Eccentric Lathe for turning gun-stocks and other irregular forms; 2. McCormick's Reaper and Mower; Hussey's Reaper and Mower; 3. Colt's Revolver; 4. Ericsson's Screw Propeller; 5. Goodyear's Hard Rubber goods; 6. Hoe's Steam Printing-Press; 7. Howe's Sewing-Machine.

The following inventions came from abroad: 1. Knitting Machines.   2. Planing Machines (greatly improved in 1828 by Woodworth).   3. Friction Matches, 1836 (gas had been introduced in 1822).   4. The Steam Fire Engine, 1841, but not brought into practical use until much later.   5. The Daguerreotype and Photograph, 1843. 6. The Diving-Dress, 1843.   On earlier American inventions, see page 201, note 1.

[2] By the Missouri Compromise (see Paragraph 243) slavery could not be extended west of the Mississippi, outside of Missouri, north of 36° 30′ (the southern boundary of Missouri).   Unless, therefore, the South got more territory annexed southwest of the Mississippi, the North would soon have the chief power in Congress.

[3] James Russell Lowell's fine poem, "The Present Crisis," expresses the feeling of the Anti-Slavery party at this time.

**285. Summary.** — The principal events of the Harrison and Tyler administrations were: (1) The death of the President; followed (2) by the Webster-Ashburton Treaty; (3) the Dorr Rebellion; (4) the opening of the first line of electric telegraph in the United States or the world; (5) the use of ether in surgery; and (6) the annexation of Texas.

## James K. Polk.

**286. Polk's Administration (Eleventh President, One Term, 1845–1849); the Question of the Possession of Oregon.** — Congress had decided to annex Texas;[1] and, when Mr. Polk[2] entered office, the first question was, what should be done about Oregon.[3] We claimed the whole country west of the Rocky Mountains, north of California (then a part of Mexico), to Alaska; that is, from parallel 42° to 54° 40'. Our claim rested on: 1. Gray's discovery of the Columbia[4] (1792); 2. Lewis and Clark's exploration (1805–1806); 3. Settlements begun by Astor (1811); 4. Treaty with Spain (1819). But England insisted that the northern part of Oregon, including the Columbia River, belonged to her; and the Hudson Bay Company hoped that the whole region would be kept a wilderness where they could hunt wild animals for the fur trade. Since 1818 Great Britain and the United States had held the disputed territory by a treaty of joint occupation.

**287. Dr. Whitman's Journey to Oregon.** — It is quite probable that the English might have got it, had it not been for the energy of Dr. Marcus Whitman of New York, who had gone as a missionary to Walla Walla[5] nine years before. He

---

[1] See Paragraph 284.

[2] James K. Polk (pronounced Poke) was born in North Carolina, 1795; died, 1849. He emigrated with his father to Tennessee in 1806; and was elected governor of that state in 1839. In 1844 he was elected President by the Democrats (George M. Dallas of Pennsylvania, Vice-President), over Henry Clay, the Whig candidate.

[3] See Paragraphs 216, 238.          [4] See note 3, on page 210.

[5] Walla Walla: now in the state of Washington, near the Oregon boundary.

went out with a wagon in which he took his bride. The English, who were alarmed at this resolute attempt of Dr. Whitman's to open up a passage on wheels to the country they
coveted, told him that his wagon would be broken to splinters
in crossing the mountains. Whitman and his young wife persisted in going on, and after many formidable upsets and
breakages they finally reached their destination, though the
wagon had to be left at Fort Boisé,[1] and brought on later.
The Indians, who had never seen a wagon before, looked on
in admiration ; they called it "chick-chick-shani-le-kai-kash,"
because, said they, it used to go "chick-chick" over the soft
grass, but "*kai-kash !*" when it struck the rocks.

**288. Dr. Whitman's Journey to the East ; how we got Oregon ;
the Treaty.** — In the autumn of 1842 Dr. Whitman resolved
to visit the East, for the double purpose of getting help for
his mission and of inducing emigrants to go out to Oregon.
It was a journey of between three and four thousand miles,
and the doctor's sufferings on the way were terrible. He had
to face winter storms in the mountains, the terrors of starvation and of attacks by Indians. But his indomitable will
kept him up and in five months he reached Boston. A small
band of emigrants had already gone out, and in the spring of
1843 a second company numbering about a thousand started
for the Columbia. Their determination was to found a new
state on the Pacific coast. Dr. Whitman went as guide to
the advance party of this great emigration. By his help they
reached the land they were seeking.[2] These men, with those
who followed, saved Oregon. By the time that Polk became
President we had such a strong hold on the territory that the
cry in 1846 was, "The British must go " — " The whole of
Oregon, or none " — " Fifty-four-forty, or fight ! " [3] But later

---

[1] Now Boizé (Boi'se) City, Idaho.    [2] See H. H. Bancroft's "Oregon," I.,
chapter xv; Blaine's "Congress," I. 55; Benton's "Thirty Years' View," II. 469;
Prof. E. G. Bourne's Historical Essays; *Am. Hist. Review*, January, 1901.

[3] In other words, we insisted that the British must give up the entire country
below 54° 40', or fight. Our claim to the territory, through Captain Gray's discovery

in the same year (1846) the United States and Great Britain made a treaty by which they agreed to divide the country between them. We took the portion between the boundary

of upper Mexico (now California), or 42°, and the parallel of 49° north, including the Columbia River; the English took the remainder, from 49°,[1] to Alaska. Our part included what is now the state of Oregon, with Washington and Idaho, and parts of Wyoming and Montana — a territory so

immense that if a map of it be placed on that of the eastern coast, it would reach from New York to Florida, and extend westward nearly to the Tennessee River, covering in all about two hundred and fifty-five thousand square miles.

**289. The Mexican War; Battles of Palo Alto and Resaca de la Palma.** — But though the Oregon Treaty settled the fact that we should not fight with Great Britain, yet we were soon at war with our next-door neighbor, the feeble republic of Mexico. Texas had been admitted as a state (1845), but the western boundary was a matter of dispute. Texas insisted that the line was at the Rio Grande [2] River; Mexico denied this, and

of the Columbia River, Lewis and Clark's expedition (see Paragraphs 216; 238, note 5), settlements, and Spanish Treaty, 1819, was better than that of the English.

[1] By the Webster-Ashburton Treaty (see Paragraph 282 and Table of Boundaries) the boundary line west, between the Lake of the Woods, Minnesota, and the Rocky Mountains, was fixed at the forty-ninth parallel (as by treaty of 1818). The treaty of 1846 extended that line through to the Pacific. The boundary is marked by mounds, heaps of stones, posts, and cast-iron pillars; the pillars are placed a mile apart.

[2] Rio Grande (Spanish pronunciation, Ree'ō Grăn'day; but it is better to pronounce it as English). Texas also claimed an immense territory on the Northwest, extending to the forty-second parallel.

declared that it was on the Nueces[1] River, about a hundred miles east of the Rio Grande.

The President commanded General Taylor to seize the strip of land between the rivers.    To quote General Grant's words, our troops were sent there "to provoke a fight."[2]   Mexico

SCALE OF MILES
0   50  100   200   300

was weak, but not cowardly.   The Mexican government ordered Taylor to leave the eastern bank of the Rio Grande, where he held Fort Brown. He refused, and the Mexicans crossed the river (April 24, 1846),* and shed the first blood.[3]   Soon after, General Taylor — or "Old Rough and Ready," as his men called him — gained the victory in the battle of Palo Alto (May 8, 1846);[4] and the next day (May 9), that of Resaca de la Palma.[5]   The Mexicans now retreated across the Rio Grande, and Taylor followed them, and took possession of the town of Matamoras.[6]

**290. Congress declares War; Battles of Monterey and Buena Vista; Conquest of California and New Mexico.** — Congress now (May 13, 1846) declared war against Mexico, and thousands of volunteers, mainly from the Southern and Southwestern States, enlisted to fight against her.

In the autumn (September 24, 1846) General Taylor attacked the Mexicans at Monterey, and took the town after a desperate battle of four days.[7]   Early the next year, Santa Anna, the

---

[1] Nueces (Nwā'sĕs; but pronounce as in English).

[2] See " Personal Memoirs of U. S. Grant," I. 68.

[3] The blood was shed on territory claimed by Mexico; but the President's message stated that it had been spilt on "*our own territory*." Abraham Lincoln, then in Congress, demanded, in a series of resolutions, known as the "Spot" resolutions, to be informed where the exact "spot" of this bloodshed was, and whether it had not been provoked by a body of armed Americans sent there by order of our government.                    [4] Palo Alto (Pah'lo Al'to, or High Trees).

[5] Resaca de la Palma (Ra-sah'ka da-lah Pal'mah, the Ravine of the Palm tree).

[6] Matamoras (Mat'a-mo'ras).   * See Polk's Message to Congress, May 11, 1846.

[7] See Hoffman's poem of "Monterey" in "Heroic Ballads," published by Ginn & Co.

Mexican president and commander-in-chief, led a force of twenty thousand men against Taylor, who had only about a fourth of that number. The battle was fought at Buena Vista,[1] in the mountains (February 23, 1847). We had the advantage of position; and, after an all day's fight, the Mexicans retreated. Among the Southern officers, Colonel Jefferson Davis of Mississippi particularly distinguished himself, and was highly commended by General Taylor.

This victory gave us possession of Northeastern Mexico, and won for General Taylor, who here fought his last battle,[2] the presidency of the United States two years later. Meanwhile (1846) an American fleet with the help of Colonel Frémont had conquered California; and General Kearney had seized Santa Fé, and with it the territory now called New Mexico.

**291. General Scott sent to Mexico; he takes Vera Cruz; Victory of Cerro Gordo.** — General Scott had now been ordered to Mexico with a second army. His plan was to land at Vera Cruz,[3] and march directly on the city of Mexico, two hundred miles distant. After nine days' fighting he took (March 27, 1847) Vera Cruz and the strong fortress of San Juan de Ulua,[4] which defended it by sea, and which was considered to be the "Gibraltar of Mexico." General Scott said that this important victory was due in great measure to the remarkable engineering skill of Captain Robert E. Lee of Virginia, who fourteen years later was to command the Confederate Army in

---

[1] Buena Vista (Bwä′nah Vees′tah, Good View).

[2] General Taylor returned to the United States in November, 1847.

[3] Vera Cruz (Vä′rah Kroos, the True Cross).

[4] San Juan de Ulua, or Ulloa (San Wahn dä Oo-loo′ah).

the Civil War. Then pushing forward, Scott fought a battle at the mountain pass of Cerro Gordo[1] (April 18, 1847), driving the Mexicans before him. Late in the summer (1847) he crossed the last ridge of mountains, and saw the spires and towers of the capital of Mexico glittering in the sun. The city is situated in a valley. It was surrounded with fortifications, and could only be reached by a few narrow causeways — or raised roads of stone — built across the marshes. Scott had about eleven thousand men to attack an army which numbered more than three to his one, while the city itself had a population of nearly two hundred thousand.

**292. Victories in the Vicinity of the City of Mexico; the City taken; the Wilmot Proviso; Results of the War.** — With heavy loss to ourselves as well as to the enemy, we fought and won in a single day (August 20, 1847) a succession of battles[2] near the city, — every one ending in victory to our arms. A few weeks later (September 8, 1847) we attacked and carried the fortified mill of Molino del Rey,[3] and five days afterwards (September 13, 1847) we took the castle of Chapultepec.[4]

The next morning (September 14, 1847) Scott's little army, now numbering only six thousand men, entered the city of Mexico, and hoisted the " stars and stripes " over the ancient palace, or so-called Halls of the Montezumas.[5] In the conquering army there was a young lieutenant from Ohio, destined to be better known at a later period of our history — his name was Ulysses S. Grant.[6]

---

[1] Cerro Gordo : Great Hill.

[2] These were the battles of Contreras, San Antonio, and Churubusco.

[3] Molino del Rey (Mō-lee'nō děl Ray) : the King's Mill.

[4] Chapultepec (Chah-pool-tay-pěk).

[5] The Mon-te-zu'mas were the rulers of Mexico at the time of the Spanish conquest by Cortez (see Paragraph 19). The palace, which we called the " Halls of the Montezumas," was built by the Spanish successors of Cortez.

[6] General Grant says, in his " Personal Memoirs," I. 53, that he considered the Mexican war " one of the most unjust ever waged by a stronger against a weaker nation." The feeling against the war in New England found witty and able expression in Lowell's " Biglow Papers " (First Series).

The fall of the city of Mexico practically ended the war, which had lasted less than two years. It is, perhaps, the only war recorded in history in which all the victories were on one side; for our troops gained every battle, and gained it in every instance against a larger force.

By a treaty of peace signed early in 1848 we obtained the territory of California and New Mexico, with undisputed possession of Texas — or in all, nearly a million of square miles.[1] While the war was going on, Congressman Wilmot, a Pennsylvania Democrat, endeavored to get a bill passed, called the "Wilmot Proviso," prohibiting slavery in any part of the territory acquired from Mexico; but the bill failed to become law. Many of the Democrats who voted for it afterward united with a part of the Whigs and with anti-slavery men, to form a new party called the "Free Soilers" — later (1856) they became the Republican party. Another result of the war was that it educated many of the officers who fought in it, or were connected with it (such men as Grant, Lee, Sherman, and "Stonewall" Jackson) for the battle-fields of the Civil War.[2]

293. **Discovery of Gold in California.** — At the close of the Mexican War Colonel Mason was left in charge of California as military governor, and William T. Sherman — since, General Sherman — acted as one of his chief officers. In the spring of 1848 two men came to the governor's headquarters at Monterey,[3] and asked to see him. They were shown into his office. Presently Colonel Mason called to Sherman to come in. On the table were several little papers containing small

[1] See Map of Territorial Growth of the U. S. We, however, paid Mexico $15,000,000 for the territory, besides assuming certain debts of hers, amounting to about $3,000,000 more. We had previously assumed the debt of Texas, of $7,500,000; so that the whole cost of the entire territory, exclusive of the expense of the war, was $25,500,000. This was thought to be an enormous outlay, and, as it had been incurred through the annexation of Texas, many people grumbled, and said that "Texas" was simply "Taxes," with the letters differently arranged.

[2] Nearly every prominent officer in both armies in our Civil War served in the war with Mexico.     [3] Monterey: about ninety miles south of San Francisco, on the coast.

bits of yellowish metal. "What is that?" said the governor to Sherman. "I touched it," adds the general, "examined one or two of the large pieces, and asked, 'Is it *gold?*'"[1]  It *was* gold. Some men had found it in digging a mill-race for a saw-mill for Captain Sutter, on a fork of the American River,[2] near Coloma, about a hundred miles northeast of San Francisco.

San Francisco was then a little village of about four hundred inhabitants. When the news of the "great find" was spread abroad, nearly every person started for the mines. Houses were left half-built; fields half-plowed. Every man that could possibly get away bought a shovel and hurried off to dig his fortune out of the golden sands.

**294. Emigration to California; the "Vigilance Committee"; Results of the Discovery of Gold.** — The next spring (1849) the "gold fever" reached the Eastern States; and a great rush of emigration, by both land and sea, began for California. Many died of sickness contracted in crossing the Isthmus of Panama; multitudes more perished on the overland route across the continent. From the Rocky Mountains to the Sierras the track of the emigrants was marked by the skeletons of horses and oxen, and by barrels, boxes, and household goods thrown away along the road. But notwithstanding the loss of life, and the fact that many turned back, discouraged at the hardships of the undertaking, still, over eighty thousand men succeeded in reaching California before the end of that year. From an insignificant settlement San Francisco suddenly sprang into a city of twenty thousand inhabitants, which has since rapidly increased, and, at its present rate of growth, will soon reach half a million. But the great majority of the emigrants hurried off to the gold diggings, where, with pan and

---

[1] "Memoirs of General W. T. Sherman," I. 68.

[2] The American River is a tributary of the Sacramento. Coloma is in El Dorado County. See Map of the Territorial Growth of the U. S.

shovel,[1] they were speedily engaged in collecting the shining particles of that precious metal which most men find it so hard to get, and also so hard to hold. In the course of the next seven years (1849–1856) between four and five hundred millions were obtained, but costing in labor, says the leading historian of California,[2] three times what the gold was actually worth. A few gained the riches they so eagerly sought, but the greater part barely made a living by the most exhausting toil.

Eagerness for wealth naturally brought bad men as well as good to this land of promise. At times these reckless adventurers made serious trouble. But the stern hand of a Vigilance Committee, organized by a majority of the best citizens of San Francisco,[3] speedily taught desperadoes and thieves that life and property must be respected.

In the end the discovery of gold had great results for good. First of all, it gave us firm possession of the Pacific coast, since it rapidly settled the wilderness of California with a population of energetic and determined men. Next, by increasing the amount of gold in circulation, it stimulated trade, industry, and commerce, not only throughout the United States, but throughout the civilized world. New lines of steamships were started, new lines of railroads built, new markets opened for goods and produce, new mills and factories established. Finally, when the gold in the sands began to give out, men then found the real, inexhaustible wealth of the country in its fields of grain,[4] its vineyards, its orange plantations, its sheep

[1] At first, much of the gold was taken from the beds of small streams and their vicinity. It was done by sifting out the sand, or washing the earth, in pans or otherwise. When the surface mining gave out, men began to cut down the hills by directing powerful streams of water against them, and then washing the gravel and dirt for gold. Most of the gold now obtained in California is from quartz rock, which is broken to pieces by stamping-mills.

[2] Bancroft's "Pacific States," Vol. XVIII.

[3] "To punish incendiaries and other criminals."

[4] Farming in California is often carried on on an immense scale. There are single fields of wheat and barley of thousands of acres in extent.

and cattle farms. These make it a true land of gold, and of gold which is forever growing, forever increasing.

**295. Summary.** — James K. Polk's presidency opened with our getting possession of Oregon. The Mexican War followed, resulting in our obtaining California and New Mexico. The period closed with the discovery of gold, and with an immense emigration to California.

## Zachary Taylor and Millard Fillmore.

**296. Taylor and Fillmore's Administrations (Twelfth and Thirteenth Presidents, One Term, 1849–1853); the Question of the Extension of Slavery.** — When General Taylor [1] became President, the North and the South were already engaged in fierce dispute in regard to the territory gained through the Mexican War. Florida had been admitted (1845) as a slave state, and Texas followed. It was the last slave state that entered the Union; next, Congress was called on to determine whether California and New Mexico should be permitted to hold slaves.

This question of the spread of slavery had now come to be of greater importance and of greater danger to the country than any other. It acted like a wedge, gradually forcing the North and the South further and further apart. The reason was that the two sections had come to be wholly unlike. At the North, the laborer was free ; whatever he earned was his own. At the South, he was not free ; and what he earned was his master's. The North with free labor had steadily increased

---

[1] General Taylor was born in Virginia, 1784. A few years later his father removed with his family to Louisville, Kentucky. Taylor entered the regular army in 1808. In 1840 he bought a plantation, and settled at Baton Rouge, Louisiana. His career in Mexico has already been traced. He was elected President by the Whigs, over Lewis Cass, the Democratic candidate, and Martin Van Buren, the Free-Soil candidate. President Taylor died July 9, 1850, and was succeeded by Vice-President Millard Fillmore. General Taylor owned a large number of slaves ; but in political action he belonged to no party, and did not favor the extension of slavery to new territory. He was a brave, true, and conscientious man.

in population and wealth; the South with slave labor had made but little real progress.   Most people at the North now considered slavery a positive evil; but a strong party at the South, under Calhoun, held, in spite of all the facts pointing to the contrary, that it was a positive good.   This difference in belief led to the struggle about the new territory.   The South was the more determined because it was only by getting new slave states — thus bringing in senators and representatives — that it could maintain its power in Congress.   If that power were once really lost, the foremost Southern leaders feared that their whole system of labor would be destroyed, that the negroes would be set free, and that they would by and by get the control of that part of the country.

297. **Dispute about Slavery; the Danger of Disunion; the Compromise of 1850 ; the Fugitive-Slave Law.** — The longer the dispute about slavery in the new territory went on, the hotter it grew.   Three methods of settlement were proposed.   The extreme Southern men said, Every citizen of the United States has the right to go to any part of the country he pleases, and take his property — including his negroes — with him.   Give us, said they, that right, and we ask no more.   But the advocates of the "Wilmot Proviso"[1] and other Free-Soil men answered, We will have no more slave states.   All territory shall come in free.   Finally, a third class said: Congress has no right to meddle in this matter, one way or the other.   The people of the territories are the sovereigns;[2] let them decide for themselves between freedom and slavery.   Their will shall be law.

Iowa (1846) and Wisconsin (1848) had recently entered the Union, making a total of fifteen free to the same number of slave states.   Now California asked to come in as a free state. If admitted, this would give the North the majority.   Presi-

[1] See Paragraph 292.

[2] This was called "Popular Sovereignty," or "Squatter Sovereignty," because it left the question to the settlers (sometimes called "squatters") of the new territories.

dent Taylor, though himself a large slaveholder, strongly favored its admission; but Calhoun and his party just as strongly opposed it. The feeling became so violent and bitter that it seemed to many that the Union must be broken up, and that, instead of one nation, we should split into a Northern and a Southern Republic.

At this time of peril, Henry Clay, "the Peacemaker," came forward in Congress with a compromise, or plan of settlement.[1] He said: 1. Let California come in as a free state. 2. In the remainder of the territory, obtained from Mexico, let the people determine for themselves how they will come in. 3. All runaway slaves found at the North shall be arrested, and, without trial by jury, they shall be returned to their masters.

Daniel Webster employed his eloquence to get Congress to vote for this compromise, including the new Fugitive-Slave Law;[2] for he believed that if it was rejected, the country would be lost. Many people at the North denounced him, as John Quincy Adams once did, as "a heartless traitor to the cause of human freedom"; but Horace Greeley, a strong Abolitionist, declared that the great majority, both North and South, agreed with Mr. Webster.[3]

[1] Clay's Compromise Bill contained so many points that it was called the "Omnibus Bill." In it he proposed to conciliate the North by: 1. Admitting California as a free state. 2. By abolishing the slave trade (but not slavery) in the District of Columbia.

On the other hand, he endeavored to conciliate the moderate party in the South by: 1. Leaving the question of slavery in New Mexico and Utah (acquired from Mexico) to the people of those territories. 2. To conciliate all parties in the South, he proposed a more effective Fugitive-Slave Law than that of 1793, which rested on a provision of the Constitution (see the Constitution, page xiv). The Omnibus Bill was passed at last, not as one, but as several bills (September, 1850).

Henry Clay, though a slaveholder, was opposed to the extension of slavery into new territory, and used all his influence to get his own state (Kentucky) to abolish slavery, but without success.

[2] Mr. Webster, however, wished to have this law modified so as to secure trial by jury to negroes arrested as fugitives, in case they denied that they were runaway slaves. His efforts to secure this change were unsuccessful, for the South insisted that no Northern jury would ever return a negro. See Curtis's "Life of Webster," II. 422, 423.    [3] See Horace Greeley's "American Conflict," I. 220, 221.

**298. Passage of the Fugitive-Slave Law; its Results; the "Underground Railroad"; the "Higher Law."** — During the debate on the Fugitive-Slave Law, President Taylor died, and was succeeded by Vice-President Fillmore. The law, with the other compromise measures, passed in the autumn of 1850, California was admitted, and it was hoped that peace was secured. But it was only a hollow peace, like the quiet of a smouldering fire, ready to break out at any moment in a conflagration.

As soon as the slave-owners of the South attempted to arrest their runaway negroes at the North there were riots and rescues. In Boston, a fugitive named Shadrach was taken from the officers and carried off to a place of safety; and in Syracuse, New York, one named Jerry received his liberty in the same way. Several Northern states now passed laws to protect negroes and prevent their being sent back to slavery. Many persons, out of pity for the escaped slaves, banded themselves together to help them privately to get to Canada. This method got the name of the "Underground Railroad"; and hundreds, if not thousands, of trembling fugitives owed their liberty to the quickness and secrecy of this peculiar system of travel.

There has always been a deep and abiding respect for law in America — because here the people themselves may be said to make the laws. But now for the first time many men began to declare, as William H. Seward of New York did in the United States Senate: Above the Constitution and all Acts of Congress there is a "Higher Law" — a divine law of justice and of freedom which compels us through conscience not to obey the order of the government, and not to return the fugitive to his master.

**299. "Uncle Tom's Cabin"; Charles Sumner and Jefferson Davis.** — This feeling of opposition was suddenly intensified throughout the North by the publication in 1852 of Mrs. Stowe's "Uncle Tom's Cabin." It was in every respect a remarkable book — one written from the heart to the heart. It meant to be truthful, to be fair, to be kind.    In a single year two hundred thousand copies were sold in this country, and in a short time the total sales here had reached half a million copies. Mrs. Stowe's object was to show what the life of the slave really was — to show its bright and happy side, as well as its dark and cruel side.    People who took up the book could not lay it down until they had finished it.    They laughed and cried, and laughed again, over " Topsy," " Eva," and " Uncle Tom " ; but they ended with tears in their eyes.    No arguments, no denials, could shake the influence of the story.    From this time onward a silent revolution was going on.    The forces for slavery and those against it were girding themselves up for the terrible struggle.    The great leaders of the nation on both sides — Clay, Webster, Calhoun — had died before the close of 1852.    New men were taking their places in Congress — Charles Sumner representing the North ; Jefferson Davis, the South.    In the battles which these two men fought in words we have the beginning of that contest which was soon to end in civil war.    Both felt that the time was very soon coming when the republic must stand wholly free or wholly on the side of slavery.

300. **Summary.** — The four chief events of the Taylor and Fillmore administrations were: (1) the debate on the extension of slavery in the new territory gained by the Mexican War; (2) the Compromise Measures of 1850, with the Fugitive-Slave Law ; (3) the publication of " Uncle Tom's Cabin " ; and (4) the beginning of the final struggle in Congress between the North and the South.

### Franklin Pierce.

301. **Pierce's Administration (Fourteenth President, One Term, 1853–1857) ; the " World's Fair " at New York City ; American Labor-Saving Machines.** — The summer following the inaugura-

tion of President Pierce[1] a great exhibition of the products and industries of all nations was held at New York (1853) in a building of glass and iron erected for it, called the "Crystal Palace." Its chief result was that it helped us as a people to compare our own work with that of Europe. It proved beyond all doubt that Americans have no equals in practical inventions and in the excellence and variety of their labor-saving machinery — their steam-printing-presses, power-looms, sewing-machines, steam-shovels, planing-machines, and the like. This was especially

Reaping-Machine, or Harvester.

the case in the exhibition of farming-implements. The reapers and mowers for cutting grain and grass showed the immense advance we had made over the slow work formerly done by hand with sickle and scythe. The French Academy of Sciences declared that Cyrus McCormick,[2] the inventor of the reaper, had

[1] Franklin Pierce was born in New Hampshire in 1804; died 1869. He was in Congress from 1837–1842, and was a brigadier-general in the Mexican War. He was elected President (William R. King of Alabama, Vice-President) by the Democrats, over General Scott, the Whig candidate. The Whig party had practically ceased to exist before the next presidential election, in 1856. The Free-Soilers humorously declared that it died "of an attempt to swallow the Fugitive-Slave Law" (which the Whig National Convention had accepted in 1852). In 1852 a new political party called the American Party, or "Know Nothings," came into existence. They had a secret organization, and their object was to exclude all but native American citizens from office, to check the power of Catholicism, and to oppose the admission of foreigners to citizenship except after very long residence here. Their motto was, "Americans must rule America." The "Know Nothings" became a national party, exerted considerable influence for a few years, and then died out.

In 1853 the present boundary between the United States and Mexico was finally established by our purchase (through General James Gadsden, the United States minister to Mexico) of the region including the Mesilla Valley (now Southern Arizona and Southern New Mexico; see Map of Growth of the U. S.) for $10,000,000.

[2] Cyrus Hall McCormick was born in Virginia, 1809. In 1834 he patented his machine for reaping grain (operated by horse-power), and later improved it so that it not only cut the grain, but bound it in sheaves. William H. Seward, then in the

"done more for the cause of agriculture than any man living." The effect on the settlement of the West was wonderful.

**302. Commodore Perry opens the Ports of Japan.** — Not long after the close of the Crystal Palace Exhibition, Commodore Perry sailed into one of the ports of Japan with the first fleet of steamers that had ever entered a harbor of that island. For over two centuries that country had been almost wholly closed to the entire world.[1] The Japanese dreaded Europeans, and they had been taught that all Americans were barbarians of the most dangerous sort. Commodore Perry succeeded in convincing them that if the Americans were barbarians, they were of an uncommonly ingenious and agreeable kind. Through his influence the government of Japan made a treaty with the United States admitting our ships to trade; and we, on the other hand, made the emperor presents of a locomotive with a train of cars, and a line of telegraph — the first ever seen in that country, which has since adopted, through our influence, both steam and electricity.

**303. The Kansas-Nebraska Act repealing the Missouri Compromise.** — It will be remembered that the Missouri Compromise of 1820 shut out slavery from the territory west and north of Missouri.[2] At the time the Compromise was made it was solemnly declared that it would stand "forever." But the end of that "forever" was now reached. The South demanded the right to carry slavery into the region of Nebraska beyond Missouri. In 1854, Senator Stephen A. Douglas of Illinois —

United States Senate, said in 1859, "Owing to Mr. McCormick's invention, the line of civilization [in the United States] moves westward thirty miles each year." And Professor Alexander Johnston says that the results of McCormick's invention "have been hardly less than that of the locomotive in their importance to the United States. . . . It was agricultural machinery that made Western farms profitable, and enabled the railroads to fill the West so rapidly." (It is still a matter of controversy whether Hussey's reaper or McCormick's came first in order of time.)

[1] The Dutch had the privilege of trading with Japan, but under restrictions which forbade their landing on the island.     [2] See Paragraph 243.

the "Little Giant," as his friends called him [1] — proposed a law entitled the Kansas and Nebraska Bill. That bill cut what was then the territory of Nebraska into two parts, of which the southern portion was called Kansas; and it left it to the settlers of these two territories to decide whether they would have slave labor or not.[2] Congress passed the bill, and thus repealed or set aside the Missouri agreement made in 1820. The North was indignant at the new law. Senator Douglas was hooted in the streets. Mass meetings were held to denounce him; and so many images of him were made and burned, that Mr. Douglas himself said that he travelled from Washington to Chicago by the light of his own blazing effigies.

### 304. The Struggle for the Possession of Kansas; Emigrants from Missouri and from New England. — Now (1854) a desperate struggle began between the North and the South for the possession of Kansas.[3] No sooner had President Pierce signed the Kansas-Nebraska Bill, thus making it law,[4] than bands of men armed with rifles commenced to pour into the territory, resolved to win it either by fraud or force. The first movement came from the slaveholders of Missouri, who crossed the Missouri River and took up lands in the new territory. Soon after, this party began a settlement which they named Atchison, in honor of Senator Atchison of Missouri.

Next, the New England Aid Society of Boston sent out a

---

[1] Senator Douglas was short in stature and stoutly built. His great intellectual ability and marked decision of character got for him the name of the " Little Giant." He died in 1861, shortly after the outbreak of the Civil War. His dying message to his sons was an entreaty that they should stand by the Union and the Constitution.

[2] The " Kansas-Nebraska Act " extended the principles of Clay's Compromise of 1850 (see Paragraph 297) (which applied only to territory acquired from Mexico) and left it to the people of Kansas and Nebraska to make their own choice about slavery.

[3] In speaking of this coming struggle, Hon. William H. Seward of New York said, in the United States Senate, 1854: "Come on, then, gentlemen of the slave states; since there is no escaping your challenge, I accept it on behalf of Freedom. We will engage in competition for the virgin soil of Kansas, and God give the victory to the side that is stronger in numbers as it is in right."

[4] See page 245, note 3.

body of armed emigrants, who settled about forty miles to the southwest of Atchison. They called their little cluster of tents and log-cabins Lawrence, because Amos A. Lawrence was treasurer of the society, which was established to aid Northern men in the double purpose of building homes in Kansas and of making the territory a free state. Thus, that part of the territory lying on the Missouri River came to be held by men favoring the introduction of slavery; while the territory somewhat further west and south was generally in the hands of those opposed to slavery.

**305. The Rival Governments of Kansas; Civil War in the Territory.** — These rival sections soon set up governments to suit themselves. The Free-state settlers had their headquarters at Topeka and Lawrence; the Slave-state settlers, at Leavenworth and Lecompton.

From 1854 to 1859 that part of the country suffered so much from the efforts of both parties to get control that it fairly earned the name of "Bleeding Kansas." During the greater part of five years the territory was torn by civil war.[1] The Free-state men denounced the opposite party as "Border Ruffians"; the "Border Ruffians" called the Free-state men "Abolitionists" and "Black Republicans."[2]

**306. Attack on Lawrence; John Brown; Assault on Charles Sumner.** — In the course of this period of violence and bloodshed the Slave-state men attacked Lawrence, plundered the town, and burned some of its chief buildings. This roused the spirit of vengeance in the heart of "Old John Brown" of

[1] Civil war (from the Latin word *civis*, a citizen): a war between citizens of the same state or country.

[2] Early in 1856 those who had opposed the Kansas-Nebraska Bill, and who were pledged to resist the extension of slavery into new territory, formed a new political party, and adopted the name of "Republicans." This was the origin of the present party of that name. Their opponents at the South nicknamed them "Black Republicans," because the party was opposed to holding the black man in bondage.

Osawatomie.[1]   He was a descendant of one of the Pilgrims
who came over in the *Mayflower*,[2] and he had made a solemn
vow to "kill American slavery."   In return for the attack on
Lawrence, Brown got together a small band, surprised a little
settlement of Slave-state men on Pottawatomie Creek, south
of Lawrence, dragged five of them from their beds, and deliberately murdered them.   Later, Brown crossed into Missouri,
destroyed considerable property, freed eleven slaves, and shot
one of the slave-owners.   The truth appears to be that each
party in Kansas was resolved to drive out the other.[3]   In the
end, the Free-state men won the victory, and Kansas following
the example of Minnesota and Oregon (1858–1859) entered
the Union without slavery (1861).

During the heated debate in Congress over the Kansas
troubles, Senator Charles Sumner of Massachusetts made a
speech denouncing slavery, and alluding to Senator Butler of
South Carolina in a way that stung the latter's friends to madness.   Representative Brooks, a kinsman of Butler's, considered
the speech an insult; he brutally assaulted Sumner, and beat
him so severely over the head with a heavy cane that he was
obliged to give up his seat in Congress for nearly four years.
In less than a year from his return (1859) South Carolina had
seceded from the Union.

---

[1] John Brown, born in Torrington, Connecticut, 1800, was executed at Charlestown, Virginia, December 2, 1859, for having attempted by armed force to liberate slaves in that state.   He was a descendant of Peter Brown, who came over in
the *Mayflower* in 1620.   When a boy, he chanced to see a slave boy cruelly beaten
by his master, and he then and there vowed (so he says) "eternal war with slavery."
In 1848 he purchased a farm in North Elba, New York, but spent a great deal of
his time in aiding runaway slaves to get to Canada.   He went out to Osawatomie,
Kansas, in 1855, to take part in making that territory a free state, and also, as he
says, to strike a blow at slavery.   Brown's party declared that they perpetrated the
"Pottawatomie Massacre" in return for the assassination of five Free-state men by
the opposite party.   (Charlestown is now included in West Virginia.)

[2] See Paragraph 73.

[3] During this administration and the preceding one some attempts were made by
armed expeditions of Americans to get possession of Cuba, and also of part of
Central America, but they ended in complete failure.

**307. Summary.** — The chief events of Pierce's administration were: (1) The "World's Fair" exhibition; (2) Commodore Perry's treaty with Japan, opening that country to trade with the United States; (3) the passage of the Kansas-Nebraska Bill repealing the Missouri Compromise; and (4) the struggle of the North and the South for the possession of Kansas.

## JAMES BUCHANAN.

**308. Buchanan's Administration (Fifteenth President, One Term 1857–1861); the Case of Dred Scott.** — Two days after President Buchanan's [1] inauguration, Chief-Justice Taney gave the decision of the United States Supreme Court in a case of great importance, known as the "Dred Scott Case." Scott was a negro slave and the son of slave parents. His master had taken him (1834) from the slave state of Missouri to the free state of Illinois, where he staid two years. He then took him to what is now Minnesota, a part of the country [2] in which Congress had prohibited slavery, [3] and finally carried him back to Missouri.

There Scott was sold to a new master; but the negro demanded his liberty, on the ground that since he had lived for a considerable time on free soil he had therefore become a free man.

**309. Decision of the U. S. Supreme Court in the Dred Scott Case; Results at the North.** — The case was carried to the United States Supreme Court. That Court [4] decided: (1) that a negro (whether bond or free), who was a descendant of slave ancestors, was not an American citizen; (2) therefore he could

[1] James Buchanan was born in Pennsylvania, 1791; died, 1868. He was elected to Congress in 1820; later, to the United States Senate; was minister to Russia; Secretary of State under Polk; and 1853 minister to England. He was elected President (John C. Breckinridge of Kentucky, Vice-President) by the Democrats, over John C. Frémont, the Republican candidate, and Millard Fillmore, the "American," or "Know Nothing," candidate.    [2] Then called the Territory of Upper Louisiana.

[3] The Missouri Compromise (1820), virtually repealed by the Kansas-Nebraska Act (1854), prohibited slavery in this territory. See Paragraphs 243, 303.

[4] Judge McLean and Judge Curtis did not agree with the other seven judges.

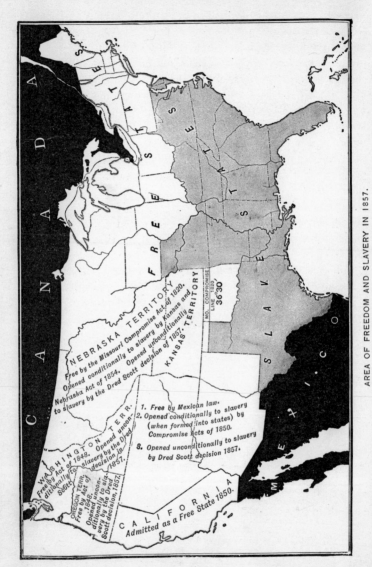

**CANADA**

**MEXICO**

NEBRASKA TERRITORY
Free by the Missouri Compromise Act of 1820.
Opened conditionally to slavery by Kansas and
Nebraska Act of 1854. Opened unconditionally
to slavery by the Dred Scott decision of 1857.

KANSAS TERRITORY

MO. COMPROMISE
LINE 1820.
36° 30′

WASHINGTON TERR.
Free by Act of 1848. Opened uncon-
ditionally to slavery by the Dred
Scott decision 1857.

OREGON TERR.
Free by Act of 1848.
Opened uncon-
ditionally to sla-
very by the Dred
Scott decision 1857.

1. Free by Mexican law.
2. Opened conditionally to slavery
(when formed into states) by
Compromise Acts of 1850.

8. Opened unconditionally to slavery
by Dred Scott decision 1857.

CALIFORNIA
Admitted as a Free State 1850.

FREE STATES

SLAVE STATES

AREA OF FREEDOM AND SLAVERY IN 1857.

(Congress abolished slavery in the District of Columbia, April 16, 1862, and prohibited it in the Territories, June 19, 1862.)

not sue (even for his liberty) in the United States Courts. It furthermore decided that Scott had not gained his freedom by going into a free state, or into a Territory where Congress had prohibited slavery, since Congress had no power to do this.

Chief-Justice Taney declared that when the Constitution was adopted negroes "had no rights which the white man was bound to respect;"[1] and lastly, that Scott's master could lawfully take his slaves into any Territory, just as he could his horses and his cattle. This decision by the highest court in the United States stirred the North like an electric shock. The people of that section believed that it practically threw open to slavery not only the Territories but even the free states.[2] The result was that many people determined that the law should not be carried out.[3] This, of course, angered the South, and greatly increased the bad feeling between the two sections.[4]

**310. The Business Panic of 1857.** — While men were excitedly discussing the Dred Scott decision, and while the danger of disunion was growing more and more threatening, a heavy business failure occurred in Cincinnati.[5] This brought down other business houses, just as when a large building falls the smaller ones whose walls rest against it often fall with it. The panic of 1837[6] was now repeated. Nearly all the banks

[1] This was no personal feeling of Judge Taney's, for he had freed his own slaves.

[2] That is, that the free states could not prevent a slaveholder from bringing his slaves with him (as Scott's master had done), and staying at least two years with them on free soil.

[3] The Northern people believed that under the Constitution slaves could only be held in those states which protected slavery by their laws, and that if a master took his negroes into a state whose laws forbade slavery, he could not hold them in bondage there.

[4] Meanwhile (1845–1846), two of the great religious denominations of the country — the Baptists and the Methodists — had split; and each was now organized as a Northern and a Southern Church; the first opposing slavery, and the second upholding it. Later (1861), the Presbyterian denomination became similarly divided; but not the Episcopal or the Roman Catholic.

[5] The Ohio Life and Trust Company failed, through the fault of its New York agent, in August, 1857.        [6] See Paragraph 274.

in the country failed,[1] many railroads could not pay their debts, thousands of merchants and manufacturers were ruined, and it seemed at one time as though all rich men must become poor, and all poor men become beggars.

The chief causes of this trouble were to be found in the results of the discovery of gold in California.[2] The increased wealth had stimulated men to overdo all kinds of business; more lines of railroad had been built in the West than the population demanded; many manufacturers had made greater quantities of goods than they could sell; and many merchants had bought more than they could pay for. The country was like a man who had worked beyond his strength — it had to stop and take a rest.

### 311. Discovery of Silver in Nevada and Colorado, and of Petroleum and Natural Gas in Pennsylvania. — But in 1859, less than two years after the panic, some of the richest silver mines ever discovered on the globe were found in the mountain region of Western Nevada.[3] The two chief of these, known as the "Bonanza"[4] mines, sent out many millions of dollars' worth of ore cast in the form of bricks. When, in the course of time, these famous "silver bricks" decreased in number for want of ore to make them, new mines that had been found (1877) in Leadville and other parts of Colorado and also in Utah, sent out a new supply of the precious metal.

In 1859 Colonel Drake sunk the first successful oil-well on

---

[1] The Chemical Bank of New York City, which had gone safely through the great panic of 1837, continued to pay all demands in gold. The State Bank of Indiana and the Kentucky banks also met all demands against them in a satisfactory manner. See Ex-Secretary of the Treasury McCulloch's "Men and Measures of Half a Century," page 133.    [2] See Paragraph 294.

[3] The mines were discovered in the Sierra Nevada Mountains, in what is called the Comstock lode (a lode is a vein or deposit of mineral).

[4] "Bonanza": a Spanish word meaning prosperity. In the West it is applied (in mining) to a very rich mass of gold or silver ore. The total yield of the mines of the Comstock lode has been over two hundred and fifty million dollars. The amount at present obtained from them is very small.

Oil Creek, near Titusville, in Northwestern Pennsylvania. Since then, petroleum [1] has flowed in streams from the wells that have been opened in Pennsylvania, Ohio, Indiana, Texas, Southern New York, and the far West. The average yield of these wells has lately been more than a hundred thousand barrels of oil a day. Lines of iron pipes, laid underground, carry the oil over hills, across rivers, through forests and farms, to Chicago, Buffalo, Philadelphia, New York, Baltimore, and other points on the Great Lakes and the seacoast. Petroleum is used not only for giving light, but it is more and more employed to oil machinery and for heating purposes.

About fifteen years after the discovery of petroleum in Pennsylvania, natural gas was found issuing from the rocks in the same region, and later in Ohio, Indiana, and other parts of the West. This gas took the place of oil and coal in Pittsburg, Indianapolis, and vicinity, for lighting streets and houses, for cooking, and for fuel in manufacturing. As Nature makes it in her laboratories underground, the gas costs practically nothing more than the expense of the tubes which conduct it from the earth. It used to be seen burning in the streets all day as well as all night, for sometimes it was cheaper to let it burn than to hire men to go round and shut it off. At one time it was proposed to convey the gas in pipes to Philadelphia, New York, and other cities, in order to supply them with light; but the supply has since fallen off in large measure.

312. **John Brown's Raid.** — In the autumn of 1859 the whole country was startled on hearing that "John Brown of Osawatomie" [2] had made a raid [3] into Virginia, seized the government buildings at Harper's Ferry, and attempted to liberate the slaves in that vicinity. John Brown's whole band consisted of only about twenty men, partly whites and partly negroes. After hard fighting, he was captured, with six of

---

[1] Petroleum: commonly known, in one of its refined forms, as kerosene oil.
[2] See Paragraph 306.     [3] Raid: a sudden invasion by a body of armed men.

his companions, and hanged at Charlestown, Virginia (December 2, 1859). On the day of his execution, he handed this paper to one of his guards: "I, John Brown, am now

Harper's Ferry in 1859.

quite certain that the crimes of this guilty land will never be purged away but with blood. I had, as I now think, vainly flattered myself that without very much bloodshed it might be done." [1] Within a year and a half from the day of his death, the North and the South were at war with each other, and a Northern regiment on its way to the contest was singing, —

> "John Brown's body lies a-mouldering in the grave,
> But his soul is marching on."

### 313. The Election of Abraham Lincoln; Secession of South Carolina. — In November, 1860, Abraham Lincoln [2] of Illinois

[1] Governor Wise of Virginia said of John Brown: "He inspired me with great trust in his integrity as a man of truth." The governor also said: "They are mistaken who take Brown for a madman. He is a bundle of the best nerves I ever saw . . . cool, collected, indomitable." In his last speech at his trial, John Brown declared that his only object had been to liberate the slaves, and that he did not intend to commit murder or treason or to destroy property. "I feel," said he, "no consciousness of guilt."

It is worthy of note that when the Republican party, which was opposed to the extension of slavery, nominated Abraham Lincoln for the presidency in 1860, it expressly denounced John Brown's attempt as "lawless and unjustifiable."

[2] Abraham Lincoln was born in Hardin County, Kentucky, in 1809. His early life was spent in toil, hardship, and poverty; but it was the independent poverty of the Western wilderness, and it made men of those who fought their way out of it.

When the boy was only eight years old he had learned to swing an axe. From that time until he came of age he literally chopped and hewed his way forward and

A Lincoln

was elected by the Republican party President of the United States, then a nation of over thirty millions. That party,

though it denounced John Brown,[1] had pledged itself to shut out slavery from the territories. The people of South Carolina believed that the election of Mr. Lincoln meant that the great majority of the North was determined to bring about the liberation of the negroes. That was a great mistake; but the Carolinians could not then be convinced to the contrary. They furthermore saw that they could no longer hope to maintain the power they

Boyhood of Lincoln.

[1] See page 286, note 1.

upward. He learned to read from two books — the spelling-book and the Bible; then he borrowed "Pilgrim's Progress" and Æsop's Fables, and would sit up half the night reading them "by the blaze of the logs his own axe had split."

In 1816 the Lincoln family moved to Spencer County, Indiana; and in 1830, to Decatur, Illinois. On this last occasion, young Lincoln walked the entire distance, nearly two hundred miles, through mud and water, driving a four-ox team. The journey took fifteen days; for even two yoke of oxen do not move quite as fast as steam. When they reached their destination, in what was then an almost unsettled country, the father and son set to work to build the log-cabin which was to be their home; and when that was finished, the young man split the rails to fence in their farm of ten acres.

Such work was play to him. He was now twenty-one; he stood six feet three and a half inches, barefooted; he was in perfect health; could out-run, out-jump, out-wrestle, and, if *necessary*, out-fight, any one of his age in the county, and "his grip was like the grip of Hercules." Without this rugged strength he could never have endured the strain that the nation later put upon him.

In 1834 he resolved to begin the study of law. A friend in Springfield offered to lend him some books; Lincoln walked there, twenty-two miles from New Salem

once possessed in Congress, for the free states now had six more senators and fifty-seven more representatives than the slave states had.[1]

On December 20, 1860, a convention met in "Secession Hall," in Charleston, and unanimously voted "that the union now subsisting between South Carolina and other states, under the name of the United States of America, is hereby dissolved." Those who thus voted said that it was no hasty resolution on their part, but that it had been under consideration for many years. The declaration of secession was welcomed in the streets with the firing of cannon and the ringing of bells. The citizens believed that they had broken up the Union, and that South Carolina had now, as its governor said, become a "free and independent State."

**314. Secession of Six other Southern States; Formation of the "Confederate States of America."** — By the first of February (1861) the states of Georgia, Mississippi, Florida, Alabama, Louisiana, and Texas — making seven in all — had likewise

---

(where he then lived), and, it is said, brought back with him four heavy volumes of Blackstone, at the end of the same day.

A few years later he opened a law-office in Springfield. In 1846 "Honest Abe," as his neighbors and friends called him, was elected to Congress; and in 1860, to the presidency of the United States, by the Republican party (Hannibal Hamlin of Maine, Vice-President). The Democratic party had split into a Northern and a Southern party. The former had nominated Stephen A. Douglas of Illinois; and the latter, John C. Breckinridge of Kentucky. The former American (or "Know-Nothing") party, which now called itself the "Constitutional Union Party," had nominated John Bell of Tennessee. Lincoln received nearly half a million more votes than Douglas, and more than a million in excess of those cast for either of the other candidates.

[1] In 1790, just after the foundation of the government, the free states (that is, the northern states; they had comparatively few slaves) had 14 senators and 35 representatives in Congress; the slave states, 12 senators and 30 representatives. From 1796 to 1812, inclusive, the free states and the slave states had an equal number in the Senate, but the free states had a majority in the House. After 1848 the free states had a majority in both Senate and House, and in the latter this majority was constantly increasing. That fact meant that the South had lost its political power, partly because slavery had failed to get a foothold in the far West, but mainly because the North had outgrown the South in population.

withdrawn from the Union.   A seceding senator rashly declared
that they had left the national government "a corpse lying in
state in Washington."  On February 4 (1861), delegates from
these states (except those from Texas, who arrived later) met
at Montgomery, Alabama.   They framed a government and
took the name of the "Confederate States of America," with
Montgomery as the capital; then they elected Jefferson Davis [1]
of Mississippi, President, and Alexander H. Stephens [2] of
Georgia, Vice-President of the Confederacy.   The Confederate
States now cast aside the Stars and Stripes, and hoisted a new
flag, the "Stars and Bars," [3] in its place.

315.  Why the South seceded; Seizure of National Property; the
*Star of the West* fired on. — What took these seven states —
soon to be followed by four more — out of the Union?   The
answer is, it was first their conviction that slavery would thrive
better by being separated from the influence of the North; and,
secondly, it was their belief in "State Rights," [4] upheld by
South Carolina as far back as Jackson's presidency.   Accord-

[1] Jefferson Davis was born in Kentucky in 1808; died, 1889.  He graduated at
West Point Military Academy in 1828.  In 1845 he was elected to Congress by the
Democrats in Mississippi, of which state he had become a resident.  He served
with distinction in the Mexican War (see Paragraph 290).  In 1847 he entered the
United States Senate, where, like Calhoun, he advocated state rights and the exten-
sion of slavery.  President Pierce made him Secretary of War.  He was United
States Senator under Buchanan.  His state (Mississippi) seceded on January 9, 1861.
Mr. Davis kept his seat in the Senate until January 21, and then, with a speech
asserting the right of secession, he withdrew to join the Southern Confederacy.

[2] Alexander H. Stephens was born in Georgia in 1812; died, 1883.  He was in
Congress as a representative of the Whigs from 1843 to 1859.  He afterwards joined
the Democrats.  He at first opposed secession, and said that it was "the height of
madness, folly, and wickedness"; but when Georgia seceded, he decided that it was
his duty to stand by his state.  After the Civil War he again entered Congress, and
in 1882 he was elected governor of Georgia.  He was a man who had the entire
respect of those who knew him.

[3] The "Stars and Bars," as the Confederate flag was popularly called, to distinguish it from the "Stars and Stripes," consisted of a blue union (the upper, inner
corner of a flag is called the *union*), containing at first seven, and later eleven, white
stars, — representing the number of the Confederate states, — arranged in a circle.
The body of the flag was made up of three very broad horizontal stripes, or "bars,"
the middle one white, the two others red.  See page 296.     [4] See Paragraph 269.

ing to that idea, any state was justified in separating itself from the United States whenever it became convinced that it was for its interest to withdraw.

In this act of secession many of the people of the South took no direct part, — a large number being, in fact, utterly opposed to it, — but the political leaders were fully determined on separation. Their aim was to establish a great slave-holding republic, or nationality, of which they should be head.[1]

President Buchanan made no attempt to prevent the states from seceding; part of his cabinet were Southern men, who were in full sympathy with the Southern leaders, and the President did not see how to act.

The seceded states seized the forts, arsenals, and other national property within their limits, so far as they could do so. Fort Sumter, commanded by Major Anderson of the United States army, in Charleston Harbor, was one of the few where the "Stars and Stripes" remained flying. President Buchanan had made an effort to send men and supplies to Major Anderson by the merchant steamer *Star of the West* (January 9, 1861); but the people of Charleston fired upon the steamer, and compelled her to go back.

All eyes were now turned toward Abraham Lincoln. The great question was, What will he do when he becomes President?

### 316. General Summary from Washington to Buchanan (1789–1861); Growth of the West; Secession    Looking back to the

---

[1] Alexander H. Stephens, Vice-President of the Confederacy, said, in a speech at Savannah, March 21, 1861, " The prevailing idea entertained by him [Jefferson] and most of the leading statesmen at the time of the formation of the old Constitution [the Constitution of the United States] was that the enslavement of the African was in violation of the laws of nature; that it was wrong in principle — socially, morally, and politically. . . . Our new government [the Southern Confederacy] is founded upon exactly the opposite idea; its foundations are laid, its corner-stone rests, upon the great truth that the negro is not equal to the white man; that slavery — subordination to the superior race — is his natural and normal condition." — McPherson's *Political History of the Rebellion*, page 103.

presidency of Washington, we see that over seventy years had elapsed since the formation of the Union. We then had a population of less than four millions; in 1861 — at the outbreak of secession — we had eight times that number, and much more than eight times the wealth possessed by us in 1789. Thus, from a small and poor nation, we had grown to be great and prosperous.

In 1789 our western boundary was the Mississippi, and there seemed no prospect that we should extend beyond it. Long before 1861 we had reached the Pacific. Our original eight hundred thousand square miles had increased to over three millions; and the original thirteen states had added to themselves twenty-one more, besides immense territories.

In 1789 New York, Boston, Philadelphia, Baltimore, and Charleston — five in all — were our only cities,[1] and they were so small that they were hardly worthy of the name. By 1861 most of these places (especially those at the North) had grown enormously in population and wealth; Brooklyn, Detroit, Cincinnati, and St. Louis had become large and flourishing cities, and we had added to them Chicago, St. Paul, Minneapolis,[2] Indianapolis, Milwaukee, New Orleans, and Galveston; with Kansas City, Salt Lake City, Portland, Seattle, and San Francisco in the far west, — all, but the last six, connected with each other by railroads and lines of telegraph.

In fact the western and northwestern part of the country had advanced "by leaps and bounds," so that every year beheld it coming more and more to the front.[3] Emigrants, miners, and other pioneers of civilization were constantly pushing forward into the vast region beyond the Mississippi. There they were building the first rude shanties of settlements

1 City is used here in its primary sense of "a large town."

2 The eastern part of what is now Minneapolis was incorporated as a city, under the name of St. Anthony, in 1860. The west side, named Minneapolis, was incorporated as a city in 1867; in 1872 the two were united under that name.

3 On the growth of the west and northwest in population and political power see: Table of Population.

which were to become known as Omaha and Denver, and they were laying the foundations of the eleven great states[1] which, with West Virginia, have since joined the Union.

But between 1789 and 1861 there was this sad difference: Washington had found and left us a united people; Buchanan, a divided people.   Seven of our states had left us; four more would go.   For many years we had been brothers; now we were fast becoming enemies.   Only let the word be spoken, and our swords would leap from their scabbards, and we would fly at each other's throats.

What had brought about this deplorable change?   Time. Time had strengthened Slavery at the South and Freedom at the North.   It was no longer possible for both to dwell together in peace under the same flag.   Either the Union must be dissolved, or those who loved the Union must fight to save it; and, before the war should end, must fight to make it wholly free.   If freedom should triumph, then lasting peace would be restored; for then the North and the South — no longer separated by slavery — would again become one great, prosperous, and united people.

[1] The eleven states are Kansas, Nevada, Nebraska, Colorado, North Dakota, South Dakota, Montana, Washington, Idaho, Wyoming, and Utah.   They entered the Union between January, 1861, and January, 1896.

# VI.

"Fourscore and seven years ago our fathers brought forth upon this continent a new nation, conceived in liberty, and dedicated to the proposition that all men are created equal. . . . We here highly resolve . . . that this nation, under God, shall have a new birth of freedom; and that government of the people, by the people, and for the people, shall not perish from the earth." — PRESIDENT LINCOLN'S *Address at Gettysburg, November 19, 1863.*

---

## THE WAR OF THE REBELLION.

### (APRIL, 1861, TO APRIL, 1865.)

### ABRAHAM LINCOLN.·

**317. Lincoln's Administration (Sixteenth President, Two Terms,[1] 1861–April 14, 1865); the President's Arrival at Washington; his Speech; his Intentions toward the Seceded States.** — President Lincoln's friends believed that it would not be safe for him to make the last part of his journey to Washington publicly; and he therefore reached the national capital secretly by a special night train.

At his inauguration (March 4, 1861) he said: "I have no

[1] Abraham Lincoln (see Paragraph 313, note 2) was elected President by the Republican party (Hannibal Hamlin, of Maine, Vice-President), in 1860, over Douglas and Breckenridge, the two candidates of the Northern and the Southern Democrats, and Bell, the candidate of the "Constitutional Union" party. He was again elected by the Republicans, in 1864 (Andrew Johnson, of Tennessee, Vice-President), over General George B. McClellan, the Democratic candidate. President Lincoln was assassinated April 14, 1865, one month and ten days after entering upon his second administration. Vice-President Johnson then became President for the remainder of the term. President Lincoln, on first entering office, chose William H. Seward, Secretary of State; Salmon P. Chase, Secretary of the Treasury; Gideon Welles, Secretary of the Navy; and Simon Cameron, Secretary of War; succeeded, January 15, 1862, by Edwin M. Stanton. During the Civil War they rendered services of inestimable value to the President and to the nation.

purpose, directly or indirectly, to interfere with the institution of slavery in the states where it exists. I believe I have no lawful right to do so; and I have no inclination to do so." But the President also declared in the same speech that he held the Union to be perpetual, and that he should do his utmost to keep the oath he had just taken "to preserve, pro-

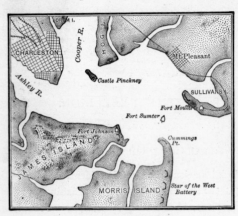

Map of Charleston Harbor.

tect, and defend it." [1] He further-more declared that the government had no intention of beginning war against the se-ceded states, but would only use its power to re-take the forts and other national property which had been seized by the Con-federacy.

At this time the general feeling throughout the Northern States was a strong desire for peace, and a willingness to assure the Southern States that their Constitutional right [2] to hold slaves should not be interfered with.

### First Year of the War, April, 1861, to April, 1862.

**318. Major Anderson's Condition at Fort Sumter; the First Gun of the War; Surrender of the Fort.** — Major Anderson now sent a message to the President, stating that he could not long continue to hold Fort Sumter unless provisions were sent to him. His entire garrison, aside from some laborers, consisted of eighty-five, officers and men; the Confederate force in

---

1 See the President's oath of office on page 196, note 4.

2 See the Constitution, page xiv, section 2, "No person held to service," etc.

Charleston was about seven thousand. The government immediately made arrangements to send the needed supplies. As soon as Jefferson Davis heard of it, he ordered General Beauregard,[1] in command of the Confederate army at Charleston, to demand the surrender of the fort. Major Anderson declined to surrender, and at daybreak, April 12, 1861, the Confederates fired the first gun at the fort. It was answered by one

Fort Sumter.

from Sumter. War had begun. For thirty-four hours nineteen batteries[2] rained shot and shell against the fort, which continued to fire back. Notwithstanding this tremendous cannonade, no one was killed on either side. But Major Anderson, finding that his ammunition was nearly exhausted, and having nothing but pork left to eat, decided to give up the fort. On Sunday (April 14), he, with his garrison, left the

[1] Beauregard (Boh'rĕh-gard).
[2] Batteries: a battery is a wall of earth or other fortification having a number of cannon mounted on it. A battery may also consist of cannon mounted on wheels and drawn by horses.

fort, and embarked for New York; he carried with him the shot-torn flag under which he and his men had fought.[1]

### 319. President Lincoln's Call for Volunteers; the Rising of the North.

— The next day (April 15, 1861) President Lincoln called for seventy-five thousand volunteers for three months' service — for few then supposed that the war, if there was really to be a war, would last longer than that. In response to the President's call the whole North seemed to rise. Men of all parties forgot their political quarrels, and hastened to the defence of the capital.

Confederate Flag.
(The Stars and Bars.)

The heart of the people stood by the Union, and by the old flag.[2] Within thirty-six hours several companies from Pennsylvania had reached Washington. They were speedily followed

The Flag Anderson carried from Fort Sumter.

by the Sixth Massachusetts Regiment — the first full regiment to march. They had to fight their way through a mob at Baltimore. There, on April 19, 1861, the day on which the Revolutionary battles of Lexington and Concord were fought, the first Union soldiers gave their lives for the preservation of the nation.[3]

---

1 Just four years, to a day, from that date, Major Anderson (then General Anderson) hoisted the same flag over the ruins of Fort Sumter.     2 See page 178, and note 4.

3 On April 18, 1861, the Confederates seized the United States arsenal at Harper's Ferry, and on the 20th the Navy Yard at Norfolk. In both cases, however, the officer in command succeeded in burning a large part of the property before the Confederates got it.

Many of the volunteers were lads under twenty, and some of them had never left home before. There were many affecting scenes when the "boys in blue"[1] started for Washington. Anxious mothers took tearful leave of sons, whom they feared they should never see again. The peril of the Republic touched men in all conditions of life, and touched them as nothing ever had before. Farmers left their ploughs, mechanics dropped their tools, clerks said farewell to their employers, college students threw down their books — all hurried to take their places in the ranks, and even lads of fifteen begged to go as drummer-boys.

On the Southern side there were the same anxious leave-takings; for it should be borne in mind that while the people of the North were eager to offer their lives for the defence of the Union, the people of the South were just as eager to give theirs to repel what they considered invasion.

**320. Secession of Four more States; General Butler's "Contrabands."** — President Lincoln's call for troops made it necessary for the remaining slave states to decide at once whether they would remain in the Union or go out. Virginia[2] joined the Confederacy; but the western part of the state had voted against secession, and later it became a separate state (1863) under the name of West Virginia. The Confederate capital was soon removed from Montgomery to Richmond. Arkansas, Tennessee, and North Carolina followed the example of Virginia; but Delaware, Maryland, Kentucky, and Missouri did not secede. By the middle of June the Confederacy consisted of eleven states; no more were added.

General Butler of Massachusetts held command of Fort Monroe[3] in Eastern Virginia. It was the only Union strong-

---

[1] The Union soldiers wore blue uniforms; the Confederates, gray.

[2] The secession of Eastern Virginia immensely increased the military difficulties with which the North had to contend. Had Virginia remained in the Union (as she seemed at one time likely to do), the war would probably have been of short duration.

[3] Commonly called Fortress Monroe, but *officially* designated Fort Monroe.

hold in the state, and was of the very highest importance. A number of slaves came to the General and begged him to set them free. He had no authority to give them their liberty. On the other hand, he was certain that if he returned these slaves to their masters they would use them in carrying on the war against the Union. Finally, General Butler got out of the difficulty by saying, These negroes are *contraband of war;* [1] then putting spades in the hands of the "contrabands," as they were henceforth called, he set them to work to strengthen the fort. General Butler's action was the first decided blow struck at the existence of slavery after the commencement of the war.

**321. Condition of the North and of the South with Respect to the War.** — In regard to the terrible struggle now about to begin between the North and the South, each of the combatants had certain advantages over the other. First, the National Government had more than twice as many men to draw on as the South. [2] Next, although unprepared for war, the North had iron-mills, ship-yards, foundries, machine-shops, and factories of all kinds. For this reason it could make everything its soldiers would need, from a blanket to a battery. Finally, it had the command of the sea, and so with its war-vessels — most of which, however, it had to buy or build — it could shut up the Southern ports and cut them off from help from abroad.

The South had the advantage (1) of being prepared for the war by having got possession of large quantities of arms and ammunition (though it had small means of making any more); (2) with the exception of General Scott and a few others who stood by the Union, it had a majority of the best-known

[1] Contraband of war: here meaning, forfeited by the customs or laws of war. General Butler's idea was that the laws of war forbade his returning anything or any property to the Confederates, or to those who sympathized with them, which they could use in carrying on the contest.

[2] The total population of the United States in 1860 was, in round numbers, 32,000,000. The Union states had about 23,000,000; the eleven seceded states about 9,000,000, of which nearly 3,500,000 were slaves.

officers in the regular army, — such men as Robert E. Lee of Virginia[1] and General Beauregard; (3) it could send all of its fighting men to the front while it kept several millions of slaves at work raising food to support them; (4) the South had the great advantage of being able to fight on the defensive, on its own soil, and so needed fewer soldiers. General Grant thought the two armies, all things considered, were about equally matched.

322. The Number and Position of the Two Armies. — President Lincoln's first call for troops was quickly followed by others, and the South likewise strengthened its side. By the summer of 1861 the Union forces probably numbered about 180,000, and those of the Confederates, 150,000. The former were under the direction of the veteran General Scott,[2] and the latter under General Beauregard.[3] The Union army was mainly in Eastern Virginia and Maryland. It extended along the banks of the Potomac from Harper's Ferry to the mouth of the river, and thence southward to Fort Monroe. The Confederate army held the country south of the Potomac, with Richmond as its fortified centre.

In Missouri the national troops, under Generals Lyon, Frémont,[4] and Halleck, got control of that state, while General

[1] General Lee was born in Virginia, 1807; died, 1870. He was a graduate of West Point, and served with distinction in the Mexican War (see Paragraph 291). When Virginia seceded, Lee, who was then a lieutenant-colonel in the United States army, said, " I recognize no necessity for this state of things," yet he felt it his duty to go with his state. He said, " With all my devotion to the Union . . . I have not been able to make up my mind to raise my hand against my relatives, my children, my home." He was made commander-in-chief of the Virginia state forces. In 1862, he received — subject to the orders of Jefferson Davis — the entire command of "the armies of the Confederacy." His management of the war showed that he was a man of great military ability, and of entire devotion to what he understood to be his duty. [2] See Paragraph 291.

[3] General Joseph E. Johnston ranked above General Beauregard, and after the battle of Bull Run (July 21, 1861), in which he took a leading part, he held command of the Confederate army of Virginia until he was wounded at the battle of Seven Pines, May 31, 1862, when General Lee took the command.

[4] General Frémont was born at Savannah in 1813. Under the authority of the

McClellan drove out the Confederates from West Virginia. In the southwest the Confederates had got possession of the Mississippi from New Orleans to Columbus, Kentucky, by building forts on the river banks. They were making preparations to do the same on the Tennessee and Cumberland rivers, and their intention was, if possible, to get the entire control of Kentucky besides.

323. The Battle of Bull Run. — The cry at the South was, "On to Washington!" It was answered by the cry of the North, "On to Richmond!" Beauregard had taken up his position at Manassas Junction on Bull Run.[1] There he could both protect the Confederate capital and threaten Washington. He had an army[2] of about 30,000. General McDowell in command, in the field, of the Union forces, had about the same number.[2] One army, as President Lincoln said, was as "green" as the other. McDowell advanced, not because he was ready, or because General Scott advised it, but for the simple reason that the North was tired of waiting and was impatient to strike a decisive blow.

The battle began on a sweltering hot Sunday in July (July 21, 1861). At first the Union troops drove the Confederates from their position. General Bee, one of the Southern leaders, rushing up to General Jackson, cried out, "General, they are

government he began the exploration of the Rocky Mountains and of an overland route to the Pacific in 1842–1844. In 1845 he set out on another exploring expedition to the Pacific coast. After the outbreak of the Mexican War he, with the assistance of American settlers in California, freed that territory from the authority of Mexico, and in the summer of 1846 he was appointed governor of the territory. By treaty with Mexico in 1847 Frémont secured California to the United States. In 1856 he was nominated to the Presidency (as the anti-slavery candidate) by the Republican party. From 1878 to 1881 he was governor of Arizona. In the summer of 1861 Frémont issued a proclamation emancipating the slaves of all persons in Missouri who were in arms against the Union; but President Lincoln refused to approve it.    [1] Run: a small stream or creek.

[2] In the Civil War the Confederates counted in battle only those of their men who were present and able to fight; but the Union officers, on the contrary, counted all as present whose names were on their army rolls. See General Grant's "Personal Memoirs," II. 290, and "The Century Company's War-Book," I. 485.

beating us back!" "We will give them the bayonet," said Jackson, quietly. Rallying his men, Bee shouted, "Look! there is Jackson standing like a stone wall!" It was true; and "Stonewall" Jackson,[1] as the Confederate general was ever after called, used "the bayonet" so effectually that the Union advance was checked, and the Southerners held their ground until heavy reinforcements came up, by rail, from the Shenandoah Valley, struck the national troops a terrible blow on the flank, and drove them from the hard-fought field. As the

SCALE OF MILES
0    25    50    75    100

Confederate General Johnston says: the Northern army fought under the great disadvantage of having to make the attack. They fled back to Washington in confusion.

**324. Results of the Defeat at Bull Run.** — Some failures are simply stepping stones to final success. The defeat at Bull

---

[1] Gen. T. J. Jackson of Va., born 1824; died 1863. He was one of the most remarkable men who fought on the side of the South. His motto was, "Do your duty, and leave the rest to Providence." His death was the heaviest personal loss the South sustained during the war. Lee called "Stonewall" Jackson his "right arm"; in his department he ranked as one of the ablest generals in the Confederacy, and was respected alike by those who fought under him and those who fought against him.

Run was such a case.  Instead of discouraging the people of the North, it roused them to new and greater effort.  At the very time the defeated and disheartened Union soldiers were pouring over the Long Bridge across the Potomac into Washington, Congress voted to raise 500,000 men and $500,000,000 to carry on the war.  The cry now was, "Drill and organize!"  General McClellan came fresh from his victories in West Virginia to take command of the army.  He taught them the great lesson, that enthusiasm without military organization is of no more use than steam without an engine.  For the next six months and more there was no general movement, but, as the newspapers said, "all was quiet on the Potomac";[1] that quiet, however, meant that both sides were now getting ready to fight in terrible earnest.

325. **Union Plan of the War.** — Gradually a plan for the war in defence of the Union took shape; it was this: 1. To maintain a strict blockade[2] of all Southern ports, and thus cut off the South from getting supplies from abroad for carrying on the war.  This arm of the Union service was of immense help, and without it the contest might have dragged on for many years longer than it did.  2. To attack and take Richmond. 3. To open the lower Mississippi, with the Tennessee and the Cumberland, which the Confederate forts had closed to navigation.  4. To break through the Confederate line in the West, march an army through to the Atlantic, and thence northward to Virginia.

326. **Blockade Runners; Confederate War-Vessels; Seizure of Mason and Slidell.** — While the Union forces were getting possession of Fort Hatteras, Port Royal, and other important

---

[1] On October 21, 1861, a body of Union troops two thousand strong was beaten by a large force of Confederates at Ball's Bluff on the Potomac, and on August 10 of the same year General Lyon was defeated and killed at the battle of Wilson's Creek, Missouri.

[2] This blockade was maintained by stationing vessels of war in front of every Southern port, thus, after a time, effectually closing them to all commerce with Europe.

points on the Southern coast, fast Southern vessels ran the gantlet of the blockade to obtain arms and ammunition ; furthermore British steamers, specially built for the work, often succeeded in evading the Union cruisers and in bringing supplies for the Confederates.   Jefferson Davis had no navy, but he succeeded in buying or building a number of war-vessels in

Running the Blockade — Union Cruiser in the Distance.

Great Britain which in time destroyed so many merchant ships owned in the North that unarmed vessels no longer dared to carry the stars and stripes.   Later, the *Alabama*, built in England, was added to the Confederate fleet and inflicted immense damage on Union commerce, for which at the end of the war England had to pay roundly.

Early in November (1861) the Confederacy undertook to send two commissioners or agents — Mason and Slidell — to Europe to get aid for the Southern cause and also to endeavor to persuade England and France to acknowledge the independence of the Confederate states.

Captain Wilkes of the United States navy stopped the British mail steamer *Trent*, on which Mason and Slidell had embarked for England, and took them both prisoners. England at once demanded that the national government should give them up. The North protested, but President Lincoln said, "We fought Great Britain in 1812 for doing just what Captain Wilkes has done. We must give up the prisoners to England." It was accordingly done, but Mason and Slidell, though they went to Europe, failed to accomplish anything of importance for the Confederacy.

**327. The *Merrimac* destroys the *Cumberland* and the *Congress*; the *Monitor*.** — When the Confederates seized the Norfolk navy yard,[1] they got possession of the United States ship of war

The " Monitor " and the " Merrimac."

*Merrimac.* Having covered the vessel with a very heavy double plating of iron, they sent her out under command of Captain Buchanan to destroy the Union war-vessels at the mouth of the James River off Fort Monroe. The Union ships were of wood; they could not resist an antagonist that was a floating fort rather than an ordinary war-vessel. The balls from their guns made no more impression on the iron shell of the monster which now attacked them, than a sparrow's bill would make on the back of an alligator. The *Merrimac* sunk the *Cumberland*, which carried down with her many sick and wounded

[1] See note 3, page 296.  The Confederates named the *Merrimac* the *Virginia*.

men;[1] she then destroyed the *Congress*. The next day (Sunday, March 9, 1862) the *Merrimac* returned to complete the destruction of the fleet; suddenly a strange little craft appeared, looking like a "cheese-box on a raft." This was the *Monitor*,[2] a new Union vessel made of iron. She was commanded by Lieutenant Worden. The *Merrimac* now found that she had got her match. After a terrific battle the Confederate vessel[3] steamed back to the navy yard at Norfolk.

The "little giant" had practically won the day. It was perhaps "the most important single event of the war." If the *Merrimac* had gained the victory, she might next have gone up the Potomac and destroyed the national capital. In that case European nations might have acknowledged the independence of the South, and demanded that the blockade be raised and the ports of the Confederacy thrown open to the commerce of the world. The United States now built more Monitors, and by the end of the year had a fleet of several hundred effective war-vessels of different kinds, both on the ocean and on the western rivers.

### 328. The War in the West; Capture of Fort Henry and Fort Donelson.

— At the West the line of the Confederate army, under General A. S. Johnston, stretched from Mill Spring, and Bowling Green, in Kentucky, through Fort Donelson on the Cumberland, and Fort Henry on the Tennessee, to Columbus on the Mississippi. General Halleck,[4] in command of the

---

[1] See Longfellow's poem on the loss of the *Cumberland*.

[2] The *Monitor* was built by Captain Ericsson, the inventor of the screw-propeller for steamships, and of the hot-air engine. She was an iron vessel of small size, sitting so low in the water that scarcely anything of her hull was visible. In the centre of her deck stood a revolving iron turret, which carried two cannon, sending solid shot weighing one hundred and sixty-six pounds. The invention of the *Monitor* revolutionized the construction of war-vessels throughout the world. Few wooden ships of war have since been built.     [3] Colonel Wood, of the *Merrimac* (or *Virginia*), speaks of slight damages, but no leak; he thinks "the battle was a drawn one," but says "the advantage was with the *Monitor*." See Century Company's War Book, I. 703.

[4] General Halleck was born near Utica, N. Y., in 1815; died 1872. He graduated at West Point and served in the Mexican War. He was appointed a major-general

greater part of the Union forces of the West, resolved to break that line, to enter the cotton states, and also to open the Mississippi. In January, 1862, General Thomas gained a victory at Mills Spring and drove the Confederates out of Eastern Kentucky. Then General Halleck ordered General U. S. Grant,[1] to start from Cairo, Illinois, and attack Fort Henry; but Commodore Foote got there first with his gun-

SCALE OF MILES
0    50    100    200    300

boats and took it (February 6, 1862). Grant then moved on Fort Donelson. The battle raged for three days in succession;

of the United States army in August, 1861. He received command of the department of Missouri (with other states) in November, and of the department of the Mississippi in March, 1862. From July 11, 1862, to March, 1864, he was general-in-chief of the armies of the United States, and had his headquarters at Washington.

[1] General U. S. Grant was born in Ohio, 1822; died in New York, 1885. He was a graduate of West Point, and served in the Mexican War (see Paragraph 292), where he was promoted for meritorious conduct in battle. In 1859 he entered into the leather and saddlery business with his father at Galena, Illinois. On the breaking out of the Civil War he raised a company of Union volunteers, and in August, 1861, he was made a brigadier-general, and took command of the department of **Cairo**. His subsequent career will be traced in the pages of this history.

No terms except an unconditional and immediate surrender can be accepted. I propose to move immediately upon your works.

I am sir: very respectfully Your obt servt—

U. S. Grant
Brig. Gen

then the Confederate General Buckner asked Grant what terms he would grant him if he gave up the fort. Grant wrote back, *"No terms except an unconditional and immediate surrender can be accepted."* [1] The Confederates were forced to agree to Grant's conditions and the first great Union victory of the war was won (February 16, 1862). Fifteen thousand prisoners — "the greatest number ever taken in any battle (up to that time) on this continent " — were captured, and also large quantities of arms. Columbus was now of no use to the Confederates and they abandoned it. The surrender of Nashville followed, and Kentucky and Tennessee were in the hands of the Union forces.

**329. Battles of Pittsburg Landing and Island Number Ten.** — Grant, with his victorious army, then moved up the Tennessee River to Pittsburg Landing or Shiloh. Here (April 6, 1862) he was attacked by General A. S. Johnston and driven back. The night after the battle, General Buell brought a large force of Union troops. The Union men now outnumbered the Confederates by seventeen thousand, and the next day Grant gained his second great victory. In his official report he said, " I am indebted to General Sherman for the success of that battle." On that hotly contested field twenty-five thousand men had fallen dead or wounded [2] — among them was General Johnston — one of the South's noblest men.[3] On

Map of Island No. 10, showing the canal cut by the Union troops in order to take the Confederate fortifications.

the following day (April 8, 1862) the Confederates on Island Number Ten, in the Mississippi, surrendered to Commodore Foote, after nearly a month's obstinate fighting. That victory was of immense importance in a military point of view,

---

[1] Hence the name sometimes given General Grant of " Unconditional Surrender Grant." See copy of General Grant's letter to General Buckner, opposite page 307.

[2] Union force, 57,000; Confederate, 40,000. Union loss, 14,000; Confederate, 11,000.

[3] After he was wounded, General Johnston sent his surgeon to attend to some wounded Union prisoners; while he was gone Johnston bled to death.

for it opened the river to the Union vessels down to Vicksburg, a distance of about three hundred miles.

**330. General Summary of the First Year of the War, April, 1861, to April, 1862.** — The Civil War began April 12, 1861, with the Confederate attack on Fort Sumter. After the surrender of that fort, the first great battle was fought in the summer at Bull Run, and resulted in the defeat of the Union army. In the spring of 1862 the battle between the *Merrimac* and *Monitor* occurred, and the *Merrimac* was forced to retreat. During the year the Union forces in the West gained the important victories of Fort Henry, Fort Donelson, Pittsburg Landing, and Island Number Ten. The general result of the year was decidedly favorable to the cause of the Union, especially in the West.

SECOND YEAR OF THE WAR, APRIL, 1862, TO APRIL, 1863.

**331. Expedition against New Orleans; how the City was defended.** — Very early in the spring of 1862 an expedition under Captain Farragut [1] and General Butler sailed from Fort Monroe to attack New Orleans, the most important city and port in the possession of the Confederate government. The approach to New Orleans was defended by two strong forts on the Mississippi, about seventy-five miles below the city.[2] These forts were nearly opposite each other, so that any vessels trying to

[1] Admiral David G. Farragut, born in Tenn. in 1801; died 1870. He entered the navy in 1812. In 1841 he was made commander, and later, captain. In 1862, after his famous victory at New Orleans, he was promoted to the rank of rear-admiral, then (1864) to that of vice-admiral, and in 1866 to that of admiral — the highest position in the United States navy; the last two grades were created for him. From 1823 to the outbreak of the Civil War, Farragut's home, when on shore, was at Norfolk, Virginia. He insisted that Virginia had been forced to secede against the will of the majority of the people of the state. From 1861 to the close of his life his home was at Hastings-on-the-Hudson.

[2] New Orleans is about one hundred and five miles from the sea. In the war of 1812 a single fort, at one of the points where those two Confederate forts stood, checked the advance of the British fleet for nine days.

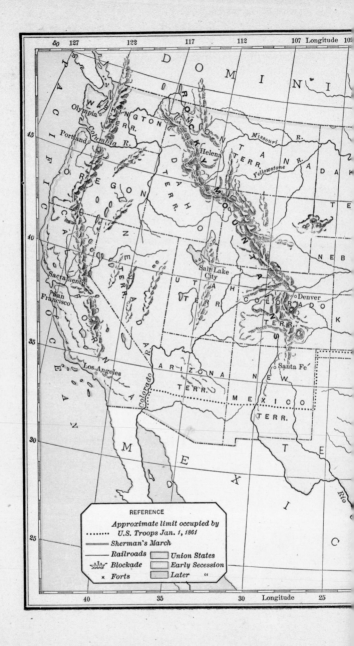

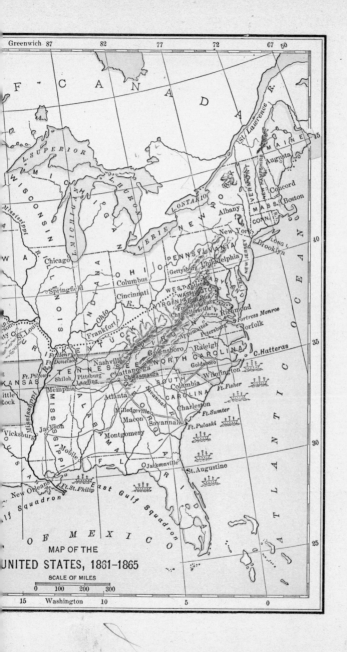

MAP OF THE

UNITED STATES, 1861–1865

SCALE OF MILES

0   100   200   300

pass between them would be exposed to a tremendous cross fire from their guns.   Just below the forts the Confederates had stretched two heavy chain cables, on hulks, across the river to check any Union war-ships that might attempt to come up, while above the forts they had stationed fifteen armed vessels — two of them ironclads like the *Merrimac.*[1] With these defences the city defied attack.

Captain Farragut had a fleet of nearly fifty wooden vessels. It was considered to be the most powerful "that had ever sailed under the American flag."   General Butler had followed him to take command of a force of fifteen thousand men, then at Ship Island,[2] near New Orleans, and with them to hold the city after its surrender.   Farragut's work, with the aid of Commander Porter's mortar-boats,[3] was to silence the forts, break through the chains, conquer the Confederate fleet, and take the city.   One of the men who took part in that work was Lieutenant George Dewey, now known as Admiral Dewey — the "Hero of Manila."

**332.  Bombardment of the Forts ; Farragut passes them and destroys the Opposing Fleet ; Capture of New Orleans.** — For six days and nights Commander Porter hammered away at the forts, and the forts did their best to hammer back.   The discharge of artillery was deafening, and the shock so severe that it killed birds and fishes.   It even broke glass in windows at Balize, thirty miles away.[4]   Porter's men were completely

[1] See Paragraph 327.

[2] Ship Island is in the Gulf of Mexico, about one hundred miles east of New Orleans.  See Map of the Territorial Growth of the United States.

[3] Mortar-boats : vessels for carrying mortars, short and very wide-mouthed cannon for firing shells.   The shells used here were hollow cast-iron balls of great size, weighing nearly three hundred pounds.   They were filled with powder, and so constructed that when they fell they would explode with tremendous violence.   The shells made a peculiar screaming, hissing noise as they flew through the air, accompanied by a train of smoke by day and of fire by night.   When one buried itself in the earth inside of one of the forts and then exploded, the result was like that of a small earthquake.

[4] See Draper's " The American Civil War," II. 331.

exhausted by their labors at the guns, and the moment they were off duty would drop down on the deck and fall fast asleep, amid the continuous roar of the battle.

Finally, Captain Farragut determined to make an attempt to cut through the chains, and run past the forts. He succeeded in doing this, and after a terrific combat, destroyed the Confederate fleet and reached New Orleans.

The river-front of the city, for a distance of full five miles, was all ablaze with burning ships, steamboats, and thousands of bales of cotton, which had been set on fire to prevent their capture by the Union forces. A party of Farragut's men landed, speedily hauled down the "stars and bars" from the public buildings, and hoisted the "stars and stripes" in their place (April 25, 1862).

Port Hudson and Vicksburg were now the only important fortified points on the Mississippi still held by the Confederates. If they could be taken, the great river of the West would once more be open from its source to the sea. But both Port Hudson and Vicksburg stood on immensely high bluffs,[1] out of the reach of the guns of the war-vessels, so that it would be exceedingly difficult, if not indeed absolutely impossible, to capture them by an attack from the river alone. For this reason an expedition against them had to be put off until a land force, as well as one by water, could be sent to make the attack.[2]

Meanwhile the Union navy had captured several important points on the coast of North and of South Carolina.

### 333. The War in Virginia; McClellan's Advance on Richmond; the Peninsular Campaign; the Weather. — Before Farragut had taken New Orleans, General McClellan with one hundred

---

[1] The banks of the river at Port Hudson are about fifty feet high, and at Vicksburg about two hundred feet high. (See Physical Geography and History, page 50.)

[2] Captain Farragut, after taking New Orleans, went up the river, captured Baton Rouge and Natchez, and attempted, but in vain, to take Vicksburg. He was now made rear-admiral.

GENERAL LEE.

thousand men, leaving about as many to defend Washington,[1] had begun an advance on Richmond from Fort Monroe. His plan was to march up the Peninsula — as the Virginians call the long and rather narrow strip of land between the James and York rivers. The Confederates did everything in their power to check his advance at Yorktown and Williamsburg, and, later, at Seven Pines or Fair Oaks. Meanwhile heavy rains compelled McClellan's army to wade, rather than march, forward through mud and water. To increase his difficulties the Chickahominy River had overflowed its banks; and as part of his army was on one side of it and part on the other, they could not act together to advantage; in fact, both parts were floundering about for weeks in a swamp, spending much of their time in building roads and bridges, and fighting the weather rather than the enemy. An immense number of men were lost by sickness.

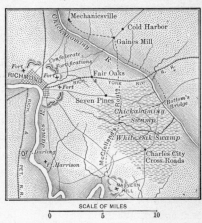

SCALE OF MILES

0          5          10

**334.** **"Stonewall" Jackson's Raid; Stuart's Raid; Results of the Peninsular Campaign.** — Early in June (1862) General Lee[2] took command of the Confederate forces,[3] shortly after "Stonewall" Jackson had gained a brilliant success.[4] "Stonewall" had started to drive General Banks's Union army out of the

---

[1] 40,000 of these were at Fredericksburg under McDowell.

[2] See page 299, note 1.

[3] General Joseph E. Johnston had been in command since the battle of Bull Run, July, 1861. He was wounded at the battle of Seven Pines, May 31, 1862, and Lee then took command.          [4] See page 301, note 1.

Shenandoah Valley, in Western Virginia, and make the authorities in Washington think that the capital was in danger of immediate attack.    With his seventeen thousand men he made Banks's nine thousand beat a hasty retreat to the Potomac; and he effectually prevented McClellan from getting any help from the forty thousand Union troops at Fredericksburg.[1] Then Lee sent General Stuart with a dashing body of cavalry to see what mischief he could do.    He rode clear round McClellan's army, tore up the railroads, burned car-loads of provisions, and made matters very awkward and uncomfortable for that general.

From June 25 to July 1 (1862), Lee and McClellan were engaged in a number of desperate fights around Richmond, known as the "Seven Days' Battles";[2] Lee captured many guns and prisoners; the Union forces retreated to James River, and McClellan and his army were recalled to the neighborhood of Washington.    In these last battles over fifteen thousand men had been lost on each side, but the Union army had accomplished nothing decisive; though it had been within sight of the spires of the Confederate capital, and of the wooden or "Quaker guns" which helped to guard it.[3]    Once the alarm there was so great that a niece of Jefferson Davis wrote to a friend, "Uncle Jeff thinks we had better go to a safer place than Richmond."    On the other hand, President Lincoln called for additional volunteers; and new forces, shouting, "We are coming, Father Abraham, three hundred thousand more," began to go forward to the aid of the government.

[1] Note 1, page 311.

[2] In the last of these battles, that at Malvern Hill, Lee's forces were driven back with heavy loss.    During the Peninsular campaign the armies of Frémont, Banks, and McDowell were united under the name of the *Army of Virginia*, and the command of this force was given to General Pope, who had been successful in the West.

[3] One of the humorous features of the war was the use of wooden cannon by the Confederates in their fortifications at Manassas, Richmond, and elsewhere.    It was some time before the Union army found out this clever trick of the "Quaker guns," which, as a "contraband" said, were "just as good to *scare* with as any others."

335. **The Second Battle of Bull Run ; Lee's Advance across the Potomac ; Battle of Antietam.**[1]— Near the last of August (1862), Lee advanced his forces against General Pope,[2] and met him in the second battle of Bull Run. "Stonewall" Jackson did the heaviest of the fighting. Pope was defeated ; but fell back in good order to Washington, and resigned his command.

Not long after, Lee crossed the Potomac above Washington, his men singing exultingly, "Maryland, my Maryland." Lee believed that thousands of the Maryland people would welcome him as their deliverer, and would join him in a march against Philadelphia. In this he was sorely mistaken. In the middle of September, "Stonewall" Jackson captured Harper's Ferry, and thus obtained a quantity of arms and some provisions. McClellan now advanced to meet Lee. At Antietam Creek (or Sharpsburg) one of the bloodiest battles of the war was fought (September 17, 1862); and the bodies of the "boys in blue" and of the "boys in gray" lay in ranks like swaths of grass cut by the scythe.[3] The result of the terrible contest was that Lee was compelled to retreat across the Potomac. McClellan followed, but he did not move rapidly enough to suit the government authorities, and the command of the army was taken from him and given to General Burnside.

336. **Battles of Fredericksburg and Murfreesboro.** — General Burnside set out to march on Richmond, but found the Confederates strongly fortified[4] on the hills around Fredericksburg, on the Rappahannock. In the battle which ensued (December 13, 1862) he was defeated and forced to fall back toward Washington. General Hooker — "Fighting Joe Hooker," as

---

[1] Antietam (An-tee'tam).          [2] See page 312, note 2.

[3] Union forces actually engaged at Antietam are estimated at about 60,000. McClellan's *available* strength was probably double that of Lee's. Confederate forces, 40,000. See Century Company's War Book, II. 603. Loss nearly 12,000 on each side. Authorities differ about the strength of the two armies. "Loss" in all cases is understood to include *wounded* as well as killed.

[4] Burnside had about 116,000 men ; Lee had nearly 80,000 strongly entrenched on and near the hills. Burnside lost 12,000 men, and Lee not quite half that number.

his men called him — now received the command of Burnside's army.

This was the last battle of the year in the East.   In the West the Union forces had beaten the enemy at Pea Ridge, Arkansas, and had taken Corinth, Mississippi; the Confederates attempted to retake it, but were driven back with frightful loss.   Bragg invaded Kentucky; Buell fought him at Perryville, and Bragg fled with his plunder and took shelter behind the Cumberland Mountains.   Grant and Sherman then moved against Vicksburg, but the Confederate Cavalry cut off Grant's supplies and Sherman was repulsed.   Next, General Rosecrans moved against Bragg.   He met the Confederate general at Murfreesboro, Tennessee (December 31, 1862).   Each had about forty thousand men.   The contest raged for three days. "The battle must be won," said Rosecrans.   The Union forces held their ground,[1] and Bragg retreated in the night.

**337. President Lincoln's Proclamation of Emancipation; its Results.** — President Lincoln had entered office resolved, as he then said, not to interfere with slavery.   But the progress of the contest convinced him that slavery was not only the real cause, but also the main strength of the war against the Union.   He believed that the time had now come when it was his duty to strike that cause and that strength a decided blow. On New Year's Day, 1863, the President issued a proclamation, freeing all the slaves in those states of the South which were still at war against the Union.   Thus by a single stroke of the pen, over three millions of negroes received (so far as the government could then give it) that most precious, yet most perilous of all rights — the ownership of themselves. No greater event is recorded in the pages of American history.   After the expiration of nearly a hundred years the nation at last made good, without exception, the words of the Declaration of Independence, which declare that "all men

[1] Union loss, 14,000; Confederate, 11,000.

*And by virtue of the power, and for the purpose aforesaid, I do order and declare that all persons held as slaves within said designated States, and parts of States, are, and henceforward shall be free; — — — — —*

*And upon this act, sincerely believed to be an act of justice, warranted by the Constitution, upon military necessity, I invoke the considerate judgment of mankind, and the gracious favor of Almighty God.*

*[L. S.]   Independence of the United States of America the eighty-seventh.*

*Abraham Lincoln*

*By the President;
William H Seward,
Secretary of State*

NOTE.— President Lincoln issued a preliminary proclamation of emancipation on Sept. 22, 1862, giving one hundred days warning to the South. In case any State chose to return to the Union within that time its slaves were not to be set at liberty by the final proclamation.

The President said: " My paramount object in this struggle is to save the Union, and is not either to save or to destroy slavery. If I could save the Union without freeing any slave, I would do it; and if I could save it by freeing all the slaves, I would do it; and if I could save it by freeing some and leaving others alone, I would also do that." Letter to Horace Greeley, Aug. 22, 1862.

are created equal "; that is, with equal natural rights to "life, liberty, and the pursuit of happiness."

Many thousands of negroes were now enlisted in the Union army; but the greater part remained quietly at work on the Southern plantations. The freedom of the whole body of slaves in the country was not accomplished until after the close of the war. Then an amendment to the Constitution[1] declared that slavery should no longer exist in the United States. That final act of emancipation has proved to be as much an advantage to the white race, both North and South, as to the negroes themselves. Free labor has brought a greater degree of prosperity than any section of the country ever obtained under slave labor. Now that the South is no longer hampered by having to hold the negroes in bondage, it has found its real strength and its true and lasting prosperity.

338. **Summary of the Second Year of the War, April, 1862, to April, 1863.** — The one great military success of the year on the part of the Union forces was the taking of New Orleans. In the East, if McClellan and his successors failed to reach Richmond, Lee, on the other hand, failed just as completely and far more disastrously in his attempted invasion of the North. The Proclamation of Emancipation gave the war a new character. Before, the North had been fighting simply to restore the Union as it was before the South seceded; but now, it was to restore the Union without slavery — to make the nation wholly *free*.

THIRD YEAR OF THE WAR, APRIL, 1863, TO APRIL, 1864.

339. **The War in the East; Battle of Chancellorsville.** — In the spring of 1863, General Hooker crossed the Rapidan, intending to advance on Richmond. But he had no sooner started than General Lee, with "Stonewall" Jackson, met him

---

[1] See Amendments to the Constitution, page xvii, Article XIII.

at Chancellorsville.[1]  Here a two days' battle was fought (May 2-3, 1863).  General Hooker had twice as many men as the Confederates, but he was badly beaten.  He might have

gained the victory; but at a critical moment he was stunned by a cannon-ball and lay senseless for many hours. During all that time his army "was without a head."

Lee, with "Stonewall" Jackson's help, not only won the battle, but drove the Union forces back across the river. But it was a dearly bought triumph to the Confederates, for Jackson fell.  His death was the heaviest loss of the kind

"Stonewall" Jackson.

which the South suffered during the war.  Chancellorsville was the last victory gained by the Confederates in Virginia in the "open country."[2]  The command of the Union army was now given to General Meade.

**340.  Battle of Gettysburg.** — A month after the battle of Chancellorsville Lee made a second [3] attempt to enter the free states and conquer a peace. He moved down the Shenandoah Valley with about seventy thousand men, crossed the Potomac in June (1863), and moved into Pennsylvania, intending to strike Harrisburg, the capital of the state, and then, if successful, to march on Philadelphia.  General Meade, with a Union force of about ninety thousand,[4] met Lee at Gettysburg.  Here one of the

---

[1] Union forces in the battle, 130,000; Confederate, 60,000.  But see note on page 300, on estimates of combatants.  Union loss, 17,000; Confederate, about 12,000. General Lee gave Jackson all the credit of the victory.

[2] See Comte de Paris, "Hist. of the War," III. 102.     [3] See Paragraph 335.

[4] Official returns estimate that Lee had at least 70,000 men, and Meade 90,000.

The "High-Water Mark Monument."

Erected at the "clump of trees" on the battlefield of Gettysburg, 1892.

This monument, dedicated June 2, 1892, was erected to commemorate the repulse, by the Union troops, of the famous charge of the Confederate column led by General Pickett, commander of a division of Longstreet's corps.

The monument consists of a large open bronze book supported by two pyramids of bronze cannon balls resting on a granite base.

The book bears the inscription: *High-Water Mark of the Rebellion;* then follow the names of the officers of the assaulting column on the left-hand page, with the names on the opposite page of the Union officers who repulsed that assault.

Beneath the book, on the front face of the base, a bronze tablet fastened to the granite block has this inscription:

"*Commands Honored.* In recognition of the Patriotism and Gallantry displayed by their respective troops who met and assisted to repulse Longstreet's Assault, the following States have contributed to erect this tablet: Maine, New Hampshire, Vermont, Massachusetts, Rhode Island, Connecticut, New York, New Jersey, Delaware, Pennsylvania, West Virginia, Ohio, Michigan, and Minnesota."

The northern face of the monument bears a second tablet giving the names of the Union infantry commands of Hancock's and Newton's corps which met Longstreet's assault; and the southern face bears a third tablet giving the names of the Confederate infantry commands of Longstreet's corps which constituted the charging column.

The battle of Gettysburg is generally considered as having been the turning-point in the terrible struggle for the mastery between the Confederate forces fighting for secession and the National forces fighting to preserve the Union.

The battles of July 1st and 2d were indecisive; the battle of the third and last day forced Lee to retreat. The efforts of the Confederates reached their high-water mark at Gettysburg, — henceforth they continued to recede.

The monument appropriately marks the spot reached by Armistead, who was leading the Confederate advance.

With his cap on the point of his sword he had penetrated a short distance within the Union lines, when he fell riddled with bullets. Then came a hand-to-hand fight which lasted a few minutes, and the remnant of Pickett's column threw down their arms. Lee's last desperate effort had failed. It was the beginning of the end.

A portion of the battlefield of Gettysburg was set apart for the burial of those who fell there in defense of the Union. It was dedicated November 19, 1863. On that occasion President Lincoln delivered his ever-memorable address, of which the following words are inscribed on one of the panels of the Soldiers' Monument.

"It is rather for us to be here dedicated to the great task remaining before us — that from these honored dead we take increased devotion to that cause for which they gave the last full measure of devotion; that we here highly resolve that these dead shall not have died in vain; that this nation, under God, shall have a new birth of freedom; and that government of the people, by the people, for the people, shall not perish from the earth."

The "Soldiers' Monument"
in the National Cemetery on the Battlefield of Gettysburg.

most important and decisive battles of the war took place. Both sides fought with the most desperate courage. The Confederates held Seminary Ridge; the Union men, Cemetery Ridge, nearly opposite. The battle lasted three days (July 1–3, 1863). On the first day, the Confederates, having far greater numbers, gained the advantage. On the second day, Lee's men made a rush to get Little Round Top, but were beaten back with heavy loss. Later, they got a foothold on Culp's Hill, but were soon driven out. On the third day, Lee sent General Pickett, with a force of fifteen thousand Confederates, to attack General Hancock on Cemetery Ridge. To reach the ridge they had to cross a mile of open ground. They came forward steadily, silently, under a terrible fire from the Union guns. Their ranks were ploughed through and through with shot and shell, but the men did not falter. They charged up the slight rise of ground and broke a part of the Union line; but they could go no further, and Pickett, with the fragments of his division, — for only fragments were left, — fell back defeated. It was the end of the most stubbornly fought battle of the war; nearly fifty thousand brave men had fallen [1] in the contest; Lee had failed; he retreated across the Potomac, and never made another attempt to invade the North. [2]

**341. The Surrender of Vicksburg and Port Hudson.** — While the great battle of Gettysburg was going on, another battle of almost or quite equal importance was being fought at Vicksburg, on the Mississippi. Vicksburg and vicinity were held by a strong Confederate force under General Pemberton. Early in the spring (1863) General J. E. Johnston (then at Chattanooga, Tennessee) moved with an army to join Pemberton. In a number of masterly battles Grant defeated Pemberton before Johnston could unite with him. He then forced him to retreat

[1] Union loss, 23,003; Confederate loss, 20,451.

[2] For this great victory and the one that followed it, President Lincoln called for a day of national thanksgiving and prayer.

to Vicksburg, and at the same time drove Johnston off the
field.    For several weeks following, Grant and Sherman,[1] with
a total force of over seventy thousand, besieged Vicksburg.
During that time the Union men were shelling the city night
and day.    Food had become so scarce that the Confederate
troops had but one "cracker" and a small piece of raw pork
a day, and the town was so knocked to pieces with shot and
shell that the women and children were forced to live in caves

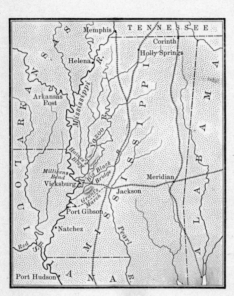

dug in the earth.
They, too, were re-
duced to a few
mouthfuls of food
a day; and when
"mule steaks" gave
out, many had to
choose between eat-
ing cats and rats or
dying of starvation.
Out of less than
thirty thousand men
the Confederates
had six thousand
sick or wounded in
hospital, besides
great numbers unfit
for active duty.
They could hold
out no longer, and on July 4 (1863), Vicksburg surrendered.
The Union troops "felt that their long and weary marches,
hard fighting, ceaseless watching by night and day" were
over.    Grant took nearly thirty-two thousand prisoners.    Fam-

---

[1] General W. T. Sherman was born at Lancaster, Ohio, in 1820.    He graduated
at West Point in 1840, and entered the regular army.    He commanded a Union
brigade at Bull Run, and, under Grant, won the battle of Pittsburg Landing (see
page 307).    In May, 1862, he was made a major-general.    He died in 1891.

ine had forced them to give up their stronghold; had they not given it up, Grant's army would have dug down or blown up this Gibraltar of the Confederacy. Before noon of that day the stars and stripes were hoisted over the Court House, and the Union men were distributing bread to the hungry, and making the place ring with, —

> "Yes, we'll rally round the flag, boys,
>   We'll rally once again,
>   Shouting the battle-cry of Freedom."

Among those that took part in the celebration of that victory was the war-eagle "Old Abe." He was a pet bird, the

Vicksburg, showing the Union Gun-Boats and the Firing from the Confederate Batteries.

hero of many battles, and was carried, perched on the flag, by one of the color-bearers of the Eighth Wisconsin Regiment. He had flapped his wings and screamed defiance in the thickest of the fight, and now he exulted with the "boys in blue" over the result. It was a great "Fourth" for the Union.

Port Hudson surrendered five days later (July 9, 1863), and thus the second part of the Union plan of the war was accomplished.  The first had been to shut the ports of the South by the blockade ; the second, to open the Mississippi River.  This had now been done, and the great river flowed in peace from Minnesota to Louisiana, and from Louisiana to the sea.

**342.  Draft Riots ;  Morgan's Raid ;  Chickamauga ;  Siege of Chattanooga.** — The last call of President Lincoln for volunteers did not bring anything like the number of men needed; and in July (1863), the government began to draft[1] the troops required.  In New York City mobs of rioters resisted the draft, but they were finally put down by armed force, and the necessary men for the army were in the end obtained.  In the South drafting had long been going on, and nearly every able-bodied man was forced to serve in the war.

During the same month General Morgan with a body of Confederate cavalry made a raid through Tennessee and Kentucky into Indiana and Ohio, burning mills, factories, and bridges, tearing up the railroads, and destroying a large amount of property ;  but he was at last captured and his men scattered.

In the course of the summer, General Rosecrans, by a series of brilliant movements, forced General Bragg to take refuge in Chattanooga, Tennessee.  In September he compelled Bragg to give up that city to him.  Shortly afterward he met the Confederate general in Georgia and fought the great battle of Chickamauga (September 19–20, 1863).  Bragg had the most men and defeated Rosecrans.  But General Thomas — the "Rock of Chickamauga," as his men called him — repulsed the enemy.  He held his position as stubbornly as a rock, and not only saved a large part of the Union army from destruction, but inflicted terrible loss on the Confederates, who greatly outnumbered him.  The Union forces now retreated to Chattanooga and were shut up there by Bragg, who besieged them for two months.

**343.  Battles of Lookout Mountain and Missionary Ridge; Sherman's Raid;  Grant, General-in-Chief.** — The Confederates held

[1] See page 189, note 6.

VIEW FROM LOOKOUT MOUNTAIN.

Lookout Mountain and Missionary Ridge, which overlook the beautiful Chattanooga Valley. General Hooker had come from Virginia, and, under Grant, he, with Sherman and Thomas, drove the enemy from the mountains in two battles (November 24–25), — one the famous "battle above the clouds," [1] the other the magnificent charge of the Union troops up Missionary Ridge. The Confederates now retreated to Dalton, Georgia.

In February, 1864, General Sherman made a raid [2] across Mississippi, and effectually destroyed the railroads centering at Meridian, by ripping up the rails, burning bridges, machine-shops, and locomotives. So little was left of the place that one of the inhabitants said, "Sherman did n't simply smash things, but he just carried the town off with him." This rendered the Confederates in that quarter helpless to attack him at Chattanooga. Shortly after this (March 3, 1864), Grant was made general-in-chief of the Union armies. At last the right man has been found. He will advance on Richmond, and Sherman will soon begin his famous march from Chattanooga to Atlanta, and from Atlanta to the sea.

344. **Summary of the Third Year of the War, April, 1863, to April, 1864.** — At the East the Confederates had gained the battle of Chancellorsville, but lost "Stonewall" Jackson. Lee's second invasion of the North had ended in his defeat at Gettysburg; at the same time Grant and Sherman were taking Vicksburg. Port Hudson surrendered a few days later, and the Mississippi was open through its entire length. In the Southwest, the Union forces, after their defeat at Chickamauga, won the brilliant victories of Lookout Mountain and Missionary Ridge. Grant was now made general-in-chief of the Union forces; he went East to manage the war there, and left Sherman in charge of the West.

[1] That of Lookout Mountain. Union forces in the campaign 60,000, loss 5800; Confederate 40,000 (?), loss 6700.

[2] From Vicksburg, destroying the roads on the way.

FOURTH AND LAST YEAR OF THE WAR, APRIL, 1864,
TO APRIL, 1865.

**345. Grant and Sherman agree on a " Hammering Campaign."**
— Early in the spring of 1864, Grant and Sherman met and
decided on a plan of action. The Confederates had been

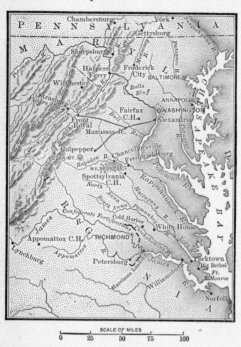

driven from the
Mississippi; they
now had two
chief centres of
power left. Lee,
with an army of
about sixty thou-
sand, held the
southern banks
of the Rapidan
and the Rappa-
hannock, thus
guarding Rich-
mond, and all the
country south of
it. Johnston, with
about seventy-
five thousand,
held Dalton,
Georgia (a town
a short distance
below Chatta-

nooga, Tennessee), and all the country south and east of it.
Grant and Sherman agreed to divide their work: the first,
with one hundred and twenty thousand men, was to move on
Lee and compel him to surrender Richmond; the second, then
at Chattanooga with an army of one hundred thousand, was
to march the same day on Johnston, beat him, and then push
his way through to the sea. This was " the famous hammer-

GENERAL GRANT.

ing campaign."[1] Grant and Sherman agreed "to hammer" together, "to hammer" with all their might, and never to leave off "hammering," until they had given the finishing blow, and permanently established peace, union, and freedom for the whole country.

**346. The Battles of the Wilderness.** — South and east of the Rapidan is a desolate region known as "the Wilderness." Much of it is covered with a scraggy growth of oak, pine, and tangled underbrush. Into the Wilderness Grant's army began to advance for the conquest of Richmond (May 4, 1864), and sitting on a log in that wilderness Grant telegraphed to Sherman at Chattanooga to begin his march into Georgia. From that time until June, or about a month in all, Grant was "hammering" at Longstreet and other noted fighters of the Confederate army, first in the thick of the Wilderness itself, then at Spottsylvania Court-House (May 8–18, 1864), then at Cold Harbor (June 3, 1864), on the edge of the fortifications of Richmond, where, it is said, ten thousand of the "men in blue" fell in twenty minutes. It was a terrible series of battles, costing the Union army a loss of many thousand men. Lee lost fewer men because he knew the country perfectly, and was acting on the defensive. Grant had vowed that he would not turn back, but would fight it out on that line if it took all summer. He did not turn back; but he had to give up his direct line of advance and take another. Lee had retreated, and entrenched himself inside the fortifications of Richmond; in order to draw him out to a battle in the open field, or to find a more favorable point of attack, Grant now moved round to Petersburg on the south of the Confederate capital.

**347. Captain Winslow sinks the *Alabama*; Early's Raid.** — Petersburg was strongly fortified, and Grant had to lay siege to it with shot and shell as he did to Vicksburg. While he

---

[1] "Hammering" in the sense of giving the Confederates no rest; Grant did this, largely, by direct attack; Sherman, largely, by indirect, or flank attack.

was busy in this way, Captain Winslow of the United States war-ship *Kearsarge* attacked the *Alabama*,[1] commanded by Captain Semmes. The fight took place off the northern coast of France (June 19, 1864). Captain Winslow gained the victory and sunk the vessel that had destroyed so many Northern merchant ships.

About the beginning of July (1864), Lee despatched General Early with a strong force to make a dash on Washington.

Grant shelling Petersburg.
(Notice the defences formed of stakes and trees in front of the Union Army.)

He succeeded in getting within half a dozen miles of that fort-girdled city, and then had to retreat up the Shenandoah Valley. He carried off with him about five thousand horses and two thousand cattle to recruit the fast-failing fortunes of the men in " Dixie's land." [2]  Later in the same month Early's

1 See Paragraph 326.

2 " For Dixie's land we take our stand,
And live or die for Dixie ! "

This was one of the most famous of the Confederate war-songs; it was originally a negro melody sung in praise of the South or " Dixie's Land."

cavalry made a raid into Pennsylvania, and burned Chambersburg.

**348. Sheridan's Raid in the Shenandoah Valley.** — Grant now (August 7, 1864) sent General Sheridan [1] with a strong force of Union cavalry to lay waste the Shenandoah Valley. This valley was one of the chief strongholds of the Confederates, and Grant was determined to destroy everything in it which could support their men. Sheridan went to work with a will, and in the course of a few weeks he had burned so many barns and mills filled with grain, and driven off so many sheep and cattle, that it was said, "If a crow wants to fly down the valley, he must carry his provisions with him." Could "Stonewall" Jackson have re-visited that beautiful country, — the pride of his heart, — he would have wept fierce tears over its heaps of desolate ashes, as the women and children of Chambersburg had wept and wrung their hands at the sight of their blazing homes.

**349. The Petersburg Mine; Sheridan's Ride.** — Meanwhile (July 30, 1864) General Burnside had undermined the Confederate fortifications at Petersburg, and placed eight thousand pounds of powder in the mine. When it was exploded, it made a deep chasm or "crater" nearly two hundred feet long. The Union soldiers rushed into the breach, hoping to enter the city ; but the Confederate fire made it a "slaughter-pen" and a gigantic grave for hundreds of brave fellows, while those who got out found themselves prisoners in the hands of Lee's army.

In September (1864) there was fighting in the Shenandoah Valley between Sheridan and Early, in which Sheridan gained the day. Later, Early took advantage of Sheridan's absence from his army to surprise the Union force at Cedar Creek in the Valley. They retreated, and the retreat soon became a

[1] General Philip H. Sheridan was of Irish descent, and was born in Albany, New York, in 1831 ; died 1888. He graduated at West Point in 1853. In 1864 he was appointed commander of all the cavalry of the Army of the Potomac, and after his famous "ride" to Winchester he was made a major-general.

panic.   Sheridan was then at Winchester, about twenty miles away.   He heard the cannon with their

> "terrible grumble, and rumble, and roar,
> Telling the battle was on once more." [1]

Mounting his horse, he hurried to the scene of disaster.   As he came up, a great cheer greeted him from the Union cavalry.   "We must face the other way!" shouted Sheridan to the retreating men.   They did face the other way, and so effectually that they speedily drove the Confederates "flying" out of that part of the Valley.

350. The War in the West; Sherman's Advance to Atlanta. — According to agreement Sherman began his advance from Chattanooga to Atlanta the same day (May 4, 1864) that Grant marched forward into the Wilderness.   Atlanta was not only a great railroad centre, but it was "the chief seat of the machine-shops, foundries, and factories of the Confederacy."   For this reason its capture would be one of the severest blows to the Southern armies that the Union forces could strike.

Sherman advanced slowly.   His march was through a rough, mountainous country, and there were sharp battles fought at Resaca (May 14–15, 1864), at Dallas (May 25–28, 1864), and at Kenesaw Mountain (June 27, 1864); but the Confederates could not check him in his march.   Of the two the soldiers would much rather have fought more battles and had less rain. For three weeks it poured most of the time night and day; while he was marching, every man had a rivulet streaming down his back, and, as the army carried no tents, he was fortunate when night came if he did not have to sleep in a puddle.

As fast as the Confederates fell back they tore up the railroad track and burned the bridges; but Sherman's men rebuilt

---

[1] See Read's poem of "Sheridan's Ride" in Ginn & Co.'s "Heroic Ballads"; then read Sheridan's own modest account of the "ride" in his "Personal Memoirs," II. 66–92.   See map showing the Shenandoah Valley on page 322.

FARRAGUT

PORTER

FOOTE

them so rapidly that "the whistle of the locomotives was always following close on the heels of Johnston's soldiers."

**351. Sherman takes Atlanta; Farragut enters Mobile Bay.** — After a series of battles with Hood, to whom Jefferson Davis had now given the command in place of Johnston, Sherman took Atlanta (September 2, 1864). He had advanced a hundred miles from Chattanooga, and in that short distance each side had lost about thirty thousand men; that meant that every

*I am going into Mobile Bay in the morning if "God is my leader" as I hope he is;*

*D. G. Farragut*

Farragut's Letter Home, written just before the Battle.

I am going into Mobile Bay in the morning if " God is my leader," as I hope he is.

D. G. FARRAGUT.

mile had cost the two armies six hundred killed and wounded. Sherman applied the torch to Atlanta, burning the foundries, mills, and machine-shops, but sparing dwelling-houses and churches. This destruction crippled the Southern armies. From that time they fought like a man with one of his arms broken : they were as brave, as resolute as ever, but they were losing ground every day.

Meanwhile Admiral Farragut attacked Mobile (August 5, 1864), stationing himself in the rigging of his vessel, where he could see every move in the battle ; after a hard fight he forced his way with his fleet past the forts, and took possession of the harbor. It was the admiral's last and greatest battle. It completely closed the port of Mobile [1] against supplies sent to the Confederates from abroad. It was thus one more important step taken toward compelling the final surrender of the South.

352. **Sherman's March from Atlanta to the Sea.** — After the fall of Atlanta, Jefferson Davis ordered the Confederate army to abandon the State of Georgia, his intention being to strike

An Incident of the March through Georgia.

General Thomas, who held Nashville. He hoped in this way to compel Sherman to turn back to help Thomas. But Sherman believed that "the Rock of Chickamauga" [2] was quite able to take care of himself; he therefore resolved to push forward. About the middle of November, 1864, Sherman cut the telegraph and railroad lines which connected him with the North. Thus "detached from all friends, dependent on its

[1] All the ports of the South had long been blockaded by Union war-vessels, but in some cases "blockade-runners" succeeded in evading these vessels, and thus a certain amount of secret commerce was carried on.    [2] See Paragraph 342.

SHERIDAN

SHERMAN

THOMAS

HOOKER

HANCOCK

own resources and supplies," his army set out on their great march to the sea, two hundred miles distant in a direct line. For four weeks Sherman and his men disappeared. The North knew nothing of his movements. But Grant had faith that his friend would not get hopelessly lost, and that sometime the country would hear from him.

Meanwhile Sherman was going forward with sixty thousand veterans, plenty of provisions, and practically no force to resist him. He cut a clean swath sixty miles wide [1] from Atlanta to

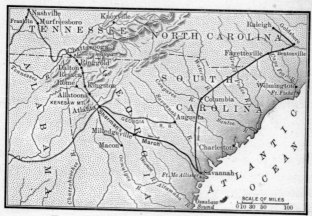

Map of Sherman's March.

Savannah, destroying railroads and whatever else could be of use to the Confederates, and eating the plantations and towns on the way bare of everything, — hay, cows, pigs, chickens; whatever, in fact, horse or man could devour disappeared before the advancing army. Along this broad track of desolation — the stern result of war — several thousand negroes followed in the wake of "Massa Sherman," shouting and singing as they trudged on.

[1] "So we made a thoroughfare for Freedom and her train,
Sixty miles in latitude, three hundred to the main."

— Soldiers' Song, *Marching through Georgia.*

**353. Thomas destroys Hood's Army.** — While Sherman was pressing forward, the Confederate General Hood — one of the best fighters in the South — moved from the vicinity of Atlanta into Tennessee to attack Thomas. A battle was fought at Franklin (November 30, 1864), in which Hood was severely repulsed. Then Hood advanced and besieged Thomas in Nashville. Thomas was deliberate in his movements, but when he did strike, it was with sledge-hammer force. He attacked Hood (December 15–16, 1864), and cut his army all to pieces. The miserable remnant, ragged, barefooted, wet to the skin by incessant winter rains, shivering and starving, escaped, as best they could, leaving their sick and wounded to die along the roadside. This ended the war in Tennessee; the Confederacy from eleven states had now practically shrunk to three, — Virginia, and North and South Carolina; the rest were either inactive, as in the case of Florida and Texas, or they were under the control of the military power of the United States.

**354. Sherman takes Savannah and moves Northward.** — In a little less than a month from the day when he left Atlanta, Sherman reached Savannah. He stormed and took Fort McAllister on the south of the city (December 13, 1864), and nine days later he sent the following message to the President, —

" SAVANNAH, GEORGIA, Dec. 22, 1864.

"To his Excellency, President Lincoln, Washington, D. C.:

"I beg to present you as a Christmas gift the City of Savannah, with one hundred and fifty heavy guns and plenty of ammunition; also about twenty-five thousand bales of cotton.

" W. T. SHERMAN, *Major-General.*" [1]

Sherman's men had long before come to the conclusion that the seacoast was not their final destination, and would call out to the General as he rode past, " Uncle Billy, I guess Grant is waiting for us at Richmond!" [2]

---

[1] General Sherman sent this message by a vessel to Fort Monroe. It reached the President on Christmas eve.    [2] See Sherman's "Memoirs," II. 179.

# SHERMAN'S ANNOUNCEMENT OF LEE'S SURRENDER.

[*Special Field Orders, No. 54.*]

> Headquarters Military Division of the
> Mississippi, in the Field, Smithfield,
> North Carolina, April 12, 1865.

The General commanding announces to the army that he has official notice from General Grant that General Lee surrendered to him his entire army, on the 9th inst., at Appomattox Court-House, Virginia.

Glory to God and our country, and all honor to our comrades in arms, toward whom we are marching!

A little more labor, a little more toil on our part, the great race is won, and our Government stands regenerated, after four long years of war.

W. T. SHERMAN, Major-General commanding.

(*See Sherman's "Memoirs."*)

The above order was issued while the Union army was marching from Goldsboro', N. C., in pursuit of Johnston's army. Johnston did not make a stand, but surrendered near Durham Station, about twenty-five miles northwest of Raleigh, N. C., April 26, 1865.

When Sherman's men learned that Lee had surrendered they went wild with excitement. They shouted, they flung up their caps, they turned somersaults in their delight.

The whole land seemed full of rejoicing that the long, terrible struggle was practically over. Confederate as well as Union soldiers were glad to see peace at hand; and a Southern woman, who heard the hurrahs of Sherman's "boys in blue" as they marched past her house, looked upon her wondering children and said, while tears streamed down her cheeks, "Now father will come home." — (See *General Jacob D. Cox: " The March to the Sea."*)

7ᵗʰ Apⁱ '65

Genⁱ

I have recᵈ your note of this date, Though not entertaining the opinion you express of the hopelessness of further resistance on the part of the Army of N. Va — I reciprocate your desire to avoid useless effusion of blood, I therefore before Considering your proposition ask the terms you will offer on Condition of its Surrender

Very respᵗ your Obᵗ Servᵗ

R E Lee
Genⁱ

Lt. Genⁱ U. S. Grant
Commdᵍ Armies of the U. States

LEE'S LETTER TO GRANT RESPECTING THE SURRENDER OF THE CONFEDERATE ARMY OF NORTHERN VIRGINIA.

They were right, and on the 1st of February, 1865, Sherman set out with his army northward.    It was a seven weeks' march through mud, rain, and swamps.    He reached Columbia, the capital of South Carolina, about the middle of February, and ordered the destruction of all buildings which might be of use to the Confederates in prolonging the war.    Unfortunately the town caught fire, and in spite of all the efforts of the Union army to extinguish the flames the greater part of the place was burned to the ground.    On his advance Sherman had to fight Johnston with a strong Confederate force near Goldsboro, North Carolina (March 19, 1865).    Meanwhile Charleston and Wilmington had been captured by Union forces: the Confederacy had lost its last seaports.

About a week later (March 27, 1865), General Sherman, leaving his victorious army at Goldsboro, went to City Point, on James River, Virginia, to consult with Grant.    A month later (April 26, 1865) Johnston surrendered to Sherman near Raleigh, North Carolina.

**355. The End of the War.** — Sheridan now made a raid south through the Shenandoah Valley, in which he destroyed the railroad and canal from Lynchburg, on the west of Richmond, nearly up to the Confederate capital.    This had the effect of cutting off a large part of the provisions for Lee's army.    Sheridan next (March 29, 1865) made a similar raid to the south of Richmond.    Lee had now only forty thousand men to Grant's one hundred thousand.    While the Confederate general was trying to guard against Sheridan, Grant threw his whole force on Petersburg and captured it (April 2, 1865).    Lee retreated from Richmond, and the next day (April 3, 1865) Grant's forces entered the capital of the Southern Confederacy, and raised the old flag over the city.    Jefferson Davis escaped to North Carolina.[1]    Lee's forces were now completely broken

[1] Jefferson Davis was captured in Georgia, May 11, 1865.    He was sent to Fort Monroe; but was released two years later.    By the end of May all the Confederate forces had surrendered and disbanded.    None of the leaders or men engaged in the

up; and many of his men were so weak from want of food that they could not shoulder a musket. On April 9, 1865, Lee surrendered to Grant at Appomattox Court-House, a little place about seventy-five miles west of Richmond. Nothing could be more nobly generous than the terms given by General Grant to the defeated Confederates. The only conditions he demanded were that the men should lay down their arms and return to their homes. Those who had horses were permitted to take them with them; for, as Grant remarked, they "would need them for the ploughing." Finally, the victorious general issued an order to serve out twenty-five thousand rations of food to Lee's half-starved men. That meant that the strife was over, and that peace and brotherhood were restored. Five days afterward (April 14, 1865), General Anderson hoisted the identical flag over Fort Sumter, under whose starry folds he had fought against Beauregard. It was exactly four years to a day since the Confederates had won their first victory in the Civil War.

Thus ended the great contest, which had cost in all probably over half a million of lives and thousands of millions of dollars.[1] The triumphant joy of those who had fought to save the Union was quenched in tears; for on the evening following the celebration at Fort Sumter (April 14, 1865), the President was shot by an assassin.[2] Many of those who had fought against him in the South wept at his death. He was the friend of every American; none of us or of our children, North or South, will ever know a more unselfish or a truer man than Abraham Lincoln.

War of Secession were brought to trial for having taken up arms against the national government; but Henry Wirz, the Swiss commandant at Andersonville, Georgia, was charged with cruel treatment of Union prisoners, and was tried and convicted by court-martial; he was hanged, November 10, 1865.

[1] The total war debt of the North was nearly $3,000,000,000; this, however, represents but a part of the expense. The greatest number of men engaged in the Union armies at any one time was about 1,000,000; in the Confederate, about 700,000.

[2] President Lincoln was shot at the theatre by John Wilkes Booth, an obscure actor, who was the leader of a conspiracy for the assassination of the President, Vice-President, the cabinet, and General Grant. Booth was pursued and shot, four of the other conspirators were hanged, and four imprisoned.

356. **The North and the South in the War.** — In the North there was sore anxiety for friends who might never return ; and sisters, wives, and mothers were mourning for those who had fallen on the battle-field or died in prison.   In the South there was the same terrible loss of life, the same mourning for those who had left their homes never to return.   The material privations and sufferings of the war fell mainly on the South.   Except at Gettysburg all the fighting was done on Southern soil.   No armies marched through the North.   Two new states — West Virginia (1863) and Nevada (1864) — had been added to the Union.   All business went on as usual, or with increased activity.   Every seaport was open, and trade and commerce flourished.   There were many quiet homes not directly touched by the hardships and horrors of the struggle, where the progress of the war was only known by newspaper reports.

Thanks to the financial ability and the unfailing energy of Secretary Chase, the government never lacked means to carry on the contest.   Whatever money could do for the equipment and comfort of the Union forces was done without stint or murmur, even when the expenses exceeded $3,500,000 a day.

In addition to all this care for the men by the government, the Sanitary and the Christian Commissions were unwearied in their great work of love and mercy among the wounded and the sick.   Once in hospital no one was ever asked on which side he had fought ; but tender hands ministered to his needs, and soothed his sufferings, whether he wore the "blue" or the "gray."

With the people of the South all was different.   Their ports were blockaded, their business ruined.   The country had no money, no manufactures ; the negroes had been set free.   In their extremity Southern ladies cut up their carpets to make blankets and clothes for the soldiers, and churches gave their bells to be cast into cannon.   Long before the final surrender there was sore want everywhere throughout the South, and everywhere the people were either suffering from the destruction necessarily caused by invading armies or from the dread of such invasion. It is a noble evidence of the fortitude of the American character that the Southern people, however mistaken in their purpose, "fought," as General Grant says, "so bravely, so gallantly and so long." [1]

**357. Summary of the Fourth and Last Year of the War, April, 1864, to April, 1865.** — This year was marked by Grant and Sherman's "hammering campaign," which ended in the destruction of the Confederate power in the West and in the East, and was followed by the surrender of Lee. The surrender of Johnston [2] soon after ended the war, and established the Union on a solid foundation of freedom for all men.

[1] See General Grant's "Personal Memoirs," II. 426.

[2] In his last orders to his troops, General Johnston said: "I earnestly expect you to observe faithfully the terms of pacification agreed upon, and to discharge the obligations of good and peaceful citizens as well as you have performed the duties of thorough soldiers in the field." Like a brave officer, Johnston led the way in the execution of this order by his own example. He died March 21, 1891, shortly after he had acted as pall-bearer at the funeral of his friend, General W. T. Sherman.

# VII.

"America is another word for Opportunity." — R. W. EMERSON, *Essay on American Civilization.*

———◦———

## RECONSTRUCTION. — THE NEW NATION.

### (1865 TO THE PRESENT TIME.)

#### ANDREW JOHNSON.

**358. Johnson's Administration (Seventeenth President, April 15, 1865, to 1869). Difficulty of the President's Task; the Grand Review; Disbanding the Armies.** — The untimely death of President Lincoln made Andrew Johnson[1] the head of the nation. The position to which the new President was thus suddenly called, was peculiarly hard and trying; for if the great heart of Lincoln had to bear the sad burden of four years of civil war, his successor had to undertake the delicate and difficult work of reconstruction, — that is, of restoring the seceded states to their former places in the Union.

Now that the war was over, the first thing to be done was to disband the armies. But multitudes wished to see the brave men who had fought to save the nation; and late in May a grand review of Grant's and of Sherman's troops took place in Washington.

For the first time since the beginning of the war, the trium-

---

[1] Andrew Johnson was born at Raleigh, North Carolina, in 1808; died 1875. He learned the tailor's trade and moved to Greenville, Tennessee. He never attended school, but was entirely self-educated. He was elected to Congress in 1843, by the Democrats, and to the United States Senate in 1857. When the Civil War broke out he took a decided stand against secession. In 1862 President Lincoln appointed him military governor of Tennessee. On Lincoln's second election to the presidency by the Republicans, Johnson was elected Vice-President. See page 293, note 1.

phant armies of the East and of the West were united. During the greater part of two days (May 23, 24, 1865), the broad avenue from the Capitol to the White House resounded with martial music, and with the strong, steady tread of a column over thirty miles long. The march of these seemingly endless regiments of sunburnt veterans, bearing their glittering muskets and their tattered, smoke-stained battle flags, festooned

The Capitol at Washington.

with flowers, was a magnificent sight. No such spectacle had ever been seen before in America; as one enthusiastic officer declared, "It was worth ten years of a man's life for him to be able to say, 'I was there.'"

But grand as the display was, something grander was to come — that was the fact that in the course of a few weeks, all these men, with many hundreds of thousands more,[1] laid down their arms and went quietly to their homes. Neither on the North-

[1] With the exception of about 50,000 men, kept as a standing army, to preserve order, all the Union troops, numbering over a million, were now disbanded. The number of Confederates disbanded was about 175,000.

In 1866 about 1500 "Fenians"—Irish citizens of the United States, who felt that England had wronged their native land—invaded Canada. Many of them had served in the war for the Union and now hoped to strike Great Britain a blow, but as the movement was discountenanced by the United States it came to nothing.

ern nor on the Southern side, says a recent writer, was there a single act of lawlessness recorded to stain their proud repute as soldiers and Americans.

**359. What the War settled.** — First, as a Southern historian admits, it "extinguished secession" as completely as water extinguishes a flame of fire. Henceforth it was understood that the Union cannot be broken. On this point the Constitution received a final and unmistakable interpretation. In the words of the Chief Justice of the Supreme Court of the United States (1868) the American Republic is "an indestructible Union composed of indestructible States." The war established the supremacy of the national Government beyond all question; but more than this, it made every heart feel that we are one nation and have a common destiny. It fixed in the minds of the people the great thought expressed by Daniel Webster: "Liberty and union, now and forever, one and inseparable."

Secondly, the war made the negro free — that was an advantage to every one, white or black, North or South; for free labor only is intelligent and profitable.

Thirdly, beyond all political and material benefits resulting from the war was the immense moral uplift involved in the result. Human slavery, with all its attendant wrongs, was forever abolished in our country. Our flag was made to represent freedom in fact as well as in name, freedom for all, and not for the privileged only. Henceforth men of every race were to be alike entitled to the blessings of our Government and the opportunities of our country.

Fourthly, the manner in which the result was accepted on both sides was itself a benefit. General Grant showed a magnanimity that has had no parallel. General Lee had fought with all his might; he was in the wrong; he applied to the Government for a pardon, as an example to his men. He said, "Remember that we are one country now. Do not bring up your children in hostility to the government of the United States. Bring them up to be Americans."[1]

**360. The President's Proclamation of Pardon; the Contest between Congress and the President.** — The President issued a proclamation of pardon (May 29, 1865) to the greater part of the people of the seceded states on condition that they would swear to "faithfully support, protect, and defend the Constitution and the Union." A majority of the inhabitants of those states took the oath. They furthermore bound themselves to accept the Thirteenth Amendment to the Constitution, which prohibited slavery, and they agreed never to demand payment of any part of the Southern war-debt.

Now came the question whether these states should be at once permitted to send representatives to Congress. The President said, Yes; but a majority in Congress said, No. The reason for this denial was that the greater part of Congress believed that it would not be safe to restore the Southern States to their full political rights until more was done to protect the negroes or "freedmen," as they were now called, in the enjoyment of their new liberty.

From this time forward the President and Congress were engaged in bitter strife with each other. Congress refused to re-admit the Southern States, and passed a number of bills[2] in favor of the "freedmen," one of which made them citizens,[3] another gave them military protection, while a third granted them power to vote in the District of Columbia. The President believed that the South would deal fairly by the "freedmen," and he therefore vetoed these bills; Congress then passed them over his veto.[4]

---

[1] See Cooke's "Life of Robert E. Lee."

[2] Civil Rights Bills, and establishment of the Freedmen's Bureau.

[3] By making the "freedmen" citizens, Congress (by the Civil Rights Bill, March, 1866) gave them the right to protection under the laws of the United States, with power to use the courts to sue for the payment of debts and the like.

[4] In case the President vetoes a bill (that is, refuses to sign it, and returns it to

**361. Congress puts the Southern States under Military Government.**—In the spring of 1867 Congress passed another bill over the President's veto. This new law divided the South into districts, each of which was to be governed by a military governor. The "freedmen" were given the right to vote, but that right was denied to all those white inhabitants who had taken a prominent part in the war against the Union. Each state was to continue under this form of government until the people of the states,—black as well as white,— should form a government accepting the Fourteenth Amendment to the Constitution. That amendment declared the negro a citizen; it made it a great disadvantage to a state to deny him the right to vote or to hold office; finally it shut out the chief white men of the South from holding any high office.[1] When these conditions should be accepted, but not before, the Southern States might send representatives to Congress.

Tennessee, President Johnson's state, having fulfilled all the conditions required, had been re-admitted in 1866.

**362. Six States re-admitted; Negro Legislators and "Carpet-Baggers."**[2]—Six states accepted these conditions;[3] four refused, but accepted them later (1870). In some of the restored states, especially in South Carolina, there were more negroes than white men. The negroes now got control of these states. They had been slaves all their lives, and were so ignorant that they did not even know the letters of the alphabet. Yet they

Congress), Congress may pass the bill without the President's signature, providing two-thirds of the members vote for it. See the Constitution, page ix, sec. 7.

[1] See the Constitution, page xviii. The Fourteenth Amendment furthermore required the South to repudiate their war-debt and to agree to the payment of the Union war-debt.

[2] "Carpet-Baggers": a nickname given by Southerners to Northern adventurers who went South after the war (with no baggage or property except a carpet-bag) for the purpose of getting office and plunder. Those Southerners who joined the "Carpet-Baggers" in their schemes were nicknamed "Scalawags."

[3] The six states which accepted (and were re-admitted June, 1868) were Alabama, Arkansas, Florida, Louisiana, North Carolina, and South Carolina. Georgia, Mississippi, Texas, and Virginia remained out until 1870.

now sat in the state legislatures and made the laws.    After
the war many industrious Northern men settled in the South,
but, besides these, certain greedy adventurers went there eager
to get political office and political spoils.    These "Carpet-
Baggers," as they were called, used the ignorant "freedmen"
as tools to carry out their own selfish purposes.    The result
was that the negro legislators, under the direction of the
"Carpet-Baggers," plundered and, for the time, well-nigh
ruined the states that had the misfortune to be subject to
their rule.[1]

After a time the white population throughout the South
resolved that they would no longer endure this state of things.
Partly by peaceable and partly by violent means they succeeded in getting the political power into their own hands, and
the reign of the "Carpet-Bagger" and the negro came to an end.

363. Congress impeaches the President; Proclamation of Full
and Unconditional Pardon; the Fifteenth Amendment. — Meanwhile the quarrel between Congress and the President was constantly growing more and more serious.    The President was not
only determined to have his own way, but also to remove from
office those who did not agree with him.    Congress now passed
the Tenure of Office Bill[2] forbidding him to dismiss even the
members of his own cabinet or private council without the
consent of the Senate.

The President denied the power of Congress to make such
a law, and he removed Edwin M. Stanton, Secretary of War,
who had been appointed by President Lincoln.    For this
refusal to obey the law Congress now (February 25, 1868) proceeded to impeach[3] the President.    On his trial thirty-five

[1] In 1868 the total debt of South Carolina was about $5,000,000.    Under four
years of "Carpet-Bag" government, or rather misgovernment, the debt was increased
to no less than $30,000,000.    Much of the debt represented simply what was stolen
from the people of the state.

[2] The Tenure of Office Act, 1867 (repealed 1887).

[3] Impeach the President: to bring him to trial.    The House of Representatives
makes the charges and the Senate tries the case — the Chief Justice presiding.    See

senators voted "guilty" and nineteen "not guilty"; as this was less than the two-thirds vote required to convict him, President Johnson was therefore acquitted. One more vote against him would have removed him from the presidency.

On the Christmas following (1868) the President issued a proclamation of full and unconditional pardon to all persons, without exception, who had taken part in the war against the Union.

Early in the year following (1869) Congress passed the Fifteenth Amendment to the Constitution.[1] The Thirteenth Amendment (passed 1865) made the negro free, the Fourteenth Amendment made him a citizen,[2] the Fifteenth finished the work and made him a *voter*. All these great changes had taken place within the short space of four years!

**364. The Atlantic Cable.** — But these political events were not the only ones in which the country was interested. It will be remembered that Professor Morse, the inventor of the telegraph, had predicted[3] that the time would come when messages would be sent across the sea by electricity.

The Atlantic Cable.

Cyrus W. Field of New York formed a company to accomplish the work by means of a wire cable laid on the bottom of the Atlantic, between Great Britain and the United States. The company lost several millions in attempting to do this, though they succeeded in laying a cable in 1858 by which messages were sent for a

the Constitution, pages viii and xiii. As only part of the Southern States had been re-admitted, the number of senators was then but 54.

[1] Ratified by the states in 1870.      [3] See page 261, note 2.
[2] See page 339.

few weeks. Not to be discouraged, Mr. Field formed a new company, and raised more money for the work. In the summer of 1866 the steamship *Great Eastern* laid a new cable between Valentia Bay, Ireland, and the port of Heart's Content, Newfoundland, thence connecting with the United States. On Friday, July 27, 1866, instantaneous communication beneath the ocean was established between the Old World and the New. This communication has never since been interrupted. Several additional cables have since been laid, and every important event which occurs in Europe is now known here as soon as it is there. News which appears in the London morning papers, and which is read at the English breakfast-tables, is read also at ours on the same day throughout the length and breadth of the United States.

365. **The Purchase of Alaska ; Payment of the National Debt.** — The next year (1867), just after Nebraska entered the Union, we purchased from Russia the territory of Alaska, embracing about 550,000 square miles. We paid a little over $7,000,000, or about what we spent in less than four days in carrying on the war [1] during the last year. This addition to our territory raised the total area of the United States to about 3,600,000 square miles, or nearly equal to that of all the countries of Europe united.

Alaska includes the islands of the Aleutian Archipelago, which extend a very long way westward. This makes San Francisco the city nearest the centre — east and west — of the United States ; the distance from that city to the eastern coast of Maine being about 3600 miles, and to Attoo, the farthest of the Aleutian islands, over 3800 miles.

Secretary Seward persuaded Congress to make this purchase, in order to extend our power on the Pacific coast. Many Congressmen thought it was a waste of money, and one called

---

[1] The average daily expenses of the war 1864-1865 were over $2,000,000, and for a time some estimates make them $3,500,000.

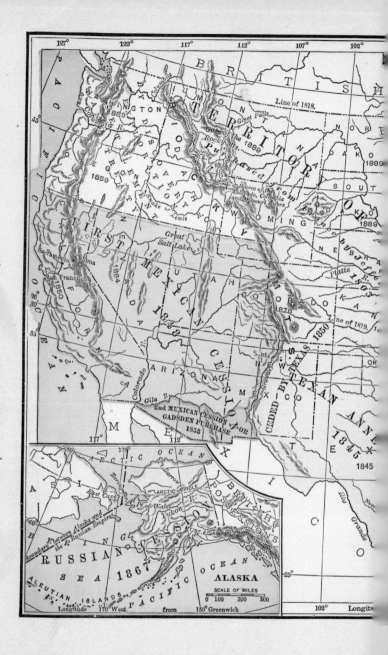

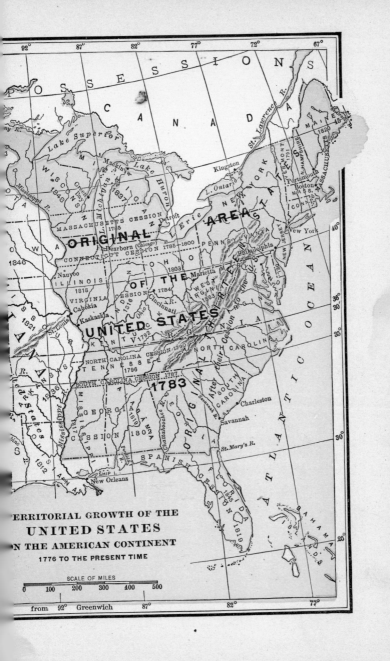

TERRITORIAL GROWTH OF THE
UNITED STATES
ON THE AMERICAN CONTINENT
1776 TO THE PRESENT TIME

SCALE OF MILES

0   100   200   300   400   500

from   92°   Greenwich   87°   82°   77°

Alaska "the refrigerator of the United States." But it promises to become a very profitable "refrigerator." Its furs,
forests, and fish are constantly increasing in value; rich deposits
of gold were found (1897) on the Yukon and on the Klondike,
a tributary of that river, and the trade in sealskins alone now
amounts to about $2,000,000 a year.[1]

Besides buying this new territory the national government
began as soon as the war was over to pay off the great war debt,
amounting to nearly $3,000,000,000,[2] — a sum so enormous
that in the longest life-time a person counting out the dollars
one by one, at the rate of sixty a minute, could not get through
even a third of it.

Before all the soldiers had been sent home we had paid off
over $30,000,000. Since then we have paid nearly $1,200,-
000,000 more. Had we continued to reduce our debt at the
same rate we should have finished paying it in about fourteen
years. No country in Europe ever voluntarily settled such a
debt.[3] To-day our credit stands as high as that of any other
nation on the globe.

**366. Summary.** — During President Johnson's administration six of the seceded states were re-admitted to the Union;
but Congress and the President did not agree, and Congress attempted by impeachment to remove the President from office.

Three amendments to the Constitution were made during
Mr. Johnson's presidency.[4] The first declared the negro free,
the second made him a citizen, the third, a voter.

---

[1] An International Commission fixed the Alaska boundary in 1903.

[2] The actual debt was $2,750,000,000. This was independent of the state debts,
which were very heavy.

[3] Between 1871 and 1873, or in less than three years, France paid Germany a war
claim of $1,000,000,000, but this payment was not voluntary, but made by the French
to rid their soil of the presence of German troops. The total debt of the United
States just prior to the war with Spain was $1,808,777,643. The war with Spain
greatly increased our debt. In 1901 it amounted to $2,151,585,743.

[4] The first of these amendments had been passed by Congress in February, 1865,
and was ratified by the necessary number of three-fourths of the states by December

The other important events were: 1. The full pardon of all persons who had fought against the Union. 2. The beginning of the payment of the national debt. 3. The laying of the Atlantic cable. 4. The purchase of Alaska.

## ULYSSES S. GRANT.

**367. Grant's Administration (Eighteenth President, Two Terms 1869-1877); Completion of the Pacific Railroad; what Railroads and Telegraphs have done for the Union.** — A little over two months after President Grant[1] was inaugurated, the last spike of a line of railroad[2] connecting the Atlantic coast with the Pacific was driven at Ogden, Utah (May 10, 1869). The blows of the sledge-hammer which drove that spike — completing the greatest work of the kind in the world — were telegraphed, as they fell, throughout the Union.

Congress granted a tract of land, in alternate sections twenty miles wide, extending from Omaha to San Francisco in

of that year. The two other amendments were passed by Congress during Mr. Johnson's term; the last was ratified during the next administration, 1870.

[1] General Ulysses S. Grant of Illinois (Schuyler Colfax of Indiana, Vice-President) was elected President by the Republicans in 1868, over Governor Horatio Seymour of New York and Francis P. Blair of Missouri, the Democratic candidates. He was re-elected in 1872 (Henry Wilson of Massachusetts, Vice-President), over Horace Greeley of New York and B. Gratz Brown of Missouri, the candidates of the Liberal Republicans and the greater part of the Democrats united.

[2] The Union Pacific Railroad, begun during the Civil War, was built westward from Omaha on the Missouri to Ogden, Utah, a distance of 1029 miles; there it met and connected with the Central Pacific Railroad, which was pushed through at the same time, from San Francisco, a distance of 878 miles. The total distance from New York to San Francisco is 3322 miles. The Northern, and the Southern Pacific, the Great Northern, and the Atchison, Topeka, and Santa Fé Railroads have since been built; and in Canada the Canadian Pacific, making six transcontinental lines in all.

In 1872 the Credit Mobilier, a company that had been engaged in the building of the first Pacific Railroad, became involved in a lawsuit in Pennsylvania. It was shown in the course of the suit that some members of Congress secretly held stock in the company, and it was supposed that the stock had been given them in order to secure their votes in behalf of the railway. After an investigation by a congressional committee, the House passed resolutions censuring two of its members; the matter was then dropped.

RELIEF MAP OF THE UNITED STATES (AND PART OF BRITISH AMERICA)

SHOWING THE FIRST TRANSCONTINENTAL RAILROAD.

The total grant made by the national Government to the "Union Pacific" and the "Central Pacific" Railroads for building 1917 miles of road was 25,000,000 acres of land and $55,092,074.

aid of this national enterprise.    During the previous thirty-five years the government gave to road, canal, and railroad corporations public lands nearly equal in area to that of the thirteen original states as they now stand.

Between Omaha and San Francisco the railroad crosses nine mountain ranges, including the Rockies and the Sierras, climbing, and then descending, over eight thousand feet.    In point of time, it is now no farther from New York to San Francisco than it was in the days of the Revolution from New York to Boston.    Then it took our forefathers between five and six days to go by wagon somewhat less than two hundred and fifty miles; now, in that time, we can cross the entire continent.

The result of this rapid means of travel is of the greatest importance to the republic.[1]    Once, members of Congress laughed at the idea that California and Oregon would be added to the United States.    They said that it would be practically impossible for such states, if added, to send representatives to the national capital, because it would take them the greater part of the year to get to Washington and back.    For that reason, they believed that the people who settled the Pacific coast would form a separate and independent republic.    The railroad and the telegraph have changed all that.    They have connected the farthest extremities of the country so closely that they have made it possible for us to extend and maintain the Union from ocean to ocean.

368.  Effect of the Pacific Railroad on Commerce with Asia, and on the Growth of the far West; the Homestead Act. — But this is not all.    The building of the Pacific Railroad entirely changed our relations with Asia.    Teas, spices, and silks formerly reached us from China and from the East Indies by ships sailing round Cape Horn.    Goods might be five or six months coming that immense distance.    Now, many of these goods

[1] Before the completion of the Pacific Railroad, a pony express, followed by a line of stage-coaches, carried the mail across the country from St. Joseph, Missouri, to San Francisco.

are shipped by steamer to San Francisco, and thence by rail across the country to the East. In a little over a month from the time a cargo of tea leaves China, it can be delivered in New York. The old navigators spent their lives in trying to find a short route to Asia; we have found it, though in a totally different way from what they expected.

Last of all, and most important as well as last, the Pacific Railroad, and the lines since built, have opened the Far West — as the region west of the Mississippi is called. Steam enabled a peaceful army of thrifty emigrants to reach that section easily, quickly, and cheaply. The unexplored region that a little more than a generation ago was given up to wild beasts and savages is now rapidly filling with population.

The liberal land laws of the United States greatly encouraged this movement. From 1830 to 1862 actual settlers on the public lands had the first right to buy one hundred and sixty acres at the very low price of $1.25 per acre. This power of pre-emption, as it was called, made the farmer independent in large measure of speculators and other would-be purchasers.

But in 1862 Congress passed the Homestead Bill. That measure actually made a present of one hundred and sixty acres to every settler on government land on condition that he built himself a home and proceeded to cultivate and improve the soil. The western emigrant's song declaring that "Uncle Sam is rich enough to give us all a farm," then became a fact. It induced scores of thousands to cross the Mississippi. Their labor has transformed the country where they settled. Kansas, Nebraska, Colorado, and the newer states west and north of them that were once treeless deserts or vast stretches of uncleared and uncultivated wilderness are to-day covered with grain-fields and fruit orchards.

Denver and many other prosperous cities and towns in neighboring states have sprung up in places where when Grant became President there were often, at the most, only a few rude cabins made of sods or logs, or a few "dug-outs," excavated in the sides of the hills.  Thus within the short period of about thirty years the railways of the West have entirely changed that part of the republic.  They have converted what was once a broad extent of unoccupied territory — sometimes, seemingly barren and worthless — into groups of rapidly growing commonwealths, rich in mines of precious metals, rich in farms, in ranches, and industries of every kind.

Some of these ranches, in the Far West, exhibit stock raising and agriculture on a scale never seen before, for they embrace from 20,000 to 30,000 acres each, and have 50,000 head of cattle or sheep. There are single wheat-fields of 13,000 acres, and single farms which extend for many miles — covered as far as the eye can see, with one mass of grain rolling in golden waves.[1]

**369. Completion of Reconstruction; the Weather Bureau; Great Fires; "Rings" and their Work.** —

Where some of our Western Railroads go — Animas Canyon, Colorado.

The reconstruction of the Southern States was completed in 1870; and in January of the following year (1871) all the states "were represented in Congress for the first time since December, 1860."  The disastrous effects of negro voting in South Carolina and some

---

[1] See *Harper's Magazine* for March, 1880, on "Dakota Wheat Fields"; Charles Dudley Warner's series of papers on the "Great West" in the same magazine for 1888; and more recent articles in "Poole's Index to Reviews" on this subject.

other states where the "freedmen" were in the majority, caused violent resistance on the part of the white inhabitants. A secret society known as the *Ku Klux Klan* was organized in various parts of the South to prevent the negroes from voting. Congress passed the "Force Bill," to give military protection to the black man. Experience has since proved that he can protect himself best by advancing in education and in habits of industry. It will be seen later on that several Southern States (1890-1899) have raised the conditions of suffrage; but the fact remains that the negro, like the white man, still has the liberty to make himself what he chooses.

Another important work accomplished by Congress in 1870 was the establishment of the Weather Bureau. This department has its headquarters at Washington, with branches in all the principal cities.

Its object is to give information of approaching storms and changes of weather. It has been the means of saving the country from heavy losses both by land and sea.

In the autumn of 1871, a great fire broke out in Chicago, which destroyed about eighteen thousand buildings valued at two hundred million dollars. During the same season, terrible forest fires caused great destruction, in Michigan, Wisconsin, and Minnesota. The year following (1872) a conflagration consumed about eighty million dollars' worth of business property in Boston. These losses greatly aggravated the panic of 1873.

In New York City it was discovered that "Boss" Tweed, one of the commissioners of public works, had been guilty, in connection with other city officers, of a series of stupendous frauds. In the course of years this "ring," as it was called, robbed the city of many millions, — so many in fact that it would have been cheaper to have had a great fire than to have kept these men in power. Eventually the "ring" was broken up, and Tweed died in Ludlow Street Jail.

A few years later (1875) a "Whiskey Ring" was exposed in

the West.   Its purpose was to cheat the government out of a large part of the tax levied on whiskey.

370. **The New Coinage Act; the Business Panic of 1873; the Centennial Exhibition; the Electric Light; the Telephone.** — Late in the winter of 1873 Congress passed a new coinage act. At that time paper money was the only kind in circulation throughout the country.   Silver dollars had not been seen for many years, and although "quarters" and ten-cent pieces were common enough, they could only be used for making small purchases and for "change."

On account of the discovery of rich silver mines in Nevada and elsewhere[1] the price of the "white metal" had fallen so much that many of the European nations stopped coining silver.

For these reasons Congress thought it best to drop "the dollar of our fathers," as it was called, and to order that nothing should be coined for home use but gold, small silver pieces, and "coppers."[2]

Later many people became alarmed at this change.   They said that the coinage act of 1873 was a mistake — or something worse; and that it was the work of wealthy men who held government bonds[3] and who were determined to have those bonds paid in nothing cheaper than gold.

The pressure brought to bear on Congress was so strong that both political parties united (1878) in repealing the act of 1873, and in passing a new law over the President's veto[4]

[1] See Paragraph 311.      [2] But the new coinage act of 1873 ordered that some very heavy pieces called "Trade Dollars" should be coined, not for use at home, but to be employed in our trade with China.

[3] Bonds: In order to get money to pay the enormous expenses of the war for the preservation of the Union the government of the United States borrowed hundreds of millions of dollars from loyal citizens and from banks.   In return, the government issued bonds, or promises to pay back the money with interest at the expiration of a certain number of years.   Not only rich people, but many persons of comparatively small means bought these bonds.   It was generally understood by those who thus lent their money to the government that it was to be paid back to them either in gold or in other coin of the same value as gold.

[4] This was President Hayes; see Paragraph 375, note 3.

which ordered that many millions of standard silver dollars should be coined and used to pay debts.

The success of the first Pacific Railroad encouraged the commencement of a second line across the continent, and eventually the number of transcontinental lines within the limits of the United States was increased to five. More railroads were built at the West than the country then demanded.[1] Multitudes of people put their savings into these new enterprises, hoping to get rich at locomotive speed. This, with other causes, brought on the failure of a large banking-house in Philadelphia, in the autumn of 1873.[2] The failure was followed by a panic like that of 1837 and of 1857.[3] In the course of a few weeks, many thousands of business men were ruined, and it became so difficult to get money that even the national government had to stop making payments on the war debt for a time, and all work on public buildings came to a standstill. The country did not fully recover from the effects of the panic for five or six years.

A leading feature of the celebration of the anniversary of the One Hundredth Year of the Independence of the United States was the opening of the Centennial[4] Exhibition in Fairmount Park, Philadelphia, in the spring of 1876. The principal buildings were immense structures of glass and iron; with numerous others, they covered a total space of about seventy-five acres. All the nations of the world sent products of their industry or their art to be exhibited; but, as in the World's Fair of 1853,[5] our own country took the lead in the display of useful inventions. The Exhibition showed what a great change

---

[1] From 1871 to the autumn of 1873 — or about two years and a half — over twenty thousand miles of railroad were built in the United States, at a cost of over a thousand millions of dollars. See, too, Paragraph 367, note 2.

[2] The banking-house of Jay Cooke & Co. They were largely interested in the building of the Northern Pacific Railroad. Their failure was the immediate cause of the panic.           [3] See Paragraphs 274 and 310.

[4] Centennial: occurring once in a hundred years; here used of the anniversary which the Exhibition commemorated.           [5] See Paragraph 301.

had taken place in the mode of doing most kinds of work. In Washington's day, and for many years later, nearly everything was done by hand; but by the time we had reached our hundredth birthday an industrial revolution had taken place. Arms of iron and fingers of steel now performed the labor, and the duty of the workman since that period has been mainly to guide and superintend a machine which is his willing, tireless servant.

Since the Exhibition, machines have multiplied with greater rapidity than ever. Two of the most remarkable novelties then exhibited were the electric light — which has since come into common use — and an instrument invented by Professor A. G. Bell of Boston, which we know to-day as the telephone. Professor Morse enabled men to send written messages to each other by electricity;[1] Professor Bell, going a step farther, enabled them to talk together in the same way, so that cities as far apart as New York or Boston and Omaha are now actually within speaking distance of each other.[2]

Since then the application of electricity to the service of man has made very rapid progress. It is employed to drive various kinds of light machinery for manufacturing, and the street-cars now generally use it in place of horses. It would seem as though the age of steam was drawing to its close and that the electric age had at length fairly begun.

[1] See Paragraph 283.

[2] A still more recent invention is the phonograph (greatly improved in 1888), invented by Thomas A. Edison, of Menlo Park, New Jersey. This remarkable instrument records sound in such a manner that it can be exactly reproduced any length of time afterward. By its use the tones of the human voice may be stored up for the future. Aside from its uses for entertainment, it is sometimes employed for business purposes in dictating to a typewriter. (The first American typewriting machine appeared in 1829, but it was not until 1874 that a greatly improved instrument began to be manufactured on a large scale.) After Mr. Edison gave the world the phonograph he invented (1896) the kinetoscope — an instrument which exhibits photographs of moving figures *in action.*

In a wholly different direction, that of astronomical instruments, Mr. Alvan Clark and his son, Alvan G. Clark, of Cambridgeport, Mass., have recently made great progress. Their telescopes now rank among the most perfect in the world. In 1886 they constructed one for the Lick Observatory, on Mount Hamilton, near San Francisco, and later one for the Yerkes Observatory in Wisconsin, which are especially noteworthy.

**371. The Treaty of Washington; the Geneva Tribunal; Indian Wars.** — In 1871 an important treaty[1] was made with Great Britain. Under that treaty the Geneva Tribunal, which met at Geneva, Switzerland (1871), decreed that England should pay the United States $15,500,000 for damages done by the *Alabama* and other Confederate war-vessels built in Great Britain.[2] In 1812 such a claim on our part would probably have led to war between the two countries. The fact that it could now be peaceably settled showed what a great change for the better had taken place in the relations of England and America.

It was unfortunate for us that we either could not or would not settle our disputes with the Western Indians in the same peaceable way. The Modocs of Southern Oregon refused to be removed from their hunting-grounds, and war ensued (1872). Later, the Sioux[3] tribes, who had been driven from the Black Hills by gold seekers, made up their minds that they would not go to Indian Territory. General Custer, one of the bravest officers of the army, attacked them in their stronghold in Montana. The Indians numbered nearly ten to his one. In a desperate fight Custer and his entire command of several hundred men were killed on the spot (1876). But in time both the Modocs and the Sioux had to yield to superior force.

A little later in the same year (1876) Colorado entered the Union as the "Centennial State."

**372. Summary.** — President Grant's administration was marked (1) by the completion of the first railroad across the continent; (2) by the admission to Congress of representatives of all the seceded states; (3) by an important treaty with England; (4) by terrible fires West and East,

[1] The Treaty of Washington referred all matters in dispute between the two countries to one or more boards of arbitrators. The Geneva Tribunal consisted of five arbitrators. The Canadian Fisheries dispute came up for settlement under this treaty, and a board of arbitration decided that we should pay Great Britain $5,500,000 for using the Canadian shores in carrying on our fishing.

[2] See Paragraph 326.          [3] Sioux: pronounced Soo.

destroying many millions of property ; (5) by a new coinage act ; (6) by a severe business panic ; and (7) by the Centennial Exhibition at Philadelphia.

## RUTHERFORD B. HAYES.

373. **Hayes's Administration (Nineteenth President, One Term, 1877–1881); Withdrawal of Troops from the South ; Railroad and Coal Strikes.** — President Hayes [1] believed that there would never be permanent peace at the South until the people of that section were allowed to manage their own affairs without the interference of the national government. He therefore withdrew the United States troops from that part of the country, trusting that the whites and the blacks would come to an understanding between themselves. From that time forward the "solid South"—that is, the solid white vote of the South—got the control, and the negro ceased to govern. It was a great relief to the whole country to have the strife over, and the President's action, though severely condemned by many of his party, was heartily approved by the great mass of the people.

In the summer (1877), extensive railroad strikes occurred throughout the Northern States west of New England. Later, many Pennsylvania coal-miners joined the strike. In all about a hundred and fifty thousand men stopped work. In Pittsburgh a mob of "roughs" and "tramps" took advantage of the strike to plunder freight-cars, and finally to set fire to the

---

[1] Rutherford B. Hayes was born in Ohio in 1822. He studied law, and settled in Cincinnati. During the Civil War he became a brigadier-general in the Union army. After the war he was twice elected governor of Ohio. In 1876 he was elected President by the Republicans (William A. Wheeler of New York, Vice-President) over Samuel J. Tilden of New York and Thomas A. Hendricks of Indiana, the Democratic candidates. Mr. Hayes had but *one* majority of the electoral votes over his opponent. The Democrats maintained that the election was not fairly conducted, and that many Democratic votes in the South had been thrown out by those whose duty it was to count them. Congress created an Electoral Commission composed of ten members of Congress and five Justices of the Supreme Court to decide the matter. After investigating the facts, they decided in favor of Mr. Hayes by a vote of 8 to 7, and he was declared elected.

railroad machine-shops and other buildings, destroying nearly $10,000,000 of property.

The President was finally obliged to send troops to Pittsburgh to prevent further destruction.

**374. Deepening the Chief Mouth of the Mississippi.** — During President Hayes's administration, the attention of Congress was particularly called to the condition of the Lower Mississippi. That great river is constantly bringing down vast quantities of sand and mud, which gradually fill up the mouths of the stream.[1]

The sand bar thus formed had increased so that it finally blocked up the passage to such an extent that large and heavily loaded ships could pass over it only with the greatest difficulty. On one occasion over fifty vessels were seen lying north of the bar, waiting for an opportunity to get to sea. Sometimes they were delayed there for days, or weeks, even, and had at last to be at great expense, paying steam tug-boats to haul them through.

Both the national government and the state of Louisiana had spent many millions trying to remove the obstructions, but they had met with only a partial degree of success.

In 1875 Captain Eads, an engineer of St. Louis, the builder of the great steel arch bridge across the Mississippi at that point, undertook to open the mouth of the river. His plan, though not new, was a most ingenious one. He had noticed that where the river was narrow the current was strong, and so deposited but little mud to fill up the channel. He said to himself, By building new banks on each side, near the mouth of the river, I can narrow the channel and increase the force of the current to such a degree that it will carry all the sand and mud out to sea. Then, if the bar is once dredged out, it will never form again.

---

[1] The waters of the Mississippi enter the Gulf by five channels or "passes"; Captain Eads's great work was on the South Pass.

Congress reluctantly gave him permission to try the experiment. He set to work, and in four years proved the truth of his idea (1879). The Mississippi, like a well-behaved river, now sweeps out its own channel, and large ocean steamers can pass up to New Orleans, or out to sea, without difficulty or expense. The saving in a single year in this way amounts to nearly two millions of dollars. Captain Eads's great work has been of immense benefit, for the foreign commerce of New Orleans is larger by far than that of any other city in the South.[1]

### 375. United States Paper Money becomes as Good as Gold; Effect on the National Debt.

The paper money called "greenbacks"[2] which the government issued during the Civil War, and with which it paid part of its enormous expenses, was worth less than gold. At one time (summer of 1864), it was worth so much less that it took nearly three dollars in "greenbacks" to purchase as much as a single dollar in gold would buy. That meant that at that time people had so little confidence in the power of the government to do as it agreed that a paper promise of payment stamped "one dollar" was worth only about thirty-five cents.

But after the war the feeling changed, especially as the government began at once to pay off its debt.[3] On this account, paper money rose steadily in value, until at last a "greenback" dollar would buy quite as much as a gold dollar.

[1] For an interesting account of Captain Eads's work, see *Scribner's Magazine*, vol. xix., "The Mississippi Jetties" (illustrated).

[2] "Greenbacks": they were so called because the backs of the bills were printed largely in green ink.

[3] In 1873 (see Paragraph 370) the United States suspended the coinage of the standard silver dollar. In 1878 Congress passed the "Bland Silver Bill," which ordered the coinage of large sums in silver dollars of $412\frac{1}{2}$ grains weight, and provided that they might be used in payment of debts by the government. As these dollars were worth then only about ninety-two cents, President Hayes vetoed the bill, on the ground that the government would be guilty of dishonesty and "bad faith" if it paid its debts in such coin. Congress, however, passed the bill over the President's veto, and it became law. Notwithstanding this law, the credit of the government continued to improve until its notes were as good as gold.

Finally, on New Year's Day, 1879, the Treasurer of the United States stood ready to give gold to those who preferred it to "greenbacks." This had such an effect in strengthening the credit of the government that it was now able to borrow all the money it wanted to meet the debt as it fell due, at very low rates of interest.

**376. Summary.** — The four most important events of Mr. Hayes's presidency were: (1) His withdrawal of troops from the South; (2) the great railroad and coal strikes; (3) the deepening of the mouth of the Mississippi; (4) the reduction of the expenses of the government in paying interest on its debt.

## James A. Garfield and Chester A. Arthur.

**377. Garfield's and Arthur's Administrations (Twentieth and Twenty-First Presidents, One Term, 1881–1885); Assassination of the President; Civil Service Reform.** — In the summer following his inauguration, President Garfield[1] was shot by a disappointed office-seeker named Guiteau.[2] He died in the autumn from the effects of the wound, and Vice-President Arthur became President.

The murder of Garfield led to an attempt on the part of Congress to relieve the President from the necessity of appointing

[1] James A. Garfield was born in Ohio in 1831; died, 1881. His early life, like that of Abraham Lincoln, was passed in hardship and poverty, in a part of the country then called the "Wilderness."

Like Lincoln, he rose above all difficulties, and made his own way by the force and integrity of his character. By dint of hard work, he fitted himself for college, and graduated at Williams College, Massachusetts, with distinction. When the war broke out, he entered the Union army, and was promoted, for his services at the battle of Chickamauga, to the rank of major-general. In December, 1863, he was elected to Congress, and later, was chosen United States Senator.

In 1880 he was elected President (Chester A. Arthur of New York, Vice-President) over General W. S. Hancock of Pennsylvania and William H. English of Indiana, the Democratic candidates. President Garfield was shot by Charles J. Guiteau, July 2, 1881. He died September 19. Vice-President Arthur then became President.

[2] Guiteau (Ge-toe') was convicted of the murder, and hanged.

thousands[1] of persons to government offices merely as a reward for their having worked, or spent money, to get him elected.

A law called the Civil Service Reform Act was passed (1883) which gave the President power to appoint commissioners to examine all persons applying for the lower grade of offices, and to recommend such as they thought showed themselves best fitted to do the work.   Out of the list they furnish, the President can then make his selection.

This method, which has received the name of Civil Service Reform,[2] takes off the President's hands (if he sees fit to use it) a vast amount of very laborious work.   It also saves his time, and spares him the vexation of having to listen to that class — found even among office-seekers — who cry night and day, like professional beggars, " Give !" "Give !"

President Arthur gladly appointed the Civil Service Commissioners ; and it seems probable that in time all appointments to the lower class of government offices will be made by examination — thus giving an equal chance to all.

378. Overflow of the Mississippi ; the East River Suspension Bridge ; Cheap Postage ; the Alien Contract Labor Act. — In the spring of 1882 the Mississippi overflowed its banks in Louisiana, doing immense damage to cotton and sugar plantations. Over a hundred thousand persons were made homeless.   The abundant aid given showed that the wealth of the country had become so great that it was easy for the nation to help any section of the republic that should really require it.

---

[1] In 1881 there were 3400 government clerks and other persons employed in the Treasury Department at Washington.   The whole number of government offices (including post-offices) was then estimated at about 140,000.   This number is, of course, constantly increasing.   The Civil Service Reform aims to fill the greater part of these offices by competitive examination, and to make their tenure permanent during good behavior, unless some good reason arises for demanding a change.

[2] Civil service : all persons in the employ of the government outside of the army and navy (that is, outside of *military* service) are said to be in the *civil* service.

The necessity for civil service reform has already been considered in Paragraphs 260 and 261.

An illustration of our steadily growing prosperity and enterprise was given during the spring of 1883 in the completion of the great East River Suspension Bridge, connecting New York City with Brooklyn. This bridge was built at a cost of nearly fifteen million dollars — an amount double that of the entire annual cost of carrying on the government of the United States in the first years of Washington's presidency. It took fourteen years to finish the structure, which has a total length of over

The East River Suspension Bridge.

a mile. The roadway is suspended by four steel-wire cables, each more than a foot in diameter, stretched from towers nearly three hundred feet in height. The bridge is divided into five avenues, — one for foot-passengers, two for carriages and wagons, and two for cable-cars. Taken as a whole, this bridge — a monument of American engineering skill — is the grandest work of the kind in the world.[1]

[1] The East River Suspension Bridge was begun by John A. Roebling (pronounced Ro'bling) of Trenton, New Jersey, the inventor of wire suspension bridges, the builder of the famous railroad suspension bridge at Niagara, and of the great suspension bridge across the Ohio at Cincinnati. Mr. Roebling only lived to complete the plan

Still another evidence of the prosperity of the country was the reduction of postage (1883) on letters, weighing not more than half an ounce, from three cents to two. Two years afterward (1885), the weight of a letter which might be sent at this low rate was increased to a full ounce. For two cents we can now send a bulky letter from Eastport, Maine, to Alaska or to San Francisco and Honolulu, Hawaii, — a distance of between five and six thousand miles, or nearly double that from New York to Liverpool.

Late in Mr. Arthur's presidency a law called the "Alien Contract Labor Act" was passed (1885). Its object was to protect American workmen against the importation of foreign workmen. The Act prohibited any Company or other persons from bringing foreigners into the United States under contract to perform labor here. The only exceptions made by this law were in the case of those who were brought over to do housework or other domestic service, and skilled workmen who should be needed here to help establish some new trade or industry.

**379. The New Orleans Cotton Centennial Exhibition; the "New South."** — In 1784, eight bags of cotton were exported from Charleston, South Carolina, to England.[1] It was the first shipment of the kind ever made from the United States. In time, this country came to supply nearly all the cotton used in Great Britain and Europe, and the value of the crop grew to be so great that it was a common saying at the South, "Cotton is king."

Samuel Slater, who came to this country from England in 1789, was the first person to establish the manufacture of cotton in the United States on a really solid foundation. Moses Brown, a Rhode Island Quaker, wrote to him in regard to

of the East River Bridge. He was succeeded by his son, W. A. Roebling, who took up the work and finished it.

[1] See Paragraph 205. See the history of cotton exportation from Charleston in "The Charleston Year-Book" for 1883 and compare the "Year-Book" for 1880.

setting up a mill, saying: "If thou canst do this thing, I invite thee to come to Rhode Island, and have the credit of introducing cotton manufacture into America."

Mr. Slater was just the man who could "do this thing"; and, trusting wholly to his memory to construct the complicated machinery required, he started a mill for cotton spinning at Pawtucket in 1790, which proved an entire success.

Francis C. Lowell of Newburyport, Massachusetts, following Mr. Slater's example, set up the manufacture of cotton cloth on an important scale in that state (1814), and later the great manufacturing city of Lowell was named in his honor.

In the winter of 1884, an exhibition[1] was opened at New Orleans — the largest cotton market in America — to mark the hundredth anniversary which had elapsed since the first export of that product, of which the "Crescent City" alone now ships nearly two millions of bales.[2]

The real importance of that Centennial Exhibition did not, however, depend on its display of any one production, but in the fact that it proved that the South had entirely changed, — that it had in fact become absolutely a "New South."

**380. The Progress made by New Orleans an Illustration of what the "New South" is doing.** — Take New Orleans itself as an illustration. Before the war, it had but a single important line[3] of railroad entering the city; now it has six trunk-lines.[4]

Before the war, it was almost wholly a commercial city, and its manufactures practically counted for nothing. To-day, its commerce is larger than ever,[5] and its manufactures are rapidly

---

[1] The buildings covered more than seventy-five acres, and the main building was the largest of the kind ever erected in the world. Important cotton exhibitions had been held in Atlanta in 1881, and at Louisville in 1883; but they did not compare in magnitude with this at New Orleans.

[2] Cotton was at first shipped in bags, but later in compressed bales of about 400 pounds weight.        [3] See Scribner's "Statistical Atlas of the United States."

[4] Trunk-lines of railroad: main lines, connecting large and important cities.

[5] Much of this increased ocean commerce is due to Captain Eads. See Paragraph 374.

increasing; it now makes great quantities of goods which it formerly bought. In 1860, the money invested in its machine-shops, mills, and workshops was so small that it was not reported; at the present time, it is probably close upon twenty-five million dollars, and the yearly wages it pays to its workmen amount to about nine million dollars.

381. **The South no longer a Purely Agricultural Country; its Manufactures; its Prosperity; the "Freedmen"; Education.** — The change that has taken place in New Orleans shows us what has been going on throughout the South. When the war broke out, it was almost purely an agricultural country; now, within the past four years alone, fourteen thousand new manu-facturing and mining enterprises have been started, including the production of cotton-seed oil,[1] and many thousands of miles of railroad have been built. Such cities as Chattanooga (Ten-nessee), Augusta and Atlanta (Georgia), and Birmingham (Alabama) are "hives of industry." Their cotton-mills, iron-mills, and other important works are fast rivalling anything in the North or West; and they possess the advantage of having their supplies of raw material — their cotton, iron, lumber — at the very doors of their factories and mills; with unlimited quantities of coal for fuel, and, in some cases, immense water-power[2] besides.

But this is not all. A new spirit shows itself in the South. Free labor is accomplishing double what slave labor did. In 1860, the South produced less than four million bales of cotton; now it produces eight millions; the white man does about half the work; the black man, the other half. The "Freedmen" share in this prosperity; and the men who, when the war broke out, could not call even themselves their own, are to-day taxed

---

[1] Before the war the seed was thrown away or burned as useless. Now nearly $50,000,000 are invested in its production. The oil is used as a substitute for olive-oil for making a superior soap, and for many other purposes.

[2] Augusta, Spartanburg and Columbus have great water-power.

for over a hundred million dollars' worth of property, which they have fairly made and just as fairly enjoy.

In education the progress has been equally great.[1] Common schools have multiplied all through the South, — they are free to black and white alike, though the schools are separate,[2] — and the negro has not only many thousand teachers of his own race, but great numbers of white teachers besides. If he cannot get on now the fault will be mainly his own.

Horace Greeley used to give this advice to the young men of his acquaintance who wanted to get a start in life : "Young man, go West." The progress of the cotton states would seem to change this advice a little, and tend to induce us to say, Young man, go West, *or* South.

382. Summary. — The principal events of the Garfield and the Arthur administrations were the assassination of President Garfield, followed by Vice-President Arthur's succession, and by an act of Congress providing for Civil Service Reform.

During Arthur's presidency, great destruction of property was caused by the overflow of the Mississippi ; but the general prosperity of the country was shown by the completion of the East River Suspension Bridge, by the reduction in the rate of letter postage, and by the immense growth and prosperity of the "New South."

[1] In 1882, Paul Tulane, of Princeton, New Jersey, but for more than half a century a resident of New Orleans, left over $1,000,000 to found a university for the education of white youth in that city. Vanderbilt University of Nashville, Tennessee, is another example of the same kind. In 1866, George Peabody of Danvers, Massachusetts (the London banker), gave a sum of money, which he later increased to $3,500,000, for the promotion of education at the South. In 1882, John F. Slater of Norwich, Connecticut, gave $1,000,000 for the education of the "freedmen" at the South. To-day the Southern States are spending very large sums on common and high-school education.

[2] The common schools for the blacks and the whites throughout the South, says the late Mr. Grady, "are separate, without exception." See "In Plain Black and White," *Century*, April, 1885. The Agricultural Colleges established throughout the Union by grants of land made by Congress have been of very great help to the South in many ways.

## GROVER CLEVELAND.

**383. Cleveland's Administration (Twenty-Second President, One Term, 1885–1889); Progress made in Civil Service Reform.** — The Republican party had held control of the government ever since the election of Abraham Lincoln; Grover Cleveland[1] was the first Democratic President that had been inaugurated for over a quarter of a century.[2]

Among the important matters to which President Cleveland gave special attention was the reform of the Civil Service,[3] which had been undertaken under President Arthur. The success of such a movement — earnestly advocated by the best men of all parties — must depend on the whole people. When the vast good which this measure promises is clearly seen, no one can doubt that the nation will thoroughly work out this reform as it has so many others.[4]

**384. The "Knights of Labor"; the "Black-List" and the "Boycott"; the "American Federation of Labor"; the Department of Labor.** — For a number of years, a large part of the laboring-men of the country had been members of a society or union known as "The Knights of Labor" (1869). The

---

[1] Grover Cleveland was born in Caldwell, New Jersey, in 1837. His father soon after moved to New York State, and his son began the study of law in Buffalo, at the age of eighteen. In 1881, he was elected mayor of that city, and the year following, he became governor of New York. In 1884, Mr. Cleveland was elected President (Thomas A. Hendricks of Indiana, Vice-President) by the Democrats, over James G. Blaine of Maine and John A. Logan of Illinois, the Republican candidates. Many "Independent Republicans," or "Mugwumps," as they were called, voted for Mr. Cleveland.

[2] James Buchanan, the last Democratic President before Cleveland, was elected in 1857, just twenty-eight years before.

[3] See Paragraph 377.

[4] The first movement toward Civil Service Reform was made in 1853, but nothing was accomplished. Presidents Grant and Hayes next took it up; since, the progress made by the Civil Service Commissioners is seen in the fact that during the year 1885 they held one hundred and fifty examinations of applicants for government positions in seventeen different states. The whole number examined was 7602; of these, 1876 received appointments from the government.

purpose of the society was to secure for its members the power of united action in all matters that concerned their interest.

In this, as in every country, there had been at times serious disputes between employers and workmen ; one object of the "Knights of Labor" was to get such disputes settled in a way satisfactory to both parties. Where this could not be done, the labor-union might order its members to quit work until they either got the terms they asked, or were compelled to accept those offered by the employers. In some instances, when the union men struck, they refused to allow men who were not "Knights of Labor" to take their places, and used force to prevent them.

The employers, on the other hand, formed combinations, or unions, to protect their own interests. In some cases they kept a "black-list" on which were recorded the names of those laboring-men who were thought to be unreasonable in their demands for higher pay or shorter hours, or whose influence over the other men was believed to be injurious. Such men often found it impossible to get work.

The "Knights," however, were not without their weapon. They could refuse to have any dealings with an employer who used the "black-list"; and furthermore, they could, and did, use their influence to prevent others from having any dealings with him. This was called "boycotting."[1] It is difficult to say whether the "black-list" or the "boycott" came first ; but in President Cleveland's administration both were extensively used, and both caused immense loss without apparently gaining any very decided advantage for either side.

More recently the "American Federation of Labor" was organized (1886) for the purpose of promoting the welfare of the great body of artisans in the United States. It is one of

---

[1] The word "boycott" came from Captain Boycott, the name of an English farmer and land agent in Ireland. In 1880 he became so much disliked that the people of the district where he lived refused to work for, buy from, sell to, or have any dealings whatever with him.

the largest and strongest organizations of the kind in the world, and probably has nearly a million of members.

Both of the above-mentioned associations exert a powerful influence on lawmaking, on the tone of a part of the newspaper press, and on the action of political parties.

That influence was shown in the creation by the government of the Department of Labor at Washington (1888), for the purpose of collecting and publishing important facts respecting the condition, rate of wages, and general progress of the laboring classes of the country. The Department is ably managed, and makes frequent reports which are of great value not only to those who sell, or hire labor, but to the whole community beside.

### 385. The Year of Strikes ; the Chicago Anarchists.

— The year 1886 may almost be called the year of labor strikes. They began very early in the spring, with the horse-car drivers and conductors in New York ; and they gradually extended, in one form or another, to points as far west as Nebraska, and as far south as New Orleans.[1]

In many cases, the strikers demanded that the working-day be shortened to eight hours ; in other cases, they asked an increase of wages. In Chicago, forty thousand men left their employments, and the greater part of the factories and workshops of the city were closed. Processions of strikers, ten thousand strong, marched through the streets, — in some cases, with all the precision of movement of a body of highly drilled troops. Soon the men engaged in handling freight at the different railroad freight-houses in the city joined their fellow-workmen, and all movement or delivery of goods came to a stop. On the day following, there was some rioting. On the evening of the next day (May 4, 1886), six or seven hundred persons gathered in the neighborhood of Haymarket Square, and were addressed by different speakers,

[1] See Appleton's " Annual Cyclopædia," 1887, " Strikes."

one of whom — an Englishman — urged the most violent measures. A large force of police was on the ground; believing that the meeting was likely to end in a serious riot, they ordered the crowd to disperse. At that moment, some one threw a dynamite bomb [1] at the police. It exploded with terrible violence, severely wounding many of the officers, and killing several.[2] Persons in the crowd then drew revolvers, and fired on the police. The officers charged on the crowd, firing rapidly, and killing and wounding a large number. The ringleaders of the mob were arrested, and brought to trial. All but one were of foreign birth. They belonged to a small but dangerous class calling themselves Anarchists.[3] The object of the Anarchist is to overthrow all forms of government, either by peaceable means, or — as in the case of the men arrested at Chicago — by murder, and the destruction of property. The workingmen of Chicago, and throughout the country, expressed their horror of such methods, and denounced the Anarchists as enemies of the interests of labor, and of society. Four of the rioters were hanged.

**386. Growth of Great Corporations and " Trusts " ; Political Questions ; Disasters.** — From the time of which we are speaking men engaged in every kind of work or enterprise have been more and more inclined to form associations. We have seen in a previous section [4] how labor organized for self-protection and to obtain shorter hours or higher wages.

In the same way capitalists have united in forming companies for carrying on business on a scale never before attempted.

The object sought by these gigantic corporations and

---

[1] These bombs were made of pieces of gas-pipe filled with dynamite, — a substance which explodes with much greater force than gunpowder.

[2] Sixty of the police were badly wounded, and seven were either killed on the spot, or died in consequence of the injuries they had received.

[3] Anarchists (An′ar-kists) : the name comes from two Greek words meaning *without a ruler or government ;* hence, in ordinary use, those who seek to overthrow all government.    [4] See Paragraph 384.

" trusts " [1] is generally to obtain more effective results, with less competition, at smaller cost, and at larger profit to the stockholders.

For instance, there were once many individual men or small companies engaged in obtaining and selling coal oil. Now the "Standard Oil Company" (organized in 1881) controls nearly the entire output of petroleum in the United States, and directly or indirectly influences the trade of the world in this important product.

So, too, companies or "trusts" have been formed, having in the aggregate hundreds of millions of capital, for the manufacture and sale of iron, steel, sugar, cotton-seed oil, tobacco, india-rubber, and other staple products.

In like manner since 1881 the Western Union Telegraph Company has absorbed by purchase or by lease nearly all the telegraph lines in the United States, while the Bell Telephone Company "practically conducts the telephone business " of the country.[2]

Again, many independent or competing railway lines have consolidated into through systems extending over thousands of miles.

The same movement is seen operating in a different way in the establishment of the great "Department Stores " of our large cities. Formerly the business they conduct was in the hands of a number of small dealers, but now a customer can buy, under one roof, almost anything he wants, from a paper of pins to a barrel of flour, or a set of parlor furniture.

These changes which have revolutionized business in great degree are of deep interest to every one. Many thoughtful persons are convinced that we can no more resist them than we could swim against the rapids of Niagara. But the Socialists

---

[1] " Trusts ": A " Trust " is a combination of several independent or rival companies so that they shall work together for the interest of all concerned.

[2] See " Statistical Abstract of the United States," prepared under the direction of the Secretary of the Treasury (1897–1899).

believe that the State should interfere, and that the time is coming when it will assume the management of railways, telegraph lines, and many other enterprises which are now under the control of corporations.

The present conditions of doing business, however necessary they may seem to be, naturally rouse questions respecting the right employment of capital and the true relations of money and labor.  Political parties find it for their interest to deal with these difficult problems — or, at least, to try to deal with them.  For many years they have been discussed and voted upon, in some form, at State and Presidential elections.

Meanwhile the natural world has had its sudden changes, tempests, and upheavals like those which disturb human affairs. In a single day (1884) a series of terrible tornadoes swept over a large part of the country east of the Mississippi.  They levelled more than ten thousand buildings to the ground, and killed or wounded several thousand persons.

Two years later (1886), an earthquake in Charleston, South Carolina, destroyed property worth $5,000,000.  Still later (1888), terrific snowstorms and blizzards wrought havoc and death in the Northwest.

But these, and all subsequent calamities, however sorrowful and ruinous they seem at the time, seldom leave any permanent mark on the history of our country.  Our productive power is now so enormous that we can recover from almost any material loss in a few years.  The most important lesson that these disasters teach us is that nothing — save national mistakes and national misdeeds — can long check our growth as a people.

387.  The Statue of Liberty. — In the autumn of 1886, the colossal statue[1] of "Liberty enlightening the World" was

---

[1] The statue is a little over a hundred and fifty feet in height.  The top of the torch is rather more than three hundred feet above the water.  The expense of the statue

unveiled and lighted in the harbor of New York.   The statue
— the largest of the kind ever made — was presented to the
United States by a great number of citizens of the Republic
of France, as a memorial of their friendly
feeling toward the people of this country,
and as an expression of their confidence
in the stability of the American government.

The statue is of bronze, and represents
the goddess, or genius, of Liberty holding
high upraised in one hand a lighted torch,
to show the way to those who are seeking
the shores of the New World.   The figure
is of great beauty; and at night the torch
serves the purpose of a guiding light to all
incoming vessels.

388. Four Im-
portant Laws (the
Presidency; the
Presidential Elec-
tions; Interstate
Railroads; Chinese
Immigrants). —
During President
Cleveland's ad-
ministration, four
very important

The Statue of Liberty.

laws were passed by Congress.   The first (1886) provided, in
case of the death or disability of both the President and the
Vice-President, that the Secretary of State (followed, if neces-

was paid by subscriptions raised in France, and the work was done by the French
sculptor, Bartholdi, at a cost of over two hundred thousand dollars.   The government
of the United States set apart Bedloe's Island, in New York Harbor, for the statue;
and three hundred thousand dollars were raised in this country to build the foundation
and pedestal on which it stands.

sary by the other six members of the Cabinet)[1] should succeed to the office of President.

The second law (1887) laid down certain rules for counting the electoral votes, in order that all uncertainty and dispute in regard to the election of the President might be avoided.

The third law (1887) — the Interstate[2] Commerce Act — was for the purpose of regulating the charges made by all railroads which pass through more than one state, the object being to secure fair and uniform rates both for passengers and freight.

The fourth law (1888) forbade any Chinese laborer to land on our shores.   The reason for this measure was that upwards of a hundred thousand Chinamen had emigrated to the United States, — most of whom remained in California, — and their cheap labor was believed to be hurtful, rather than helpful, to the country.

Other immigrants, it was said, come here to make the United States their permanent home ; but the Chinaman comes simply to get what he can out of the country ; he then leaves it forever.   He can live on a few cents' worth of rice a day, he has no family to support, and so he can afford to work for wages on which an ordinary laborer would starve.   On this account, Congress considered itself justified in shutting out such a class from a land whose doors have hitherto stood wide open to all the world.[3]

**389. Summary.** — The principal events of President Cleveland's administration were: (1) The widely extended labor strikes; (2) the Anarchist riot in Chicago; (3) the growth of

---

[1] The Cabinet now consists of nine officers: 1. The Secretary of State; 2. The Secretary of the Treasury; 3. The Secretary of War; 4. The Attorney-General; 5. The Postmaster-General; 6. The Secretary of the Navy; 7. The Secretary of the Interior; 8. The Secretary of Agriculture (1889); 9. The Secretary of Commerce and Labor (1903).          [2] Interstate: between states.

[3] As a matter of fact, the law has thus far accomplished less than was expected ; since Chinamen come over in large numbers to British America, and then quietly cross the line into the United States.

labor unions, and of great corporations; (4) the passage of four important laws relating to the succession and the election of the President, Interstate Commerce, and Chinese Immigration.

## BENJAMIN HARRISON.

390. **Harrison's Administration (Twenty-Third President, 1889–1893); Opening of Oklahoma; how Cities spring up in the Far West.** — In the centre of Indian Territory there was a large district (now a territory) called, in the Indian language, Oklahoma,[1] or the "Beautiful Land." This tract was finally purchased from the Indians by the United States early in 1889.

On the 22d of April, of that year, some fifty thousand persons were waiting impatiently on the borders of Oklahoma for President Harrison's[2] signal giving them permission[3] to enter and take up lands in the coveted region. At precisely twelve o'clock, noon, of that day, the blast of a bugle announced that Oklahoma was open to settlement. Instantly an avalanche of human beings rushed wildly across the line, each one eager to get the first chance. Towns made of rough board-shanties and of tents sprang up in all directions. The chief of these were

---

[1] See Map of the United States, page 372.

[2] Benjamin Harrison was born at North Bend, Ohio, in 1833. He is a grandson of President W. H. Harrison (see Paragraph 281), and his great-grandfather, Benjamin Harrison, was one of the signers of the Declaration of Independence. Mr. Harrison studied law, and opened an office at Indianapolis. In 1862 he entered the Union army as a second lieutenant of Indiana volunteers. Later, he was commissioned colonel of the Seventieth Indiana Regiment. Near the close of the war he received the title of brigadier-general of volunteers. In 1880 he was elected United States Senator. In 1888 he was elected President by the Republicans (Levi P. Morton of New York, Vice-President) over Grover Cleveland of New York, and Allen G. Thurman of Ohio, the Democratic candidates.

The chief political issue in the election was the question whether the United States should adopt the Democratic policy of a reduction of tariff, or that of Protection advocated by the Republicans.

[3] President Harrison's proclamation declared that no one who entered and occupied lands in Oklahoma before twelve o'clock, noon, of April 22, 1889, should be permitted to acquire rights to lands there by such entrance and occupation. This was what kept the "boomers," as they were called, back.

Oklahoma City and Guthrie. At the end of four months, the latter had a population of about five thousand, with four daily papers and six banks; and arrangements, since completed, were made to start a line of street cars, and light the city with electricity.

**391. The Celebration of the Washington Centennial ; the Johnstown Disaster.** — A week after the opening of Oklahoma, the centennial anniversary of the inauguration of Washington,[1] and of the beginning of our government under the Constitution,[2] was celebrated in New York City. The celebration[3] began with a naval review, followed by a military review by President Harrison; and closed, on the third day, with a grand procession of all the trades and industries of the chief city of America.

In May (1889) a terrible disaster visited Western Pennsylvania. The breaking of a dam let loose a flood which rushed down a long narrow valley choking it with ruins, and dashing to pieces the greater part of Johnstown. In all, several thousand lives and property worth ten millions were destroyed.

**392. Congress of the Three Americas ; the Department of Agriculture; Admission of Six New States ; Our New Ships of War ; Woman-Suffrage.**[4] — In the autumn (1889), representatives of the leading governments of Central and of South America, with those of the Republic of Mexico, met representatives chosen by the United States in a conference or congress held at Washington.[5] The object of the congress was to bring about

[1] See Paragraphs 196 and 199.

[2] The centennial celebration of the framing of the Constitution by the Constitutional Convention, in 1787, was held at Philadelphia, September 15–17, 1887.

In 1888, Ohio celebrated the hundredth year of the first settlements made at Marietta, Cincinnati, and other points; and a grand exhibition — open for four months — was held at Cincinnati, to show the results of the century's progress.

[3] April 29 to May 1, 1889.          [4] Suffrage: the right and power to vote.

[5] Popularly called the "Pan-American Congress" (from Pan, a Greek word, meaning *all*).

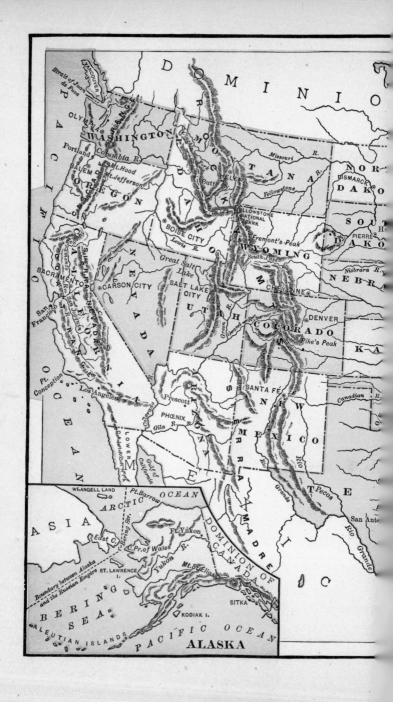

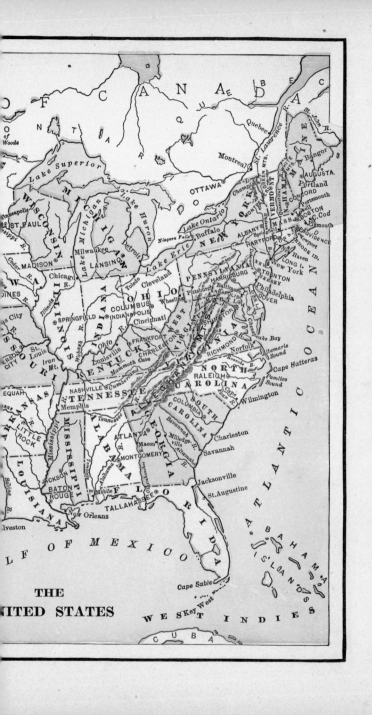

THE
NITED STATES

a closer union of the Americas, for purposes of trade and of mutual advantage.

In 1889 the Department of Agriculture was included in the chief executive departments. It has charge of all matters which are of public interest to the farming population. The Secretary is a member of the President's Cabinet.[1]

In November (1889) the President declared the four new states of Montana, Washington, North Dakota, and South Dakota admitted to the Union. The next summer (1890) Idaho and Wyoming were added. The admission of Utah (1896) raised the number of states to forty-five, and the flag of the republic will bear forty-five stars to represent them.

The power of the American nation manifests itself not only on the continent, but on the ocean. The old, worn-out wooden vessels which made up a large part of our navy, were gradually replaced (1884–1899) by a fleet of magnificent steel war-steamers and battle-ships, named generally after states and cities.[2]

The state of Wyoming was the first admitted to the Union, since the adoption of the Constitution, in which women may vote[3] and hold office the same as men. Colorado (1893) followed the example of Wyoming, and (1894) elected three women to the legislature. Utah and Idaho likewise granted (1896) equal suffrage to men and women.

**393. The New Pension Act; the Sherman Silver Purchase and Coinage Act; the McKinley Protective Tariff.** — In 1890 Congress passed three very important laws relating directly or

[1] See note on the President's Cabinet on page 370.  [2] The total number of vessels in the United States navy January, 1899, was 77; and 53 in process of construction or contracted for. By April, 1902, the total number built or building was 138.

[3] Women voted in New Jersey from 1800 to 1807. Since 1869 they have voted at all elections in Wyoming. A law granting them similar power in Washington (then a territory) was declared unconstitutional by the territorial Supreme Court. Partial woman suffrage (especially the power to vote on questions relating to schools) now exists in a majority of the states. In 1893 the people of Colorado voted an Amendment to the State Constitution by which suffrage was granted to women on the same conditions as to men; the Constitution of Utah (1895) gives equal suffrage to men and women.

indirectly to getting, coining, or spending money. The first was the new Pension Act. This added nearly 480,000 names to the list of "invalid soldiers" or their widows to whom the government pays a sum of money each year. The whole number of pensioners[1] at the beginning of 1899 was nearly a million. This number will probably be increased by the late war with Spain. They draw nearly $400,000 a day, or more than $145,000,000 a year.[2] Next, Congress passed the Sherman Silver Purchase and Coinage Act. It directed the Treasurer of the United States to buy (if offered) 4,500,000 ounces, or more than 140 tons of silver each month. Provision was made for coining this silver into dollars.[3]

In the autumn Congress enacted the McKinley Tariff.[4] Its main object was to protect American products, such as wool for example, and American manufactures against foreign competition.[5]

[1] Pensions and Pensioners : see page 226, note 1. The states which formed the Southern Confederacy in the Civil War grant pensions to "invalid soldiers" (or their widows) who fought on that side.

[2] The Commissioner of Pensions reported (1898) the total number of pensioners then on the rolls at 993,714. In 1898, Congress appropriated $145,000,000 for pensions ; the expenses of the Pension Bureau will be about $4,000,000 more.

[3] The Director of the Mint states that between 1873 and 1889 the value of the silver dollar fell gradually from a fraction over 100 cents in 1873, to about 72 cents in 1889. In 1890 it rose to 81 cents; in 1891 it averaged 76 cents; in 1892, 67 cents; and in 1893, 61 cents. He attributes the fall in value first to the fact that a number of European countries, including Germany and Austria, long since ceased coining silver except for use as "change"; but secondly and chiefly, he believes silver has depreciated because of the enormous increase in the amount mined. In 1873 the world's production of the "white metal" was $81,800,000; by 1892 it had risen to $196,605,000, an increase of 140 per cent. See "Report of the Director of the Mint" for 1893, pages 21–26. On the other hand, President Andrews, of Brown University, contends that silver has not really fallen in value or in purchasing power, but that the value of gold has risen. See "Andrews' History of the United States," II. 276. In 1898 the actual average value, by weight, of a silver dollar was about 45 cents. See Report of the Secretary of the Treasury for 1898.    [4] Tariff : see page 246, note 1.

[5] The McKinley Tariff contained certain provisions (called Reciprocity or "Fair Trade" Measures) which permitted some foreign articles to be admitted free of duty provided the country from which we imported them admitted American products free. When the McKinley Tariff was repealed in 1894 the Reciprocity Measures were repealed with it; but were later re-enacted.

**394. The Census of 1890; the Patent Office Centennial; the Immigration Act ; the Homestead Strike ; Extension of Civil Service Reform.** — The Centennial census of the United States (1890) reported the total population at over 62,000,000.[1] Since the first national census was taken in 1790 we had gained more than 58,000,000 of people, and had taken possession of the entire breadth of the continent, from ocean to ocean. It is expected that by 1915, or perhaps sooner, we shall number a round hundred millions.

The next spring (1891) the Patent Office at Washington celebrated its hundredth birthday. It issued its first patent (for making potash for the manufacture of soap) in 1790; by 1891 it had issued more than 450,000. These patents show that American genius has entered every field which thought and skill can occupy. Our labor-saving machines are the most wonderful in the world. They are driven by hand, by horse-power, by wind, water, steam, and electricity, and they do so many kinds of work that it is getting to be difficult to think of any that they cannot do.[2]

Perhaps no single invention in the latter part of the nineteenth century has had more remarkable results in certain directions than the "safety bicycle," introduced in 1889. It has had a very decided influence on outdoor exercise, especially of women, on health, dress, social habits and manners, and on the improvement of roads.

[1] The exact number in 1890 was 62,622,250; in 1790 it was 3,929,214. The census of 1890 showed that since 1880 the centre of population had moved westward nearly 50 miles. See map of Movement of Population on page 194.

[2] Among the inventions of the nineteenth century, not previously mentioned, attention may be called to the following : The Gatling gun, smokeless powder, fixed ammunition, breech-loading cannon ; the Westinghouse air-brake for cars, the automatic electric signals, the interlocking safety switch, the automatic car-coupler, vestibule trains, the Pullman and the Wagner palace cars ; the compressed-air drill, the sandblast for cutting designs on glass ; the electric search-light, electric welding and heating ; the self-binding reaper and harvester ; aluminum ware ; enamelled kitchen ware ; dyes made from coal tar ; wood paper ; wire nails, gimlet-pointed screws, plain and barbed wire fence ; the cash-carrier for stores, the passenger elevator ; ocean steamers built of steel with water-tight bulkheads and twin screws ; the hydraulic

During Harrison's presidency the "Farmers' Alliance" began to take an active part in national politics. In 1891 our immigration laws were amended. A Superintendent of Immigration was appointed, and it was ordered that no foreigners should land on our shores if proved to be paupers or criminals, insane or idiotic, suffering from dangerous contagious disease, or who were likely on any account to become a public burden.

The second event was the great strike (1892) for higher wages by the workmen in the Carnegie Steel Works at Homestead near Pittsburgh. Battles were fought between the strikers and a force of detectives hired by the company to protect their works. Firearms were used on both sides, and on both sides a number were killed. Eventually the Governor of Pennsylvania sent a military force to occupy the town and restore order.

Just before leaving office the President (1893) extended the Civil Service Reform[1] so as to make it include a larger number of persons holding government positions.

**395. Summary.** — Aside from the opening of Oklahoma and the admission of six new states (in two of which women may vote and hold office the same as men), the principal events of Harrison's administration were: 1. The building of many new ships of war; 2. The passage of the new Pension Act, the Sherman Silver Purchase and Coinage Act, and the McKinley Protective Tariff; 3. The Census Report, the Patent Office Celebration, the Homestead Strike, the amendment of our immigration laws, and the Extension of Civil Service Reform.

dredge; the gas engine, the Corliss engine; the voting machine; the tin-can-making machine; water gas; Yale, combination, and time locks; the bicycle, the horseless carriage, and wireless telegraphy.

Among the most noteworthy scientific discoveries of the century (not previously mentioned) are: Spectrum analysis, dynamite, the use of cocaine as a local anæsthetic in producing insensibility to pain, the X or Roentgen Ray used in surgery (and to some extent in the arts) for seeing and photographing objects otherwise invisible to the eye, the use of antiseptics in surgical operations, and finally the discovery and treatment of disease germs; and the production of liquid air.

[1] Civil Service Reform: see pages 357, note 1, and 363.

## GROVER CLEVELAND.[1]

**396. Cleveland's (Second) Administration (Twenty-Fourth President, 1893–1897); the Introduction of the Australian or Secret Ballot.** — Soon after Harrison became President (1889) a new kind of ballot or voting-paper was used by the people of Massachusetts for the first time in the United States. It was called the Australian ballot, because it was introduced here from that country. One great fault in the old system of election was that the bystanders could see how each one voted. This often prevented a man from voting independently. The Australian method is this: First, an officer hands the voter a printed ballot having on it the names of all the candidates of the different political parties. Next, the voter, passing behind a railing, enters a narrow booth or stall, where no one can overlook him, and makes a cross opposite such candidates as he chooses. Finally, he folds his ballot so that no one can see what names he has marked, and, in the presence of an officer, deposits it in the ballot-box. When Mr. Cleveland was elected to his second term of office (1892) many states had adopted the Australian ballot or one resembling it. No less than forty-three states use it; and it seems probable that in the course of a few years the two remaining states will adopt some form of secret ballot.

**397. The World's Columbian Exposition; "Hard Times"; Repeal of Two Important Acts; the Behring Sea Case.** — In October

---

[1] Grover Cleveland (see page 363, note 1) was elected a second time by the Democrats (Adlai E. Stevenson of Illinois, Vice-President) over Benjamin Harrison (see page 371, note 2), the Republican candidate for re-election. The political question was practically the same as in the previous presidential election (see page 371, note 2). At this election a new party calling themselves the "People's Party," or "Populists," voted for James B. Weaver of Iowa for President. Out of a total of 444 "electoral votes," cast for all presidential candidates, he received 22, but none east of Kansas, which gave him 10. The "Populists" in their platform declared themselves in favor of the union of the labor forces of the United States to secure: 1. The ownership of all railroad, telegraph, and telephone lines by the national government; 2. Free coinage of silver in its present ratio of 16 ounces of silver to 1 of gold; 3. The establishment of postal savings banks; 4. The prohibition of all alien ownership of land.

1892 the public schools throughout the Union celebrated the four hundredth anniversary of the discovery of America by Columbus. At the same time the magnificent buildings of the World's Columbian Exposition[1] at Chicago were dedicated. The next spring (1893) President Cleveland opened the great Fair to the public. It proved to be a brilliant success in every respect. During the six months of its continuance this grand object-lesson of the industry and art of all nations was visited by upwards of twenty-seven millions of people.

But the summer brought "hard times" to multitudes. There had been a money panic[2] in the spring which was followed by many disastrous failures. Property of all kinds fell in value, and immense numbers of people who depended on the work of their hands for their daily bread were thrown out of employment. Great strikes in the coal mines and on one of the leading coal railroads increased the distress.

Before the presidential election the Republicans and the Democrats had both declared themselves on the side of "honest money," and had resolved that they would make every dollar, whether gold, silver, or paper, as good as any other.

President Cleveland believed that the Sherman Silver Purchase and Coinage Act of 1890 was doing harm to the country. He called a special meeting of Congress (1893) which repealed the purchase clause in the act. This put a stop to the further buying of great quantities of silver, and checked the making of silver dollars.[3]

The next year (1894) Congress repealed another important law, commonly called the "Force Act"[4] (passed in 1870, amended in 1871), which had permitted the general government to order troops to be present at elections. Meanwhile (1893) a serious dispute in regard to the Behring Sea was

---

[1] Exposition: a word now often used for exhibition.
[2] Panic: see pages 253, note 1, 283, 350.
[3] Silver Act: see page 374.       [4] Force Act: see page 348.

settled.   We claimed that when we bought Alaska,[1] we bought the right to control Behring Sea and could close it against English and other foreign seal-hunters.   The foreign seal-hunters denied our right to shut the sea.   We seized a number of their vessels.   Finally after a long and hot dispute we agreed that the question should be left to a commission[2] to decide.   They reported that Behring Sea must remain open, but that the seals should be properly protected, and not killed by everybody at all times.   This protection was what we most wished to secure.   We got it, as we did the damages for the destruction done by the *Alabama*,[3] by peaceful means.   The more such bloodless victories any nation can win the better for it and for the world.

**398. The Coxey " Industrial Army ";[4] the Pullman Strike; more " Hard Times "; Hawaii.[5]** — The next spring (1894) a horse-dealer, named Coxey, started from Ohio to lead an "army" of the unemployed to Washington to demand relief from the government.   Similar "armies" began their march from the Pacific States and from Texas.   In all they numbered five or six thousand persons.   Part of them were honest men seeking work, part were young fellows who joined for "the fun of the thing"; others were simply "tramps" and criminals.   When hungry these "armies" begged bread, or helped themselves to it without asking; when tired of marching, and they soon got tired, they captured trains and travelled by steam.   Coxey with his so-called "industrial army" reached the national capital, but accomplished nothing, and his followers soon disbanded and disappeared.

Shortly after this, several thousand workmen employed in building Pullman cars at Pullman, near Chicago, struck for

---

[1] Alaska : see page 342.

[2] Behring Sea Commission : this commission consisted of seven eminent men chosen by the United States, the British Empire, France, Italy, and Norway and Sweden.                     [3] *Alabama :* see page 352, note 2.

[4] Or *"Army of the Commonweal of Christ."*     [5] Hawaii (Hah-wy′ee).

higher wages.   Next, the men on a number of western railroads struck in order to stop the use of these cars until the
Pullman Company should raise the rate of wages.   For a time
trains ceased running between Chicago and San Francisco and
other points.   Much railroad property was destroyed, and the
President felt compelled to send United States troops to Chicago and to certain points in California to protect the carrying of the mails and to maintain order.   Meanwhile (1894) a
new money panic [1] did enormous damage to all kinds of business and for a time made it harder than ever for men to get
work.

On the Fourth of July (1894) the Republic of Hawaii or of
the Sandwich Islands was established.   It was modeled on
our government, and President Cleveland formally recognized
Hawaii as a "free, sovereign, and independent republic." [2]   But
it was not destined to remain long in that condition, for four
years later (1898) the islands were annexed to the United
States.[3]

**399. The Wilson Tariff ; Important Extension of Civil Service
Reform.** — After a long and bitter contest Congress enacted
(1894) a modified form of what was originally called the Wilson Tariff.   It reduced protective duties about one-fourth, and
admitted wool, salt, and lumber free.[4]   It furthermore condemned "trusts" and all combinations in restraint of lawful
trade which affected imports in any way.

President Cleveland made very important additions to the
number of persons employed by the government who came

[1] Panic: see pages 253, note 1, 283, 350, and 378.

[2] In 1893 a part of the inhabitants of Hawaii rose in revolution, overthrew the
queen's government and organized a provisional government which sought annexation
to the United States.   President Harrison submitted the treaty of annexation to the
Senate, and they had it under consideration when President Cleveland came into
power.   He withdrew the treaty on the ground that it did not appear to represent
the wishes of the majority of the people of Hawaii.

[3] On the annexation of Hawaii, see Paragraph 417.

[4] See page 374, and page 246, note 1.

under the rules of the Civil Service Reform.[1]  About ninety thousand places — or nearly one-half of all government positions — are now filled by competitive examination.  Once the applicants for such places begged them as a favor, and if they got them they never knew how soon they might be turned out; now the holders can expect to retain them so long as they show themselves faithful and capable.  All political parties are interested in helping forward this great reform.

**400.  The Atlanta Exhibition; the Admission of Utah; the "New West."** — In the autumn of 1895 the "Cotton States and International Exhibition" was opened at Atlanta, Georgia.  It furnished fresh evidence of the astonishing progress which the South has made since the war.  Cotton is now manufactured very largely in the region where it is produced, and the Southern output of coal and iron is steadily increasing.

It is interesting to see that the "freedmen" share in the general progress.  The Southern States have given generous sums to promote the education of the colored people, and the "Negro Building" at the Atlanta Exhibition showed that many of them are making good use of their new opportunities for self-improvement and for the acquisition of property.

Early in 1896 Utah was admitted to the Union; this gives the Republic a total of forty-five states.  The admission of Utah naturally calls attention to the marvelous growth of the "New West" in population, wealth, and industrial enterprise.  Thousands of miles of railroads have been constructed in that section during the last ten years, cities and towns have multiplied, mines of precious metals have been opened, and cattle ranches, sheep ranches, and grain farms are yielding food products on a gigantic scale.

**401.  The Venezuela Question; the General Arbitration Treaty.** — In his third annual message (1895) President Cleveland

---

[1] Civil Service Reform : see pages 357, note 1, 363, and 376.  The whole number of government positions, exclusive of the army and navy, at the close of 1894, was about 190,000.

expressed the hope that the long-standing dispute between England and Venezuela respecting the boundary line of British Guiana might be settled by a joint committee of arbitration. Unless some decisive action should be taken, he feared that the interests of our own nation might be seriously affected. England, however, took no steps in the direction suggested, and the President thereupon urged Congress to give him power to appoint a commission to determine "the true divisional line between the Republic of Venezuela and British Guiana." The President made the appointment, but while the commissioners were engaged in their work an agreement was made between England and the United States by which the Venezuela controversy was amicably settled shortly after the Presidential election[1] (1896).

At the beginning of 1897 a general treaty of arbitration was signed by representatives of the United States and England for the purpose of disposing of any questions which might arise between the two nations, but as the Senate did not ratify the treaty it came to nothing.

**402. Summary.** — The chief events of Cleveland's second administration were: (1) the introduction at presidential elections of the Australian or secret ballot; (2) the opening of the World's Columbian Exposition and the Atlanta Exhibition; (3) the financial panic of 1893; the repeal of the Sherman Act and of the "Force Act"; (4) the settlement of the Behring Sea controversy and of the Venezuela dispute; (5) the Coxey "Industrial Army" movement, the Pullman strike, and the recognition of the Republic of Hawaii; (6) the passage of the Wilson Tariff in a modified form, the extension of Civil Service Reform, and the admission of Utah.

1 In 1896 the Democrats nominated William J. Bryan of Nebraska to the presidency on a free-silver platform and the "People's Party," or "Populists" (see note 1 on page 377), accepted Mr. Bryan as their candidate. The Republicans nominated Major William McKinley of Ohio. They declared themselves unalterably "opposed to the free coinage of silver except by international agreement with the leading commercial nations of the world."

## WILLIAM McKINLEY.[1]

**403. McKinley's Administration (Twenty-Fifth President, 1897–1901); the Dingley Tariff.** — In his inaugural address the President declared himself for "sound money," for strict economy in the management of the government, for the advancement of Civil Service Reform,[2] and for the maintenance of peace with all the nations of the earth.

The government was in great need of money to meet its expenses; Congress passed the Dingley Tariff[3] act "to provide revenue for the support of the government, and to encourage the industries of the United States."[4]

The Dingley Tariff (1) levies duties on wool and certain other raw materials, which the Wilson Tariff[5] admitted free; (2) it generally imposes higher rates on silks, woolens and other woven fabrics; (3) it keeps in force the sections of the Wilson Tariff which forbade all persons forming combinations to restrain trade in any articles imported into the United States or to raise their market price.

**404. Enormous Increase in Exports; General Grant's Tomb; the Congressional Library.** — During the last few years our

[1] William McKinley was born in 1843 in Niles, Ohio. He enlisted in the Civil War, and was promoted for gallant service to the rank of major. After the war he began the practice of law in Canton, Ohio. In 1876 the Republicans elected him to Congress. In 1890 he introduced the McKinley tariff. In 1896 the Republican vote, supplemented by the votes of many "Gold Democrats," elected him President of the United States (Garrett A. Hobart, of New Jersey, Vice-President) over William J. Bryan, the Democratic and Populist candidate. The great question at the election was whether the United States should adopt the free coinage of silver advocated by the regular Democratic Party and by the Populists, but opposed by the Republicans and the "Gold Democrats." Mr. McKinley was re-elected President by the Republicans in 1900 (Theodore Roosevelt, of New York, Vice-President) over William J. Bryan. The Democrats demanded "Free Silver" and the ultimate independence of the Philippines; the Republican platform upheld the gold standard; and pledged self-government, as far as practicable, to the Philippines.

[2] See page 381, note 1.    [3] The tariff gets its name from the late Nelson Dingley, a Representative from Maine, who originated the measure.

[4] See Dingley Tariff (Preamble).    [5] See Paragraph 399.

exports have increased enormously. In 1898 we shipped to Europe and other countries breadstuffs, provisions, and cattle valued at more than $500,000,000. Great Britain now depends on us for the greater part of her food supply. American beef has crowded "the roast beef of Old England" off the table; and when the traveller calls for bread, the waiter is pretty sure to bring him a loaf made of Minnesota flour.

We also export immense quantities of cotton, petroleum, leather, and tobacco.

Within the memory of men now living we did not send any manufactured iron or steel abroad; on the contrary, we once imported most of our tools and even the locomotives and the rails for our railroads. To-day we can underbid the world

Grant's Tomb, Riverside Park, New York City.

in the manufacture of iron, steel, and copper. We are sending American locomotives and American rails to Russia, China, Japan, and, in some cases, to Great Britain; and we have constructed steel bridges in Egypt, and electric street-car lines through Cairo to the Pyramids. Our manufactured copper, our tools, hardware, and machinery are being exported in constantly increasing quantities. American sewing-machines, watches, type-writers, bicycles, and revolvers can now be found in every large city in Europe, unless they are shut out by tariff.

In twenty-five years — and twenty-five years is a very short space in the life of a nation — our exports have more than doubled. In 1898 they were over $1,200,000,000, or almost twice the value of our imports; our exports have since greatly increased.

The architectural progress of our country was marked in 1897 by two noteworthy events. In the spring General Grant's tomb was dedicated. It is a superb white granite edifice standing on the banks of the Hudson in Riverside Park, New York. Over the entrance are cut the significant words of the great commander: "Let us have peace."

Congressional Library Building, Washington.

In the autumn the magnificent Congressional Library Building in Washington was opened. It is an imposing granite structure facing the capitol; it has room for nearly six million volumes, and is perhaps the finest building of the kind in the world.

**405. "Greater New York"; Growth and Government of American Cities.** — On New Year's Day, 1898, the charter of "Greater New York" went into operation. The metropolis now includes Brooklyn and a number of suburban towns. It covers an area of nearly 360 square miles, — or a territory more than one-fourth that of the state of Rhode Island, — and its population is estimated at over 3,500,000.

This makes New York the largest city in the world except London.

The rapid growth of cities is one of the most remarkable features in our history. In 1790, when the first census was taken, we had only six cities which had more than 8000 inhabitants. Philadelphia came first with 42,000 and New York next with 33,000. By the census of 1890, the total number of cities in the United States was 438. In 1790 only about three persons in a hundred lived in cities, while according to the census of 1890 nearly thirty in a hundred — or almost one-third of the entire population — lived in them.

This great change makes the good government of the United States depend very largely on the good government of our cities. If they are intelligently, honestly, and efficiently managed, all will probably go well; but if they are badly managed, all is likely to go wrong. The decision of this momentous question rests with the voters in our cities now, but it will soon rest with those who are to-day pupils in the public schools. In a few years you who are at present studying the history of your country will be called upon to take a hand in making its history. Your votes will then turn the scale, and America will be whatever you choose it shall be.

**406. Revised State Constitutions in the South and West.** — Within the past ten years (1891–1898) several states have adopted new or amended constitutions. Mississippi, South Carolina, and Louisiana now require every voter to be able to read a section of the State Constitution or to pay a certain amount of taxes, or both.

This change in the conditions of suffrage is expected to exclude the great majority of the negroes from the polls, and to give the white race the entire control. Several other southern states which have a very large black population are discussing the adoption of similar provisions respecting the ballot.

In 1898 South Dakota amended its constitution for the purpose of giving the people of the state a more direct voice in making its laws. The amendment provides that whenever five per cent of the voters — or fifty in a thousand — shall ask for the enactment of a law the question shall be decided at a special election. If, on the other hand, the same number object to any law which the legislature has enacted, the question of retaining it must be decided in the same way.[1]  This method has been in operation in the republic of Switzerland for many years, but South Dakota is the first state here to make trial of it.

**407. Spanish Possessions in the Sixteenth Century.** — It will be remembered that at the close of the sixteenth century Spaniards were the only white men who had planted permanent colonies in North America.[2]  They, too, held the West Indies, the greater part of South America, the Philippines, and other groups of islands in the east. The king of Spain could then boast with truth "that the sun never set on his dominions."

As late almost as the beginning of the nineteenth century Spain still held the greater part of the West Indies, Mexico, Florida, and the whole vast territory between the Mississippi River and the Pacific, which is now part of the United States.

In less than twenty-five years from that time Spain had been forced to sell or had lost[3] all of her immense possessions on the mainland of North America. The only important islands she had left in the West Indies were Cuba and Porto Rico.

---

[1] This power is called the right of *initiative* and of *referendum;* because the people initiate or originate legislation in the one case, while in the other they approve or reject the law which has been referred to them.

[2] See Paragraphs 31 and 44.

[3] See Paragraphs 215, 238, and Map of the U. S. in 1792 on page 209.  Napoleon forced Spain to give up the great province of Louisiana to him; in 1803 he sold it to us; Spain felt obliged to sell us Florida, and at the same time (1819) to give up all claims to Oregon; and Mexico freed herself from Spain by revolution.

**408. The Revolution in Cuba ; War for Independence.** — Spain's oppressive treatment of Cuba caused great discontent, and for many years there was danger of open revolt. The southern slave states coveted the island, which is as large as Pennsylvania and is almost in sight from Key West, Florida. In 1845 the United States offered Spain $100,000,000 for Cuba, but met with a flat refusal. Later, several armed expeditions tried to seize the island on behalf of the South. In 1854 the American ministers to Great Britain, France, and Spain met at Ostend, in Belgium, to discuss the Cuban question. They sent a despatch called the "Ostend Manifesto" to the secretary of state at Washington. This famous manifesto declared that so long as Cuba should belong to Spain it would be dangerous to our peace, and that if Spain should continue to refuse to sell us the island we should be justified in taking it by force.

In 1868 a rebellion broke out in Cuba[1] which lasted ten years. In the spring of 1895 a new uprising occurred, and the Revolutionists declared themselves for "independence or death."[2] This revolt in Cuba excited the people of the Spanish colony of the Philippines to declare their independence.

President Cleveland said that if the war in Cuba should go on it must end in "the utter ruin of the island." He took the ground that rather than see that, it would be our duty to put a stop to the conflict. When President McKinley entered office the Cuban war was still raging, and an enormous amount of American property on the island had been destroyed.

---

[1] The last census taken in Cuba (1887) reported the total population at over 1,600,000, consisting of (1) a small number of native Spaniards, who held nearly every position of power and trust ; (2) the white creoles, who constituted the great bulk of the people ; (3) mulattoes, free negroes, and Chinamen.

[2] The progress of the rebellion developed three parties : (1) the Revolutionists, who demanded absolute separation from Spain ; (2) the Autonomists, who asked for "home rule" — that is, the management of all local affairs — without separation from Spain ; (3) the Spanish party in power, who opposed any change whatever. A very large number of Cuban farmers — called "*pacificos*" — wished to remain neutral ; all they asked was to be let alone and allowed to cultivate their farms in peace ; but neither the Revolutionists nor the Spanish military authorities would permit this.

Many small Cuban farmers wished to keep on with their work and take no part in the struggle. But the Revolutionists drove them from their farms, or hanged them if they refused to give help; on the other hand, General Weyler, the Spanish commander, forced scores of thousands to come within the towns held by his troops. There they died of pestilence and starvation. General Lee, our consul at Havana, reported that in a single town of 14,000 inhabitants nearly half the people starved to death in a single year.

**409. Demands made on Spain by the United States; Reforms granted.** — The United States protested against this terrible state of things; finally, President McKinley demanded that Spain should put an end to it without further delay.

The result was that the Spanish government called General Weyler back and sent out General Blanco to grant reforms. He tried to relieve the starving peasants, and he offered the Revolutionists peace and "home rule." But the Revolutionists did not trust Spanish promises. They demanded independence, and would take nothing less; and when General Blanco sent an officer to Gomez, the Revolutionist leader, to propose peace, Gomez had the man shot as a spy.

**410. The Destruction of the *Maine*; Report of the Court of Inquiry.** — Such was the situation in Cuba when an event occurred which suddenly changed everything. The United States had sent Captain Sigsbee in command of the battle-ship *Maine* to pay a friendly visit to Havana. On the night of February 15, 1898, the *Maine*, while lying in the harbor of that port, was destroyed by an explosion. Two officers and two hundred and sixty-four of her crew were killed. The terrible news acted like an electric shock on the people of our country.

The United States appointed a naval Court of Inquiry to make an investigation. After a long and careful examination the court reported that, in their opinion, "the *Maine* was destroyed by the explosion of a submarine mine." The court found no evidence showing whether the explosion was caused by accident or design, and they accused no one of having been guilty of the act.

The Spanish government expressed their regret at the "lamentable incident." They declared they believed that the explosion resulted from causes within the ship itself, and urged that the whole question should be referred to a committee of persons chosen by different nations.[1] This proposal the United States declined to accept.

**411. The President's Message; the Resolutions adopted by Congress.** — In April, 1898, President McKinley sent a special message to Congress. He declared that in the "name of humanity," in the "name of civilization," and "in behalf of endangered American interests," the "*war in Cuba must stop.*"

Shortly afterward it was moved in Congress that the United States recognize the Cuban Republic. The motion failed. Then both Houses of Congress resolved (April 19, 1898) "that the people of Cuba are, and of right ought to be, free and independent."[2] In the same resolutions Congress demanded that Spain should give up all sovereignty over Cuba; in case Spain refused, they authorized the President to use the land and naval forces of the United States to compel the Spaniards to leave the island.

Finally, Congress resolved that when peace should be made in Cuba, we would "leave the government and control of the island to its people."

**412. We prepare for War with Spain; the Call for Volunteers; the Call for Money; the Navy; War declared.** — Spain refused to grant our demands and the country saw that we must fight.

[1] See Paragraph 371, Settlement of the *Alabama* case by an international committee of arbitration.

[2] Compare the words of the motion of Richard Henry Lee of Virginia in 1776; see the Declaration of Independence, in the Appendix, page 1, note 1.

The President called for 200,000 volunteers. A million of men stepped forward, saying: "Here am I; take me."

But in war, money is as necessary as men — for those who fight must be fed, clothed, armed, and paid. Congress had already placed $50,000,000 in the President's hands to buy ships and complete coast defences. Later, after the contest had actually begun, Congress gave the Secretary of the Treasury power to borrow $200,000,000 to pay the soldiers and the men in the navy, and for other expenses. Only three per cent interest was offered for the money, but the people of the United States were so eager to lend it to the government, even at that low rate, that they came forward not with $200,-000,000, but with seven times more than was called for.

Congress next proceeded to pass a war revenue act. The object of it was to meet the various expenses of the war and those which the war has since made necessary. The act levied taxes of different kinds;[1] and required stamps, purchased from the government, to be placed on bank checks,[2] telegraphic despatches, insurance policies, and many other kinds of business paper. These taxes brought into the United States Treasury from $175,000,000 to $200,000,000 annually. The entire act, with a few exceptions, was repealed in 1902.

In a contest with Spain, the navy necessarily came into play first. The President sent Captain William T. Sampson[3] with a fleet of war-ships to blockade Havana and other ports of Cuba. He also ordered Commodore W. S. Schley to organize a "flying squadron" of fast, armed steamers at Fort Monroe. This "flying squadron" was to be used as occasion might require. Congress then declared war (April 25, 1898).

### 413. The Battle of Manila. — Commodore George Dewey, who had been with Farragut at the battle of New Orleans,[4]

---

[1] It imposed a tax on patent medicines, tobacco, beer; there was also a tax on legacies, varying from 75 cents on each $100 up to $15 on each $100.   [2] Repealed, 1901.
[3] Captain Sampson had the rank of Acting Rear Admiral.   [4] See Paragraph 331.

was in command of our Asiatic squadron at Hong Kong, China. The President telegraphed to him to proceed at once to Manila, the capital of the Philippines,[1] and "capture or destroy" the Spanish squadron which guarded that important port. Our plan was to attack Spain through her colonies of Cuba and the Philippines, and so strike her two heavy blows at the same time — one on one side of the world, the other on the other.

Commodore Dewey had only six ships of war. The Spaniards at Manila held a fortified port; they had twice as many vessels as Dewey had, but they were not equal in size or armament to our squadron; last of all the enemy, though brave men and good fighters, had never learned how to fire straight.

On May 1, 1898, Commodore Dewey sent a despatch to the President. He reported that he had just fought a battle in which he had destroyed every vessel of the Spanish squadron without losing a man. A French officer, who witnessed the fight, said that the American fire was "something awful" for its "accuracy and rapidity."

Congress voted the thanks of the nation to the "Hero of Manila," and he was promoted to the rank of Rear-Admiral; after the war he was made Admiral (1899), and Captain Sampson and Commodore Schley were made Rear-Admirals.

Soon after Dewey's splendid victory the President sent General Wesley Merritt to him with reinforcements. He and his men sailed from San Francisco direct to Manila.

**414. Cervera's Squadron "bottled up"; Hobson's Exploit.** — Shortly before the battle of Manila Admiral Cervera left the Cape Verde Islands with a Spanish squadron consisting of four armed cruisers and three torpedo-boat destroyers. Nobody in America knew whether Cervera was headed for Cuba or whether he meant to shell the cities on our eastern coast.

Commodore Schley set out with his "flying squadron" to

1 See Map of the United States and Dependent Territories on page 396.

DEWEY

SAMPSON

SCHLEY

find the enemy. It was at length discovered that Cervera had entered the harbor of Santiago on the southeast coast of Cuba. When the Commodore found where the Spanish ships had taken refuge, he said with a grim smile : "They will never get home." They never did.

A few days later Captain Sampson sailed in command of a number of war-ships for Santiago. One of his squadron was the battle-ship *Oregon*, built on the Pacific coast. It had come from San Francisco, through the Straits of Magellan — an exciting voyage of over thirteen thousand miles — in order to take part in the fight.

The entrance to the harbor of Santiago is long, narrow, and crooked; furthermore, it was protected by land batteries and submarine mines. This made it very hazardous for our ships to attempt to enter to attack the enemy.

On the other hand, Cervera's vessels could not come out without running the risk of destruction from our fleet, which watched the entrance to the harbor as a cat watches a rat-hole. But though Cervera's ships were "bottled up," there was danger that they might slip out, under cover of darkness or fog, and so elude our guns.

Captain Sampson resolved to "cork the bottle" and prevent the Spaniards from escaping. Lieutenant Hobson, a young officer from Alabama, begged permission to undertake the experiment, which seemed to everybody like rushing straight into the jaws of death. With the help of seven sailors, all as daring as himself, Hobson ran the coal-ship *Merrimac* into the Santiago channel and sank the vessel part way across it. The Spaniards captured Hobson and his men. They soon exchanged them for Spanish prisoners of war held by us; and when the leader landed in New York, he found himself the hero of the day.

**415. Fighting near Santiago; the "Rough Riders"; Destruction of Cervera's Squadron.** — A few weeks later General Shafter landed a strong force near Santiago to coöperate with Captain Sampson in the capture of that city.    A sharp skirmish with

Colonel Roosevelt.

the enemy showed the fighting qualities of our "regulars" and of the regiment of "Rough Riders,"[1] who here fought on foot.

A week afterward (July 1–2, 1898) our men stormed up the steep heights of El Caney and San Juan,[2] overlooking the city of Santiago.    In spite of defences made of barbed wire, and all other devices of the enemy, they drove the Spanish, with heavy loss, pellmell into the city.

Captain Sampson then went down the coast a short distance to confer with General Shafter about making an attack on the city.    Meanwhile, Commodore Schley, of the flagship *Brooklyn*, and the commanders of the other vessels of the fleet, were keeping a sharp lookout for Cervera; for though Hobson had risked his life in sinking the *Merrimac*, yet he had only succeeded in half corking the bottle.

Not long after Captain Sampson left, a great shout went up from the *Brooklyn*: "The Spaniards are coming out of the harbor!"    Both sides opened fire at the same moment (July 3, 1898).    But the Spanish Admiral's squadron of six vessels proved to be no match for our fleet of six vessels, comprising four powerful battle-ships.[3]

[1] At the beginning of the war Theodore Roosevelt resigned the office of Assistant Secretary of the Navy in order to raise a force of volunteer cavalry.    Col. Leonard Wood took command of this regiment, in which Roosevelt held the position of lieutenant colonel.    The regiment was popularly known as "Roosevelt's Rough Riders." It included "cowboys" from the West and college graduates and the sons of wealthy families from the East.

[2] San Juan (San Whan).    Lodge's "War with Spain," pp. 125, 129–130, says that while the "Rough Riders," led by Colonel Roosevelt, showed themselves the equal of any men in the field for desperate fighting, yet this battle "was pre-eminently the battle of the American regulars, of the flower of the American standing army."

[3] Our fleet, then off Santiago (July 3, 1898), consisted of six war-ships, among

In a few hours nothing was left of the enemy's squadron ut helpless, blazing wrecks; and Cervera himself was taken risoner. Spain still had a few war-ships left, but she kept hem at home to protect her coast. So far as we were con-erned her sea-power was destroyed, and the war on the ocean ʋas over.

**416. The End of the War.** — Shortly after this decisive defeat he Spaniards surrendered Santiago. A few days later Spain sked, through the French ambassador at Washington, on what erms we would be willing to make peace. On August 12, 1898, he Secretary of State and the French ambassador signed a pro-ɔcol,[1] or first draft for a treaty of peace, the full terms of which ʋere to be decided later.

The President at once ordered all fighting on land and sea ɔ stop. General Nelson A. Miles, Commander of the Army of he United States, was then at the head of a body of troops in 'orto Rico.[2] He was preparing for a decisive battle when the 'resident's order to suspend hostilities arrived. The Spanish overnor of the island then surrendered to General Miles.

Before the President's despatch could reach the Philippines, Rear-Admiral Dewey and General Merritt had attacked and aken Manila (August 13, 1898).

**417. Annexation of Hawaii [3]; the Treaty of Peace.** — After )ewey's splendid victory at Manila in the spring of 1898,

---

hich were the battle-ships *Iowa, Indiana, Oregon,* and *Texas.* The battle-ship *Iassachusetts,* with other war-ships, and Captain Sampson's flag-ship, the *New York,* ere east of Santiago. Cervera had four first-class cruisers, but no battle-ships.

[1] Protocol (prŏ′tō-kŏl), the first draft of any public document on which a treaty is ɔ be based.   [2] Porto Rico or Puerto Rico.

[3] See Paragraph 398. Hawaii (Hah-wy′ee); the Hawaiian group consists of welve islands having a total area of about 7000 square miles. The Hon. James ryce in a recent article on Hawaii gives their estimated population at about 137,000; f this number some 14,000 are Americans and English; 75,000 are natives; 40,000 re Japanese and Chinese; and lastly there are about 9000 Portuguese. Only a small roportion of the total population can speak English.

Captain Mahan and other eminent men in our navy urged the annexation of Hawaii.

They believed that we needed the islands as a military base of defence and of naval operations in the Pacific.

When the question came up in the United States Senate there was strong opposition. A number of Senators declared that the people of the Republic of Hawaii had not been fully and fairly consulted, and that the great majority of them were unfit for self-government. But Congress passed a joint resolution to annex; and on July 7, 1898, Hawaii became a part of the territory of the United States.

The Peace Commission, appointed by the American and the Spanish governments, met in Paris in the autumn (1898). They completed their work and signed the treaty in December.

By the terms of the treaty Spain (1) gave up all right and title to Cuba; (2) she ceded Porto Rico,[1] and Guam the largest island in the Ladrones,[2] to the United States; (3) finally Spain ceded the entire group of the Philippines[3] to us, on payment by us of $20,000,000 for the public works which the Spanish government had constructed in those islands.

When the question of ratifying the treaty came before the Senate,[4] a part of the members objected to our taking posses-

---

[1] Porto Rico, with its three small dependent islands, has an area of over 350 square miles, and is therefore nearly three times as large as the state of Rhode Island. According to the last census (1887) it had a population of whites, negroes, and mulattoes estimated at over 800,000.

[2] Guam (see Map on page 396) is about 100 miles in circumference; it has a few inhabitants; it was seized by the United States, during the war with Spain, as a naval port.

[3] The Philippines (see Map on page 396) comprise over 400 islands, many of which are very small. They have a total area of over 114,000 square miles. Luzon the largest of the islands of which Manila is the capital, has an area of nearly 40,000 square miles and is therefore nearly as large as the state of Ohio. The Philippines have a population estimated at from 9,000,000 to 11,000,000. The greater part of the inhabitants are (1) Malays, (2) savage tribes of an undersized negro-like race, and (3) Chinese.

[4] The President may make a treaty provided two-thirds of the Senators present vote in favor of it. See the Constitution in the Appendix, page xii, Section 2.

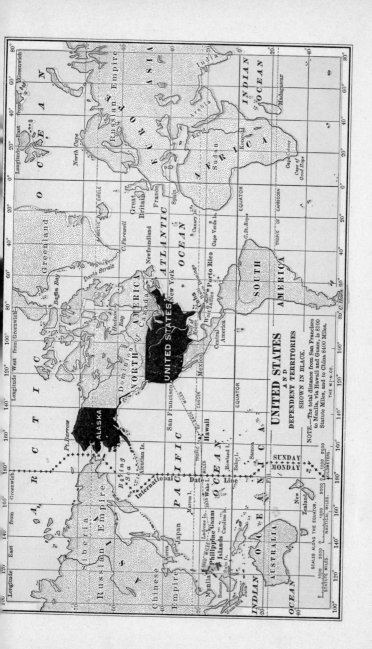

UNITED STATES
AND
DEPENDENT TERRITORIES

SHOWN IN BLACK.

NOTE.—The total distance from San Francisco
to Manila, via Hawaii and Guam, is 8100
Statute Miles, and to China 8400 Miles.

THE M/N. CO.

SCALES ALONG THE EQUATOR.

0    1000   2000   3000
STATUTE MILES

0    1000   2000
NAUTICAL MILES

0    1000    2000   3000
KILOMETERS

SUNDAY
MONDAY

International Date Line

sion of the Philippines. They contended that we could not give the semi-civilized or barbarous people of those islands the rights and privileges of American citizenship; and that, on the other hand, we could not hold them under permanent military rule without violating the spirit of the American Republic. They urged, too, that the expense and difficulty of governing so distant a territory would be very great, and that there would be serious danger of our getting into war with some of the nations of Europe over questions that would arise about the islands.

They wished to amend the treaty so that it would simply make us the guardians over the Philippines, as in the case of Cuba, until the people of those islands should be able to govern them.

But a large majority of the Senate held that the Philippines would be safer, and in every way better off, if they became a part of the United States. They argued that we have no choice; the war, said they, has forced us to annex distant islands; it has thus made us a "world-power"; and our trade interests with China and the far East demand that we should own the whole Philippine group. We can hold them, they said, as we do Alaska, under some form of territorial government, until we see our way to do differently.

While the discussion was going on the natives attacked our forces at Manila. A fierce battle ensued, with the result that General Otis and Rear-Admiral Dewey drove back the insurgents with terrible loss. The news of the battle was at once sent to Washington. The next day, February 6, 1899, the Senate met to take action on the treaty with Spain. Fifty-seven Senators voted for the treaty as it stood, against twenty-seven who voted against it. The result was that the treaty was ratified by one more than the two-thirds majority which the Constitution requires.[1] The whole Philippine group, and the islands of Porto Rico and Guam now belong to the United States.

[1] See the Constitution in the Appendix, page xii, Section 2.

Territorially considered, the results of the war were: 1. We obtained important possessions in the Atlantic and the Pacific, all of which we shall be called upon to defend and develop, if we decide to continue to hold them all. 2. The United States became the guardian of Cuba, with the intention of remaining so until the people of that island should either establish an independent republic or become members and citizens of the American Union. At that time many thought it probable that Cuba would eventually join the ranks of the Southern States, and so add one more star to our national flag.

In the meantime the Spanish had withdrawn from Cuba. At noon on New Year's Day, 1899, the Spanish flag was hauled down at Havana and the Stars and Stripes were hoisted above the palace and the castle of that ancient city. The Spanish general then bade a sorrowful farewell to the beautiful island. Spain, once so rich in American possessions,[1] does not now own a single foot of land on this side of the Atlantic.

418. The Cost of the War in Money and Life ; Work of the "Red Cross" and of the Women of America. — The direct cost of the war with Spain was about $130,000,000 ; but the increased expenses of the government in consequence of the war have been very heavy. We shall have to maintain a much larger standing army than we did formerly ; for we must preserve order in Porto Rico and the Philippines, and we must hold ourselves ready to protect the freedom of Cuba. We shall have to build more ships of war ; and we must pay pensions to the disabled soldiers and sailors who fought against Spain, and to the widows of those who were killed or died of disease.

No successful campaign in the records of our history was ever fought at such small cost of life in battle ; the total loss in the entire hundred days being only 402 ; but many times that number died from disease.

The war showed the wonderful fighting power of our navy

[1] See Paragraph 407.

and of our land forces — both "regulars" and volunteers.   It united the Union and the Confederate veterans under the old flag; and it brought the "Red Cross Society"[1] and the women of America to the front in their noble work of ministering to the wounded, the sick, and the dying.

419. The "Trans-Mississippi Exposition"; Cheap Lands; Agricultural Prosperity; the Preservation of Forests; National Wealth. — While the war with Spain was going on, the "Trans-Mississippi Exposition" was opened at Omaha, Nebraska (June 1, 1898).   The object of this grand fair was to exhibit to the world the marvellous growth and resources of the states and territories west of the Mississippi.

Spain held that vast region for nearly three hundred years, and expected to hold it forever.[2]   Through it Coronado wandered in his search for gold.[3]   Fifty years ago the greater part of it was an unexplored wilderness.   Not a single mile of railroad penetrated the country; and the school maps of that day marked a central portion, covering many thousand square miles, with the forbidding name: "GREAT AMERICAN DESERT."

The building of railroads [4] and the generous offer by the government of cheap lands, and finally of free lands, made rapid changes in that part of the country.

Under the Homestead Act, to which reference has been made,[5] every permanent settler receives 160 acres of land

[1] The "Red Cross Society" was organized in Geneva, Switzerland, in 1864, by delegates from the chief nations of the world.   Its object is to take care of all sick and wounded soldiers, whether friends or enemies, who may need immediate help. Miss Clara Barton is the President of the "American National Red Cross."   Miss Helen Gould, of New York, and other wealthy society women in different parts of the country, contributed very large sums for the relief of the soldiers and sailors in the war, and in some cases they or their friends acted as nurses in the hospitals.

[2] See Paragraphs 215, 286, and Map of the U. S. in 1792 showing the Province of Louisiana, and the Oregon country.   The remainder of what had been Spanish territory we gained through the annexation of Texas and the cessions made by Mexico at the close of the Mexican war and in 1853.      [4] See Paragraphs 255, 270, 368.

[3] See Paragraph 21.                         [5] See Paragraph 368.

practically free of charge.   It is estimated that between 1862 and the present time, Western farmers have taken up over 170,000,000 acres, or over 260,000 square miles.   This enormous area is more than four times the size of England and Wales, and nearly six times larger than Pennsylvania.   Forty years ago it was the home of the buffalo, and the hunting-ground of the Indian; now it is cultivated by men who own it, live on it, and prosper by it.

A noted writer has said that it is a great thing for any one to make two ears of corn or two blades of grass grow where only one grew before.   But the "Trans-Mississippi Exposition" showed that the Western farmer has done even better than this; for he has made corn grow where it never grew before, and in some cases he has made grass spring up where not a blade of it was ever seen.

The liberal government policy which gave homesteads to tens of thousands of hard-working, thrifty settlers, and thereby enriched the country, did not stop there; it also gave large tracts of land to each state to establish agricultural colleges. More than sixty of these educational institutions have been founded.   In many cases they have been productive of great good; and, if well managed, they will sow the seed for a harvest of still greater good.

The year 1898 was one of almost unexampled agricultural prosperity for the United States.   The West raised enormous crops of grain.   The foreign demand put up the price.   Millions of bushels were sent abroad which were paid for in gold, filling the farmer's pockets and adding largely to the wealth of the country.

But progress has been made in other directions equally important to agriculture, and to the country at large.   An old maxim tells us that a "penny saved is a penny got." This holds as true of millions of dollars as it does of pennies.

One great source of waste in the United States has been the needless destruction of great areas of forest.   Where the trees covering a large extent of country are cut down or burned, the streams in that section often become devastating torrents in the spring, and then suddenly dry up in hot weather. This condition of things has a direct effect on the cultivation of the soil and on the production of agricultural wealth.

Since 1891 the general government and a number of state governments have turned their attention to the preservation of forests.

Ten years ago the total forest area in the United States, not including Alaska and Indian reservations, was about 480,000,000 acres. This is an immense and seemingly inexhaustible extent of wood-land; but great as it is, it is rapidly disappearing. Forest fires every year destroy about 430,000 acres of timber worth $20,000,000.

The lumberman's axe, the saw-mill, and the pulp-mill demand almost incredible quantities of wood for lumber, for the manufacture of paper, and for various kinds of hollow ware, such as pails and tubs.

The United States now sets apart certain forest districts in order to preserve them and preserve the streams which rise in them. Furthermore, many states, notably those at the West which have great areas of treeless plains, have appointed one day in the year, called "Arbor Day," for tree-planting. By these means it is hoped that the good work of saving the woods and in some cases of actually creating them may in time prove of great benefit to the whole country.

Taking the Republic as a whole, no nation in the world shows greater thrift than our own highly favored land. The first three savings-banks in America were established in 1816–1817 in Philadelphia, Boston, and New York. In 1820 the total deposits in these institutions amounted to but little more than a million of dollars. To-day they reach nearly two thousand times that sum! The greater part of this mass of money is the result of years of patient toil by an army of workers who believe in Franklin's advice: "Save and have."

The steady growth of these banks is an index of the general

growth in prosperity which is going on to a greater or less extent among all classes. The estimated increase of the real and personal property of the United States from 1880 to 1890 was nearly 50 per cent. The census returns of 1900 showed that the "true valuation" or fair selling price of the total property of the country on the eve of the beginning of the twentieth century fell only a little short of $100,000,000,000.

It is pleasant to know that side by side with this great accumulation of property there is wise and generous giving. President Eliot of Harvard University says that no people anywhere have equalled our countrymen in what they have done and are doing for the support of schools, churches, and charities.

Figures prove the truth of this statement. In the last six years private citizens of the United States gave more than $200,000,000 to help forward the cause of education, to establish libraries and art museums, to endow homes for friendless children, and for the aged poor, and hospitals for the sick and the suffering.[1]

**420. American Women; the "Open Door" in China; the Samoan Islands; The Hague Treaty.** — Half a century ago a meeting was held in Worcester, Mass. (1850), in behalf of American women who wished to secure the right to vote. Since then remarkable changes have taken place in their condition.

Great opportunities have been opened to them for higher education; their power to hold property has been largely extended; they can now practically enter any field of work they choose; finally, they have obtained the power to vote in some measure in many States and in full measure in four.[2]

[1] In 1901 the gifts and bequests for these purposes amounted to more than $107,360,000.    [2] See Paragraph 392.

NOTE. — It is proper to state that American women are by no means agreed about the question of equal suffrage. One association is laboring with all its might to extend the power of women to vote, while another association is laboring just as hard against it; both believe that they are doing what is best for the true interests of their sex.

Within a few years five of the great nations of Europe, with Japan, obtained control of important ports and sections of territory in China. England wished to have all of these made free to the commerce of the world, but the other five nations refused to give their consent. Early in 1900 we obtained that privilege — called the "open door." It gives every American the same right to buy or sell goods in China that any citizen of any foreign state possesses.

Since then a treaty with Great Britain and Germany has divided the control of the Samoan Islands so that we now hold sovereignty over two of them while Germany governs the remaining islands.

Next, the Senate ratified The Hague Peace Conference Treaty. By this agreement the United States, with the principal nations of Europe and with Japan, bind themselves to maintain a perpetual Court [1] of Arbitration at the capital of Holland. The object of the Court is to do away, as far as possible, with war between the nations signing the treaty.[2]

**421. The Gold Standard Act; the Porto Rican Act; Hawaii; the Isthmian Canal.** — When the American government first went into operation the silver dollar was made the chief measure of value.[3] In 1900 a great change took place, and notwithstanding strong opposition an act was passed which makes the gold dollar the standard measure of value. Whatever other money the United States issues must now come up to this new standard.

When Congress came to establish a government for Porto Rico[4] there was great difference of opinion as to what it would be best to do. A large number of members believed that all commerce should be as free between the United States and Porto Rico as it is between the different States and Territories.

[1] In the past the United States has settled many serious disputes with other countries by arbitration. See the *Alabama* case (page 352 and Note 2) and the Behring Sea case (pages 378, 379). [2] The Hague Tribunal decided its first case — between Mexico and the United States (1902) — in our favor. [3] See Paragraphs 202, 370, 393, 397. [4] See page 397.

But Congress at length by a very small majority decided to impose a light duty on merchandise sent from the United States to Porto Rico, or sent from Porto Rico to the United States.[1] This duty was to be levied not quite two years at the longest; the revenue was to be expended for the people. Entire freedom of trade between the United States and Porto Rico was established in 1901.

Under the Constitution Congress has complete power over all territory belonging to the United States.[2] Acting in accordance with that power, Congress provided (1900) a government for the "people of Porto Rico." This gave the island a legislature which can make laws provided they receive the approval of Congress. Unlike Hawaii, since organized as a Territory, the Porto Ricans cannot send a delegate to represent them in Congress.[3]

Ever since we came into possession of California there has been talk of digging a canal across the isthmus of Panama or by way of Lake Nicaragua.[4] In 1903 we ratified a treaty with Colombia for the right of a water way across the isthmus; but Colombia declined to grant it. The people of the isthmus then declared themselves independent. In 1904 we made a canal treaty with the new Republic of Panama, by which for $10,000,-000 we secured control of a strip of territory ten miles in width, extending from the Atlantic to the Pacific. We then purchased the unfinished French Panama Canal for $40,000,000. We shall now push the work to completion. Our trade with the Pacific demands it, and our vessels of war demand it just as strongly.

**422. Census of 1900 ; Exports ; Congress and Our New Territorial Possessions ; Cuba ; the Philippines.** — The twelfth census (1900) returned the total population of the United States at

---

[1] The duty was 15 per cent of that levied by the Dingley Tariff — see Paragraph 403.

[2] See the Constitution, page xiv, section 3.    [3] Arizona, New Mexico, Oklahoma, and Hawaii are represented in Congress by a delegate sent by each Territory. These delegates sit in the House of Representatives and take part in debate, but cannot vote.    [4] Treaties for a canal were ratified with England in 1850 and 1901.

WILLIAM McKINLEY.

over 76,000,000.[1] This shows a gain of nearly 21 per cent over the population reported by the census of 1890.[2] Statistics proved that our commerce was keeping pace with our growth in numbers, since the value of our exports for 1900 exceeded the enormous sum of $1,450,000,000. To-day we stand at the head of the nations of the world in the magnitude of our foreign trade.[3]

Late in the spring of 1901 the United States Supreme Court handed down a decision of great importance respecting the islands acquired by us as the result of the war with Spain. The Court decided that, under the Constitution, Congress has full power to deal as it sees fit with our new territorial possessions.

Meanwhile Congress authorized the President to leave the control of Cuba to its people on certain conditions. The chief of these were first, that the Cubans should maintain their independence, and next, that they should acknowledge the right of the United States to take steps, if necessary, to preserve that independence, and also to protect life, property, and individual liberty in that island. These conditions were accepted,[4] and on May 20, 1902, the United States formally recognized the new Republic of Cuba.

The insurrection which began in the Philippines[5] in 1899 continued until Aguinaldo,[6] the Filipino leader, was captured in the spring of 1901. He was induced to take the oath of allegiance to the United States. He then issued an address to his countrymen, telling them he believed that further resistance on their part would be useless. Since that time civil

---

[1] The exact figures are 76,304,799. This total includes 89,670 persons stationed abroad in the service of the United States and the 154,001 inhabitants of Hawaii.

[2] See Paragraph 394.

[3] Compare Paragraph 404. The total exports of the United States in 1900 amounted to $1,453,013,659. This was nearly $35,000,000 more than the amount returned by Great Britain, our chief commercial rival and until recently the leading exporting nation of the globe.

[4] By a vote (16 to 11) of the Cuban Constitutional Convention.

[5] See page 397.        [6] Aguinaldo: English pronunciation, Ah-gwe-nal′do.

government has been established to a considerable extent in the islands, and many public schools have been opened. These are encouraging signs, and they seem to show that permanent peace has been generally established.

**423. The Pan-American Exposition ; the Assassination of President McKinley.** — In the spring of 1901 the Pan-American Exposition[1] was opened at Buffalo, New York. In one very important respect it was unlike any other exhibition hitherto held in this country, for it was especially designed to show the progress made by the nations of North, South, and Central America in agriculture, manufactures, and the arts. Furthermore, its object was to unite all the nations of the American Continent in closer commercial intercourse for their common benefit.

President McKinley visited the Exposition in September and made his last speech on that occasion. He then expressed the hope that the exhibition would tend to bring the United States into broader and freer trade relations with foreign countries.

The next day (September 6) the President gave a public reception at the Exposition. While holding this reception he was treacherously shot by a young man who came forward to shake hands with him. The assassin[2] was an avowed Anarchist,[3] whose object was to destroy the government. The wickedness of the crime was only equalled by its folly — for our history proves[4] that the murder of the Chief Magistrate of the American Republic cannot overthrow the Republic itself. Mr. McKinley died of his wounds about a week later (September 14), and under the

[1] See Paragraph 392 and note 5.

[2] Leon F. Czolgosz (Chol'gosh), the assassin, was the son of emigrants from Poland; he was born in the United States. He was executed at Auburn, N. Y., October 29, 1901.

[3] See Paragraph 385 on page 366.

[4] See the murder of Lincoln, page 332, and of Garfield, page 356.

THEODORE ROOSEVELT.

provisions of the Constitution Vice-President Roosevelt[1] became President.

The day of the funeral at Canton, Ohio (September 19), was solemnly kept not only throughout the Union, but in great measure throughout the civilized world. It was in very truth a day of mourning and of prayer. Moved by a common impulse, men of all political parties joined in paying their heartfelt tribute of sorrow to the memory of a man who had held the highest place in the gift of the American people.

**424. The Great Coal Strike ; Wireless Telegraphy ; the Pacific Cable.** — Early in the spring of 1902 the United Mine Workers in the anthracite or hard coal mines of Pennsylvania asked for an increase of wages and shorter hours. They threatened to strike unless their demands were granted, but finally offered to leave the matter to the decision of the Arbitration Committee of the National Civic Federation,[2] an organization of prominent men formed for the purpose of settling labor disputes in a way that shall be satisfactory to all concerned.

But the managers of the coal railways declined to accept the offer, on the ground that the committee could not have the practical knowledge of mining necessary for dealing with the questions coming before them.

On May 12 the workers belonging to the Union, numbering more than 140,000, struck, and for the first time since the first shovelful of hard coal was dug in Pennsylvania,[3] all of the anthracite mines were shut down.

The strike lasted a little more than five months. It was finally settled (October 21, 1902) by both parties pledging themselves to abide for three years by the decisions of a Coal

[1] See page 383, note 1, and page xii (Paragraph second) of the Constitution of the United States. Compare, too, Paragraph 388, on page 369, on the Presidential Succession Act.

[2] The Civic Federation organized in 1902 consists, first, of a number of well-known capitalists ; secondly, of leading representatives of the labor unions ; thirdly, of a number of men of high standing who represent the interests of the general public.      [3] See Paragraph 270.

Strike Commission [1] appointed by President Roosevelt. The Commission, after thoroughly investigating all sides of the controversy, made their report (March 21, 1903).

They unanimously awarded a moderate increase of wages and some reduction in hours of labor. They furthermore required that future disputes should be settled by arbitration, and that all men engaged in the mines, whether members of the Union or independent workers, should be equally protected in their right to labor.

The Commission estimated the cost of the strike to all parties directly concerned in it at nearly $100,000,000. But no figures could adequately show the loss and suffering endured by the public; for although the mines were reopened in the autumn of 1902, coal came in very slowly. At one time even rich men could not buy a ton of it, and throughout the winter millions of people had to choose between doing without fuel or paying enormous prices for it.

It will be remembered that Americans laid the first telegraphic cable to Europe.[2] In the last month of 1902 they finished laying a cable between San Francisco and Hawaii. The line was then carried to Manila, where it connects with one to Hong Kong. On the Fourth of July, 1903, President Roosevelt sent a message, over this cable, around the world.

Meanwhile President Roosevelt, on January 19, 1903, sent a message of congratulation to King Edward of England by Marconi's wireless telegraph from the station at Wellfleet on Cape Cod. This was the first telegram sent from this country, through the air, across the Atlantic. It marked another step forward in that wonderful development of electrical science which began in this country, by Dr. Franklin's experiments, more than a century and a half ago.[3]

---

[1] The Commission consisted of seven members, namely: Judge George Gray of the United States Circuit Court, Thomas H. Watkins, Gen. John M. Wilson, E. W. Parker, E. E. Clark, Bishop John L. Spalding, and Hon. Carroll D. Wright.

[2] See Paragraph 364.                    [3] See Paragraph 152.

**425. Acts of Congress** (1901–1904); **the Louisiana Purchase Exposition ; Election of 1904.** — The Fifty-Seventh Congress passed three laws regulating trusts,[1] suspended the duty on the importation of foreign coal for a year, provided a civil government for the Philippines and voted $3,000,000 for the relief of the inhabitants who were suffering from scanty harvests. Congress also passed a new Immigration Act[2] under which anarchists[3] are forbidden to enter the United States, enacted an irrigation law for reclaiming desert lands in certain parts of the country west of the Mississippi, renewed the Chinese Exclusion Act,[4] and created the Department of Commerce and Labor.[5]

In 1904 we ratified a treaty with the new Republic of Panama[6] for the construction of the Panama Canal. On November 8, Theodore Roosevelt of New York was elected President of the United States, with Charles W. Fairbanks of Indiana Vice-President.

On the last day of April (1904) the "Louisiana Purchase Exposition" was opened at St. Louis. It commemorated that day, when, a hundred years ago, we more than doubled the area of our country by the acquisition of the Louisiana territory.[7]   It showed the marvelous growth of that part of the great West lying between the Mississippi and the Rocky Mountains. It was well worth while to celebrate such progress by a World's Fair planned on the grandest scale ever yet adopted for such an exhibition.

**426. Some Things Americans are doing in the Twentieth Century ; how Disasters are met.** — (1) We work to save time, — "the stuff," as Franklin said, "of which life is made."

The American steam shovels are cutting a passage for ships across the Isthmus of Panama,[8] from ocean to ocean. This will make the voyage from New York to San Francisco 8000 miles shorter than that around South America.

[1] See Paragraph 386.  [4] See Paragraph 588.  [7] See Paragraphs 215, 216.
[2] See Paragraph 394.  [5] See Paragraph 388, note 1.  [8] See Paragraph 421.
[3] See Paragraph 423.  [6] See Paragraph 421.

Next, the State of New York is engaged in deepening and enlarging the Erie Canal.[1] When that great work is done immense new boats, moved by steam, will go from Buffalo to New York City in six days — just half the time they take now. They will carry millions of bushels of grain from the West[2] at rates much lower than at present. This will make bread cheaper in the Eastern States and in Europe as well.

Finally, we are improving and extending our railroads. We have many more miles of steam roads than all the countries of Europe combined.[3] Furthermore, we are increasing the speed of our trains. By so doing we save time to every passenger and on every car load of freight; here time is money.

(2) We are trying to save health, without which life is hardly worth living. We are working for the children so that they may grow up with strong bodies and active minds. We are endeavoring to secure pure food, and our cities and villages are making efforts to obtain cleaner streets and better drinking water.

It was only about fifty years ago that New York planned the first great pleasure ground in this country and named it Central Park. To-day every leading American city has one or more such open spaces where all can freely enjoy fresh air and sunshine.

But not satisfied with doing this good work we have laid out National Parks on a generous scale. They will preserve some of the grandest mountain, river, and forest scenery in the world. We have one such park in the Yosemite[4] Valley in California, another in the valley of the Yellowstone River in Wyoming, a third at Mt. Rainier[5] in the State of Washington, and a fourth at Crater Lake in Oregon. These, with some smaller ones, like

[1] See Paragraphs 250, 251.

[2] Much of this grain will come from Minnesota through the Soo Ship Canal (connecting Lake Superior with Lake Huron) which carries nearly double the freight carried by the Suez Canal.

[3] The total length of railroads of the United States at the close of 1904 exceeded 212,000 miles, and at the beginning of 1906 it probably amounted to about 217,000 miles. Europe has in all only about 150,000 miles.

[4] Yosemite (Yŏ-sĕm′ĭ-tĕ).

[5] Rainier (Rā′neer).

the Big Tree Park in California, cover a space a little larger than the States of Rhode Island and Delaware put together.[1]

Now, President Roosevelt recommends that we make a national park of the Grand Canyon of the Colorado River in Arizona. To that he hopes to add Niagara Falls, so that they may both become the common property of American citizens for all time.

(3) We are taking steps to save the farming land and the forests of our country, so that neither shall be wasted. The Government at Washington employs a number of trained men who devote their whole time to this most important work.

They examine the soils of the different states and territories to see what crops will grow best on them. They try experiments with trees, plants, grasses, vegetables, grains, seeds, fruits, and flowers. Through their labors our farmers are converting swamps, sand hills, and stony places into broad fertile fields. In this way too we are drawing new riches from the earth, — the mother of nearly all the riches we possess, whether they come from cotton plantations, grain, corn, rice, or sugar fields, fruit orchards, dairy and poultry farms, cattle ranches, or from mines, quarries, and forests.

(4) But going beyond these things, we are beginning to try to save the wear and tear of human life. Not very much has been done in this direction yet, but we look forward with hopeful hearts. We believe that the time will come when we shall be able to settle all labor disputes in a friendly way. Then strikes and lockouts will practically cease. Better work will be done and better results obtained.

Last of all, and best, as well as last, we are trying to see what can be done to save the needless destruction of human life by foolish and hasty wars. If we look at it in one way the prospect does not seem bright; for perhaps the world never before saw so many men in uniform with guns in their hands as we see now. But there is another side to the picture, for

[1] Our national parks have a total area of 3312 square miles.

never before have there been so many wise and thoughtful men resolved to do all in their power to hold back nations from unnecessary fighting.

We can truthfully say that, in the main, the influence of America is on the side of peace. In 1905 President Roosevelt persuaded Japan and Russia to end their terrible war. In the same year the United States made a treaty or agreement with Mexico and a number of the republics of Central America and of South America which promises to prevent many useless quarrels. A movement is on foot to make such a treaty with England, Germany, France, and other nations of Europe.

In these four ways we Americans are trying to save time, health, the good earth on which we live, and human life. There are 17,000,000 children in our public schools, who, we hope, will grow up to take part in this beneficent work.

But recent events show that Americans are developing another kind of power. They are manifesting their ability to face and overcome widespread disaster.

Reference has been made[1] to the conflagrations which occurred in Chicago (1871), in Boston (1872), and to the Charleston earthquake (1886). These calamities were followed by the Galveston hurricane (1900), which destroyed more than 6000 lives, property valued at $18,000,000, and which swept away much of the very ground on which the city stood. Four years later (1904) the great Baltimore fire burned up property worth upwards of $50,000,000. In both cases the citizens have more than made good the devastation.[2]

In the spring of 1906 came a still heavier blow. The California earthquake wrought havoc far beyond anything the country had ever before experienced. The shock was felt over a strip of coast about one hundred miles in length. Its destructive force showed itself on the greatest scale at San Francisco,

[1] See Paragraphs 369 and 388.
[2] Galveston has recently completed an immense sea wall to protect the city in the future.

where scores of costly buildings were overthrown. Fire completed the work of devastation. The loss of life was comparatively small, but the business portion of the city was ruined. More than 200,000 persons were rendered homeless, and property estimated at $350,000,000 was destroyed.

This appalling disaster roused the sympathy of the entire world. People in all parts of the globe made haste to offer their assistance. America never knew before how many friends she had.

At home, the whole population, even to the school children, rose up to send instant supplies of money, food, and clothing to the stricken city. It was a demonstration of the fact that North, South, East, and West form but one country and one people, and that the blow which strikes the remotest part is felt by all.

On the other hand, the inhabitants of San Francisco showed their wonderful power of self-help. They immediately set to work to begin life again. They proved what Americans have proved more than once, that is, that strength of heart and strength of will can find ways to turn loss into gain. Standing in the midst of confusion and desolation, they have set their hands to the work and have bravely resolved that a new and grander city shall rise above the ruins and the ashes of the old.

**427. General Summary.** — In this book we have endeavored to trace the progress of our country from its earliest period to the present time. We have seen it grow from a few feeble colonies, planted along the Atlantic coast, to a group of thirteen sturdy and independent states.

We have followed the development of that commonwealth of states and their added territories into a great, prosperous, and powerful nation, which numbered at the last census (1900) over 76,000,000 of people,[1] and which now not only extends from ocean to ocean, but also embraces important islands in both the Atlantic and the Pacific.

[1] The official returns of the census of 1900 give a population of 76,304,799.

With the single exception of Russia in Asia,[1] the American Republic controls the largest portion of the earth's surface[2] under the management of any one government on any one of the grand divisions of the globe.

Here every advantage is open. Education is absolutely free. Millions of acres of Western lands are free. Here, and here only, among the leading civilized nations, no colossal standing army eats up the daily earnings of the people.[3] Here every law springs, or may spring, directly from the will of the majority.

These facts prove the truth of the motto chosen for this book. They show that **America means Opportunity.** In closing this brief history can we do better than ask, each one of himself, What use do I intend to make of this opportunity? The whole future of the Republic for good or ill, for growth or decay, for glory or shame, depends on the way in which we individually answer this question.

[1] The Chinese Empire is not excepted, because, in the first place, authorities differ very widely as to its area (the Encyclopædia Britannica estimating it at only about 3,000,000 square miles); and next, for the reason that Warren and others state that a large part of the country is only "nominally" subject to the emperor.

[2] The area of the United States, including Alaska, but not including Hawaii or our other island dependencies, is over 3,560,000 square miles; adding the islands, it would be nearly 3,700,000 square miles.

[3] The leading standing armies of Europe are: Russia, over 835,000; France, nearly 500,000; Germany, over 562,000; Great Britain, over 220,000. In February, 1901, Congress passed an act permitting the standing army of the United States to be increased to 100,000 men.

# DECLARATION OF INDEPENDENCE.

IN CONGRESS, JULY 4, 1776.

## A DECLARATION BY THE REPRESENTATIVES OF THE UNITED STATES OF AMERICA, IN CONGRESS[1] ASSEMBLED.

WHEN, in the course of human events, it becomes necessary for one people to dissolve the political bands which have connected them with another, and to assume, among the powers of the earth, the separate and equal station to which the laws of nature and of nature's God entitle them, a decent respect to the opinions of mankind requires that they should declare the causes which impel them to the separation.

---

[1] The First Continental or General Congress met in Carpenters' Hall, Philadelphia, September 5, 1774. It consisted of forty-four delegates, representing eleven of the thirteen colonies. Later, eleven more delegates took their seats, and all of the colonies were represented except Georgia, which promised to concur with " her sister colonies " in their effort to maintain their rights as English subjects. Peyton Randolph of Virginia was elected President of the Congress. Among the distinguished men who had assembled there, were Washington, Patrick Henry, Richard Henry Lee, John Dickinson, William Livingston, John Jay, John Adams, Samuel Adams, Roger Sherman, and the Rutledges of South Carolina.

On the 14th of October, the Congress adopted a *Declaration of Colonial Rights.* On the 26th, a *Petition to the King*, asking the redress of their wrongs, was drawn up.

The Second Continental Congress (at which Georgia was represented) met in Philadelphia, in the State House (Independence Hall), May 10, 1775. A second *Petition to the King* was adopted, and Washington was appointed commander-in-chief of the Continental army, though Congress still denied any intention of separating from Great Britain, and earnestly expressed a desire for the peaceful settlement of all difficulties.

The King's Proclamation, declaring the Colonies in rebellion, and calling for volunteers to force them to submit to taxation without representation, and other unjust measures, finally convinced the delegates to Congress of the impossibility of our continuing our allegiance to the English crown.

On June 7, 1776, Richard Henry Lee of Virginia moved "That these United Colonies are, and of right ought to be, *free and independent states.*" John Adams of Massachusetts seconded the motion.

Later, a committee of five — Thomas Jefferson of Virginia, John Adams of Massachusetts, Benjamin Franklin of Pennsylvania, Roger Sherman of Connecticut, and Robert R. Livingston of New York — was appointed to draft the Declaration of Independence. Jefferson drew up the paper, though a few alterations were made in it by the committee and by Congress.

It was adopted on the evening of July 4, 1776, and signed by John Hancock, President of Congress, and Charles Thomson, Secretary. On August 2, 1776, it was signed by the members, representing all the thirteen states.

We hold these truths to be self-evident:— That all men are created equal; that they are endowed by their Creator with certain unalienable rights; that among these are life, liberty, and the pursuit of happiness. That, to secure these rights, governments are instituted among men, deriving their just powers from the consent of the governed; that, whenever any form of government becomes destructive of these ends, it is the right of the people to alter or to abolish it, and to institute a new government, laying its foundation on such principles, and organizing its powers in such form, as to them shall seem most likely to effect their safety and happiness. Prudence, indeed, will dictate, that governments long established should not be changed for light and transient causes; and accordingly all experience hath shown that mankind are more disposed to suffer while evils are sufferable, than to right themselves by abolishing the forms to which they are accustomed. But when a long train of abuses and usurpations, pursuing invariably the same object, evinces a design to reduce them under absolute despotism, it is their right, it is their duty, to throw off such government, and to provide new guards for their future security. Such has been the patient sufferance of these colonies; and such is now the necessity which constrains them to alter their former systems of government. The history of the present King of Great Britain is a history of repeated injuries and usurpations, all having in direct object the establishment of an absolute tyranny over these states. To prove this, let facts be submitted to a candid world.

He has refused his assent to laws the most wholesome and necessary for the public good.

He has forbidden his governors to pass laws of immediate and pressing importance, unless suspended in their operation till his assent should be obtained; and when so suspended, he has utterly neglected to attend to them.

He has refused to pass other laws for the accommodation of large districts of people, unless those people would relinquish the right of representation in the legislature—a right inestimable to them, and formidable to tyrants only.

He has called together legislative bodies at places unusual, uncomfortable, and distant from the depository of their public records, for the sole purpose of fatiguing them into compliance with his measure.

He has dissolved representative houses repeatedly, for opposing, with manly firmness, his invasions on the rights of the people.

He has refused, for a long time after such dissolutions, to cause others to be elected, whereby the legislative powers, incapable of annihilation, have returned to the people at large for their exercise; the State remaining, in the mean time, exposed to all the dangers of invasions from without, and convulsions within.

He has endeavored to prevent the population of these States; for that purpose obstructing the laws for the naturalization of foreigners; refusing to pass others to encourage their migration hither, and raising the conditions of new appropriations of lands.

He has obstructed the administration of justice, by refusing his assent to laws for establishing judiciary powers.

He has made judges dependent on his will alone for the tenure of their offices, and the amount and payment of their salaries.

He has erected a multitude of new offices, and sent hither swarms of officers to harass our people and eat out their substance.

He has kept among us in times of peace, standing armies, without the consent of our legislatures.

He has affected to render the military independent of, and superior to, the civil power.

He has combined with others to subject us to a jurisdiction foreign to our constitutions, and unacknowledged by our laws; giving his assent to their acts of pretended legislation:

For quartering large bodies of armed troops among us;

For protecting them, by a mock trial, from punishment for any murders which they should commit on the inhabitants of these States;

For cutting off our trade with all parts of the world;

For imposing taxes on us without our consent;

For depriving us, in many cases, of the benefits of trial by jury;

For transporting us beyond seas, to be tried for pretended offences;

For abolishing the free system of English laws in a neighboring province, establishing therein an arbitrary government, and enlarging its boundaries, so as to render it at once an example and fit instrument for introducing the same absolute rule into these colonies;

For taking away our charters, abolishing our most valuable laws, and altering, fundamentally, the forms of our governments;

For suspending our own legislatures, and declaring themselves invested with power to legislate for us in all cases whatsoever.

He has abdicated government here, by declaring us out of his protection, and waging war against us.

He has plundered our seas, ravaged our coasts, burned our towns, and destroyed the lives of our people.

He is at this time transporting large armies of foreign mercenaries to complete the works of death, desolation, and tyranny, already begun with circumstances of cruelty and perfidy scarcely paralleled in the most barbarous ages, and totally unworthy the head of a civilized nation.

He has constrained our fellow-citizens, taken captive on the high seas, to bear arms against their country, to become the executioners of their friends and brethren, or to fall themselves by their hands.

He has excited domestic insurrection among us, and has endeavored to bring on the inhabitants of our frontiers the merciless Indian savages, whose known rule of warfare is an undistinguished destruction of all ages, sexes, and conditions.

In every stage of these oppressions we have petitioned for redress in the most humble terms; our repeated petitions have been answered only by repeated injury. A prince whose character is thus marked by every act which may define a tyrant, is unfit to be the ruler of a free people.

Nor have we been wanting in our attentions to our British brethren. We have warned them, from time to time, of attempts by their legislature to extend an unwarrantable jurisdiction over us. We have reminded them of the circumstances of our emigration and settlement here. We have appealed to their native justice and magnanimity; and we have conjured them, by the ties of our common kindred, to disavow these usurpations, which would inevitably interrupt our connections and correspondence. They, too, have been deaf to the voice of justice and consanguinity. We must, therefore, acquiesce in the necessity which denounces our separation, and hold them, as we hold the rest of mankind, enemies in war, in peace friends.

We, therefore, the Representatives of the United States of America, in General Congress assembled, appealing to the Supreme Judge of the world for the rectitude of our intentions, do, in the name and by the authority of the good people of these colonies, solemnly publish and declare, That these united Colonies are, and of right ought to be, free and independent states; that they are absolved from all allegiance to the British crown, and that all political connection between them and the state of Great Britain is, and ought to be, totally dissolved; and that, as free and independent states, they have full power to levy war, conclude peace, contract alliances, establish commerce, and do all other acts and things which independent states may of right do. And, for the support of this declaration, with a firm reliance on the protection of Divine Providence, we mutually pledge to each other our lives, our fortunes, and our sacred honor.

The foregoing Declaration was, by order of Congress, engrossed, and signed by the following members: —

### JOHN HANCOCK.

#### NEW HAMPSHIRE.

JOSIAH BARTLETT,
WILLIAM WHIPPLE,
MATTHEW THORNTON.

#### MASSACHUSETTS BAY.

SAMUEL ADAMS,
JOHN ADAMS,
ROBERT TREAT PAINE,
ELBRIDGE GERRY.

#### RHODE ISLAND.

STEPHEN HOPKINS,
WILLIAM ELLERY.

#### CONNECTICUT.

ROGER SHERMAN,
SAMUEL HUNTINGTON,
WILLIAM WILLIAMS,
OLIVER WOLCOTT.

#### NEW YORK.

WILLIAM FLOYD,
PHILIP LIVINGSTON,
FRANCIS LEWIS,
LEWIS MORRIS.

#### NEW JERSEY.

RICHARD STOCKTON,
JOHN WITHERSPOON,
FRANCIS HOPKINSON,
JOHN HART,
ABRAHAM CLARK.

#### PENNSYLVANIA.

ROBERT MORRIS,
BENJAMIN RUSH,
BENJAMIN FRANKLIN,
JOHN MORTON,
GEORGE CLYMER,
JAMES SMITH,
GEORGE TAYLOR,
JAMES WILSON,
GEORGE ROSS.

#### DELAWARE.

CÆSAR RODNEY,
GEORGE READ,
THOMAS M'KEAN.

#### MARYLAND.

SAMUEL CHASE,
WILLIAM PACA,
THOMAS STONE,
CHARLES CARROLL, of Carrollton.

#### VIRGINIA.

GEORGE WYTHE,
RICHARD HENRY LEE,
THOMAS JEFFERSON,
BENJAMIN HARRISON,
THOMAS NELSON, JR.,
FRANCIS LIGHTFOOT LEE,
CARTER BRAXTON.

#### NORTH CAROLINA.

WILLIAM HOOPER,
JOSEPH HEWES,
JOHN PENN.

#### SOUTH CAROLINA.

EDWARD RUTLEDGE,
THOMAS HAYWARD, JR.,
THOMAS LYNCH, JR.,
ARTHUR MIDDLETON.

#### GEORGIA.

BUTTON GWINNETT,
LYMAN HALL,
GEORGE WALTON.

*Resolved*, That copies of the Declaration be sent to the several assemblies, conventions, and committees, or councils of safety, and to the several commanding officers of the continental troops; that it be proclaimed in each of the United States, at the head of the army.

# CONSTITUTION OF THE UNITED STATES.[1]

WE, the People of the United States, in order to form a more perfect union, establish justice, insure domestic tranquillity, provide for the common defence, promote the general welfare, and secure the blessings of liberty to ourselves and our posterity, do ordain and establish this CONSTITUTION for the United States of America.

## ARTICLE I.

SECTION I. All legislative powers herein granted shall be vested in a Congress[2] of the United States, which shall consist of a Senate and House of Representatives.

---

[1] Before the Declaration of Independence, July 4, 1776, the Thirteen Colonies were subject to the king of Great Britain. From July 4, 1776, the United States of America were governed by a Continental or General Congress, until March 1, 1781, when the states adopted a constitution, called the "Articles of Confederation and Perpetual Union between the States." The Confederation had no president, no supreme court; and consisted of a single house of Congress, made up of delegates elected by the legislatures of the states. Under this constitution Congress continued to govern — in so far as a body with no practical authority can be said to govern — until March 4, 1789; but on May 14, 1787, a convention of delegates from all the states, except Rhode Island, met in Philadelphia "to form a *more perfect union*" (see the opening words of the Constitution above). The whole number of delegates that attended was fifty-five, but only thirty-nine signed the Constitution. The Articles of Confederation had been made by the *States* only; but as the opening words of the new compact declare, "We, *the People*," made the Constitution.

George Washington presided over the convention, and Benjamin Franklin, Robert Morris, James Madison, Rufus King, Roger Sherman, Alexander Hamilton, John Dickinson, Charles C. Pinckney, Charles Pinckney, J. Rutledge, and Gouverneur Morris, were among its distinguished members.

Madison, Hamilton, Washington, and Franklin took the leading part in the great work of drafting the new Constitution, and after its adoption by the convention, Madison and Hamilton used their influence, with great effect, to urge its ratification by the states, especially by New York (see their papers in the *Federalist*).

After a stormy session of nearly four months, during which the convention several times threatened to break up in hopeless dispute, the Constitution was at last adopted. (For the compromises on which it rested, see page 192, note 3.)

While the members of the convention were signing the Constitution (for its leading provisions, see page 194), the venerable Dr. Franklin, then aged eighty-one, rose and said: "I have often, in the course of the session, and the vicissitudes of my hopes and fears as to its issue, looked at the sun [painted on the wall back of the president's chair], without being able to tell whether it was rising or setting; but now, at length, I have the happiness to know that it is a *rising*, and not a setting sun."

The Constitution was then submitted to the thirteen states. In 1788 eleven had ratified it (Rhode Island and North Carolina declining then, though they gave their assent before the close of 1790), and on March 4, 1789, the new Constitution went into operation, although, owing to delays, Washington was not inaugurated as the first President until April 30 of that year.

[2] Congress assembles on the first Monday in December; the first, or "long session," usually closes some time in the following summer; the second, or "short session," closes, by law, at noon on March 4. Each Congress exists two years.

SECTION 2. The House of Representatives shall be composed of members chosen every second year by the people of the several States, and the electors in each State shall have the qualifications requisite for electors of the most numerous branch of the State Legislature.

No person shall be a representative who shall not have attained to the age of twenty-five years, and been seven years a citizen of the United States, and who shall not, when elected, be an inhabitant of that State in which he shall be chosen.

Representatives and direct taxes shall be apportioned among the several States which may be included within this Union, according to their respective numbers,[1] which shall be determined by adding to the whole number of free persons, including those bound to service for a term of years, and excluding Indians not taxed, three-fifths of all other persons.[2] The actual enumeration shall be made within three years after the first meeting of the Congress of the United States, and within every subsequent term of ten years, in such manner as they shall by law direct. The number of representatives shall not exceed one for every thirty thousand, but each State shall have at least one representative: and until such enumeration shall be made, the State of New Hampshire shall be entitled to choose three; Massachusetts, eight; Rhode Island and Providence Plantations, one; Connecticut, five; New York, six; New Jersey, four; Pennsylvania, eight; Delaware, one; Maryland, six; Virginia, ten; North Carolina, five; South Carolina, five; and Georgia, three.

When vacancies happen in the representation from any State, the executive authority thereof shall issue writs of election to fill such vacancies.

The House of Representatives shall choose their Speaker[3] and other officers; and shall have the sole power of impeachment.

SECTION 3. The Senate of the United States shall be composed of two senators from each State, chosen by the Legislature thereof, for six years; and each senator shall have one vote.

Immediately after they shall be assembled in consequence of the first election, they shall be divided as equally as may be into three classes. The seats of the senators of the first class shall be vacated at the expiration of the second year; of the second class, at the expiration of the fourth year; of the third class, at the expiration of the sixth year, so that one-third may be chosen every second year; and if vacancies happen by resignation, or otherwise, during the recess of the Legislature of any State, the executive thereof may make temporary appointments until the next meeting of the Legislature, which shall then fill such vacancies.

No person shall be a senator who shall not have attained to the age of thirty years, and been nine years a citizen of the United States, and who shall not, when elected, be an inhabitant of that State for which he shall be chosen.

The Vice-President of the United States shall be president of the Senate, but shall have no vote, unless they be equally divided.

---

[1] At present (census of 1890) one representative is sent to Congress for every 173,901 persons; this will hold good until 1903.

[2] "Persons" meaning *slaves*. This has been amended (by Amendments XIII. and XIV.), and is no longer in force.

[3] The Speaker presides. Other officers are the clerk, sergeant-at-arms, door-keeper, etc.

The Senate shall choose their other officers,[1] and also a president *pro tempore*, in the absence of the Vice-President, or when he shall exercise the office of President of the United States.

The Senate shall have the sole power to try all impeachments: When sitting for that purpose, they shall be on oath or affirmation. When the President of the United States is tried, the Chief-Justice shall preside: and no person shall be convicted without the concurrence of two-thirds of the members present.

Judgment in cases of impeachment shall not extend further than to removal from office, and disqualification to hold and enjoy any office of honor, trust, or profit under the United States; but the party convicted shall nevertheless be liable and subject to indictment, trial, judgment, and punishment, according to law.

SECTION 4. The times, places, and manner of holding elections for senators and representatives shall be prescribed in each State by the Legislature thereof; but the Congress may at any time, by law, make or alter such regulations, except as to the places of choosing senators.

The Congress shall assemble at least once in every year, and such meeting shall be on the first Monday in December, unless they shall by law appoint a different day.

SECTION 5. Each house shall be the judge of the elections, returns, and qualifications of its own members, and a majority of each shall constitute a quorum to do business; but a smaller number may adjourn from day to day, and may be authorized to compel the attendance of absent members, in such manner, and under such penalties, as each house may provide.

Each house may determine the rules of its proceedings, punish its members for disorderly behavior, and, with the concurrence of two-thirds, expel a member.

Each house shall keep a journal of its proceedings, and from time to time publish the same, excepting such parts as may in their judgment require secrecy, and the yeas and nays of the members of either house on any question shall, at the desire of one-fifth of those present, be entered on the journal.

Neither house, during the session of Congress, shall, without the consent of the other, adjourn for more than three days, nor to any other place than that in which the two houses shall be sitting.

SECTION 6. The senators and representatives shall receive a compensation[2] for their services, to be ascertained by law, and paid out of the treasury of the United States. They shall in all cases, except treason, felony, and breach of the peace, be privileged from arrest during their attendance at the session of their respective houses, and in going to and returning from the same; and for any speech or debate in either house, they shall not be questioned in any other place.

No senator or representative shall, during the time for which he was elected, be appointed to any civil office under the authority of the United States, which shall have been created, or the emoluments whereof shall have been increased, during such time; and no person holding any office under the United States, shall be member of either house during his continuance in office.

---

[1] The chief of these are the secretary, sergeant-at-arms, door-keeper, etc.

[2] $5000 a year, with twenty cents for every mile necessarily travelled in coming to and returning from the Capital.

SECTION 7. All bills for raising revenue shall originate in the House of Representatives; but the Senate may propose or concur with amendments as on other bills.

Every bill which shall have passed the House of Representatives and the Senate, shall, before it become a law, be presented to the President of the United States; if he approve, he shall sign it, but if not, he shall return it, with his objections, to that house in which it shall have originated, who shall enter the objections at large on their journal, and proceed to reconsider it. If after such reconsideration, two-thirds of that house shall agree to pass the bill, it shall be sent, together with the objections, to the other house, by which it shall likewise be reconsidered, and if approved by two-thirds of that house, it shall become a law. But in all such cases the votes of both houses shall be determined by yeas and nays, and the names of the persons voting for and against the bill shall be entered on the journal of each house respectively. If any bill shall not be returned by the President within ten days (Sunday excepted) after it shall have been presented to him, the same shall be a law, in like manner as if he had signed it, unless the Congress by their adjournment prevent its return, in which case it shall not be a law.

Every order, resolution, or vote to which the concurrence of the Senate and House of Representatives may be necessary (except on a question of adjournment) shall be presented to the President of the United States; and before the same shall take effect, shall be approved by him, or being disapproved by him, shall be repassed by two-thirds of the Senate and House of Representatives, according to the rules and limitations prescribed in the case of a bill.

SECTION 8. The Congress shall have power to lay and collect taxes, duties, imposts, and excises, to pay the debts and provide for the common defence and general welfare of the United States; but all duties, imposts, and excises shall be uniform throughout the United States;

To borrow money on the credit of the United States;

To regulate commerce with foreign nations, and among the several States, and with the Indian tribes;

To establish a uniform rule of naturalization, and uniform laws on the subject of bankruptcies throughout the United States;

To coin money, regulate the value thereof, and of foreign coin, and fix the standard of weights and measures;

To provide for the punishment of counterfeiting the securities and current coin of the United States;

To establish post-offices and post-roads;

To promote the progress of science and useful arts, by securing, for limited times, to authors and inventors the exclusive right to their respective writings and discoveries;

To constitute tribunals inferior to the Supreme Court;

To define and punish piracies and felonies committed on the high seas, and offences against the law of nations;

To declare war, grant letters of marque and reprisal, and make rules concerning captures on land and water;

To raise and support armies, but no appropriation of money to that use shall be for a longer term than two years;

To provide and maintain a navy;

To make rules for the government and regulation of the land and naval forces;

To provide for calling forth the militia to execute the laws of the Union, suppress insurrections and repel invasions;

To provide for organizing, arming, and disciplining the militia, and for governing such part of them as may be employed in the service of the United States, reserving to the States respectively the appointment of the officers, and the authority of training the militia according to the discipline prescribed by Congress;

To exercise exclusive legislation in all cases whatsoever over such district (not exceeding ten miles square) as may, by cession of particular States, and the acceptance of Congress, become the seat of the government of the United States, and to exercise like authority over all places purchased by the consent of the Legislature of the State in which the same shall be, for the erection of forts, magazines, arsenals, dockyards, and other needful buildings; — And

To make all laws which shall be necessary and proper for carrying into execution the foregoing powers, and all other powers vested by this Constitution in the government of the United States, or in any department or officer thereof.

SECTION 9. The migration or importation of such persons as any of the States now existing shall think proper to admit, shall not be prohibited by the Congress prior to the year one thousand eight hundred and eight, but a tax or duty may be imposed on such importation, not exceeding ten dollars for each person.[1]

The privilege of the writ of habeas corpus shall not be suspended, unless when in cases of rebellion or invasion the public safety may require it.

No bill of attainder or ex-post-facto law shall be passed.

No capitation or other direct tax shall be laid, unless in proportion to the census or enumeration herein before directed to be taken.

No tax or duty shall be laid on articles exported from any State.

No preference shall be given by any regulation of commerce or revenue to the ports of one State over those of another; nor shall vessels bound to, or from, one State, be obliged to enter, clear, or pay duties in another.

No money shall be drawn from the treasury but in consequence of appropriations made by law; and a regular statement and account of the receipts and expenditures of all public money shall be published from time to time.

No title of nobility shall be granted by the United States: And no person holding any office of profit or trust under them, shall, without the consent of the Congress, accept of any present, emolument, office, or title, of any kind whatever, from any king, prince, or foreign state.

SECTION 10. No State shall enter into any treaty, alliance, or confederation; grant letters of marque and reprisal; coin money; emit bills of credit; make anything but gold and silver coin a tender in payment of debts; pass any bill of attainder, ex-post-facto law, or law impairing the obligation of contracts, or grant any title of nobility.

No State shall, without the consent of the Congress, lay any impost or duties on imports or exports, except what may be absolutely necessary for executing its

---

[1] " Person " meaning *slave;* referring to the foreign slave-trade, abolished in 1808.

inspection laws; and the net produce of all duties and impost, laid by any State on imports or exports, shall be for the use of the treasury of the United States; and all such laws shall be subject to the revision and control of the Congress.

No State shall, without the consent of Congress, lay any duty of tonnage, keep troops, or ships-of-war, in time of peace, enter into any agreement or compact with another State, or with a foreign power, or engage in war, unless actually invaded, or in such imminent danger as will not admit of delay.

## ARTICLE II.

SECTION 1. The executive power shall be vested in a President of the United States of America. He shall hold his office during the term of four years, and, together with the Vice-President, chosen for the same term, be elected, as follows:

Each State shall appoint, in such manner as the Legislature thereof may direct, a number of electors, equal to the whole number of senators and representatives to which the State may be entitled in the Congress: but no senator or representative, or person holding an office of trust or profit under the United States, shall be appointed an elector.

[The electors shall meet in their respective States, and vote by ballot for two persons, of whom one at least shall not be an inhabitant of the same State with themselves. And they shall make a list of all the persons voted for, and of the number of votes for each; which list they shall sign and certify and transmit sealed to the seat of the government of the United States, directed to the president of the Senate. The president of the Senate shall, in the presence of the Senate and House of Representatives, open all the certificates, and the votes shall then be counted. The person having the greatest number of votes shall be the President, if such number be a majority of the whole number of electors appointed; and if there be more than one who have such majority, and have an equal number of votes, then the House of Representatives shall immediately choose by ballot one of them for President; and if no person have a majority, then from the five highest on the list the said house shall, in like manner, choose the President. But in choosing the President, the votes shall be taken by States, the representation from each State having one vote; a quorum for this purpose shall consist of a member or members from two-thirds of the States, and a majority of all the States shall be necessary to a choice. In every case, after the choice of the President, the person having the greatest number of votes of the electors shall be the Vice-President. But if there should remain two or more who have equal votes, the Senate shall choose from them by ballot the Vice-President.[1]]

The Congress may determine the time of choosing the electors, and the day on which they shall give their votes; which day shall be the same throughout the United States.[2]

---

[1] This paragraph in brackets has been set aside by the XII. Amendment.

[2] The electors are chosen on the Tuesday following the first Monday in November, next before the expiration of a presidential term. They vote (by Act of Congress of Feb. 3, 1887) on the second Monday in January following, for President and Vice-President. The votes are counted, and declared in Congress on the second Wednesday of the next February.

No person except a natural born citizen, or a citizen of the United States at the time of the adoption of this Constitution, shall be eligible to the office of President; neither shall any person be eligible to that office who shall not have attained to the age of thirty-five years, and been fourteen years resident within the United States.

In case of the removal of the President from office, or of his death, resignation, or inability to discharge the powers and duties of the said office, the same shall devolve on the Vice-President, and the Congress may by law provide for the case of removal, death, resignation, or inability, both of the President and Vice-President, declaring what officer shall then act as President; and such officer shall act accordingly until the disability be removed, or a President shall be elected.

The President shall, at stated times, receive for his services a compensation [1] which shall neither be increased nor diminished during the period for which he shall have been elected, and he shall not receive within that period any other emolument from the United States, or any of them.

Before he enter on the execution of his office, he shall take the following oath or affirmation : — " I do solemnly swear (or affirm) that I will faithfully execute the office of President of the United States, and will, to the best of my ability, preserve, protect, and defend the Constitution of the United States."

SECTION 2. The President shall be commander-in-chief of the army and navy of the United States, and of the militia of the several States, when called into the actual service of the United States; he may require the opinion, in writing, of the principal officer in each of the executive departments, upon any subject relating to the duties of their respective offices; and he shall have power to grant reprieves and pardons for offences against the United States, except in cases of impeachment.

He shall have power, by and with the advice and consent of the Senate, to make treaties, provided two-thirds of the senators present concur; and he shall nominate, and by and with the advice and consent of the Senate shall appoint ambassadors, other public ministers and consuls, judges of the Supreme Court, and all other officers of the United States, whose appointments are not herein otherwise provided for, and which shall be established by law : but the Congress may by law vest the appointment of such inferior officers, as they think proper, in the President alone, in the courts of law, or in the heads of departments.

The President shall have power to fill up all vacancies that may happen during the recess of the Senate, by granting commissions which shall expire at the end of their next session.

SECTION 3. He shall from time to time give to the Congress information [2] of the state of the Union, and recommend to their consideration such measures as he shall judge necessary and expedient; he may, on extraordinary occasions, convene both houses, or either of them, and in case of disagreement between them with respect to the time of adjournment, he may adjourn them to such time as he shall

---

[1] The President now receives $50,000 a year; the Vice-President, $8000. **Previous to** 1873 the President received but $25,000 a year.

[2] The Presidents, beginning with Jefferson, have done this by messages sent to Congress. Washington and Adams read speeches or messages to that body.

think proper; he shall receive ambassadors and other public ministers; he shall take care that the laws be faithfully executed, and shall commission all the officers of the United States.

SECTION 4. The President, Vice-President, and all civil officers of the United States, shall be removed from office on impeachment for, and conviction of, treason, bribery, or other high crimes and misdemeanors.

## ARTICLE III.

SECTION 1. The judicial power of the United States shall be vested in one Supreme Court, and in such inferior courts as the Congress may from time to time ordain and establish. The judges, both of the Supreme and inferior courts, shall hold their offices during good behavior, and shall, at stated times, receive for their services a compensation which shall not be diminished during their continuance in office.

SECTION 2. The judicial power shall extend to all cases, in law and equity, arising under this Constitution, the laws of the United States, and treaties made, or which shall be made, under their authority; — to all cases affecting ambassadors, other public ministers, and consuls; — to all cases of admiralty and maritime jurisdiction; — to controversies to which the United States shall be a party; — to controversies between two or more States; — between a State and citizens of another State; [1] — between citizens of different States; — between citizens of the same State claiming lands under grants of different States, and between a State, or the citizens thereof, and foreign states, citizens or subjects.

In all cases affecting ambassadors, other public ministers and consuls, and those in which a State shall be party, the Supreme Court shall have original jurisdiction. In all other cases before mentioned, the Supreme Court shall have appellate jurisdiction, both as to law and fact, with such exceptions and under such regulations as the Congress shall make.

The trial of all crimes, except in cases of impeachment, shall be by jury; and such trial shall be held in the State where the said crimes shall have been committed; but when not committed within any State, the trial shall be at such place or places as the Congress may by law have directed.

SECTION 3. Treason against the United States shall consist only in levying war against them, or in adhering to their enemies, giving them aid and comfort.

No person shall be convicted of treason unless on the testimony of two witnesses to the same overt act, or on confession in open court.

The Congress shall have power to declare the punishment of treason, but no attainder of treason shall work corruption of blood, or forfeiture, except during the life of the person attainted.

## ARTICLE IV.

SECTION 1. Full faith and credit shall be given in each State to the public acts, records, and judicial proceedings of every other State. And the Congress may by

---

[1] But compare Amendment XI.

general laws, prescribe the manner in which such acts, records, and proceedings shall be proved, and the effect thereof.

SECTION 2. The citizens of each State shall be entitled to all privileges and immunities of citizens in the several States.

A person charged in any State with treason, felony, or other crime, who shall flee from justice, and be found in another State, shall, on demand of the executive authority of the State from which he fled, be delivered up, to be removed to the State having jurisdiction of the crime.

No person [1] held to service or labor in one State, under the laws thereof, escaping into another, shall, in consequence of any law or regulation therein, be discharged from such service or labor, but shall be delivered up on claim of the party to whom such service or labor may be due.

SECTION 3. New States may be admitted by the Congress into this Union; but no new State shall be formed or erected within the jurisdiction of any other State; nor any State be formed by the junction of two or more States, or parts of States, without the consent of the Legislatures of the States concerned as well as of the Congress.

The Congress shall have power to dispose of and make all needful rules and regulations respecting the territory or other property belonging to the United States; and nothing in this Constitution shall be so construed as to prejudice any claims of the United States, or of any particular State.

SECTION 4. The United States shall guarantee to every State in this Union a republican form of government, and shall protect each of them against invasion, and on application of the Legislature, or of the Executive (when the Legislature cannot be convened) against domestic violence.

## ARTICLE V.

The Congress, whenever two-thirds of both houses shall deem it necessary, shall propose amendments to this Constitution, or, on the application of the Legislatures of two-thirds of the several States, shall call a convention for proposing amendments, which, in either case, shall be valid to all intents and purposes, as part of this Constitution, when ratified by the Legislatures of three-fourths of the several States, or by conventions in three-fourths thereof, as the one or the other mode of ratification may be proposed by the Congress; provided that no amendment which may be made prior to the year one thousand eight hundred and eight shall in any manner affect the first and fourth clauses in the ninth section of the first article; and that no State, without its consent, shall be deprived of its equal suffrage in the Senate.

## ARTICLE VI.

All debts contracted, and engagements entered into, before the adoption of this Constitution, shall be as valid against the United States under this Constitution, as under the confederation.

---

[1] " Person " here means *slave*. This was the original Fugitive Slave Law. It now has no force, since, by Amendment XIII. to the Constitution, slavery is prohibited.

This Constitution, and the laws of the United States which shall be made in pursuance thereof; and all treaties made, or which shall be made, under the authority of the United States, shall be the supreme law of the land; and the judges in every State shall be bound thereby, anything in the Constitution or laws of any State to the contrary notwithstanding.

The senators and representatives before mentioned, and the members of the several State Legislatures, and all executive and judicial officers, both of the United States and of the several States, shall be bound by oath or affirmation to support this Constitution; but no religious test shall ever be required as a qualification to any office or public trust under the United States.

## ARTICLE VII.

The ratification of the Conventions of nine States shall be sufficient for the establishment of this Constitution between the States so ratifying the same.

Done in conventions, by the unanimous consent of the States present, the seventeenth day of September, in the year of our Lord one thousand seven hundred and eighty-seven, and of the independence of the United States of America the twelfth.

In witness whereof, we have hereunto subscribed our names.

GEORGE WASHINGTON,
*President, and Deputy from Virginia.*

NEW HAMPSHIRE.
JOHN LANGDON,
NICHOLAS GILMAN.

MASSACHUSETTS.
NATHANIEL GORHAM,
RUFUS KING.

CONNECTICUT.
WILLIAM SAMUEL JOHNSON,
ROGER SHERMAN.

NEW YORK.
ALEXANDER HAMILTON.

NEW JERSEY.
WILLIAM LIVINGSTON,
DAVID BREARLEY,
WILLIAM PATERSON,
JONATHAN DAYTON.

PENNSYLVANIA.
BENJAMIN FRANKLIN,
THOMAS MIFFLIN,
ROBERT MORRIS,
GEORGE CLYMER,
THOMAS FITZSIMONS,
JARED INGERSOLL,
JAMES WILSON,
GOUVERNEUR MORRIS.

DELAWARE.
GEORGE READ,
GUNNING BEDFORD, JR.,
JOHN DICKINSON,
RICHARD BASSETT,
JACOB BROOM.

MARYLAND.
JAMES M'HENRY,
DANIEL OF ST. THOMAS
JENIFER,
DANIEL CARROLL.

VIRGINIA.
JOHN BLAIR,
JAMES MADISON, JR.

NORTH CAROLINA.
WILLIAM BLOUNT,
RICHARD DOBBS SPAIGHT,
HUGH WILLIAMSON.

SOUTH CAROLINA.
JOHN RUTLEDGE,
CHARLES C. PINCKNEY,
CHARLES PINCKNEY,
PIERCE BUTLER.

GEORGIA.
WILLIAM FEW,
ABRAHAM BALDWIN.

*Attest:*   WILLIAM JACKSON, *Secretary.*

## AMENDMENTS

To the Constitution of the United States, ratified according to the Provisions of the Fifth Article of the Foregoing Constitution.

ARTICLE I.[1] — Congress shall make no law respecting an establishment of religion, or prohibiting the free exercise thereof; or abridging the freedom of speech, or of the press; or the right of the people peaceably to assemble, and to petition the government for redress of grievances.

ARTICLE II. — A well-regulated militia being necessary to the security of a free State the right of the people to keep and bear arms shall not be infringed.

ARTICLE III. — No soldier shall, in time of peace, be quartered in any house, without the consent of the owner; nor in time of war but in a manner to be prescribed by law.

ARTICLE IV. — The right of the people to be secure in their persons, houses, papers, and effects, against unreasonable searches and seizures, shall not be violated, and no warrants shall issue, but upon probable cause, supported by oath or affirmation, and particularly describing the place to be searched, and the persons or things to be seized.

ARTICLE V. — No person shall be held to answer for a capital, or otherwise infamous crime, unless on a presentment or indictment of a grand jury, except in cases arising in the land or naval forces, or in the militia, when in actual service in time of war and public danger; nor shall any person be subject for the same offence to be twice put in jeopardy of life or limb; nor shall be compelled in any criminal case to be a witness against himself, nor to be deprived of life, liberty, or property, without due process of law; nor shall private property be taken for public use, without just compensation.

ARTICLE VI. — In all criminal prosecutions, the accused shall enjoy the right to a speedy and public trial, by an impartial jury of the State and district wherein the crime shall have been committed, which district shall have been previously ascertained by law, and to be informed of the nature and cause of the accusation; to be confronted with the witnesses against him; to have compulsory process for obtaining witnesses in his favor, and to have the assistance of counsel for his defence.

ARTICLE VII. — In suits at common law, where the value in controversy shall exceed twenty dollars, the right of trial by jury shall be preserved, and no fact tried by a jury shall be otherwise re-examined in any court of the United States than according to the rules of common law.

ARTICLE VIII. — Excessive bail shall not be required, nor excessive fines imposed, nor cruel and unusual punishments inflicted.

---

[1] The first ten amendments were offered in 1789, and adopted before the close of 1791. They were largely the work of James Madison. They were adopted, says Judge Story, in order to "more efficiently guard certain rights already provided for in the Constitution, or to prohibit certain exercises of authority supposed to be dangerous to the public interests."

ARTICLE IX. — The enumeration in the Constitution of certain rights shall not be construed to deny or disparage others retained by the people.

ARTICLE X. — The powers not delegated to the United States by the Constitution, nor prohibited by it to the States, are reserved to the States respectively, or to the people.

ARTICLE XI.[1] — The judicial power of the United States shall not be construed to extend to any suit in law or equity, commenced or prosecuted against any of the United States by citizens of another State, or by citizens or subjects of any foreign state.

ARTICLE XII.[2] — The electors shall meet in their respective States, and vote by ballot for President and Vice-President, one of whom, at least, shall not be an inhabitant of the same State with themselves; they shall name in their ballots the person voted for as President, and in distinct ballots the person voted for as Vice-President; and they shall make distinct lists of all persons voted for as President, and of all persons voted for as Vice-President, and of the number of votes for each, which list they shall sign and certify, and transmit sealed to the seat of the government of the United States, directed to the president of the Senate; — the president of the Senate shall, in the presence of the Senate and House of Representatives, open all the certificates, and the votes shall then be counted; — the person having the greatest number of votes for President, shall be the President, if such number be a majority of the whole number of electors appointed; and if no person have such majority, then from the persons having the highest numbers not exceeding three on the list of those voted for as President, the House of Representatives shall choose immediately, by ballot, the President. But in choosing the President, the votes shall be taken by States, the representation from each State having one vote; a quorum for this purpose shall consist of a member or members from two-thirds of the States, and a majority of all the States shall be necessary to a choice. And if the House of Representatives shall not choose a President whenever the right of choice shall devolve upon them, before the fourth day of March next following, then the Vice-President shall act as President, as in the case of the death or other constitutional disability of the President. The person having the greatest number of votes as Vice-President, shall be the Vice-President, if such number be a majority of the whole number of electors appointed; and if no person have a majority, then from the two highest numbers on the list, the Senate shall choose the Vice-President; a quorum for the purpose shall consist of two-thirds of the whole number of senators, and a majority of the whole number shall be necessary to a choice. But no person constitutionally ineligible to the office of President shall be eligible to that of Vice-President of the United States.

ARTICLE XIII.[3] — *Section* 1. Neither slavery nor involuntary servitude, except as a punishment for crime, whereof the party shall have been duly convicted, shall exist within the United States, or any place subject to their jurisdiction.

*Section* 2. Congress shall have power to enforce this article by appropriate legislation.

---

[1] Proposed in 1794; adopted 1798. A number of states have, at different times, taken advantage of this amendment to repudiate their debts.          [2] Adopted 1804.

[3] This confirmed the Proclamation of Emancipation; it was adopted in 1865.

ARTICLE XIV.[1] — *Section* 1. All persons born or naturalized in the United States, and subject to the jurisdiction thereof, are citizens of the United States and of the State wherein they reside. No State shall make or enforce any law which shall abridge the privileges or immunities of citizens of the United States; nor shall any State deprive any person of life, liberty, or property, without due process of law, nor deny to any person within its jurisdiction the equal protection of the laws.

*Section* 2. Representatives shall be appointed among the several States according to their respective numbers, counting the whole number of persons in each State, excluding Indians not taxed. But when the right to vote at any election for the choice of electors for President and Vice-President of the United States, representatives in Congress, the executive or judicial officers of a State, or the members of the Legislature thereof, is denied to any of the male inhabitants of such State, being twenty-one years of age, and citizens of the United States, or in any way abridged, except for participation in rebellion or other crime, the basis of representation therein shall be reduced in the proportion which the number of such male citizens shall bear to the whole number of male citizens twenty-one years of age in such State.

*Section* 3. No person shall be a senator or representative in Congress, or elector of President or Vice-President, or hold any office, civil or military, under the United States, or under any State, who having previously taken an oath as a member of Congress, or as an officer of the United States, or as a member of any State Legislature, or as an executive or judicial officer of any State, to support the Constitution of the United States, shall have engaged in insurrection or rebellion against the same, or given aid or comfort to the enemies thereof. But Congress may, by a vote of two-thirds of each house, remove such disability.

*Section* 4. The validity of the public debt of the United States, authorized by law, including debts incurred for payment of pensions and bounties for services in suppressing insurrection or rebellion, shall not be questioned. But neither the United States nor any State shall assume or pay any debt or obligation incurred in aid of insurrection or rebellion against the United States, or any claim for the loss or emancipation of any slave; but all such debts, obligations, and claims shall be held illegal and void.

*Section* 5. Congress shall have power to enforce, by appropriate legislation, the provisions of this article.

ARTICLE XV.[2] — *Section* 1. The right of citizens of the United States to vote shall not be denied or abridged by the United States, or by any State, on account of race, color, or previous condition of servitude.

*Section* 2. Congress shall have power to enforce this article by appropriate legislation.

---

[1] Adopted 1868. The object of sections 1 and 2 was to make the freedmen (negroes), emancipated during the Civil War, *citizens* of the United States.

[2] Adopted 1870. Its object was to give the freedmen (negroes) the right to *vote*.

## TABLE OF STATES AND TERRITORIES.

| NO. | NAME OF STATE. | DERIVATION OF NAME. | DATE OF ADMISSION. | BY WHOM SETTLED. | FIRST SETTLEMENT. | DATE OF SETTLEMENT. | SQUARE MILES. | POPULATION IN 1790. | POPULATION IN 1900. |
|---|---|---|---|---|---|---|---|---|---|
| 1 | *Delaware.* | In honor of Lord Delaware. | 1787 | Swedes. | Christiana, near Wilmington. | 1638 | 2,050 | 59,096 | 184,735 |
| 2 | *Pennsylvania.* | Name given by Charles II.— Meaning Penn's Woods. | 1787 | English. | Philadelphia. | 1683 | 45,215 | 434,373 | 6,302,115 |
| 3 | *New Jersey.* | In honor of Sir George Carteret, governor of the British Island of Jersey. | 1787 | Dutch. | Bergen. | 1617 | 7,815 | 184,139 | 1,883,669 |
| 4 | *Georgia.* | In honor of George II. | 1788 | English. | Savannah. | 1733 | 59,475 | 82,548 | 2,216,331 |
| 5 | *Connecticut.* | From the Indian — Long River. | 1788 | English. | Wethersfield. | 1634? | 4,990 | 238,431 | 908,355 |
| 6 | *Massachusetts.* | From the Indian — The Great Hills — from the Blue Hills near Boston. | 1788 | English. | Plymouth. | 1620 | 8,315 | 378,717 | 2,805,346 |
| 7 | *Maryland.* | In honor of Queen Henrietta Maria, wife of Charles I. | 1788 | English. | St. Mary's. | 1634 | 12,210 | 319,728 | 1,190,950 |
| 8 | *South Carolina.* | In honor of Charles II.; derived from *Carolus*, the Latin for Charles. | 1788 | English. | Old Charleston? | 1670? | 30,570 | 249,073 | 1,340,316 |
| 9 | *New Hampshire.* | Named by John Mason, in remembrance of Hampshire, England. | 1788 | English. | Dover? | 1627? | 9,305 | 141,899 | 411,588 |
| 10 | *Virginia.* | In honor of Queen Elizabeth, the "Virgin Queen." | 1788 | English. | Jamestown. | 1607 | 42,450 | 748,308 includig W. Va. | 1,854,184 |
| 11 | *New York.* | In honor of the Duke of York, who became James II. | 1788 | Dutch. | Fort Orange (Albany). | 1623 | 49,170 | 340,120 | 7,268,012 |
| 12 | *North Carolina.* | In honor of Charles II.; derived from *Carolus*, the Latin for Charles. | 1789 | English. | Albemarle? | 1663? | 52,250 | 393,751 | 1,893,810 |

## TABLE OF STATES AND TERRITORIES (Continued).

| NO. | NAME OF STATE. | DERIVATION OF NAME. | DATE OF ADMISSION. | BY WHOM SETTLED. | FIRST SETTLEMENT. | DATE OF SETTLEMENT. | SQUARE MILES. | POPULATION IN 1790. | POPULATION IN 1900. |
|---|---|---|---|---|---|---|---|---|---|
| 13 | *Rhode Island.* | Either from a fancied resemblance of the Island of Rhode Island to the Isle of Rhodes in the Mediterranean, or from the Dutch Rood or Red Island. | 1790 | English. | Providence. | 1636 | 1,250 | 69,110 | 428,556 |
| 14 | Vermont. | From the French—Green Mountains. | 1791 | English. | Fort Dummer (near Brattleborough). | 1724 | 9,565 | 85,416 | 343,641 |
| 15 | Kentucky. | From the Indian—At the Head of a River; or meaning, according to other authorities, The Dark and Bloody Ground. | 1792 | English. | Harrodsburg. | 1774 | 40,400 | 73,077 | 2,147,174 |
| 16 | Tennessee. | From the Indian—River of the Big Bend. | 1796 | English. | Watauga. | 1769 | 42,050 | 35,791 | 2,020,616 |
| 17 | Ohio. | From the Indian—Beautiful or Beautiful River. | *1803 | Americans. | Marietta. | 1788 | 41,060 |  | 4,157,545 |
| 18 | Louisiana. | From the French—In honor of Louis XIV. of France. | 1812 | French. | About 38 miles below New Orleans. | 1700 | 48,720 |  | 1,381,625 |
| 19 | Indiana. | From the word Indian. | 1816 | French. | Vincennes. | 1702 | 36,350 |  | 2,516,462 |
| 20 | Mississippi. | From the Indian—Great and Long River, or Father of Waters. | 1817 | French. | Natchez. | 1716 | 46,810 |  | 1,551,270 |
| 21 | Illinois. | From the union of an Indian and a French word—Tribe of Men. | 1818 | French. | Cahokia. | 1682 | 56,650 |  | 4,821,550 |
| 22 | Alabama. | From the Indian—A Place of Rest. | 1819 | French. | Near Mobile Bay. | 1702 | 52,250 |  | 1,828,697 |

* The most recent authorities (see King's "History of Ohio" in *The Commonwealth Series*, and the article "Ohio" in the *Encyclopædia Britannica*) give the date of 1803 instead of 1802, the date usually given heretofore.

## TABLE OF STATES AND TERRITORIES (Continued).

| NO. | NAME OF STATE. | DERIVATION OF NAME. | DATE OF ADMISSION. | BY WHOM SETTLED. | FIRST SETTLEMENT. | DATE OF SETTLEMENT. | SQUARE MILES. | POPULATION IN 1790. | POPULATION IN 1900. |
|---|---|---|---|---|---|---|---|---|---|
| 23 | Maine. | The Main Land. | 1820 | English. | Pemaquid. | 1625 | 33,040 | 96,540 | 694,466 |
| 24 | Missouri. | From the Indian — Muddy, or Muddy River. | 1821 | French. | Fort Orleans (near Jefferson City). | 1719 | 69,415 | | 3,106,665 |
| 25 | Arkansas. | From the Indian *Kansas* (Smoky Water) and the French *Arc*, a bow. | 1836 | French. | Little Rock. | 1690? | 53,850 | | 1,311,564 |
| 26 | Michigan. | From the Indian — A weir or dam of twigs for catching fish. | 1837 | French. | Mackinaw. | 1680? | 58,915 | | 2,420,982 |
| 27 | Florida. | From the Spanish *Pascua Florida* — Flowery Easter, hence Flowery, or Land of Flowers. | 1845 | Spanish. | St. Augustine. | 1565 | 58,680 | | 528,542 |
| 28 | Texas. | Perhaps from an Indian word meaning Friends. | 1845 | French. | Lavaca, on the coast. | 1685 | 265,780 | | 3,048,710 |
| 29 | Iowa. | The French form of an Indian word applied by the Sioux to the "Gray-snow Tribe," and meaning the "Drowsy" or the "Sleepy Ones." | 1846 | Americans. | Dubuque. | 1833? | 56,025 | | 2,231,853 |
| 30 | Wisconsin. | From the Indian — Wild or Rushing River (applied to the rapids of the Wisconsin). | 1848 | French. | Green Bay. | 1669? | 56,040 | | 2,069,042 |
| 31 | California. | From the Spanish — The name first occurs in a Spanish work of fiction (1510); it was there given to an imaginary island abounding in gold. | 1850 | Spanish. | San Diego. | 1769 | 158,360 | | 1,485,053 |
| 32 | Minnesota. | From the Indian — Cloudy or Whitish Water. | 1858 | Americans. | Fort Snelling. | 1819 | 83,365 | | 1,751,394 |
| 33 | Oregon. | Either from the Indian — River of the West, or from the Spanish — Wild Marjoram, which grows there in great abundance. | 1859 | Americans. | Astoria. | 1811 | 96,030 | | 413,536 |

# TABLE OF STATES AND TERRITORIES (Concluded).

| NO. | NAME OF STATE. | DERIVATION OF NAME. | DATE OF ADMISSION. | BY WHOM SETTLED. | FIRST SETTLEMENT. | DATE OF SETTLEMENT. | SQUARE MILES. | POPULATION IN 1790. | POPULATION IN 1900. |
|---|---|---|---|---|---|---|---|---|---|
| 34 | Kansas. | From the Indian — Smoky Water. | 1861 | Americans. | Atchison? | 1854 | 82,080 | | 1,470,495 |
| 35 | West Virginia. | From Virginia. | 1863 | English. | | | 24,780 | included in 1790 in Va. | 958,800 |
| 36 | Nevada. | From the Spanish Sierra Nevada (Snowy mountain ridge),— Snowy. | 1864 | Americans. | Genoa, at the base of the Sierras. | 1850 | 110,700 | | 42,335 |
| 37 | Nebraska. | From the Indian—Water Valley, or Shallow River. | 1867 | Americans. | Bellevue (near Omaha). | 1847 | 77,510 | | 1,068,539 |
| 38 | Colorado. | From the Spanish — Red or Colored (referring to the color of the rocks). | 1876 | Americans. | Denver? | 1859? | 103,925 | | 539,700 |
| 39 | North Dakota. | From the Indian — Leagued or Allied (referring to the confederation or league of the Sioux tribes). | 1889 | English. | Pembina. | 1812 | 70,795 | | 319,146 |
| 40 | South Dakota. | From the Indian — See above. | 1889 | Americans. | Yankton? | 1859? | 77,650 | | 401,570 |
| 41 | Montana. | From the Latin Mons, a mountain,— The Land of Mountains. | 1889 | Americans. | Helena? | 1861? | 146,080 | | 243,329 |
| 42 | Washington. | In honor of George Washington. | 1889 | Americans. | Tumwater. | 1845 | 69,180 | | 518,103 |
| 43 | Idaho. | From the Indian — Diadem of the Mountains. | 1890 | Americans. | Pioneer City? | 1862 | 84,800 | | 161,772 |
| 44 | Wyoming. | From the Indian — Great Plains. | 1890 | Americans. | Cheyenne. | 1867 | 97,890 | | 92,531 |
| 45 | Utah. | " " " " — Mountain Home. | 1896 | Americans. | Salt Lake City. | 1847 | 84,970 | | 276,749 |

Total population in 1790, 3,929,214. Total population in 1880, 50,189,200; in 1890, 62,622,250; in 1900, 76,304,799. Five territories: (1) New Mexico, (2) Arizona, (3) Alaska, (4) Indian Territory, (5) Oklahoma; the District of Columbia, the islands of Hawaii, Guam, the Philippines, Porto Rico; and the Dependency of Cuba.

NOTE. — Authorities disagree on a number of the dates and place of settlement of states. The Census Report of 1900 makes the area of the *entire* United States 3,690,822 square miles. The area of the Territories is as follows: Alaska, 590,884 sq. m.; New Mexico, 122,460 sq. m.; Arizona, 112,920 sq. m.; Indian Territory, 31,000 sq. m.; Oklahoma, 38,830 sq. m.; the District of Columbia, 60 sq. m. The area of our Island possessions is estimated as follows: Guam, 201 sq. m.; Hawaii, 6449 sq. m.; Porto Rico, 3435 sq. m.; the Philippines, 110,542 sq. m.; Samoa, 81 sq. m.
The ? indicates conflict of authorities or lack of positive information.

| NO. | PRESIDENT. | STATE. | TERM OF OFFICE. | BY WHAT PARTY ELECTED. | VICE-PRESIDENT. | SECRETARY OF STATE. |
|---|---|---|---|---|---|---|
| 1 | George Washington. | Virginia. | Two terms; 1789–1797. | Whole people. | John Adams. | Thomas Jefferson.<br>Edmund Randolph.<br>Timothy Pickering.<br>Timothy Pickering. |
| 2 | John Adams. | Massachusetts. | One term; 1797–1801. | Federalists. (But see note 2, p. 206.) | Thomas Jefferson. | John Marshall. |
| 3 | Thomas Jefferson. | Virginia. | Two terms; 1801–1809. | Republicans or Democratic Republicans. | Aaron Burr.<br>George Clinton. | James Madison. |
| 4 | James Madison. | Virginia. | Two terms; 1809–1817. |  | George Clinton.<br>Elbridge Gerry. | Robert Smith.<br>James Monroe. |
| 5 | James Monroe. | Virginia. | Two terms; 1817–1825. |  | Dan'l D. Tompkins. | James Monroe. |
| 6 | John Quincy Adams. | Massachusetts. | One term; 1825–1829. | House of Rep. | John C. Calhoun. | JohnQuincy Adams. |
| 7 | Andrew Jackson. | Tennessee. | Two terms; 1829–1837. | Democrats. | John C. Calhoun.<br>Martin Van Buren. | Henry Clay.<br>Martin Van Buren.<br>Edward Livingston.<br>Louis McLane.<br>John Forsyth. |
| 8 | Martin Van Buren. | New York. | One term; 1837–1841. | Democrats. | Rich'd M. Johnson. | John Forsyth. |
| 9 | William H. Harrison. | Ohio. | One month; 1841. | Whigs. | John Tyler. | Daniel Webster. |
| 10 | John Tyler. | Virginia. | 3 yrs. 11 mos.; 1841–1845. | Whigs. | ............ | Hugh S. Legaré.<br>Abel P. Upshur.<br>John C. Calhoun. |
| 11 | James K. Polk. | Tennessee. | One term; 1845–1849. | Democrats. | George M. Dallas. | James Buchanan. |
| 12 | Zachary Taylor. | Louisiana. | 1 yr. 4 mos.; 1849, 1850. | Whigs. | Millard Fillmore. | John M. Clayton. |
| 13 | Millard Fillmore. | New York. | 2 yrs. 8 mos.; 1850–1853. | Whigs. |  | Daniel Webster.<br>Edward Everett. |
| 14 | Franklin Pierce. | N. Hampshire. | One term; 1853–1857. | Democrats. | William R. King. | William L. Marcy. |
| 15 | James Buchanan. | Pennsylvania. | One term; 1857–1861. | Democrats. | J. C. Breckinridge. | Lewis Cass.<br>Jeremiah S. Black. |
| 16 | Abraham Lincoln. | Illinois. | 1 term and 6 w'ks; 1861–1865. | Republicans. | Hannibal Hamlin.<br>Andrew Johnson. | William H. Seward.<br>William H. Seward. |
| 17 | Andrew Johnson. | Tennessee. | 3 yrs. 10½ mos.; 1865–1869. | Republicans. |  | William H. Seward. |
| 18 | Ulysses S. Grant. | Illinois. | Two terms; 1869–1877. | Republicans. | Schuyler Colfax.<br>Henry Wilson. | Elihu B. Washburne.<br>Hamilton Fish. |
| 19 | Rutherford B. Hayes. | Ohio. | One term; 1877–1881. | Republicans. | Wm. A. Wheeler. | William M. Evarts. |
| 20 | James A. Garfield. | Ohio. | 6 mos. 15 dys.; 1881. | Republicans. | Chester A. Arthur. | James G. Blaine. |
| 21 | Chester A. Arthur. | New York. | 3yrs. 5 mos. 15 dys.; 1881–'85. | Republicans. |  | F.T.Frelinghuysen. |
| 22 | Grover Cleveland. | New York. | One term; 1885–1889. | Democrats. | Thos. A. Hendricks. | Thomas F. Bayard. |
| 23 | Benjamin Harrison. | Indiana. | One term; 1889–1893. | Republicans. | Levi P. Morton. | James G. Blaine. |
| 24 | Grover Cleveland. | New York. | One term; 1893–1897. | Democrats. | Adlai E. Stevenson. | Walter Q. Gresham. |
| 25 | William McKinley. | Ohio. | 1 term and pt. of 2d; '97–'01. | Republicans. | Garret A. Hobart. | John Sherman. |
| 26 | Theodore Roosevelt. | New York. | Part of one term. | Republicans. |  | John Hay. |
| 27 | Theodore Roosevelt. | New York. | 1905– | Republicans. | Chas. W. Fairbanks. | John Hay. |

## PRINCIPAL DATES IN AMERICAN HISTORY

[The * marks the most important dates.]

—◆◆◆—

### I. THE PERIOD OF DISCOVERY, 1000–1507.

The coming of the Northmen, 1000.
*Columbus discovers the West Indies (San Salvador), 1492.
Letter of Columbus describing his voyage, 1493.
*The Cabots discover the *Continent* of North America, 1497.
Voyages of Amerigo Vespucci to South America, 1499–1503.
Amerigo Vespucci publishes an account of his voyages, 1504.
*Waldseemüller publishes a geography in which he suggests that the New World be called AMERICA, 1507.

### II. ATTEMPTS AT EXPLORING AND COLONIZING NORTH AMERICA, 1509–1587.

Diego Columbus (son of Christopher Columbus), governor of San Domingo, conquers Cuba, 1509.
*Ponce de Leon discovers and names Florida, 1513.
*Balboa discovers the Pacific, 1513.
Cortez conquers Mexico, 1519.
*Magellan's voyage round the globe, 1519–1521.
Verrazzano explores the coast of North America (?), 1524 (?).
Cabeza de Vaca discovers one of the mouths of the Mississippi, 1528.
Cartier discovers the St. Lawrence and names Montreal, 1535.
*De Soto's expedition (he discovers the main stream of the Mississippi), 1539–1542.
Huguenot settlement at Port Royal (not permanent), 1563.
Huguenot settlement on the St. John's River, Florida (broken up by the Spaniards), 1564.
*The Spaniards settle St. Augustine, Florida (the oldest town in the United States), 1565.

Sir Martin Frobisher's voyages (in search of a Northwest Passage), 1576.
*Sir Francis Drake sails round the world (visits the western coast of North America and names it New Albion), 1577–1579.
Sir Humphrey Gilbert's voyages (takes possession of Newfoundland), 1578, 1583.
*The Spaniards settle Santa Fé, New Mexico (the second oldest town in the United States), 1582.
*Sir Walter Raleigh sends out his first expedition to North America (the country named Virginia in honor of Queen Elizabeth), 1584.
Sir Walter Raleigh sends out colonies to settle (Roanoke Island) "Virginia" (not permanent), 1585, 1587.

### III. OPENING OF THE SEVENTEENTH CENTURY; PERMANENT ENGLISH AND FRENCH SETTLEMENTS; THE THIRTEEN COLONIES. (1602–1763.)

Gosnold's expedition to Northern Virginia (New England), 1602.
*Jamestown, Virginia, settled (the first permanent English settlement made in America), 1607.
Sir George Popham attempts to make a settlement in Maine, 1607.
*The French settle Quebec (first permanent French settlement in America), 1608.
*Henry Hudson explores the Hudson River, 1609.
*John Rolf begins the cultivation of tobacco at Jamestown, Virginia, 1612.
*The Dutch take possession of New Netherland (New York), 1614.
*The House of Burgesses (the first lawmaking assembly in America) meets at Jamestown, 1619.
*Negro slavery is introduced into Virginia, 1619.
*Landing of the Pilgrims at Plymouth, 1620.

The Dutch build Fort Orange (Albany), 1622.

First permanent English settlement made (at Pemaquid Point) in Maine, 1625.

*The Dutch purchase Manhattan Island (New York City) of the Indians, 1626.

Settlement of Dover, New Hampshire, 1627.

Settlement of Salem, Massachusetts, 1628.

*Settlement of Boston, 1630.

Settlement of Portland, Maine, 1632.

*Settlement of St. Mary's, Maryland, 1634.

*The first English Catholic Church established in America, 1634.

* Religious toleration granted in Maryland to all *Christians*, 1634.

*Settlements begun in Connecticut (Wethersfield and Windsor), 1635.

*A public school is established in Boston, 1635.

*Settlement of Providence, Rhode Island, by Roger Williams, 1636.

*Religious toleration granted in Rhode Island to all persons (whether Christians or not), 1636.

*Harvard College founded, 1636.

The Pequot War, 1637.

New Haven, Connecticut, settled, 1638.

Delaware settled by the Swedes, 1638.

*The Connecticut Constitution (the first written constitution framed by the people in America), 1639.

First printing-press in New England, 1639.

First New England Confederacy, 1643.

Clayborne's Rebellion in Maryland, 1645.

Coming of the Quakers to New England, 1656.

The English settle in North Carolina, 1663.

The Regicides come to New England, 1663.

The English seize New Netherland (New Amsterdam becomes New York City), 1664.

The English settle Elizabeth, New Jersey, 1664.

The Connecticut and the New Haven colonies united, 1664.

*French exploration of the West begins, 1669.

*Settlement of Old Charleston (South Carolina), 1670.

*King Philip's War, 1675.

*Bacon's Rebellion in Virginia, 1676.

*William Penn settles Philadelphia, Pennsylvania, 1683.

*La Salle explores the Mississippi, 1682.

First war with the French and the Indians ("King William's War"), 1689.

The Salem Witchcraft, 1692.

William and Mary College (Virginia) founded, 1692.

*Cultivation of rice begun in South Carolina, 1693.

Yale College founded, 1701.

The French establish a colony at Mobile, 1701.

Second war with the French and the Indians ("Queen Anne's War"), 1702.

*The *Boston News Letter*, the first newspaper published in America, 1704.

New Orleans founded by the French, 1718.

Benjamin Franklin begins his "Poor Richard's Almanac," 1732.

Oglethorpe settles Savannah, Georgia, 1733.

Cultivation of indigo begun in South Carolina, 1741.

Third war with the French ("King George's War"), 1744.

Louisburg taken, 1745.

*Benjamin Franklin discovers that lightning and electricity are identical, 1752.

Washington sent as a commissioner to the French, 1753.

The fourth French and Indian War, 1754.

*The Albany Convention, 1754.

The Rev. Jonathan Edwards publishes his work on the "Freedom of the Will," 1754.

Braddock's defeat, 1755.

*Fort Duquesne taken by the English and named Fort Pitt (Pittsburgh), 1758.

*Wolfe takes Quebec, 1759.

*Treaty of peace, 1763.

Pontiac's War, 1763.

## IV. THE REVOLUTION; THE CONSTITUTION. (1765-1788.)

*Parliament passes the Stamp Act, 1765.

Repeal of the Stamp Act, 1766.

The Declaratory Act, 1766.

Duties laid on glass, paints, paper, and tea, 1767.

British troops sent to Boston, 1768.

The Boston Massacre (March 3), 1770.

Destruction of the *Gaspee* (June 10), 1772.

All duties repealed except that on tea, 1773.

*The "Boston Tea-Party" (December 16), 1773.

General Gage appointed military governor, 1774.

*Parliament closes the port of Boston (June 1), 1774.

*The first Continental Congress meets at Philadelphia (September 5), 1774.

The battle of Lexington (April 19), 1775.

The battle of Concord (April 19), 1775.

The siege of Boston begins (April 20), 1775.

Ethan Allen takes Ticonderoga (May 10), 1775.

Crown Point taken (May 11), 1775.

*Washington appointed commander-in-chief (June 15), 1775.

*Battle of Bunker Hill (June 17), 1775.

Washington takes command of the Continental Army at Cambridge, Massachusetts (July 3), 1775.

General Montgomery takes Montreal (November 13), 1775.

Montgomery and Arnold attack Quebec (Montgomery killed) (December 31), 1775.

Paine's " Common Sense " (January 5), 1776.

*The British evacuate Boston (March 17), 1776.

The British fail in their attack on Fort Moultrie, South Carolina (June 28), 1776.

*Declaration of Independence (July 4), 1776.

*Battle of Long Island (August 27), 1776.

Battle of White Plains, New York (October 28), 1776.

Fort Washington taken (November 16), 1776.

*Washington retreats across New Jersey and crosses the Delaware (November 19 to December 8), 1776.

*Washington gains the victory of Trenton, New Jersey (December 26), 1776.

*Washington victorious at Princeton, New Jersey (January 3), 1777.

He goes into winter quarters at Morristown, New Jersey, 1777.

Arrival of Lafayette in summer of 1777.

*American victory at Bennington, Vermont (August 16), 1777.

British victory at Brandywine Creek, Pennsylvania (September 11), 1777.

Battle of Bemis Heights, New York (September 19), 1777.

*Howe enters Philadelphia (September 26), 1777.

British victory at Germantown, Pennsylvania (October 4), 1777.

*American victory at Stillwater, New York (October 7), 1777.

*American victory at Saratoga, New York ; Burgoyne surrenders (October 17), 1777.

Washington goes into winter quarters at Valley Forge, Pennsylvania (December 11), 1777.

*France acknowledges the independence of the United States (February 6), 1778.

*The British evacuate Philadelphia (June 18), 1778.

Battle of Monmouth, New Jersey (June 28), 1778.

Indian massacre at Wyoming, Pennsylvania (July 3), 1778.

Indian massacre at Cherry Valley, New York (November 11), 1778.

The British take Savannah, Georgia (December 29), 1778.

" Mad Anthony " Wayne takes Stony Point (July 15), 1779.

*Victory of Paul Jones off coast of England (September 23), 1779.

British conquest of Georgia, 1779.

British capture of Charleston, South Carolina (May 12), 1780.

British victory at Camden, South Carolina (August 16), 1780.

*Arnold's treason (September), 1780.

American victory at King's Mountain, South Carolina (October 7), 1780.

*General Greene takes command of the American army at the South, 1780.

*American victory at Cowpens, South Carolina (January 17), 1781.

*Greene's retreat northward, 1781.

British gain battle of Guilford Court-House, North Carolina (March 15), 1781.

British success at Hobkirk's Hill, South Carolina (April 25), 1781.

British retreat from Eutaw Springs, South Carolina (September 8), 1781.

Benedict Arnold and Cornwallis invade Virginia, 1781.

*American victory of Yorktown (October 19), 1781.

The war suspended, 1782.

*Treaty of peace with Great Britain (September 3), 1783.

Shays' Rebellion in Massachusetts, 1786.

*The Federal Convention frames the Constitution, 1787.

The ordinance concerning the Northwest Territory, 1787.

*The states accept the Constitution, 1788.

## V. THE UNION; NATIONAL DEVELOPMENT. (1789–1860.)

**WASHINGTON** inaugurated President of the United States (two terms), 1789–1797.

*Organization of the departments of the government ; formation of the Cabinet, 1789.

Revenue Tariff imposed, 1789.

First Census, 1790.

Cincinnati (settled 1788) named, 1790.

United States Bank established, 1791.

United States Mint established, 1792.

Gray enters and names the Columbia, 1792.

# PRINCIPAL DATES IN AMERICAN HISTORY. xxvii

Organization of political parties begun, — *Federalists* and *Anti-Federalists* or *Democratic-Republicans*, a name later shortened to *Democrats*, — 1792.

*Whitney invents the cotton-gin, 1793.

The Whiskey Rebellion, 1794.

Jay's treaty with Great Britain, 1795.

**ADAMS'S ADMINISTRATION** (one term, 1797-1801).

The X. Y. Z. Papers, — War with France, 1798.

*The Alien and the Sedition Laws, 1798.

Peace made with France, 1799.

Death of Washington, 1799.

*The city of Washington made the national capital, 1800.

**JEFFERSON'S ADMINISTRATION** (two terms, 1801-1809).

War with Tripoli, 1801.

*Purchase of Louisiana, 1803.

*Lewis and Clark's expedition, 1804.

Peace with Tripoli, 1805.

The *Leopard* and the *Chesapeake*, 1807.

*The Embargo, 1807.

Burr's expedition and trial, 1807.

*Fulton's steamboat (August 11), 1807.

The importation of slaves forbidden, 1808.

The Non-Intercourse Act, 1809.

**MADISON'S ADMINISTRATION** (two terms, 1809-1817).

End of the Non-Intercourse Policy, 1810.

First steamboat on the Ohio and the Mississippi, 1811.

Great earthquake in the Southwest, 1811.

Battle of Tippecanoe, 1811.          [1812.

*War declared against Great Britain (June 18), Hull surrenders Detroit (August 16), 1812.

*The *Constitution* takes the *Guerrière* (August 19), — many American victories on the sea follow, 1812.          [1813.

*Perry's victory on Lake Erie (September 10), Jackson's victory at Tohopeka, Alabama (March 27), 1814.

Battle of Chippewa (July 5), 1814.

Battle of Lundy's Lane (July 25), 1814. [1814.

*The British take Washington (August 24),

*Macdonough's victory on Lake Champlain (September 11), 1814.

Hartford Convention (December 15), 1814.

Treaty of peace signed at Ghent (December 24), 1814.

*Jackson's victory at New Orleans (January 8), 1815.

**MONROE'S ADMINISTRATION** (two terms, 1817-1825).

First Seminole War, 1718.

The first steamship — the *Savannah* — (American) crosses the Atlantic, 1819.

*Purchase of Florida, 1819.

*The Missouri Compromise, 1820.

*Extension of National Road, 1822.

*The Monroe Doctrine, 1823.

High Protective Tariff established, 1824.

Lafayette visits the United States, 1824.

**ADAMS'S (J. Q.) ADMINISTRATION** (one term, 1825-1829).

*The Erie Canal opened, 1825.

*The temperance reform begun, 1826.

*Ground broken at Baltimore for the first railroad, 1828.

So-called "Tariff of Abominations," 1828.

*Publication of Webster's "Dictionary," — *Irving, Cooper, Bryant*, — 1828.

**JACKSON'S ADMINISTRATION** (two terms, 1829-1837).

*General removal of government officers, 1829.

*The first steam railroad opened (at Baltimore), 1830.

*Garrison begins the publication of the *Liberator* (January 1), 1831.

President vetoes the U. S. Bank Bill, 1832.

Tariff of 1832.

*Nullification in South Carolina, 1832.

"Compromise Tariff," 1833.

Chicago founded, 1833.

The *New York Daily Sun*, the first one-cent newspaper, appears, 1833.

*McCormick's reaper, 1834.

Rise of the *Whig* party, 1834.

Second Seminole War, 1835.

Coal comes into extensive use, 1835.

Great fire in New York City, 1835.

*Rise of American Literature, — *Whittier, Longfellow, Holmes, Lowell, Emerson, Bancroft, Prescott, Hawthorne, Poe*, — 1835.

**VAN BUREN'S ADMINISTRATION** (one term, 1837-1841).

*Business panic, 1837.

Repudiation of state debts, 1838.

Congress refuses to receive petitions for the abolition of slavery in the District of Columbia, 1838.          [1839.

*Beginning of the American Express System,

The Mormons settle Nauvoo, 1839.

*The first line of steamships between Europe and America (Cunard) established, 1840.

*The government establishes an independent treasury with sub-treasuries, 1840.

**HARRISON AND TYLER'S ADMINISTRATIONS** (one term, 1841-1845).

Death of President Harrison (April 4), 1841.
*Ashburton Treaty, 1842.
Tariff of 1842.
" Dorr Rebellion," Rhode Island, 1842.
Anti-rent troubles in New York State, 1842.
Dr. Whitman leaves Oregon for Washington (October 3) (returns, 1843), 1842.
*Morse completes the first line of electric telegraph and sends the first message (May 24), 1844.
*The President signs the bill for the annexation of Texas (March 1), 1845.
*Morton's discovery of the anæsthetic uses of ether, 1845.

**POLK'S ADMINISTRATION** (one term, 1845–1849).

*Texas admitted to the Union (December 20), 1845.
Great increase in emigration to the United States begins, 1845.
*Treaty settling the Oregon boundary, 1846.
*Elias Howe invents the sewing-machine, 1846.
Protective duties taken off (1846). Revenue Tariff established ; this continued until 1861.
*War declared against Mexico (May 13), 1846. (The battles of Palo Alto and Resaca de la Palma, May 8 and 9, 1846, were fought before the formal declaration of war.)
Conquest of California, 1846.
New Mexico conquered, 1846.
Battle of Monterey (September 24), 1846.
Battle of Buena Vista (February 23), 1847.
Battle of Contreras (August 20), 1847.
Battle of Chapultepec (September 13), 1847.
The city of Mexico taken (September 14), 1847.                              [1848.
Treaty of Peace with Mexico (February 2),
*Discovery of gold in California, spring of 1848.
The Mormons emigrate to Utah, 1848.
Great movement of emigrants and gold-diggers to California, beginning in the spring of 1849.

**TAYLOR AND FILLMORE'S ADMINISTRATION** (one term, 1849–1853).

Death of President Taylor (July 9), 1850.
Clay's " Omnibus Bill," 1850.
*Passage of the Fugitive Slave Law (included in the " Omnibus Bill "), 1850.
The Maine prohibition law passed, 1851.
Rise of the American or " Know-Nothing " party, 1852.
*" Uncle Tom's Cabin " published, 1852.

**PIERCE'S ADMINISTRATION** (one term, 1853–1857).

*Purchase of Arizona and New Mexico, 1853.
Opening of the World's Fair at New York, 1853.
Perry's treaty with Japan, 1854.
*Passage of the Kansas-Nebraska Bill, 1854.
*The struggle for the possession of Kansas begins ; first appearance of John Brown, 1855.
Assault on Senator Sumner, 1856.
*Rise of the Republican party, 1856.

**BUCHANAN'S ADMINISTRATION** (one term, 1857–1861).

*The Dred Scott decision, 1857.
Tariff of 1857.
*Business panic, 1857.
First Atlantic Cable (soon failed), 1858.
*Discovery of silver in Nevada and Colorado, and of petroleum in Pennsylvania, 1859.
*John Brown's raid on Harper's Ferry (October 16), 1859.
*Election of Abraham Lincoln, 1860.
*Secession of South Carolina (December 20), 1860.
Steamer *Star of the West* fired on by the Secessionists (January 9), 1861.
*Formation of the Southern Confederacy (February 4), 1861.
Jefferson Davis elected President of the Confederacy (February 18), 1861.
Morrill Tariff, 1861.

# VI. THE CIVIL WAR. (1861–1865.)

**LINCOLN'S ADMINISTRATION** (one term and part of second, 1861 to April 14, 1865).

*Bombardment and surrender of Fort Sumter (April 13), 1861.
*President Lincoln's call for 75,000 volunteers (April 15), 1861.
Seizure of arms at Harper's Ferry by Confederates (April 18), 1861.
Bloodshed at Baltimore (April 19), 1861.
Seizure of Norfolk Navy Yard by Confederates (April 20), 1861.
*Secession of Virginia, Arkansas, Tennessee, and North Carolina, making the whole number of states in the Confederacy eleven (May–June), 1861.
General Butler declares fugitive slaves *contraband of war*, 1861.
Union victory of Rich Mountain, West Virginia (July 21), 1861.
*Confederate victory of Bull Run (July 21), 1861.

Confederate victory of Wilson's Creek, Missouri (August 10), 1861.

Union capture of Fort Hatteras, North Carolina (August 29), 1861.

Union capture of Port Royal, South Carolina (November 7), 1861.

Union capture of Mason and Slidell (*Trent* affair) (November 8), 1861.

Union victory of Mill Spring, Kentucky (January 19), 1862.

Union victory at Fort Henry, Tennessee (February 6), 1862.

Union capture of Roanoke Island, North Carolina (February 8), 1862.

*Grant takes Fort Donelson, Tennessee (February 16), 1862.

Union victory at Pea Ridge, Arkansas (March 5-8), 1862.

*The *Monitor* fights the *Merrimac* (or *Virginia*) (March 9), 1862.

*Grant's victory at Pittsburg Landing or Shiloh, Tennessee (April 6-7), 1862.

*Union capture of Island No. Ten, Mississippi River (April 8), 1862.

Union capture of Fort Pulaski, Georgia (April 11), 1862.

*Farragut takes New Orleans (April 25), 1862.

†Battle of Williamsburg, Virginia (May 5), 1862.

"Stonewall" Jackson drives Banks out of the Shenandoah Valley (May 26), 1862.

Union capture of Corinth, Mississippi (May 30), 1862.

Union victory of Fair Oaks, Virginia (May 31), 1862.

Lee takes active command of the armies around Richmond (June 3), 1862.

The "Seven Days' Battles" around Richmond (June 25 to July 1), 1862.

Pope's campaign in Virginia (Confederates victorious) (August), 1862.

Second battle of Bull Run (Confederate victory) (August 30), 1862.

"Stonewall" Jackson takes Harper's Ferry (September 15), 1862.

*Union victory at Antietam (Sept. 17), 1862.

Bragg invades Kentucky (September), 1862.

†Battle of Perryville, Kentucky (Oct. 8), 1862.

*Confederate victory at Fredericksburg, Virginia (December 13), 1862.

Union victory of Murfreesboro', Tennessee (December 31 to January 2), 1862.

*Lincoln's Proclamation of Emancipation (January 1), 1863.

Union victory of Arkansas Post (January 11), 1863.

*Act establishing National Banks (February 23), 1863.

Confederate victory of Chancellorsville, Virginia (May 2-3), 1863.

*Union victory of Gettysburg, Pennsylvania (July 1-3), 1863.

*Grant takes Vicksburg (July 4), 1863.

Union victory at Helena, Arkansas (July 4), 1863.

*Union capture of Port Hudson on the Mississippi (July 9), 1863.

Draft riots in New York City (July 13-16), 1863.

Morgan's raid into Ohio (July), 1863.

Confederate victory of Chickamauga, Georgia (September 19-20), 1863.

Confederates besiege Chattanooga, Tennessee (October-November), 1863.

Confederates besiege Knoxville, Tennessee (November 18-29), 1863.

Union victory at Lookout Mountain, Tennessee (November 24-25), 1863.

Sherman destroys Meridian, Mississippi (February 3 to March 5), and the railroads centering there, 1864.

Grant made lieutenant-general (March 3), 1864.

Confederate capture of Fort Pillow, Tennessee (April 12), 1864.

†Battle of the Wilderness, Virginia (May 5-7), 1864.

†Battle at Spottsylvania Court-House, Virginia (May 8-18), 1864.

Union victory at Resaca, Georgia (May 14-15), 1864.

Union victory at Dallas, Georgia (May 25-28), 1864.

Confederate victory at Cold Harbor, Virginia (June 3), 1864.

Siege of Petersburg, Virginia, begun (June), 1864.

The *Kearsarge* sinks the *Alabama* (June 19), 1864.

Confederate victory at Kenesaw Mountain, Georgia (June 27), 1864.

Union victories at Atlanta, Georgia (July 20-28), 1864.

Early's raid on Washington (July), 1864.

Early burns Chambersburg, Pennsylvania (July 30), 1864.

Confederate success at the Petersburg mine, Virginia (July 30), 1864.

---

† Battles so marked were indecisive.

*Farragut enters Mobile Bay (August 5), 1864.

*Sherman takes Atlanta, Georgia (September 2), 1864.

*Union victory at Winchester, Virginia (September 19), 1864.

*Union victory at Cedar Creek, Virginia ("Sheridan's Ride") (October 19), 1864.

*Sherman's march from Atlanta to Savannah (November 12 to December 21), 1864.

Union victory at Franklin, Tennessee (November 30), 1864.

Sherman takes Fort McAllister, Georgia (December 13), 1864.

*Thomas gains decisive Union victory at Nashville, Tennessee (December 15-16), 1864.

*Sherman takes Savannah, Georgia (December 21), 1864.

Union capture of Fort Fisher, North Carolina (January 15), 1865.

Sherman marches northward (February to March), 1865.

Union capture of Columbia, South Carolina (February 17), 1865.

Union capture of Charleston, South Carolina (February 18), 1865.

Union capture of Wilmington, North Carolina (February 21), 1865.

Union victory at Averysboro', North Carolina (March 15), 1865.

Union victory at Bentonville, North Carolina (March 19), 1865.

Sheridan's raid on Lynchburg, Virginia (March), 1865.

Union victory at Five Forks, Virginia (April 1), 1865.

Union capture of Petersburg, Virginia (April 2), 1865.

*Grant takes Richmond, Virginia (April 3), 1865.

*Lee surrenders to Grant (April 9), 1865.

General Anderson raises the Union flag over Fort Sumter, South Carolina (April 14), 1865.

*Assassination of Lincoln (April 14), 1865.

### VII. RECONSTRUCTION; THE NEW NATION. (1865 TO THE PRESENT TIME.)

### JOHNSON'S ADMINISTRATION (April 15, 1865, to 1869).

Review of Grant's and of Sherman's armies at Washington (May 23-24), 1865.

Gradual disbanding of the Union armies, 1865.

The President's proclamation of pardon (limited) (May 29), 1865.

Reorganization of Southern States, 1865.

*The Thirteenth Amendment to the Constitution accepted by the states, 1865.

*Payment of the National Debt begun, 1865.

Tennessee re-admitted to the Union, 1866.

*The second Atlantic Cable laid, 1866.

Reconstruction acts passed over the President's veto, 1867.

Tenure of Office Act, 1867 (repealed, 1887).

*Purchase of Alaska, 1867.

Impeachment of the President, 1868.

*Six states re-admitted to the Union, 1868.

The Burlingame Treaty with China, 1868.

*The Fourteenth Amendment to the Constitution accepted by the states, 1868.

*The President's proclamation of full and unconditional pardon (Christmas), 1868.

### GRANT'S ADMINISTRATION (two terms, 1869-1877).

*The Pacific Railroad completed (May 10), 1869.

*Organization of the "Knights of Labor," 1869.

*Completion of the reconstruction of Southern States (all re-admitted to the Union), 1870.

*Weather Bureau established, 1870.    [1870.

*Fifteenth Amendment to the Constitution, Tweed Ring in New York, 1871.

Ku-Klux Klans, 1871.

*Great fire at Chicago and Western forest fires, 1871.

*Treaty of Washington, 1871.

*Great fire at Boston, 1872.

Settlement of the *Alabama* claims, 1872.

Modoc War, 1872.

*Business panic, 1873.

Whiskey Ring, 1875.

*Centennial celebration and exhibition (electric light and Bell telephone exhibited), 1876.

Sioux War—death of General Custer, 1876.

*Electoral Commission, 1877.

### HAYES'S ADMINISTRATION (one term, 1877-1881).

The President withdraws all troops from the South, 1877.

*Great railroad strikes, 1877.

*The telephone begins to come into general use, 1877.

Yellow fever at the South, 1878.

Silver dollars restored (remonetization of silver), 1878.

*Resumption of specie payment (January 1), 1879.

*Eads's improvement of the navigation of the Mississippi, 1879.

Treaty with China, 1880.

**GARFIELD'S AND ARTHUR'S ADMINISTRATIONS** (one term, 1881-1885).

*Assassination of the President (July 2), 1881.

Death of the President (September 19), 1881.

Overflow of the Mississippi, 1882.

*Passage of the Edmunds Bill punishing plural marriages and polygamy in the Territories, 1882.

Electric lights begin to come into general use, 1883.

Completion of the East River Suspension Bridge, 1883.

*Civil Service Reform Commission, 1883.

*Reduction in rates of letter-postage (to two cents), 1883, 1885.

Cincinnati riot, 1884.

New Orleans Exhibition, 1884.

**CLEVELAND'S ADMINISTRATION** (one term, 1885 to 1889).

Progress in civil service reform, 1885.

Extensive labor strikes, 1886.

Anarchist riot at Chicago, 1886.

The Charleston earthquake, 1886.

The Statue of Liberty completed at New York, 1886.

Presidential Succession Act, 1886.

Interstate Commerce Act, 1887.

Chinese Immigration Act, 1888.

The Mills Tariff, 1888.

Western "blizzards," 1888.

**HARRISON'S ADMINISTRATION** (one term, 1889-1893).

Opening of the Oklahoma lands to settlers (April 22), 1889.

Centennial celebration of the inauguration of Washington (April 29 to May 1), 1889.

The Johnstown disaster (May 31), 1889.

*Electricity begins to be extensively used for driving light machinery and propelling street cars, 1889.

A number of new steel war-ships added to the Navy, 1889.

Trouble with Germany relative to Samoa; settled by conference, 1889.

*Introduction of the Australian or Secret Ballot (Massachusetts), 1889.

Congress of the Three Americas (Pan-American Congress) (October 2), 1889-1890.

The "Squadron of Evolution" sails from Boston for Lisbon (December 7), 1889.

*The United States Supreme Court(the Chief-Justice and two associate justices dissenting) affirms the Edmunds Law of 1882

punishing plural marriages and polygamy in the Territories, dissolves the Mormon Church corporation, and declares its property forfeited to the United States, 1890.

Formation of the Farmers Alliance at the South and in sections of the West, 1890.

New Pension Act, 1890.

*The first State (Wyoming) having full woman suffrage, admitted, 1890.

Act against Trusts and Combinations, 1890.

*The Sherman Silver Purchase Act (directing the Secretary of the Treasury to purchase 4,500,000 ounces of Silver monthly), 1890; (repealed 1893).

*The Mormon Church renounces plural marriages and polygamy, 1890.

Great Sioux reservation (9,000,000 acres) opened to white settlers, 1890.

Indian lands (3,000,000 acres) opened in Minnesota to white settlers, 1890.

*Passage of the McKinley (Protective) Tariff, 1890.

Mississippi adopts a new Constitution (denying the right of future secession from the Union), 1890.

The eleventh or centennial Census taken, showing a total population of 62,622,250, 1890.

Italian murderers lynched at New Orleans, 1891.

International Copyright Act, 1891.

Difficulty with Chili on account of assaults on American seamen, 1891.

Behring Sea (Seal Fishery) controversy between England and the United States submitted to arbitration, 1891.

Hawaiian Protectorate, 1892.

Chili apologizes to the United States, 1892.

Louisiana refuses to re-charter the Louisiana Lottery, 1892.

Chinese Exclusion Law, 1892.

Great floods at the West (more than $30,000,-000 of property destroyed), 1892.

Great Strike at Homestead, Pa., 1892.

Organization of the People's Party, 1892.

Columbus celebration, 1892.

*Extension of Civil Service Reform by President Harrison, 1893.

**CLEVELAND'S ADMINISTRATION** (1893-1897).

*Opening of the Columbian Exposition at Chicago (May 1), 1893.

International Naval Review at New York, 1893.

*Financial Panic (July-Aug.), 1893.

*Behring Sea Commission's decision, 1893.

Terrible Cyclone at the South (Aug. and Oct.), 1893.

The Cherokee Strip opened (Sept.), 1893.

*Repeal of the Sherman Silver Bullion Purchase Act of 1890 (Nov. 1, 1893).

*By Amendment to the State Constitution Colorado grants full suffrage to women, 1893.

The Louisiana State Lottery ceases to exist (Dec. 31), 1893.

*Repeal of the Federal Election or "Force Acts" (of 1870–1871), 1894.

Extended Coal Strike begins (April), 1894.

The Coxey "Industrial Army" marches into Washington (May), 1894.

Lexow Committee begins its sessions in New York City, 1894.

*Pullman Car and Railway Strike, Federal troops sent to Chicago (July), 1894.

Labor Day made a legal national holiday, 1894.

Financial Panic and Depression, 1894.

Recognition of the Republic of Hawaii (Aug.), 1894.

*Modified Wilson Tariff Act (Aug.), 1894.

Full Amnesty granted to the Mormons, 1894.

New York adopts a New State Constitution, 1894.

*Important extension of Civil Service Reform (Nov.–Dec.), 1894.

The Atlanta Exhibition, 1895.

The Admission of Utah, 1896.

Settlement of the Venezuela Question, 1896.

**McKINLEY'S AND ROOSEVELT'S ADMINISTRATIONS** (two terms, 1897–1904).

Passage of the Dingley Tariff, 1897.

Opening of the Congressional Library Building, 1897.

Great increase in American Exports, 1897–1898.

Charter of "Greater New York" goes into operation (Jan. 1), 1898.

South Dakota amends its Constitution, 1898.

The Revolution in Cuba, 1898.

*The Destruction of the *Maine* (Feb. 15), 1898.

President McKinley's message on Cuba, 1898.

*War with Spain declared (April 25), 1898.

*Battle of Manila (May 1), 1898.

The "Trans-Mississippi Exposition" opens (June 1), 1898.

Hobson's Exploit (June 3),1898.

*The War Revenue Act (June 13), 1898.

Fighting at Las Guasimas or Siboney (June 24), 1898.

*Battles of El Caney and San Juan (July 1–2), 1898.

*Destruction of Cervera's fleet (July 3), 1898.

*Annexation of Hawaii (July 7), 1898.

*Peace Protocol signed (Aug. 12), 1898.

The Spanish forces evacuate Cuba (Jan. 1), 1899.

*Treaty of Peace between United States and Spain ratified (Feb. 6), 1899.

*Population of the United States, 1900, 76,304,799.

*The "Open Door" in China, 1900.

*Gold Standard Act, 1900.

*Hague Court of Arbitration established, 1900.

Re-election of President McKinley (Theodore Roosevelt, Vice-President) (Nov.), 1900.

*Decision of the United States Supreme Court respecting our new island territories (May 27), 1901.

Pan-American Exposition, 1901.

*Assassination of President McKinley (Sept. 6), 1901.

Theodore Roosevelt becomes President (Sept. 14), 1901.

*The Great Anthracite Coal Strike, 1902.

The American Pacific Cable, 1902.

President Roosevelt's Wireless Telegram to King Edward (Jan. 19), 1903.

Department of Commerce and Labor created, 1903.

Chinese Exclusion Act renewed, 1904.

*The Isthmian Canal Treaty, 1904.

**ROOSEVELT'S ADMINISTRATION** (1905–1909).

*The President induces Japan and Russia to end their war, 1905.

*Enlargement of the Erie Canal begun, 1905.

Work on the Panama Canal, 1905.

*The San Francisco earthquake, 1906.

# A SHORT LIST OF BOOKS ON AMERICAN HISTORY.

### Bibliography.

Channing and Hart's Guide to the Study of American History (1492–1865).
Adams's Manual of Historical Literature.
References in Winsor's Narrative and Critical History of America, 8 vols.
Foster's References to United States History.
Hinsdale's How to Study and Teach History.
Mace's Method in History.

### Historical Geography and Maps.

Hart's Epoch Maps of the United States (no text).
Scribner's Statistical Atlas of the United States.
MacCoun's Historical Geography of the United States (revised edition).
Gannett's Boundaries of the States (no maps).
Shaler's United States, 2 vols.

## General Histories.

*Winsor's Narrative and Critical History, 8 vols. (to 1887, but not including the period of the Civil War).
*Bancroft's United States, 6 vols. (revised edition) (to 1789).
*Hildreth's United States, 6 vols. (to 1821).
*Bryant and Gay's United States, 5 vols. to 1896 (revised edition).
Johnston's United States (reprinted from the Encyclopædia Britannica) (1607 to 1889).
*Higginson's Larger History of the United States (to 1837).
Schouler's United States, 6 vols. (1783–1865).
*Hart's Epochs of American History, 3 vols. (1492–1889).          [ (1492–1889).
*Scribner's American History Series, 5 vols.
*Goldwin Smith's United States (1492–1871).
McMaster's United States, 4 vols. (1784–1820).

### Works of Reference.

Lalor's Cyclopædia of U. S. History, 3 vols.
Appleton's Annual Cyclopædia.

Harper's Book of Facts.
Larned's History for Ready Reference, 5 vols.
Richardson's Messages and Papers of the Presidents, 10 vols. (1789–1901).
Hart's Source Book of American History.
Macdonald's Select Documents of United States History.
Ford's American Politics.
Old South Leaflets.
Hart and Channing's American History Leaflets.
Hart's American History Told by Contemporaries, 4 vols.
Jameson's Dictionary of United States History.
Stanwood's The Presidency.
Wright's Industrial Evolution of the United States.
Moore's History of Congress.
Wilson's Rise and Fall of the Slave Power, 3 vols.
Johnston's American Politics.
Von Holst's Constitutional History of the United States, 8 vols. (to 1859).
Lossing's Cyclopædia of U. S. History (revised edition).
Poole's Index to Reviews.
Bryce's American Commonwealth, 2 vols. (revised edition).
Curtis's Constitutional History of the United States, 2 vols. (to 1865).
Wilson's The State.
Macy's Civil Government of the U. S.
Putnam's Great Cities of the Republic (a series of vols.).
Scudder's American Commonwealths (a series of volumes giving the histories of the states, by eminent writers).
Sparks's American Biography, 25 vols.
Morse's American Statesmen (a series of volumes by able writers).
Appleton's Cyclopædia of American Biography, 6 vols.
Warner's American Men of Letters (a companion series of vols. to the American Statesmen series).
Harper's The First Century of the Republic (1776–1876).
The North American Review for January, 1876 (covering the general progress of the country from 1776 to 1876 in a series of articles on Religion, Politics, Science, Political Economy, Law, and Education).

* Books so marked begin with the earliest period of American History.

The Statesman's Year Book (American edition).
The American Historical Review.
The Magazine of American History.
The Magazine of Western History.

## I. PERIOD OF DISCOVERY (1492–1521).

Help's Columbus.
Irving's Columbus.
Irving's Companions of Columbus.
Winsor's Columbus.
§Major's Select Letters of Columbus (Hakluyt Soc. Pub.).
Fiske's North America, 2 vols.
Higginson's American Explorers.
Vogel's Century of Discovery.
Markham's The Sea Fathers.
§Hakluyt's Divers Voyages touching the Discovery of America.
Bourne's Voyages (The Cabots).
Nicholl's Sebastian Cabot.

## II. PERIOD OF EXPLORATION AND SPANISH COLONIZATION OF AMERICA (1509–1587).

Irving's Companions of Columbus, with Hakluyt, as above.
Higginson and Vogel, as above.
Parkman's Pioneers of France in the New World.
T. Irving's Conquest of Florida.
§De Soto's Discovery and Conquest of Florida (Hakluyt Soc. Pub.).
Barrow's Sir Francis Drake.
Jones's Sir Martin Frobisher.
Edwards's Sir Walter Ralegh [Raleigh].
Towle's Sir Walter Ralegh [Raleigh].
Cooke's Virginia.[1]
On the Indians, see
  Ellis's The Red Man and the White Man.
  Parkman's Jesuits in N. America (Introduction).
  Schoolcraft's Indian Tribes, 6 vols.
  Morgan's League of the Iroquois.
  Drake's Indian History for Young Folks.
  Bancroft's Native Races of the Pacific Coast.

## III. PERIOD OF PERMANENT ENGLISH AND FRENCH SETTLEMENTS (1607–1763).

Lodge's English Colonies.
Grahame's United States, 4 vols.
Doyle's The English in America, 3 vols.
§Winthrop's New England, 2 vols.
Palfrey's New England, 5 vols.

Drake's Making of New England.
Fiske's The Beginnings of New England.
Lowell's Essays : New England Two Hundred Years Ago.
§Jefferson's Notes on Virginia.
Thwaites' Colonies, 1492–1750.
§Captain John Smith's Works (Arber).
Brown's Genesis of U.S. (Virginia, 1607–16).
Cooke's Virginia.[1]
Brodhead's New York, 2 vols.
O'Calligan's New York, 2 vols.
Roberts's New York, 2 vols.[1]
Barry's Massachusetts, 3 vols.
§Hutchinson's Massachusetts, 4 vols.
§Young's Chronicles of the Pilgrims.
§Brook's Olden Time Series, 5 vols.
§Earle's Colonial Days.
§Bradford's Plymouth (Deane's edition).
Goodwin's Pilgrim Republic.
Eggleston's Beginners of a Nation.
Ellis's The Puritan Age in Massachusetts.
Oliver's Puritan Commonwealth (compare Thornton's Reply).
Winsor's Memorial History of Boston, 4 vols.
Lowell Lectures (1869), The Early History of Massachusetts.
Arnold's Rhode Island, 2 vols.
Greene's Rhode Island.
Johnston's Connecticut.[1]
Browne's Maryland.[1]
McVeagh's Pennsylvania.[1]
Williamson's North Carolina.
Moore's North Carolina, 2 vols.
Trescott's South Carolina.[1]
Sanborn's New Hampshire.
Scott's New Jersey.[1]
Jones's Georgia, 2 vols.
Vincent's Delaware, 2 vols.
Goldwin Smith's Lectures on Am. Colonies.
Weeden's Economic Hist. of N. E., 2 vols. (1620–1789).
Seeley's Expansion of England (First Part).
Roosevelt's Winning of the West, 4 vols. (1769–1807).
Winsor's Explorations in the Mississippi Basin (1697–1763).
‡Parkman's Frontenac.
‡Parkman's Old Régime in Canada.
‡Parkman's Jesuits in North America.
‡Parkman's The Discovery of the Great West.
‡Parkman's Wolfe and Montcalm, 2 vols.
‡Parkman's Conspiracy of Pontiac.
‡Parkman's Fifty Years of Conflict, 2 vols.
Johnson's History of the French War.
Drake's Making of the Great West.
Hinsdale's The Old Northwest.
*Biography.* See Sparks's American Biography for Lives of Nathaniel Bacon, Daniel Boone, Lord Baltimore (Calvert), Jonathan Edwards, John Eliot, Patrick Henry, Anne Hutchinson, John Ledyard, Cotton Mather, Governor Oglethorpe, Jas. Otis,

---

§ Early or contemporaneous history.
[1] In Scudder's "American Commonwealth" Series.
‡ These works all deal, more or less directly, with our relations with the French and the Indians in the Colonial Period.

Sir W. Phips, William Penn, Count Rumford (Benj. Thompson), Captain John Smith, Roger Williams, Governor Winthrop; Bigelow's Benjamin Franklin, 3 vols.; Montgomery's Franklin (Ginn & Co.).

## IV. THE REVOLUTION AND THE CONSTITUTION (1763-1789).

Frothingham's Rise of the Republic.
Greene's American Revolution.
Ludlow's War of Independence.
Lodge's American Revolution, 2 vols.
Lecky's American Revolution, Edited by Prof. Woodburn.
Hosmer's Governor Thomas Hutchinson.
Sabine's Loyalists of the Revolution, 2 vols.
Lossing's Pictorial Field-Book of the Revolution, 2 vols.
Fiske's American Revolution, 2 vols.
Coffin's The Boys of '76.
Abbot's Blue-Jackets of '76.
Abbott's Revolutionary Times.
Scudder's America One Hundred Years Ago.
McMaster's People of the United States (Vol. I., 1784-1790).
Winsor's Handbook of the Revolution.
Landon's Constitutional Hist. of the U. S.
Von Holst's Constitutional History of the United States, Vol. I.
§The Federalist.
Fiske's Critical Period in American History.
Story's Constitution of the U. S., 3 vols.
Curtis's History of the Constitution of the United States, Vol. I.
Macy's Civil Government (revised edition, Ginn & Co.).
Wilson's The State.
*Biography.* Parker's Historic Americans, Bigelow's Franklin, 3 vols., Hosmer's Samuel Adams,[1] Morse's John Adams,[1] Greene's General Greene, 2 vols., Lodge's Washington, 2 vols.,[1] Fiske's Irving's Washington and his Country (Ginn & Co.), Sparks's American Biography, Lodge's Hamilton,[1] Gay's Madison,[1] Roosevelt's Gouverneur Morris.[1]

## V. THE UNION NATIONAL DEVELOPMENT (1789-1861).

McMaster's People of the United States, Vols. II., III., IV. (1790-1820).
Rhodes's United States, 3 vols. (1850-1861).
Von Holst's Constitutional History of the United States, 8 vols.
Maclay's History of the United States Navy, 2 vols.
Schouler's United States, 6 vols. (1783-1865).
Tucker's United States, 4 vols. (1607-1841).

Adams's United States, 9 vols. (1801-1817).
H. H. Bancroft's Pacific States, Vols. VIII. to XXXII., inclusive.
Coffin's Building the Nation.
Johnson's War of 1812.
Abbot's Blue-Jackets of 1812.
Lossing's Field-Book of the War of 1812.
Cooper's Naval History.
Ripley's War with Mexico, 2 vols.
Jay's Mexican War.
Bishop's History of American Manufactures, 2 vols.
Shaler's United States, 2 vols.
Tuckerman's American Art.
Nichol's American Literature.
Richardson's American Literature, 2 vols.
Johnston's American Politics.
Johnston's American Orations, 4 vols.
Benton's Thirty Years' View, 2 vols.
Webster's Great Speeches (Whipple's edition).
McCulloch's Half Century (1833-1883).
§Dwight's Travels in New York and New England, 4 vols. (1796-1821).
§Lewis and Clark's Expedition, 1804, 2 vols.
§Breck's Recollections (Scudder).
§Quincy's Figures of the Past.
Scudder's American Commonwealths.
*Biography.* See in Morse's American Statesmen Series (Houghton & Mifflin), the Lives of John Adams, J.Q. Adams, Benton, Calhoun, Clay, Jackson, Jefferson, Madison, Monroe, Randolph, Washington and Webster; in Sparks's American Biography, the Lives of Fulton and Rumford; Redpath's John Brown, Johnson's Garrison, Prime's Morse, Rice's Morton, Abbott's Kit Carson, Upham's Frémont, Parton's Famous Americans, Mrs. Stowe's Men of Our Times, Hunt's American Merchants; Roosevelt's and Lodge's Hero Tales from American History.

## VI. THE PERIOD OF THE CIVIL WAR (1861-1865).

Draper's Civil War, 3 vols.
Greeley's American Conflict, 2 vols.
The Comte de Paris's Civil War, 4 vols.
Scribner's Campaigns of the Civil War, 12 vols.
Abbot's Battle-Fields of '61.
Abbot's Blue-Jackets of '61.
Johnson's Short History of the War.
Coffin's Four Years of Fighting.
Coffin's Drum-Beat of the Nation.
Coffin's Marching to Victory.
Coffin's Redeeming the Republic.
Coffin's Freedom Triumphant.
Thayer's Youth's History of the Civil War.
Dodge's Bird's-Eye View of the Civil War.
Nichol's Story of the Great March.
Conyngham's Sherman's March.
Blaine's Twenty Years of Congress, 2 vols. (1860-1880).

§ Early or contemporaneous history.
[1] In Morse's "American Statesmen" Series.

The Century Company's War-Book, 4 vols.

McPherson's Political History of the Rebellion.

Swinton's Decisive Battles of the War.

Dana's Recollections of the Civil War.

Pollard's Lost Cause (Confederate).

Stephens's War between the States, 2 vols. (Confederate).

Davis's Rise and Fall of the Confederate Government (Confederate), 2 vols.

Ropes's The Civil War, 2 vols.

Cooke's Wearing of the Gray (Confederate).

Johnston's Narrative of the War (Confederate).

*Biography.* Nicolay and Hay's Abraham Lincoln, Holland's Lincoln, Herndon's Lincoln, 3 vols., Thayer's Lincoln, Carpenter's Six Months in the White House, McClellan's Own Story, Roman's Beauregard, 2 vols., Badeau's U. S. Grant, 3 vols., Grant's Personal Memoirs, 2 vols., Sherman's Memoirs, 2 vols., Sheridan's Memoirs, 2 vols., Farragut's Life of Farragut, Schuckers's Life of S. P. Chase, Cooke's Robert E. Lee, Cooke's "Stonewall" Jackson, Johnston and Browne's Life of Alexander H. Stephens, Alfriend's Life of Jefferson Davis, Pollard's Life of Jefferson Davis.

## VII. RECONSTRUCTION.—THE NEW NATION (1865 TO THE PRESENT TIME).

McPherson's Political History of Reconstruction.

McPherson's Political Handbooks (1870–1894). [1895].

Andrews's Last Quarter of a Century (1875–

Wilson's Lives of the Presidents (1789–1893).

Curry's The South.

Johnston's American Politics.

Bryce's American Commonwealth, 2 vols.

Badeau's Grant in Peace.

Thayer's Garfield.

McCulloch's Men and Measures of Half a Century.

King's The Great South, 1875.

Harper's First Century of the Republic.

The North American Review, Jan., 1876.

Blaine's Twenty Years of Congress, 2 vols. (1860–1880).

Bancroft's Pacific States, vols. on California, Utah, Oregon, Alaska, etc.

Appleton's Annual Cyclopædia, 1865–1899.

Thayer's The New West.

Ballou's The New Eldorado (Alaska).

McClure's The South.

Bruce, The Plantation Negro as a Freeman.

Herbert's Noted Men of the Solid South.

Fiske's American Political Ideas (The Future of America).

Shaler's United States, 2 vols.

Whitney's United States (Physical Geography and Statistics).

Morris's War with Spain.

Harper's History of the War with Spain, 3 vols.

NOTE. — Many valuable articles relating to the history of the United States during this period will be found in *The Century, The Atlantic, Harper's Magazine, Scribner's Magazine, The Nation, The North American Review,* and *The Forum.* For a general index to reviews and magazines, see Poole's Index.

# TABLE OF BOUNDARIES OF THE UNITED STATES.

*(The student of American History should bear in mind that the political boundaries of the United States have been determined to a very large degree by the natural boundaries of: 1. coast lines; 2. rivers and lakes; 3. watersheds; 4. mountain ranges.)*

I. (1783) By the final Treaty of Peace of 1783 the boundary of the American Republic (see " Map of U. S. in 1783 ") was fixed, in general terms, as follows: The line separating the United States from the British possessions began at the Bay of Fundy and ran to " the northwest angle of Nova Scotia," thence " to the Highlands," and thence "along the said Highlands which divide those rivers that empty themselves into the river St. Lawrence, from those which fall into the Atlantic Ocean." Thence the line ran westerly along the 45th parallel, the middle of the St. Lawrence, and the middle of the Great Lakes to the Lake of the Woods. On the west, the line separating the United States from the Spanish province of Louisiana was drawn from the Lake of the Woods to the head-waters of the Mississippi and thence down the middle of that river to the 31st parallel — or the frontier of the Spanish province of West Florida. On the south, the line extended due east from the Mississippi along the 31st parallel to the Chattahoochee River in Georgia and thence to the sea as shown on the map. (See " U. S. Statutes at Large," VIII., 80; Macdonald's " Select Documents of U. S. History "; Winsor's " America," VII.; Gannett's " Boundaries of the U. S."; Hinsdale's " Bounding the Original U. S." in " Mag. of Western History," II., 401; Hart's " Epoch Maps of American History.")

Much of the region through which the northern boundary ran was an unexplored wilderness and the line was largely pure guesswork. This was the case west of Lake Superior, and notably so in the northeast, between what is now the State of Maine and the British possessions. The result was that for nearly sixty years this northeast line was a subject of angry dispute and the controversy was not finally settled until the negotiation of the Webster-Ashburton Treaty of 1842. (See Winsor's " America," VII.; and Benton's " Thirty Years in the U. S. Senate," II., 421.)

II. (1795) Spain refused to recognize the southern boundary of the United States as determined by the Treaty of Peace of 1783 (see above, No. I.). She claimed that her province of West Florida extended 110 miles north of the 31st parallel and that the true boundary line, separating her possessions in that quarter from the United States, extended due east from the Mississippi from the mouth of the Yazoo to the Chattahoochee River in Georgia.

In 1795 Spain relinquished her claim to the disputed territory, and, furthermore, granted to the United States the free navigation of the lower Mississippi, besides conceding the temporary right of deposit (or storage for merchandise) at the port of New Orleans. (See "U. S. Statutes at Large," VIII., and Winsor and Hinsdale, as above.)

III. (1803)   In 1803 the United States purchased the province of Louisiana, which Spain had receded to France. That immense territory extended from the mouth of the Mississippi northward to its source, and had the Rocky Mountains as its natural boundary on the west. We bought the country without receiving any definite limits, and hence further negotiations became necessary with respect to boundary lines (see below).

IV. (1818)   In consequence of the above purchase of Louisiana a treaty made by us with Great Britain in 1818 extended the northern line of the United States from the Lake of the Woods (see above, No. I.) westward along the 49th parallel to the Rocky Mountains. The same treaty provided that the country west of the Rocky Mountains, north of the 42d parallel (or the recognized Spanish frontier), and known as the Oregon country, should be held jointly by the United States and Great Britain.

V. (1819–1825)   In 1819 Spain sold Florida to us, and in the treaty defined the unsettled western boundary of Louisiana (see above, Nos. III. and IV.) by an irregular line which began at the Gulf of Mexico and approximately followed the watershed south and west of the tributaries of the Mississippi to the 42d parallel. At the same time Spain agreed to renounce all claims to the Oregon country. This was to us a most important concession. Six years later (1825) a treaty made with Russia fixed the northern limit of the Oregon country (before unsettled) at 54° 40', or what is now the southern boundary of Alaska.

VI. (1842)   In 1842 the Webster-Ashburton Treaty (see Index under "Treaty") settled the long dispute over the northeastern boundary (see above, No. I.) and reaffirmed the line of 1818 to the Rocky Mountains (see above, No. IV.).

VII. (1845)   In 1845 we annexed Texas; the boundary question was settled by the Mexican War.

VIII. (1846)   In 1846 a treaty made by us with Great Britain divided the Oregon country between the two nations by extending the boundary line of the 49th parallel (see above, No. IV.) from the Rocky Mountains to the Pacific. (See in general the "Map of Acquisitions of Territory.")

IX. (1848–1867)   All subsequent United States boundary lines on the continent (see map cited above) were determined by Mexican cessions in 1848, the Gadsden Purchase in 1853, and the Alaska Purchase in 1867.

X. (1898–1899)   The islands recently acquired by the United States present no difficulties respecting boundaries.

## POPULATION OF THE UNITED STATES AT EACH CENSUS.

| Year. | Population. | Population Living in Cities. | Inhabitants of Cities in each 100 of the Total Population. |
|---|---|---|---|
| 1790 | 3,929,214 | 131,472 | 3.35 |
| 1800 | 5,308,483 | 210,873 | 3.97 |
| 1810 | 7,239,881 | 356,920 | 4.93 |
| 1820 | 9,633,822 | 475,135 | 4.93 |
| 1830 | 12,866,020 | 1,864,509 | 6.72 |
| 1840 | 17,069,453 | 1,453,994 | 8.52 |
| 1850 | 23,191,876 | 2,897,586 | 12.49 |
| 1860 | 31,443,321 | 5,072,256 | 16.13 |
| 1870 | 38,558,371 | 8,071,875 | 20.93 |
| 1880 | 50,155,783 | 11,318,547 | 22.57 |
| 1890 | 62,622,250 | 18,284,385 | 29.20 |
| 1900 | 76,304,799 | 24,992,199 | 33.10 |

All places having a population of 8000 and over are classed as *cities*.

## POPULATION OF THE FREE AND THE SLAVE STATES, 1790–1860.

| Year. | Free States. | Slave States. (Including Negroes.) |
|---|---|---|
| 1790 | 1,968,455 | 1,961,372 |
| 1800 | 2,684,616 | 2,621,316 |
| 1810 | 3,758,910 | 3,480,902 |
| 1820 | 5,152,372 | 4,485,819 |
| 1830 | 7,006,399 | 5,848,312 |
| 1840 | 9,733,922 | 7,334,433 |
| 1850 | 13,599,488 | 9,663,997 |
| 1860 | 19,128,418 | 12,315,372 |

## REPRESENTATION IN CONGRESS FROM 1790 TO 1903.

| YEAR. | SENATE. | | HOUSE OF REPRESENTATIVES. | | RATIO OF REPRESEN-TATION.[1] |
|---|---|---|---|---|---|
| | FREE STATES. | SLAVE STATES. | FREE STATES. | SLAVE STATES. | |
| 1790 | 14 | 12 | 35 | 30 | 30,000 |
| 1793 | 16 | 14 | 57 | 48 | 33,000 |
| 1796 | 16 | 16 | 57 | 49 | 33,000 |
| 1803 | 18 | 16 | 76 | 65 | 33,000 |
| 1813 | 18 | 18 | 103 | 78 | 35,000 |
| 1816 | 20 | 18 | 103 | 78 | 35,000 |
| 1821 | 24 | 24 | 105 | 81 | 35,000 |
| 1823 | 24 | 24 | 123 | 90 | 40,000 |
| 1833 | 24 | 24 | 141 | 99 | 47,700 |
| 1837 | 26 | 26 | 142 | 100 | 47,700 |
| 1843 | 26 | 26 | 135 | 88 | 70,680 |
| 1848 | 30 | 30 | 140 | 91 | 70,680 |
| 1853 | 32 | 30 | 144 | 90 | 93,423 |
| 1860 | 36 | 30 | 147 | 90 | 93,423 |
| 1863 | 72 | | 243 | | 127,381 |
| 1873 | 76 | | 293 | | 131,425 |
| 1883 | 76 | | 325 | | 151,911 |
| 1893 | 88 | | 356 | | 173,901 |
| 1903 | 90 | | 386 | | 194,182 |

[1] The number of representatives is fixed by Congress every ten years (Constitution, Art. I. sect. 2). By the last act (1902) it was provided that there should be one representative for every 194,182 persons; this will hold good until 1913. To find the electoral vote, add together the number of Senators and Representatives; *e.g.*, the electoral vote in 1790 was 91.

## THE SECTIONS IN 1870.

| SECTIONS. | POPULATION IN 1870. | SENATE. | HOUSE. | ELECT. VOTES. |
|---|---|---|---|---|
| THE SOUTH : (Ala., Ark., Ala., Ga., Ky., La., Md., Miss., N. C., S. C., Tenn., Tex., Va., W. V.) | 12,032,225 | 28 | 92 | 120 |
| THE NORTHWEST : (Ill., Ia., Ind., Ks., Mich., Minn., Mo., Neb., O., Wis.) | 12,702,299 | 20 | 98 | 118 |
| THE MIDDLE STATES : (Del., N. J., N. Y., Penn.) | 8,941,625 | 8 | 68 | 76 |
| NEW ENGLAND : (Conn., Mass., Me., N. H., R. I., Vt.) | 3,187,924 | 12 | 28 | 40 |
| THE PACIFIC : (Cal., Col., Nev., Or.) | 889,789 | 8 | 7 | 15 |
| Total | 38,925,598 | 76 | 293 | 369 |

☞ The total population includes Territories and Indians.

## THE SECTIONS IN 1880.

| SECTIONS. | POPULATION IN 1880. | SENATE. | HOUSE. | ELECT. VOTES. |
|---|---|---|---|---|
| THE SOUTH | 16,188,757 | 28 | 106 | 134 |
| THE NORTHWEST | 17,229,810 | 20 | 114 | 134 |
| THE MIDDLE STATES | 10,644,233 | 8 | 70 | 78 |
| NEW ENGLAND | 4,010,438 | 12 | 26 | 38 |
| THE PACIFIC | 1,296,367 | 8 | 9 | 17 |
| Total | 50,155,783 | 76 | 325 | 401 |

☞ The total population includes Territories and Indians. The Apportionment Act of Feb. 25, 1882, took effect March 3, 1883.

## THE SECTIONS IN 1890.

| SECTIONS. | POPULATION IN 1890. | SENATE. | HOUSE. | ELECT. VOTES. |
|---|---|---|---|---|
| THE SOUTH | 19,370,094 | 28 | 111 | 139 |
| THE NORTHWEST | 22,362,279 | 24 | 128 | 152 |
| THE MIDDLE STATES | 12,869,293 | 8 | 73 | 81 |
| NEW ENGLAND | 4,700,745 | 12 | 27 | 39 |
| THE PACIFIC | 2,606,495 | 16 | 17 | 33 |
| Total | 62,622,250 | 88 | 356 | 444 |

☞ The new States of Montana, Washington, Idaho, Wyoming, and Utah are classed with the Pacific States. The Dakotas are classed with the Northwest. The total population includes the Territories. The Apportionment Act of Feb. 7, 1891, took effect March 3, 1893. The next apportionment will take effect in 1903.

# QUESTIONS FOR EXAMINATION.

*(These questions cover the principal topics of the history. It is believed that the headings of the paragraphs will be found to answer all the purpose of questions for ordinary recitations.)*

*1. When and where was Columbus born? What was the earth then supposed to be? What countries were then laid down on the maps?

2. What was the Atlantic called? Why? Who were the Northmen?

3. What discoveries did the Northmen make in 850? In 1000? Is it known where Vinland was? Did the discovery of America by the Northmen have any result? Why not?

4. Did Columbus learn anything of America from the Icelanders? What country did Columbus wish to reach?

5. What can you say of Marco Polo? What was the first motive of Columbus?

6. What was his second motive? How was trade with the Indies then carried on?

7. What change in trade with India occurred in 1453? What did the Portuguese attempt to do?

8. What did Diaz accomplish? What was the plan of Columbus? State his three reasons.

9. What mistake did he make? From whom did Columbus seek help?

10. How did the council regard his proposed voyage?

11–12. What help did he finally receive? When did he sail? What route did he take? How was he equipped for the voyage? What conviction did he have?

13–15. What is said of the voyage? Variation of the needle? Feeling of the crew? When and why did Columbus change his course? When and where did he land? What did Columbus believe this land to be? What did he call the natives? Why?

16. When did Columbus return to Spain? What about his letter?

17. How did the Pope divide the world? Was Spain satisfied with the discoveries of Columbus? Where and how did he die?

18–19. Who discovered the *continent* of North America? Where? When?

20–21. How did America get its name?

21–23. What was it thought to be? Who first discovered it to be an independent continent?

23–24. What was the great merit of Columbus? What voyages are mentioned in the Summary?

25–26. What did Ponce de Leon discover? Why did he name the land Florida?

26–27. When and where did Balboa discover the Pacific? When did Cortez land in Mexico?

28. What exploration did Cartier make? What did Cabeza de Vaca discover?

29–30. Describe De Soto's expedition. What great river did he discover?

31. Where was he buried? Who were the Huguenots? Where did they attempt to settle?

32–33. What did Menendez do? What is said of St. Augustine? What of De Gourgues?

33–34. What did Frobisher and Davis try to do? What were the results?

34–35. Describe Gilbert's voyages; Drake's voyage. What country did he call New Albion?

36. What expedition did Raleigh send out, and with what result?

36–37. When did he send out his first colony to Virginia? What new root and new weed did the colonists discover?

* The figures refer to pages.

37-38. What happened to his second colony?

39-40. What white settlers did this country have in 1600? What was America found to be? How is America superior to Europe? What is said of the influence of the geography of America on its history (see page 50)?

40-47. What can you say about the Indians? Their appearance? Mode of life? What was their most ingenious work? How were they governed? What was wampum used for? How was the Indian bound by customs? What was the totem? What was the Indian's religion? What about his self-control, his torturing captives, his respect for courage? What about the Indian and the White Man? What did the Whites learn from the Indians? What influence did the Indians have on the early history of the country?

47-48. What effects did the discovery of America have on Europe in regard to geographical knowledge, enterprise, precious metals, commerce, new products, sugar, cotton, rice, and coffee? what effect on men's minds?

49-50. Summarize the settlements of the Spaniards and others in America.

51-53. Describe Gosnold's expedition. Did England need America? Why? What is said of the London and the Plymouth Companies? What is a Charter? What were the three most important articles of the Charter?

53-57. When did the first colony sail? Of what did the colony consist? What is said of Captain John Smith? Where did the colonists settle? Did they own any land? Could they vote? Did they own what they raised? How did they get on the first summer? What about Pocahontas? What happened in the summer of 1608? What did the colonists resolve to do?

57-58. What did Governor Dale do? What did he give the settlers?

58-59. What effect did the raising of tobacco have?

60-62. What met in Jamestown in 1619? What is said about women's coming to Virginia? When did negro slavery begin in America? What about white apprentices? Who had now settled in the North? When did Virginia become a royal province? What about Sir William Berkeley?

63-66. Who were the Puritans? The Cavaliers? What famous men in Virginia descended from the Cavaliers? What were the Navigation Laws? Who was Nathaniel Bacon, and what did he do?

67-74. Describe Hudson's expedition. Who took possession of the country? What did they name it? What is said of Fort Orange? What of Peter Minuit? Who were the Patroons? What can you say of Peter Stuyvesant? Who claimed the country? What happened in 1664?

75-76. Who first claimed New Jersey? How did it get the name of New Jersey? What about the Friends, or Quakers?

77-79. What about religious liberty in England in 1607? Who were the Separatists? To what country did they first go? Why did the Separatists or Pilgrims come to America in 1620?

79-82. Describe the sailing of the *Mayflower*. What land did the colonists first see? What did they do there? Where did they finally land? How were public matters settled and the laws made? What about Governor Bradford and the Indians? Of what did Plymouth colony finally become part?

82-90. Where did Endicott plant a colony? When did Winthrop come, and where did he finally settle? What is said of the emigrants who came in the next ten years? How was Massachusetts governed? Who could vote? What did the people do for a living? Who was Roger Williams? Why did he leave Massachusetts? What about Mrs. Hutchinson? How did Williams influence the Narragansett Indians? What is said of public schools, of Harvard College, of John Eliot?

90-93. What was the object of the New England Confederacy? What about the coming of the Friends, or Quakers? What did the Puritans do to the Friends? What did the king do?

93-95. Describe King Philip's War. What about the Salem witchcraft? When did Massachusetts become a royal province? What is said of Andros? What of the new Charter?

96-98. Where and by whom was New Hampshire first settled? Why was it so named? What of Exeter? Of Londonderry?

98-103. Describe the first settlements in Connecticut. What about the Pequot

War? What about the Connecticut Constitution? What about the New Haven colony? What of the Regicides, of Andros and the Charter?

103–108. Who were the Catholic Pilgrims? Where did they settle? What was the first English Catholic church in America? Who made the laws of the colony? How about religious freedom? What is said of the Clayborne and Ingle rebellion? What was done in regard to Catholic worship in Maryland? What happened when Lord Baltimore got his rights again? What was done when the king took possession? What is said of Mason and Dixon's line?

108–111. What did Roger Williams do in 1636? Why did he name the place Providence? What is said of religious liberty in the colony? What other settlements were made in Rhode Island? What is said of the Charter?

111–113. Who first settled Delaware? Where? What happened to the colony? What was the first state to enter the Union?

113–117. How did the name Carolina originate? Where was the first settlement made? What is said of Charleston? What about the Huguenots? What was the "Grand Model"? When was the province divided into North and South Carolina? What is said of rice? Of indigo? Of Charleston in 1773?

118–122. Why did Charles II. give William Penn a large tract of land? What did the king name it? What did Penn intend to do in America? Where was the first settlement made? What is said of the "Great Law"? Of the Great Treaty? Of Philadelphia?

122–126. Why did General Oglethorpe wish to establish a colony in America? Why was the province named Georgia? Where did the colonists settle? What about silk culture? Did the colonists have much freedom? When did Georgia become a royal province?

126–131. Who first explored the West? Describe Joliet and Marquette's expedition. What did La Salle do? Who founded Mobile? Who New Orleans? How much of the country did the English hold? What had France got possession of? What did France mean to do? What forts did the French build?

131–142. When did war with the French begin? When did it end? How many wars are usually mentioned? Did the Indians take any part? What can you say of Louisburg? What of the great line of French forts? What of the Ohio Company? Who went as a messenger from the governor of Virginia to the French? What results did the journey have? What is said of the Albany Convention? What of Braddock's expedition? What of William Pitt? How did the name Pittsburgh originate? What is said of the fall of Quebec? What did the French and Indian War settle?

142–151. What was the population of the thirteen colonies in 1763? What about foreign trade? Did all the colonies have the same form of government? How did the farmers live? What is said of the life in cities and on plantations? What about travel, letters, hospitality, laws? What of education, of books? What did Edwards write? What did Franklin? What about Franklin and electricity?

152–169. What is said of George III.? How did he interfere with American commerce? What happened in Boston? Why did the king propose to tax the colonists? Why did they object? What about the Stamp Act? What of the Declaratory Act? The Boston Massacre? The New Taxes? What about the "Boston Tea Party"? What did Parliament do? What did Massachusetts do? Describe the British expedition to Lexington and Concord. How did it end? Describe the taking of Ticonderoga and Crown Point. Who was appointed commander of the Continental Army? What is said of Bunker Hill and the battle? When and where did Washington take command of the army? Describe the expedition against Quebec. How did Washington drive the British out of Boston? What about Fort Moultrie? What is said of "Common Sense"? Did the Americans seek to separate from Great Britain? What is said of the Declaration of Independence?

169–180. What did the British hope to do in New York? What is said of Washington? Describe the battle of Long Island. In what direction did Washington retreat? What is said of Fort Washington? Of Lee? Describe Washington's retreat across New Jersey. The victory of Trenton. What did Robert Morris do for Washington? How did Washington outwit Cornwallis? What is said of Burgoyne's expedition? Describe the battle of Oriskany; of Bennington. Describe Howe's expedition to Pennsylvania. What is said of the Saratoga battles? What did France do? What help did Franklin render?

180–188. What was the condition of Washington's army at Valley Forge? What did England offer in the spring of 1778? What is said of the battle of Monmouth? Of Lee? What did the British do next? Why? Speak of Savannah; of Wayne's victory; of Paul Jones. What of Charleston? What of Marion and Sumter? What of battle of Camden? Of King's Mountain? Speak of Arnold's treason; and of the winter at Morristown. What is said of General Greene? Of Cowpens? Of Guilford Court House? What did Cornwallis resolve to do? What is said of Greene's victories in South Carolina? Describe the "Crowning Victory of War." How did the news affect Lord North? Give summary of the Revolution.

188–195. What of George III.'s speech? When was peace made? What was the condition of United States? How about money? About trade between the states? What is said of Shays' Rebellion? What of the Northwest Territory? When and where did the Convention meet to make a new Constitution? What did they accomplish? What is said of Alexander Hamilton? What four things did the Constitution accomplish? What amendments to the Constitution were adopted? What were they called, and why? Give summary of the period.

195–203. What is said of political parties? Of the election of Washington? Of his inauguration? Whom did Washington choose for his cabinet? How did the government raise money? What did Hamilton do with a large part of this money? What did the government do in 1790, 1791, and 1792? What is said of "Citizen" Genet? What of emigration to the West? What great invention was made in 1793? What came of it? Speak of the Whiskey Rebellion; of Jay's Treaty.

204–206. What is said of France? Of the "X. Y. Z." papers? What were the Alien and the Sedition Laws? What illustrious man died in 1799?

206–214. Of what party was President Jefferson? Where was he inaugurated? What was thought of the probable extent of the Republic? Why? What about the war with Tripoli? What great territory did Jefferson purchase? What advantage did it secure us? Describe Lewis and Clark's expedition. What about the French and English war? What was the Embargo Act? What effect did it have? What was the Non-Intercourse Act? What results did it have? What is said of Aaron Burr? What about "Fulton's Folly"? What of the *Savannah*? What did Congress do in 1807? What did Jefferson say of slavery?

214–225. What is said of Madison's attempt to re-open trade with Great Britain? What of Napoleon? Speak of Tecumseh's conspiracy; of the Henry letters. What caused the War of 1812? Speak of General Hull; of the *Constitution* and the *Guerrière*; of Perry's victory; of Jackson's. What is said of Chippewa and of Lundy's Lane? What of the British capture of Washington? Describe Macdonough's victory. What is said of Fort McHenry? What of Jackson at New Orleans? What results did the war have?

225–234. What is said of Monroe? What of his journey through the North? What was the Seminole War? What did Spain do with Florida? What great question now came up? What change of feeling had occurred? How did slavery divide the country? How did the North and South feel about the extension of slavery? What was the Missouri Compromise? What about the National Road? What is the Monroe Doctrine? Speak of the visit of Lafayette.

234–240. Describe the building of the Erie Canal and its results. What about "Steam Wagons"? What was the first railroad opened in the United States? Of what did railroads convince people? What is said about Drinking Habits and the Temperance Cause?

240–252. Who was the first President from the West? How did he begin his administration? What is said about removal of government officers and employes? What is said about the "Spoils system"? What is said of Garrison? What did Channing say? What happened in Virginia? What was done at the North? What about Abolition Societies? What petitions were sent to Congress? What was the result? Why did the President put an end to the United States Bank? Why did South Carolina resist the duty on imported goods? What was Nullification? What is said of Webster's reply to Hayne? What debt do we owe Daniel

Webster? What did the President do? Speak of the growth of the country. What is said about railroads and canals? What about coal? What of the Express System? What is said about Indian wars at the West and in Florida? What of Chicago? Who were our first painters? Our first writers? What appeared in 1833?

252–258. What is said of the panic of 1837? What did the government establish? What can you say of the Mormons? Where did they finally go? What happened in 1840? What is said of emigrants? Of ocean steamships? Of the growth of the West?

258–263. What was Harrison called? How long did he live after he became President? What is said about Tyler? What of the Dorr Rebellion, the Webster-Ashburton Treaty, the Anti-renters? What about the Electric Telegraph? Who discovered that ether would control pain? What country did we annex in 1845?

263–272. What is said of Oregon? What of Dr. Whitman? How did we finally get Oregon? Why did the Mexican War break out? What battles can you mention? What countries did we conquer? What is said of General Scott? What important city did he take? What was there remarkable about the war? What did we obtain by the treaty of peace? What was the Wilmot Proviso? What is said of the discovery of gold in California? What results did it have?

272–276. What is said about slavery? What were Clay's plans of compromise? What important law was passed, and what were its results? What can you say of "Uncle Tom's Cabin"? of Sumner and Davis?

276–282. What did the "Crystal Palace" exhibition of 1853 prove? What is said about the reaper invented by McCormick? Who opened the ports of Japan? What was the Kansas-Nebraska Act? What happened in Kansas? How did Kansas enter the Union at last? What happened to Charles Sumner?

282–292. What was the Dred Scott case? What was Judge Taney's decision? How did the North feel about it? What can you say of the panic of 1857? What was discovered in Nevada and Colorado? In Pennsylvania? How is much of the oil sent to market? What was John Brown's raid, and how did it end? Who was elected President in 1860? What did the people of South Carolina think of the election? What did they do? What did six other Southern States do? Why did the South secede? What did the Confederacy seize? What did President Buchanan try to do? What is said of the growth of the United States between 1789 and 1861? What sad difference was there between 1789 and 1861? What had caused the difference? What must now happen in regard to the Union?

293–308. What did President Lincoln say at his inauguration? What did he intend to do? What is said of Major Anderson? What next happened? What did the President do when he heard of the surrender of Fort Sumter? What states now seceded? How many did that make in all? Name them. To what place was the Confederate capital now removed? What did General Butler do with fugitive slaves? What was the condition of the North with respect to the war? of the South? Speak of the number and position of the two armies. What is said of the battle of Bull Run? How did "Stonewall" Jackson get his name? What results did the defeat at Bull Run have? What was the Union plan of the war? What is said of the Union blockading fleet? What about the Confederate blockade-runners and war-vessels? What of Mason and Slidell? What can you say of the *Merrimac*? What of the *Monitor*? What about the war in the West? What did General Grant write to General Buckner? What is said of the battle of Pittsburg Landing? Of Island No. 10? What was the general result of the first year of the war?

308–315. Describe the expedition against New Orleans. What noted naval commander in the late war with Spain was with Farragut at New Orleans? What was the result of the expedition? What is said of Port Hudson and Vicksburg? What did McClellan do? What was the result of the Peninsular Campaign? What about the second battle of Bull Run? Describe Lee's advance. What happened at Antietam? What is said of the battle of Fredericksburg? Of Murfreesboro? What did the President do on New Year's Day, 1863? What has been the result? What was the North fighting for before the Proclamation? What afterwards?

315–321. What is said of the battle of Chancellorsville? What of Gettysburg? Who made a famous charge at Gettysburg? Can you describe it? What was the result of the battle? What can you say about Vicksburg? How did many of the people have to live during the siege? How did the siege end? On what day? What about Port Hudson? What had now been done? What about the draft riots; Morgan's raid? Where was a severe battle fought September 19-20? Why was General Thomas called "the Rock of Chickamauga"? Speak of Missionary Ridge and Lookout Mountain. What did Sherman do at Meridian? Who was now made general-in-chief of the Union armies?

322-334. What did Grant and Sherman now decide to do? What order did General Grant send to Sherman from the "Wilderness"? Where were the battles of the Wilderness fought? What is said of them? Did Grant turn back? What did he do? Where and by whom was the *Alabama* taken? What was Early's raid? Describe Sheridan's raid in the Shenandoah Valley. What is said of the Petersburg mine? What of Sheridan's ride? What did Sherman do in the West? What important city did he take? What is said of Farragut? What did Sherman determine to do? What did he accomplish? What is said of Thomas? To how many states had the Confederacy now shrunk? What message did Sherman send to the President? Where did his men think they were going? Describe Sherman's march northward. What did Sheridan do on the west of Richmond? on the south? What did Grant then capture? What did Lee do? What happened the next day? Describe Lee's surrender. What happened at Fort Sumter on April 14, 1865? What had the war cost? What happened at Washington on the evening of April 14, 1865? What can be said of the North in the war? Of the South? What did the war establish?

334-344. Describe the military review in Washington. What next occurred? What three things did the war settle? What is said of the President's proclamation of pardon? What question now came up? How did the President and Congress disagree? What was the result? What did Congress do in the spring of 1867? What is said of the Fourteenth Amendment? What of Tennessee? How many states came back? What about the others? What is said about the negroes? About the "Carpet-Baggers"? After a time what happened? Why did Congress impeach the President? What was the result? What did the President do the next Christmas? What did Congress do in 1869? What is said of the Thirteenth Amendment? Of the Fourteenth? Of the Fifteenth? What had Professor Morse predicted? What did Cyrus Field do? What result has the cable had? What territory did Congress purchase in 1867? What can you say about it? What can you say about the payment of the war-debt?

344-353. What great work was completed shortly after Grant became President? Describe the road. What is said of the railroad and the telegraph? What of the effect of the Pacific road on commerce with Asia? On the growth of the Far West? What is said about the Homestead Act? What is said about Western farms and ranches? When was reconstruction completed? What is said about the Weather Bureau? What is said about the "Force Bill"? What happened at the West in 1871? What at the East in 1872? What is said of "Boss" Tweed"? Of the "Whiskey Ring"? What is said about the new Coinage Act? What happened in 1873? What is said of the Centennial Exhibition? What great change has taken place since Washington's day? What were two of the most remarkable novelties exhibited? What is said of electricity? What treaty was made in 1871? What was one of its results? What wars shortly after occurred?

353-356. What is said of the election of President Hayes? (See note 1.) How was the dispute finally settled? (See note 1.) What action did the President take respecting the South? What is said of the negro? What happened in 1877? What great work did Captain Eads accomplish? What is said about the "greenbacks"? What was done on New Year's Day, 1879? What was the result?

356-362. When was President Garfield assassinated? What did Congress do? What effect does the Civil Service Reform have? What happened in Louisiana in 1882? Describe the East River Bridge. What about letter postage? What was the Alien Contract Labor Act? What is said of the New Orleans Exhibition? What did it prove? What great change has taken place in New Orleans? What is said of the South before the war and since? What about free labor? Cotton? Cottonseed oil? (Note 1.) What of the Freedmen? Of education?

363-371. What is said of President Cleveland? What did he try to do? How did he succeed? What was one object of the "Knights of Labor"? What is said of the "Black List"? Of the "Boycott"? Of the "American Federation of Labor"? Of the "Department of Labor"? What happened in 1886? What occurred at Chicago? What is said about the growth of great corporations and "trusts"? What is a "trust"? (See note 1, p. 367.) What happened at Charleston in 1886? What at the West in 1884 and in the winter of 1888? What is said about the permanent effect of these disasters on our country? What can you say about the Statue of Liberty? What four important laws were passed during Cleveland's presidency?

371–376. Where is Oklahoma? Describe the opening of Oklahoma. What event was celebrated in New York in the spring of 1889? Describe the Johnstown disaster. What is said of the Congress of the three Americas? What new states were admitted in November, 1889? What two in 1890? What is the whole number of states in the Union? How many stars has our flag now? What is said of our new ships-of-war? What about woman suffrage (or right to vote) in Wyoming? in Colorado? in Utah? What is said about the new Pension Act; the Sherman Silver Act; the McKinley Protective Tariff? What about the Census of 1890; the Patent Office; Centennial? What is said of the Immigration Act of 1891? The Homestead strike? What of the extension of Civil Service Reform?

377–382. Describe the Australian or Secret Ballot. What is said of the Columbian Exposition? What of "Hard Times"? What two important acts were repealed in 1893 and 1894? Give an account of the Behring Sea case. How was it settled? What is said of the Coxey "industrial army"? What about the Pullman strike? What of "Hard Times"? What of the Republic of Hawaii? What is said of the Wilson Tariff? What about extension of Civil Service Reform in 1894? How many places are now filled by examination? What is said of the Atlanta Exhibition of 1895? What about Utah in 1896? What of the "New West"? What was the Venezuela Question? How was it settled? What is said of a general treaty of arbitration?

383–423. Give an account of the Dingley Tariff. What is said about the increase in our exports? What do we now send abroad? Where does Great Britain get the larger part of her food supply? What about American iron and steel, machinery, tools, and labor-saving inventions? What was the total value of our exports in 1898? Describe Grant's tomb and the Congressional Library Building. What is said of "Greater New York"? What about the growth of cities in America since 1790? What is said about the government of American cities? What may your vote do? What is said of the revised state Constitutions of three Southern states? What about the amended Constitution of South Dakota? What possession did Spain have in North America in the sixteenth century? What did she have at the beginning of the nineteenth century? What about twenty-five years later? What is said of the revolution in Cuba? What demands did the United States make on Spain? What did Spain do? Describe the destruction of the *Maine*. What did President McKinley say in his message to Congress? What resolutions did Congress adopt? What preparations did we make for war with Spain? Give an account of the battle of Manila. How was Cervera's squadron "bottled up"? What did Hobson do? What happened near Santiago? What happened to Cervera's squadron? What is said about the end of the war? What about the annexation of Hawaii? What does the Treaty of Peace give the United States? What was said in Congress against ratifying the Treaty? What was said in its favor? How and when was the question decided? When did the Spanish forces leave Cuba? What did the war with Spain cost in money and life? What is said of the "Red Cross" and of the women of America? What about the "Trans-Mississippi Exposition"? What of Cheap Lands? What of agricultural prosperity at the West? What about the preservation of forests? What of "Arbor Day"? What of savings-banks and national prosperity? What of gifts? What is said about American women? China? Samoan Islands? Hague Treaty? What of the Gold Standard Act?

The Porto Rican Act? Hawaii? The Isthmian canal (and see § 425)? Census of 1900? What is said of our exports for 1900? What did the Supreme Court decide in 1901? What is said of Cuba? What about the Pan-American Exposition? What terrible event happened in the autumn of 1901?

424-427. Give an account of the great anthracite coal strike of 1902. What is said of the American Pacific cable? Who sent the first wireless telegram from this country to England? Mention some Acts of Congress (1901–1904). Who was elected President of the United States in 1904? What is said of the Louisiana Purchase Exposition? What four very important things are Americans trying to do in the twentieth century? How do we meet disaster? What is said of Galveston, Baltimore, and the San Francisco earthquake? What is said in the "General Summary" of the growth of the American Republic? What advantages does this country offer? What do these facts prove? What question ought each one to ask himself? What depends on the answer to this question?

# TOPICAL ANALYSIS FOR SLATE AND BLACKBOARD.

*The figures refer to the numbered paragraphs.*

FIRST PERIOD. — THE DISCOVERY AND NAMING OF AMERICA. (1000–1521.)

**The Northmen.**
- 2. Who were they?
- 2. Iceland.
- 2. Greenland.
- 2. "Leif the Lucky."
- 2. Vinland.
- 3. Results of the discovery of America by the Northmen.

**Geographical knowledge.**
- 1. Ideas about the earth in 1436.
- 1. The "Sea of Darkness."

**Columbus.**
- 1. Birth of Columbus.
- 3. Visits Iceland.
- 4. What he wished to do.
- 4. Marco Polo's book.
- 4. First motive or object of Columbus.
- 5. His second motive.
- 5. Trade with the Indies. (Venice, Genoa.)
- 6. Portuguese voyages. (Results.)
- 7. Plan of Columbus. (How far right, how far wrong.)
- 8. He seeks assistance.
- 9. He sails. (Vessels; Canary Islands; equipment for the voyage.)
- 10. Incidents of the voyage. (Compass, crew, birds.)
- 11. Land! (The *West* Indies; the Indians.)
- 12. Return. (Letter of Columbus; division of the world.)
- 13. Disappointment of Spain.
- 13. Death of Columbus. (What he had accomplished.)

**The Cabots.**
- 14. John.
- 14. Sebastian.
- 14. Henry VII.'s note-book.
- 14. England's claim to America.

**Origin of the name America.**
- 15. Amerigo Vespucci.
- 15. What happened in 1507.
- 15. Did Amerigo Vespucci deserve the honor he received?

**Effects of the discovery of America on Europe.**

- 43. (1) Geographical knowledge.
- 43. (2) Spain, Portugal, France, and England.
- 43. (3) The precious metals.
- 43. (4) Trade and navigation.
- 43. (5) New products.
- 43. (6) Sugar, cotton, rice, coffee.
- 43. (7) Effects on men's minds. (Opportunity.)
- 44. Summary of the section. (Spaniards, French, English.)

Effects of the geography of America on its history. (See map, pages 50, 51.)

THIRD PERIOD. — PERMANENT ENGLISH AND FRENCH SETTLEMENTS.
(1602–1763.)

**The English and the French establish permanent colonies.**
**I. Virginia (1607).**

- 45. Opening of the 17th century; Gosnold.
- 46. England's need of America; the king grants a charter to settle Virginia. (Articles of the charter; instructions.)
- 47. The London Company; Captain John Smith.
- 48. Jamestown; condition of the colonists.
- 49. Their sufferings; search for the Pacific; Pocahontas.
- 50. Gold! The French in Canada; what the colony owed Smith; Jamestown abandoned.
- 51. Lord Delaware; the new charter; Governor Dale; the great reform. (Gift of land.)
- 52. Cultivation of tobacco. (Four effects.)
- 53. Virginia becomes practically self-governing. (The house of Burgesses; wives.)
- 54. Negro slaves; white "apprentices."
- 54. What settlements were made at the North.
- 55. Virginia loses her charter; Governor Berkeley; Puritans and Cavaliers.
- 56. Berkeley restored to power; the Navigation Laws; the king gives away Virginia. (Other English colonies.)
- 57. Condition of the Virginia colonists; the Bacon rebellion. (Results.)
- 58. Summary of the Virginia colony.

**The Dutch settle New Netherland.**
**II. New York (1614).**

- 59. Henry Hudson.
- 60. The Indians.
- 61. The Dutch take possession of New Netherland; the English and the French.
- 62. Purchase of Manhattan Island.
- 63. The Patroons. (Van Rensselaer.)
- 64. Peter Stuyvesant; New Amsterdam. (The English claim the country; they seize it.)
- 65. Summary of New Netherland or New York.

**III. New Jersey (1617).**

- 66. Dutch claim; English claim.
- 66. English get possession. (Name New Jersey.)
- 67. The Friends or Quakers. (Treaty with the Indians; government of the colony.)
- 68. Summary of New Jersey.

**The wars of the English with the French and the Indians (1689–1763).**

135. War with the French and Indians; (1) " King William's War." (Schenectady, Haverhill, Acadia.)
135. (2) " Queen Anne's War." (Deerfield, Annapolis, Nova Scotia.)
136. (3) " King George's War "; Louisburg. (Results.)
137. (4) The " French and Indian War." (Object; the French forts.)
138. The Ohio Company; Governor Dinwiddie's messenger.
139. Results of Washington's journey.
140. The Albany Convention; Franklin's snake; Braddock.
141. Braddock's defeat; Washington.
142. Acadian exiles; William Pitt. (Louisburg; Fort Duquesne; the French driven back to Canada.)
143. Fall of Quebec; Pontiac.
144. What the war settled. (France and the West in 1759; treaty of 1763; what America was to become; Spain; the English flag at the end of 1763.)
145. Four results of the wars between the English and the French.

**General state of the country in 1763.**

146. The thirteen colonies in 1763. (" Making roots.") The population.
147. Language, religion, social rank; cities; trade.
148. Government of the colonies; law. (" Don't tread on me.") Unity of the people.
149. Farm life. (The houses; the fires; food; the store; recreation.)
150. City life; the Southern Plantations. (Dress; life then and life now.)
151. Travel; letters; hospitality; severe laws.
152. Education; books; Edwards; Franklin. (Electricity.)
153. Summary of the colonial period.

FOURTH PERIOD. — THE REVOLUTION; THE CONSTITUTION. (1763–1789.)

**The Revolution. (1. The colonists resist taxation without representation. 1764–1775.)**

154. American commerce; the new king. (What he was and what he did.)
155. The king proposes to tax the colonies; object of tax; protest of the Americans. (Pitt and Burke.)
156. The Stamp Act.
157. Resistance of the Colonies to the Act.
158. Repeal of the Act; the Declaratory Act; the Boston Massacre; the *Gaspee*.
159. The new taxes; their object; the " Boston Tea-Party."
160. Parliament closes the port of Boston. (General Gage; Patrick Henry; the first Continental Congress; Massachusetts; the " Minute Men.")

**The formation and adoption of the Constitution (1787–1789).**

196. The convention of 1787; the Constitution.
196. Alexander Hamilton. (The "Ship of State.")
197. What four things were accomplished by the Constitution.
198. Summary. (What John Adams said.)


FIFTH PERIOD. — THE UNION; NATIONAL DEVELOPMENT. (1789–1860.)

**I. Washington's Administration. (Two terms, 1789–1797.)**

(*Washington. See note 2, page 136, and the section on the Revolution.*)
199. Political parties; election and inauguration of Washington.
200. Washington's Cabinet; how the government obtained money.
201. Payment of three great debts. (Hamilton.)
202. The first census; the U. S. Bank; the Mint. (Decimal coinage.)
203. "Citizen" Genêt; Washington's proclamation.
204. Emigration to the West. (Boone.) Marietta, Cincinnati. (The first Western newspaper.) War with the Indians and results.
205. The Cotton-gin and its four results.
206. The Whiskey rebellion.
207. Jay's treaty; three new states.
208. Summary of Washington's presidency.

**II. John Adams's Administration. (One term, 1797–1801.)**

(*Sketch of John Adams. See note 2, page 204.*)
209. Trouble with France; the "X. Y. Z. Papers." (Pinckney; war; "Hail Columbia.")
210. The Alien and the Sedition Laws; death of Washington.
211. Summary of John Adams's presidency.

**III. Jefferson's Administration. (Two terms, 1801–1809.)**

(*Jefferson. See note 2, page 206.*)
212. Republican simplicity; the new capital.
213. Probable extent of the republic. (Means of travel.)
214. The Pirates of Tripoli; war; results.
215. Purchase of Louisiana; four results.
216. Lewis and Clark. (Oregon.)
217. The French and English war; the *Leopard* and the *Chesapeake*.
218. The Embargo; the Non-Intercourse Act.
219. Aaron Burr.
220. "Fulton's Folly." (Western steamboats; the *Savannah*.)
221. Importation of slaves forbidden. (Jefferson and slavery.)
222. (Summary of Jefferson's Presidency.)

# INDEX.

*(The references are to pages.)*

# ANNOUNCEMENTS

# LEADING FACTS OF HISTORY SERIES

By D. H. MONTGOMERY

*A Series of Sterling Text-Books on History for Schools, Academies, and Colleges*

THE BEGINNER'S AMERICAN HISTORY. Cloth. 258 + xviii pages. Fully illustrated with new maps and pictures. List price, 60 cents; mailing price, 70 cents.

AN ELEMENTARY AMERICAN HISTORY. 12mo. Cloth. 306 + xlii pages. Illustrated. List price, 75 cents; mailing price, 85 cents.

THE LEADING FACTS OF AMERICAN HISTORY. Cloth. xii + 406 + 82 pages. With colored maps and full-page illustrations. List price, $1.00; mailing price, $1.15.

THE STUDENT'S AMERICAN HISTORY. For higher schools and colleges. Cloth. xvi + 548 + lx pages. Illustrated. List price, $1.40; mailing price, $1.55.

THE LEADING FACTS OF ENGLISH HISTORY. Cloth. 420 + lxxix pages. List price, $1.12; mailing price, $1.25.

THE LEADING FACTS OF FRENCH HISTORY. Cloth. 328 + xxvii pages. With illustrations and maps. List price, $1.12; mailing price, $1.25.

MR. MONTGOMERY'S histories are universally acknowledged to be, in their departments, unequaled in scholarship, in true historic insight and temper, in interest, and in class-room availability. They are admittedly the leading text-books on their subjects. Their popularity and wide use have been duly proportionate to their merits. Hundreds of schools and colleges have used them with the greatest satisfaction.

In brief, the attractive and enduring qualities of Mr. Montgomery's books have proved them preëminently superior to all other historical text-books.

## GINN & COMPANY PUBLISHERS

# STUDENT'S AMERICAN HISTORY

*REVISED EDITION*

A Text-Book for Higher Schools and Colleges

By D. H. MONTGOMERY

---

12mo. Cloth. 612 + lvii pages. With maps and illustrations. List price, $1.40;
mailing price, $1.60

---

IN this thorough revision of a widely used text-book particular attention has been given to the leading political features, to questions of constitutional history, and to the opening and settlement of the West and its influence on the development of the nation. New maps and illustrations have been added, and the system of cross references has been extended.

The "Student's American History" is more than a mere record of events. It is a philosophical treatment of the rise and development of the nation both socially and politically. It is as attractive in style and as interesting in its manner of statement as the earlier books by this author, and is excellently adapted for the use of advanced students. Especial attention is given to the political and constitutional phases of the subject. Emphasis is laid on cause and effect as illustrated in American history, numerous facsimiles of original documents are shown, and nearly fourteen hundred references to other authorities are cited. The last impression of the book includes a list of important decisions of Chief Justice Marshall and an account of the accession of President Roosevelt.

GINN & COMPANY Publishers

# REFERENCE BOOKS IN HISTORY

GINN & COMPANY PUBLISHERS

# TEXT-BOOKS ON HISTORY

| | List Price | Mailing Price |
|---|---|---|
| Abbott's History and Description of Roman Political Institutions | $1.50 | $1.60 |
| Allen's Short History of the Roman People | 1.00 | 1.10 |
| Blaisdell's Stories from English History | .40 | .50 |
| Blaisdell's Story of American History | .60 | .75 |
| Blaisdell and Ball's Hero Stories from American History | .50 | .60 |
| Channing and Hart's Guide to the Study of American History | 2.00 | 2.15 |
| Cooper, Estill, and Lemmon's History of Our Country | 1.00 | 1.15 |
| Droysen's Outline of the Principles of History | 1.00 | 1.10 |
| Emerton's Introduction to the Study of the Middle Ages | 1.12 | 1.25 |
| Emerton's Mediaeval Europe (814–1300) | 1.50 | 1.65 |
| Feilden's Short Constitutional History of England | 1.25 | 1.35 |
| Getchell's Mediaeval History by Library Method | .50 | .55 |
| Gurney's Reference Handbook of English History | .75 | .85 |
| Hodder's Outline Maps for an Historical Atlas of the United States | .40 | .45 |
| Kemp's History for Graded and District Schools | 1.00 | 1.10 |
| Lawler's Essentials of American History | 1.00 | 1.10 |
| Mace's Method in History | 1.00 | 1.10 |
| Montgomery's Beginner's American History | .60 | .70 |
| Montgomery's Leading Facts of American History | 1.00 | 1.15 |
| Montgomery's Leading Facts of English History | 1.12 | 1.25 |
| Montgomery's Leading Facts of French History | 1.12 | 1.25 |
| Montgomery's Student's American History | 1.40 | 1.55 |
| Myers' Ancient History | 1.50 | 1.65 |
| Myers' Eastern Nations and Greece | 1.00 | 1.10 |
| Myers' General History | 1.50 | 1.65 |
| Myers' History of Rome | 1.00 | 1.10 |
| Myers' History of Greece | 1.25 | 1.40 |
| Myers' Outlines of Mediaeval and Modern History | 1.50 | 1.65 |
| Myers' Mediaeval and Modern History (Revised Edition) | | |
|    Part I. The Middle Ages | 1.10 | 1.20 |
|    Part II. The Modern Age | 1.25 | 1.40 |
| Myers' Rome: Its Rise and Fall | 1.25 | 1.40 |
| Myers and Allen's Ancient History | 1.50 | 1.65 |
| Robinson's Introduction to the History of Western Europe | 1.60 | 1.80 |
| Riggs' Studies in United States History | .60 | .65 |
| Webster's History of Commerce | 1.40 | 1.55 |

# GINN & COMPANY Publishers